The
Psychology
of Written
Composition

THE PSYCHOLOGY OF EDUCATION AND INSTRUCTION

A series of volumes edited by:
Robert Glaser and **Lauren Resnick**

The Psychology of Written Composition

CARL BEREITER

MARLENE SCARDAMALIA

Ontario Institute for Studies in Education

LEA Lawrence Erlbaum Associates, Publishers
1987   Hillsdale, New Jersey   London

To Theodore and Bianca
To the memory of Walter and Charlotte

Lawrence Erlbaum Associates, Inc., Publishers
365 Broadway
Hillsdale, New Jersey 07642

Library of Congress Cataloging-in-Publication Data

Bereiter, Carl.
   The psychology of written composition.

   Bibliography: p.
   Includes index.
   1. Rhetoric—Psychological aspects. 2. Written
communication—Psychological aspects. I. Scardamalia,
Marlene, 1944–   . II. Title.

P301.5.P75B47   1987   808′.001′9   86-19955
ISBN 0-85859-647-5
ISBN 0-8058-0038-7 (pbk)
Printed in the United States of America
10 9 8 7 6 5 4 3 2

Contents

Foreword

Only a few years ago, research on writing was a neglected field within cognitive science. By that time, reading and reading comprehension had become familiar and major topics of interest, with an expanding data base and deepening theoretical understanding. But writing was left largely unexplored. Of course, there was no lack of investigation or concern with writing: The study of writing has an old and rich tradition within rhetorics and education, and over the centuries writing teachers have accumulated a great deal of knowledge. But cognitive science researchers did not seem to know how to design the right kind of experiments, nor how to theorize about writing processes within the new framework. The study of writing continued to remain at Levels 1 and 2, as Bereiter and Scardamalia describe in chapter 2; that is, writing research relied on informal observation, introspection, and correlational methods. The kind of approach that characterizes cognitive science—experimentation, analysis, and model building, Bereiter and Scardamalia's levels 3 to 6—has taken a long time to take hold in the area of writing research.

This has all changed very quickly within the last few years. Task analyses, experimental studies, and the first models and theories began to appear; in schools, a "writing crisis" was diagnosed, joining and sometimes even replacing the more familiar "reading crisis." Books on writing from a cognitive perspective appeared. Newsletters were started to disseminate the new knowledge beyond the research community. Progress has been rapid, and writing research has assumed its rightful place within the study of the higher cognitive processes.

Bereiter and Scardamalia's *Psychology of Written Composition* marks a highpoint in this development. Their book makes contributions at three levels. First, it significantly expands the data base upon which our understanding of writing rests. We have learned a great deal about writing processes in the last few years, both through experiment, protocol analyses, and observation, and Bereiter and Scardamalia have a lot more to tell us. Secondly, the book presents an original theory, or at any rate, the beginnings of a theory of writing and the development of writing skills, emphasizing the control processes in writing. Their views are bound to have a strong impact on future theorizing and model building in this field. Last but not least, Bereiter and Scardamalia fulfill a very important bridging function between the older literature on writing in educational psychology and the new cognitive approach. Since they know and understand both viewpoints, they are able use a great deal of the pre-cognitive work to help us formulate our present concerns. Many cognitive scientists who are interested in writing lack the background to deal with the older literature on their own; Bereiter and Scardamalia make it possible for them to integrate some of these findings. This is a real service, since there is, after all, no point in continually reinventing the wheel.

The Psychology of Writing and Cognitive Theory.   One notion that might be entertained concerning the relation between the psychology of writing and cognitive theory would be that the former is nothing more than a particular domain of application of the latter, just as building bridges is an engineering application of physics. Perhaps this would be the ideal state of affairs in the distant future, but, alas, nothing could be further from the truth at present. It is not possible to derive from cognitive theory a model of the writing process—cognitive theory is not yet sufficiently detailed or sufficiently complete to support such a complex application. Our knowledge about general cognitive processes is still fragmentary, incomplete, unsystematic, and unreliable in several areas. At best, it serves as a local constraint on writing research or helps us to understand and relate the findings uncovered by the research to other phenomena. Indeed, in this situation, the general theory receives more from the "applied" field than it gives: Writing research itself contributes greatly to the development and elaboration of our ideas about cognition in general. In grappling with such complex phenomena as writing, we learn to sort out the basic elements of a general cognitive theory—perhaps more so than from the more traditional concentration on the elementary processes themselves.

Thus, Bereiter and Scardamalia's work suggests that writing research is becoming an integral part of the cognitive science enterprise, where the methods of cognitive science—from experiment to model building and simulation—will be routinely employed. (This is not quite the case yet: Both in terms of formal theorizing and computer simulation, the writing field still has some catching-up to do.) On the other hand, Bereiter and Scardamalia also demonstrate that research on writing provides an excellent opportunity and challenge for cognitive science. Writing research today is basic research, contributing its share and constraining the general theory of cognitive processes.

Cognitive Principles.   It is instructive to examine some of the ways in which Bereiter and Scardamalia make use of general principles from cognitive science in their own work on writing. Most fundamentally, Bereiter and Scardamalia manage to take over from current research on reading comprehension some useful notions about the units of representation at various levels. Explanations and interpretations differ, whether they are concerned with the actual words used and their linear organization into phrases, sentences, and paragraphs, or with the propositional meaning-units at the semantic level with their hierarchical structure, or directly with the objects, events, and states-in-the-world which are being written about, as they are reflected in the writer's memory organization and knowledge. Similarly, Bereiter and Scardamalia find the distinction between micro and macroprocesses useful in accounting for writing processes as it has been in theories of reading comprehension. Thus, while reading and writing strategies are of course different, the general framework of comprehension models appears to be readily exportable.

Throughout this book, the authors emphasize the role of control strategies. Cognitive theory today is characterized by a particular kind of architecture based on the distinction between fixed structures and flexible control processes. The structures establish the constraints within which the control processes can operate. The development of writing skills consists to a large extent in acquiring suitable control strategies. Structural changes (e.g., the knowledge structures of the writer) interact with the development of control strategies, creating a very rich and complex pattern of experimental results and observations. The structure/strategy distinction provides Bereiter and Scardamalia with one means of systematic analysis in the face of all this complexity.

Another characteristic of current theorizing about information processing relies on arguments about resource limitations and resource assignments for competing demands. Of particular interest in this connection are short-term memory limitations and their consequences for the writing process. At some stage in the development of models of writing behavior, formal process models that trace quantitatively the implications of various resource limits on writing processes may be required.

We write about what we know, what we have experienced, what we remember. Writing, therefore, always involves memory retrieval (plus, of course, a great deal else). Retrieval processes have been studied intensively for some time by memory researchers. It is interesting, instructive, and a little depressing to note, therefore, how little memory theory has to offer writing research in this respect. We know a lot about memory retrieval in list-learning experiments, and the principles derived from these studies are certainly relevant to the concerns of Bereiter and Scardamalia. What they would need, however, are not merely some general principles, but explicit models of information retrieval in various writing environments that could be used as subcomponents in theories of writing processes. Such models are only available today in rudimentary versions or not at all. There is some work appearing today on models for the retrieval of personal experiences and some work on general knowledge retrieval. However, the latter, for instance, at best deals with the situation that Bereiter and Scardamalia have called "knowledge telling." All the more complex strategies, where writing researchers could really use some help and guidance from their colleagues in the memory laboratories, remain unexplored. Indeed, if you want to know about knowledge retrieval, other than the simplest cases, you are better off turning to research on writing than to general cognitive theory. I am confident that this situation will change, and change soon, but at present it is still the general theory that has some catching up to do. Clearly, what I would regard as the applications field is leading and guiding the basic research effort—not the other way round! *Perspectives for Cognitive Science.*   Writing research, of course, has its own fields of application: in education, the teaching of writing at all levels, and more recently, in the design of software systems to support writing. Bereiter and Scardamalia concentrate on the educational implications of their work. Once again, it is not so much the case that they formulate a theory of writing, and then investigate its implications for education. Instead, they never lose sight of their educational concerns, which guide every phase of their work. This perspective has important consequences for the way they present their research in this book: It tempers theoretical analysis with a healthy dose of common sense. This common sense affects neither the sharpness nor the depth of their analysis, but it helps keep the real complexity of the problem in view. Bereiter and Scardamalia make theoretical predictions that are unhedged and testable, yet they are very aware of boundary conditions. In other words, their educational perspective helps them to do analytic research on a real, complex problem, without turning that problem into a laboratory version that is a mere shadow of the original.

The other application area of writing research—software tools for the writer—is one in which there is currently a considerable interest. A great many of such writing tools are being developed, and there appears to be a ready market for them. This development, unfortunately, proceeds for the most part without a serious theoretical basis. Software tools are developed, but tools for what? What really are the problems writers need tools for? Until such questions are answered more satisfactorily than is possible by intuition and first-order task analyses, progress in this field will probably remain restricted. *The Psychology of Written Composition* and similar work will help to change this state of affairs. What we are doing, or should be doing, in writing instruction as well as in the construction of writing tools, may soon be based on a sound theoretical foundation—and that emerging theory of writing promises to become a major component of cognitive science and a significant influence on it.

—Walter Kintsch

Preface

The subject of this book is the mental activities that go into composing written texts. For brevity we will often refer to the subject simply as *writing,* but the term should not be taken too literally. In this book we are not concerned with the physical act of writing, except insofar as it influences other processes. The mental activities of writing considered in our research are the same kinds of higher mental processes that figure in cognitive research on all aspects of human intelligence. They include goal setting, planning, memory search, problem solving, evaluation, and diagnosis. Writing is, of course, easily recognized as an activity in which a good deal of human intelligence is put to use. Its neglect, until very recently, by cognitive scientists is, however, easy to understand. Cognitive research has been gradually working its way from well-defined to ill-defined problems, from tasks that draw on limited knowledge to tasks that draw on large bodies of knowledge, and from tasks that are easily constrained experimentally to ones that are more susceptible to intentions of the participants. On all of these counts, writing lies far out on the yet-to-be-reached end of the continuum.

Theorizers about the composing process face a difficulty that is not faced by theorizers about even such closely related processes as reading. It is that people will judge your theory against an elaborate set of intuitions of their own, formed from their own experience as writers. Reading, along with many other cognitive processes, tends to go on with little conscious awareness of the process itself. But writers, especially when grappling with a difficult task, tend to be keenly aware of at least certain aspects of what is going on in their minds. This is no accident, we shall argue: Skilled writers need to be able to exert a measure of deliberate control over the process. As a by-product, however, experienced writers tend to have rich intuitive theories, in contrast to which the theoretical propositions emerging from a young science are likely to seem rather thin. It is perfectly reasonable to insist that a psychology of writing should not violate our intuitions—at least not without putting up a good argument. But it is not reasonable to insist that a psychology of writing in this day and age should do justice to all our intuitions. For our intuitions about what goes on in writing range across all dimensions of the human spirit.

A theory of writing that could explain writing in all its fullness could pretty much send all other psychological theories packing. We believe it is a mistake, however, to try to build a psychology so as to encompass the widest possible range of intuitions. Such efforts win plaudits, but they neglect the basic task of science, which is to tell us things we do not already know.

In an effort to find out things about the nature of the composing process that are not already intuitively known, we have concentrated on comparisons between the composing processes of unskilled writers and those of more expert writers. The body of intuitive knowledge about writing is, after all, knowledge accumulated by people of mature intellect for whom writing is a significant enough activity that they have taken the trouble to introspect about it. Is writing basically the same process for beginners, with a few parameters set differently, or does it follow a qualitatively different model? These are questions we have pursued through comparative studies of older and younger writers, writers of the same age, skilled and less skilled, coupled with experimental and instructional interventions designed to reveal aspects of writing that are normally hidden from examination.

The upshot of this research is that we have come to believe that there are distinctly different strategies that involve writers in different kinds of thinking when they write. These differences have structure and are not simply a matter of more of this or less of that. Producing discourse without a conversational partner—which is what writing amounts to—is a formidable task for novices. To cope with it they devise a simplifying strategy. Expertise in writing does not come from refining this strategy or from mastering the use of it. Expertise comes from subordinating the simple strategy to another that is a great deal more complex. In the following chapters we present evidence leading up to this view of writing competence and investigate what is involved in moving from the simpler to the more complex strategy.

The book is aimed at three classes of readers. One is people who are generally interested in cognition or cognitive development, and who we hope will find that research on writing contributes knowledge relevant to understanding major issues in these fields. Another class is people primarily interested in writing, but who are curious about how the mind copes with this task. We believe that the story to be told about the composing process is sufficiently fascinating and garnished with surprises to repay the effort of wading through some psychological jargon and experimental details in order to get the story. The final class of people is instructional psychologists. Instruction is both a goal and a tool of our research. That is, we use instructional interventions to test theoretical ideas but also have an eye on devising instructional approaches that are effective for difficult-to-acquire abilities.

Because the book does include instructional research, it may be helpful to say a few words about how it relates to what is currently happening in the teaching of writing. There is a reform movement afoot, concerned with making writing a more substantial, meaningful, and successful experience for students. A salient notion guiding this movement is that children have a great deal more natural aptitude for writing than is revealed under traditional school conditions (Graves, 1983). It is easy to see how our claim that novices and experts follow qualitatively different models could be construed as a denial of children's natural aptitude for writing.

In point of fact, we also argue that children have a great deal of competence that is not manifested in their typical school writing. Differences have to do with interpretation. Some take the finding of how much better students write when they are in a supportive environment and allowed to write on what really matters to them, to mean that we already know enough to sweep away the obstacles to expert competence. We are struck by how much more dependent novices are than experts on environmental supports on particular genres—most particularly the personal experience narrative—and on the topic of writing. We see a major unsolved educational problem in enabling students to sustain high-level parts of the composing process independently, in a variety of genres and topics, not simply those most suited to their strategy.

Educationally, our interest is in what it takes for students to grow beyond their dependencies and acquire the autonomous competence of the expert writer. As for the issue of what children can and cannot do at a certain age, it is probably safe to declare that this is always a false issue as far as contemporary developmental psychology is concerned. Cognitive developmental psychology tends to be concerned with what develops and how (see, e.g., Siegler, 1978). But *when* it develops is of interest only insofar as issues of synchrony and asynchrony, prerequisite conditions, and the like are concerned. In the pages that follow we present strong contrasts between mature and immature competence in writing. But it is the contrast between two different executive systems for composing that is of interest. There is good reason to believe that many educated adults follow the immature model. This is, in fact, a reason for believing that the study of these contrasting models is of educational as well as psychological importance. If someone could show us a seven-year-old who followed the mature model or (better yet) could show us an educational program that turned out children who follow the mature model, this would be of considerable interest but would not undermine claims we make about these models.

In both instructional and noninstructional research, our persistent interest has been *the effects of the composing process on the ideational content of what is written.* Language production itself has been considered mainly insofar as it may aid or interfere with the processing of content. When writing is viewed from the standpoint of language, it often seems that children do a better job of expressing what is on their minds than adults do of expressing what is on theirs, and so the challenge to writing instruction becomes that of preserving and nurturing the early genius. When writing is viewed from the standpoint of ideational content, however, it becomes clear that children have something important to learn. Mature competence is not merely a more sophisticated way of expressing what is on one's mind. It is a whole different way of interacting with one's knowledge, a cultural attainment of a high order, and one that we are only beginning to have inklings about how to develop.

BACKGROUND OF THE BOOK

The authors began research on writing in 1976. Our previous collaborative research had been on working memory capacity and intelligence (Bereiter & Scardamalia, 1979). What motivated us to study writing was not the "writing crisis," which was just beginning to grab attention at that time, but rather the belief that cognitive research had progressed to the point where research on the mental processes of composition could be profitable. During the next 8 years we and our coworkers completed about 120 studies, which form the empirical basis of this book.

With the upsurge of interest sparked by the "writing crisis," numerous conferences and edited book projects arose, to which we contributed papers. We chose this medium for publishing our findings because our research was moving very rapidly and book chapters provided an opportunity to integrate a number of studies at one time. The various chapters were written with a view to minimizing redundancy and to producing a coherent body of documentation. Coherence was militated against, however, by having the chapters scattered through many different books, so that even the most assiduous reader would be unlikely to read all of the chapters, much less read them in an order that would convey the cumulative force of the research program. The present volume is an attempt to convey such a sense of the whole. It consists of 12 previously published documents, along with two newly written chapters intended to introduce and sum up the research, and a variety of prefaces and postscripts to tie chapters together and to report more recent findings. The previously published chapters have been edited to remove major redundancies, but have not been revised to incorporate the virtues of hindsight. Consequently the reader will see some variations among the chapters in emphasis and interpretation. We hope that these variations will add breadth rather than confusion to the book's message.

Acknowledgments

The research on which this book is based was undertaken with initial grants from York University and the Ontario Institute for Studies in Education (OISE), later augmented by grants from the Alfred P. Sloan Foundation and the Social Sciences and Humanities Research Council of Canada, and with continuing support from the Ontario Ministry of Education, through its block grant to OISE. An award from the National Institute of Education, funded by the Spencer Foundation, made possible the purchase of computing equipment that greatly facilitated later stages of the research and also the preparation of this book. Grants from the Sloan Foundation were especially important both in providing released time from teaching duties and in supporting the free-ranging exploration of problems that eventually led to the central findings of the research program.

Of the many people whose contributions we would like to acknowledge, first thanks must go to those who have worked with us on writing research projects as research associates, assistants, or students. The total list would run to dozens, but among them we would like especially to cite the following, who made sustained contributions not only to the conduct of the research but to the intellectual life of the research program: Valerie Anderson, Bill Baird, Bob Bracewell, Clare Brett, Jud Burtis, Suzanne Hidi, Roz Klaiman, Pamela Paris, Rosanne Steinbach, Jacqueline Tetroe, Larry Turkish, and Earl Woodruff.

Fellow researchers whose interest and ideas have helped us greatly include Robert de Beaugrande, Ann Brown, Joseph Campione, Robbie Case, Allan Collins, Bryant Fillion, Linda Flower, Jim Greeno, Dick Hayes, Walter Kintsch, Juan Pascual-Leone, and Ian Pringle. A critical reading of the entire manuscript by Andre Carus contributed more than a just noticeable difference to such coherence as this book has managed to achieve.

The writing research projects have taken experimenters into scores of classrooms, often for repeated visits, and almost always at the wrong time of year. That so many teachers and principals have invited us back bespeaks not only forbearance but a truly impressive commitment to the hope of educational improvement through research. We would especially like to thank Roberta Charlesworth who, as Director of English for the North York, Ontario, schools, was unflagging in her dedication to excellence through knowledge and imagination.

The research program also owes much to its project secretaries, Carol Broome, succeeded by Yvonne Lucas. Barbara White assisted in a number of valuable ways in bringing this book to completion. But the main burden for handling manuscript preparation and references has fallen on Carolyn Taylor, whose competence and perseverance have been a marvel to us.

Finally, we wish to thank the following publishers for permission to reprint papers or to quote material from their publications:

Ablex Publishing Corporation
Teachability of reflective processes in written composition (with Rosanne Steinbach) *Cognitive Science, 8,* 173–190. Copyright © 1984 by Ablex Publishing Corporation and used by permission.

Academic Press, Inc.
The role of production factors in writing ability. (with H. Goelman), in M. Nystrand (Ed.) *What writers know: The language, process, and structure of written discourse,* pp. 173–210. Copyright © 1982 by Academic Press, Inc. and used by permission.

Lawrence Erlbaum Associates
From conversation to composition: The role of instruction in a developmental process. In R. Glaser (Ed.) *Advances in instructional psychology (Vol. 2),* pp. 1–64. Copyright © 1982 by Lawrence Erlbaum Associates and used by permission.

How children cope with the cognitive demands of writing. In C. H. Frederiksen & J. F. Dominic (Eds.) *Writing: The nature, development and teaching of written communication,* pp. 81–103. Copyright © 1981 by Lawrence Erlbaum Associates and used by permission.

Information-processing demand of text composition. In H. Mandl, N. Stein & T. Trabasso (Eds.) *Learning and comprehension of text,* pp. 407–428. Copyright © 1984 by Lawrence Erlbaum Associates and used by permission.

Cognitive coping strategies and the problem of "inert knowledge". In S. S. Chipman, J. W. Segal, & R. Glaser (Eds.), *Thinking and learning skills: Current research and open questions (Vol. 2).* Copyright © 1985 by Lawrence Erlbaum Associates and used by permission.

Part I
Central Concepts

Chapter 1
Two Models
of Composing Processes

1 Chomsky (1980) has argued that if we want to advance our understanding of the mind as a biological entity, we should study what it does easily and well. In particular, we should study those abilities that people acquire most naturally, with the least dependence on the environment. If that is to be the role of cognitive psychology, what becomes of instructional psychology? For if instructional psychology has a province, it is the province of things that have proved difficult to learn, that are believed to require substantial and purposely arranged contributions from the environment.

We would suggest that there are, in fact, complementary roles for a psychology of the easy and a psychology of the difficult, and that a complete cognitive science needs to encompass both. Research on cognition in infants and young children makes it increasingly evident that human beings come into the world already primed for certain kinds of knowledge. That is, they either already possess the knowledge in embryonic form or possess some kind of innate readiness to acquire it. Such appears to be the case not only with grammar, which is Chomsky's prime example, but also number (Gelman & Gallistel, 1978) and perceptual organization (Spelke, 1982). On the other hand, human beings are distinguished by their ability to acquire expertise— that is, to develop high levels of ability and knowledge of kinds that do not arise naturally out of everyday living but that require sustained effort over long periods of time. Hayes (1981) has concluded that in all those areas where top levels of expertise are equated with genius, it takes 10 years of sustained effort to achieve the necessary knowledge and skill.

In the preceding paragraph we conflated easy with natural and difficult with requiring special provisions for learning. Obviously there is no strict correlation between the naturalness and the difficulty dimensions. Walking comes naturally, yet infants work hard at it. One must be taught how to drive a car, but it is not difficult for most people to learn. The key distinction, for which we have found no convenient labels, is between those kinds of abilities that are almost inevitably acquired through ordinary living (including ordinary living in school classrooms) and those that require some special effort to transcend naturally occurring limitations. With due recognition that the terms do not fully condense the intended meanings, we shall refer to the two kinds of abilities as *natural* and *problematic.*

A complete cognitive science needs to account for both ends of the natural-to-problematic continuum. But more than that, it needs to consider possible interactions, such as the following:

> To what extent are the more problematic kinds of human capabilities built up from more naturally acquired capabilities?
> To what extent may naturally acquired abilities stand in the way of development of more expert ways of performing the same functions?

In this book we want to consider written composition from the standpoint of naturally acquired and more problematic human capabilities, with a view toward issues like the two just raised. By looking at both the easy and the hard aspects and their interaction, we hope to contribute to understanding both the mind's natural capabilities and what is involved in going beyond those natural capabilities.

WRITING AS BOTH NATURAL AND PROBLEMATIC

Writing—by which we mean the composing of texts intended to be read by people not present—is a promising domain within which to study the relationship between easy and difficult cognitive functions. On the one hand, writing is a skill traditionally viewed as difficult to acquire, and one that is developed to immensely higher levels in some people than in others. Thus it is a suitable domain for the study of expertise. On the other hand, it is based on linguistic capabilities that are shared by all normal members of the species. People with only the rudiments of literacy can, if sufficiently motivated, redirect their oral language abilities into producing a written text. Indeed, children lacking even the most rudimentary alphabetism can nevertheless produce written characters that have some linguistic efficacy (Vygotsky, 1978).

There is, indeed, an interesting bifurcation in the literature between treatments of writing as a difficult task, mastered only with great effort, and treatments of it as a natural consequence of language development, needing only a healthy environment in which to flourish. Convincing facts are provided to support both views. On the one hand we have evidences of poor writing abilities, even among relatively favored university students (Lyons, 1976) and professional people (Odell, 1980). On the other hand we have numerous reports of children taking readily to literary creation when they have yet scarcely learned to handle a pencil (Graves, 1983). While children's writing is unquestionably recognizable as coming from children, it often shows the kind of expressiveness and flair that we associate with literary talent.

One could perhaps dismiss such contradictory findings as due to the application of different standards of quality. It may, in short, be easy to write poorly and difficult to write well. But that is a half truth which obscures virtually everything that is interesting about writing competence.

The view of writing that emerges from our research is more complex than either the "it's hard" or the "it's easy" view or any compromise that might be struck between them. We propose that there are two basically different models of composing that people may follow. It is possible to write well or poorly following either model. One model makes writing a fairly natural task. The task has its difficulties, but the model handles these in ways that make maximum use of already existing cognitive structures and that minimize the extent of novel problems that must be solved. The other model makes writing a task that keeps growing in complexity to match the expanding competence of the writer. Thus, as skill increases, old difficulties tend to be replaced by new ones of a higher order. Why would anyone choose the more complex model? Well, in the first place it seems that not very many people do, and it is probably never used to the exclusion of the simpler model. But for those who do use it, the more difficult model provides both the promise of higher levels of literary quality and, which is perhaps more important for most people, the opportunity to gain vastly greater cognitive benefits from the process of writing itself.

One way of writing appears to be explainable within a "psychology of the natural." It makes maximum use of natural human endowments of language competence and of skills learned through ordinary social experience, but it is also limited by them. This way of writing we shall call *knowledge telling.* The other way of writing seems to require a "psychology of the problematic" for its explanation. It involves going beyond normal linguistic endowments in order to enable the individual to accomplish alone what is normally accomplished only through social interaction—namely, the reprocessing of knowledge. Accordingly, we shall call this model of writing *knowledge transforming*.

A two-model description may fit many other domains in addition to writing. Everyday thinking, which is easy and natural, seems to follow a different model from formal reasoning, which is more problematic (Bartlett, 1958). Similar contrasts may be drawn between casual reading and critical reading, between talking and oratory, between the singing people do when they light-heartedly burst into song and the intensely concentrated effort of the vocal artist.

In each case the contrast is between a naturally acquired ability, common to almost everyone, and a more studied ability involving skills that not everyone acquires. The more studied ability is not a matter of doing the same thing but doing it better. There are good talkers and bad orators, and most of us would prefer listening to the former. And there are surely people whose formal reasoning is a less reliable guide to wise action than some other people's everyday thought. What distinguishes the more studied abilities is that they involve deliberate, strategic control over parts of the process that are unattended to in the more naturally developed ability. That is why different models are required to describe these processes.

Such deliberate control of normally unmonitored activity exacts a price in mental effort and it opens up possibilities of error, but it also opens up possibilities of expertise that go far beyond what people are able to do with their naturally acquired abilities. In the case of writing, this means going beyond the ordinary ability to put one's thoughts and knowledge into writing. It means, among other things, being able to shape a piece of writing to achieve intended effects and to reorganize one's knowledge in the process. The main focus of this book is on the development of these and other higher-level controls over the process of composition.

FROM CONVERSATION TO KNOWLEDGE TELLING TO KNOWLEDGE TRANSFORMING

Although children are often already proficient users of oral language at the time they begin schooling, it is usually some years before they can produce language in writing with anything like the proficiency they have in speech. Longitudinal studies by Loban (1976) suggest that the catch-up point typically comes around the age of twelve. The most immediate obstacle, of course, is the written code itself. But that is far from being the only obstacle.

Others of a less obvious nature are discussed in Chapter 3. These less obvious problems have to do with generating the content of discourse rather than with generating written language. Generating content is seldom a problem in oral discourse because of the numerous kinds of support provided by conversational partners. Without this conversational support, children encounter problems in thinking of what to say, in staying on topic, in producing an intelligible whole, and in making choices appropriate to an audience not immediately present.

In order to solve the problems of generating content without inputs from conversational partners, beginning writers must discover alternative sources of cues for retrieving content from memory. Once discourse has started, text already produced can provide cues for retrieval of related content. But they are not enough to ensure coherent discourse, except perhaps of the stream-of-consciousness variety. Two other sources of cues are the topic, often conveyed by an assignment, and the discourse schema. The latter consists of knowledge of a selected literary form (such as narrative or argument), which specifies the kinds of elements to be included in the discourse and something about their arrangement. Cues from these two additional sources should tend to elicit content that sticks to a topic and that meets the requirements of a discourse type. In essence, the knowledge-telling model is a model of how discourse production can go on, using only these sources of cues for content retrieval—topic, discourse schema, and text already produced.

The main features of the knowledge-telling model are diagrammed in Figure 1.1. The diagram indicates a composing process that begins with a writing assignment. It could also begin with a self-chosen writing project, however, so long as there is some mental representation of the task that can be analyzed into identifiers of topic and genre or discourse type. The task might, for instance, be to write an essay on whether boys and girls should play on the same sports teams. Depending on the sophistication of the writer, the topic identifiers extracted from this assignment might be *boys, girls,* and *sports* or *amateur sports* and *sexual equality.* According to the model, these topic identifiers serve as cues that automatically prime associated concepts through a process of spreading activation (Anderson, 1983). This process does not ensure that the information retrieved will be relevant, but there is a built-in tendency toward topical relevance. As Anderson explains, "spreading activation identifies and favors the processing of information most related to the immediate context (or sources of activation)" (Anderson, 1983, p. 86). Naturally, the appropriateness of the information retrieved will depend on the cues extracted and on the availability of information in memory. For instance, one would expect that the cues, *amateur sports* and *sexual equality,* would have a greater likelihood of eliciting information fitting the intent of the assignment than would the cues, *boys, girls,* and *sports,* provided the writer had knowledge stored in memory related to those cues. In either case, however, the retrieval is assumed to take place automatically through the spread of activation, without the writer's having to monitor or plan for coherence.

Cues related to discourse type are assumed to function in much the same way. The assignment to write an essay on whether boys and girls should play on the same sports teams is likely to suggest that what is called for is an argument or *opinion essay.* Again, the cues actually extracted will depend on the sophistication of the writer. Some immature writers may have an opinion-essay schema that contains only two elements—*statement of belief* and *reason*

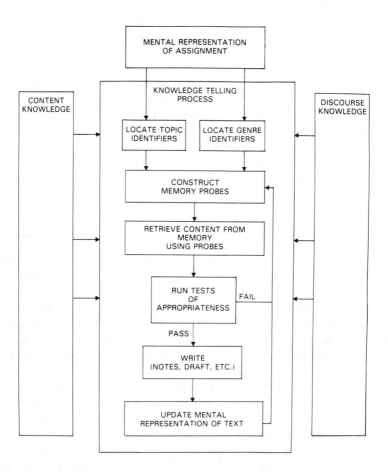

Figure 1.1. Structure of the knowledge-telling model.

(see Chapter 4). Others may have more complex schemas that provide for multiple reasons, anticipation of counterarguments, and so on. In any case, it is assumed that these discourse elements function as cues for retrieval of content from memory, operating in combination with topical cues to increase the likelihood that what is retrieved will not only be relevant to the topic but also appropriate to the structure of the composition. Thus, the cues, *boys, girls, sports,* and *statement of belief* would be very likely to produce retrieval of the idea that boys and girls should or should not play on the same sports teams, an appropriate idea on which to base the opening sentence of the essay.

According to the model shown in Figure 1.1, an item of content, once retrieved, is subjected to tests of appropriateness. These could be minimal tests of whether the item "sounds right" in relation to the assignment and to text already produced or they could be more involved tests of interest, persuasive power, appropriateness to the literary genre, and so on. If the item passes the tests it is entered into notes or text and a next cycle of content generation begins. Suppose, for instance, that the first sentence produced in our example is "I think boys and girls should be allowed to play on the same sports teams, but not for hockey or football." The next cycle of content generation might make use of the same topical cues as before, plus the new cues, *hockey* and *football,* and the discourse schema cue might be changed to *reason.* A likely result, therefore, would be retrieval of a reason why boys and girls should not play hockey or football together. Content generation and writing would proceed in this way until the composition was completed.

This way of generating text content was described for us by a 12-year-old student as follows:

> I have a whole bunch of ideas and write down until my supply of ideas is exhausted. Then I might try to think of more ideas up to the point when you can't get any more ideas that are worth putting down on paper and then I would end it.

Knowledge telling provides a natural and efficient solution to the problems immature writers face in generating text content without external support. The solution is efficient enough that, given any reasonable specification of topic and genre, the writer can get started in a matter of seconds and speedily produce an essay that will be on topic and that will conform to the type of text called for. The solution is natural because it makes use of readily available knowledge—thus it is favorable to report of personal experience—and it relies on already existing discourse-production skills in making use of external cues and cues generated from language production itself. It preserves the straight-ahead form of oral language production and requires no significantly greater amount of planning or goal-setting than does ordinary conversation. Hence it should be little wonder if such an approach to writing were to be common among elementary school students and to be retained on into university and career.

KNOWLEDGE TELLING VERSUS KNOWLEDGE TRANSFORMING

In the preceding discussion of the knowledge-telling model, it was allowed that there could be large differences in outcome depending on the writer's knowledge of the topic of discourse and on the writer's sophistication in the literary genre. In addition, of course, quality of the written product will vary depending on language abilities, such as diction and syntactic fluency, that are not dealt with in the knowledge-telling model. With all this allowance for individual differences and for improvement through learning, it is not obvious that a second model is required to account for the different ways writers go about generating text content.

Consider, however, the following description by Aldous Huxley of his composing process:

> Generally, I write everything many times over. All my thoughts are second thoughts. And I correct each page a great deal, or rewrite it several times as I go along. . . . Things come to me in driblets, and when the driblets come I have to work hard to make them into something coherent. (Cited in *Writers at Work,* 2nd series, 1963, p. 197.)

The process described here does not sound like merely a more sophisticated or elaborate version of the process sixth-graders describe of writing down thoughts that they already have in their minds. The process Huxley describes is one in which the thoughts come into existence through the composing process itself, beginning as inchoate entities ("driblets") and gradually, by dint of much rethinking and restating, taking the form of fully developed thoughts. This is the process that we shall call "knowledge transforming." It is a process that cannot be accounted for by the knowledge-telling model and that seems to require a differently structured model.

This reworking or transforming of knowledge has been described in a variety of ways by professional writers (Lowenthal, 1980; Murray, 1978; Odell, 1980). But is it, then, a process found only in exceptionally talented people who have made writing their life's work? No. As studies to be reported in later chapters will show (see especially Chapters 8 and 14), evidence of a knowledge-transforming approach to writing can be found even among people who have no particular talent for or commitment to writing, some of whom would even be judged to be bad writers by literary standards.

Where are writers who use knowledge-transforming strategies to be found? We find them among talented young students, undergraduate and graduate students in psychology, education, and English, but they could probably be found among people at advanced levels in any intellectual discipline. These are people who, like Huxley, actively rework their thoughts. While they may not have Huxley's skill in expressing those thoughts, they are used to considering whether the text they have written says what they want it to say and whether they themselves believe what the text says. In the process, they are likely to consider not only changes in the text but also changes in what they want to say. Thus it is that writing can play a role in the development of their knowledge.

To account for this interaction between text processing and knowledge processing, it is necessary to have a model of considerably greater complexity than the model of knowledge telling. Such a model is sketched in Figure 1.2. It will be noted that the knowledge-telling process, as depicted in Figure 1.1, is still there, but it is now embedded in a problem-solving process involving two different kinds of problem spaces. In the content space, problems of belief and knowledge are worked out. In the rhetorical space, problems of achieving goals of the composition are dealt with. Connections between the two problem spaces indicate output from one space serving as input to the other. For instance, a writer might be working in the rhetorical space on a problem of clarity and might arrive at the decision that she needs to define the concept of *responsibility* that she is building her argument around. This is a content problem, however, and so one might imagine a message going from the rhetorical problem space to the content problem space, saying "What do I really mean by *responsibility?*" Work on this problem within the content space might lead to determining that responsibility is not really the central issue after all but that the issue is, let us say, *competence to judge.* This decision, transferred to the rhetorical space, might initiate work on problems of modifying the text already written so as to accommodate the change in central issue. This work might give rise to further content problems, which might lead to further changes in the writer's beliefs, and so on until a text is finally created that successfully embodies the writer's latest thinking on the subject.

It is this kind of interaction between problem spaces that we argue, in Chapter 12, is the basis for reflective thought in writing. Writing is not always problematic, of course, and often we write things that have been so thoroughly thought out and rehearsed on other occasions that there is no need to reflect on them. Some writers, furthermore, may intentionally

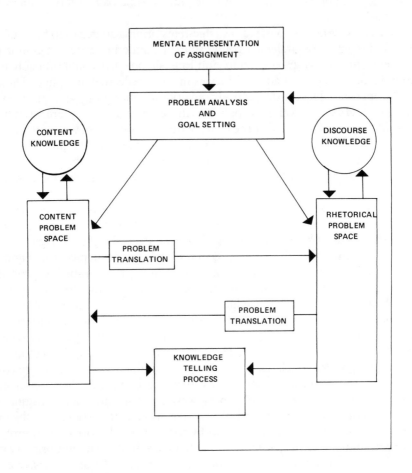

Figure 1.2.   Structure of the knowledge-transforming model.

suppress problem-solving operations until a first draft is completed. In all of these cases, knowledge telling might function much as we described it in the preceding section. In this way, knowledge telling remains one of the capabilities of the knowledge-transforming model. But the distinctive capabilities of the knowledge-transforming model lie in formulating and solving problems and doing so in ways that allow a two-way interaction between continuously developing knowledge and continuously developing text.

OBSERVABLE DIFFERENCES BETWEEN KNOWLEDGE TELLING AND KNOWLEDGE TRANSFORMING

The studies to be reported in this book are for the most part experimental studies that try to bring hidden aspects of the composing process to light. In this introductory chapter, however, we will confine ourselves to more directly observable manifestations of different approaches to composition.

It might seem that the way to begin is by showing pieces of writing that exemplify knowledge telling and knowledge transforming. That would be misleading, however. Knowledge telling and knowledge transforming refer to mental processes by which texts are composed, not to texts themselves. You cannot tell by reading this chapter whether we have engaged in problem-solving and knowledge-transforming operations while writing it or whether we have simply written down content that was already stored in memory in more or less the form presented here. You would have had to overhear, for instance, our deliberations about referring to knowledge telling as "easy" versus referring to it as "natural" to judge the extent to which a rhetorical problem led us to revise our thinking about a matter of substance.

When we see a typical example of what Macrorie (1976) calls "Engfish"—a string of vacuous assertions dressed up in the student's impression of academic diction—we feel fairly confident that we are looking at a product of knowledge telling. But it is impossible to be sure. The student's assertion that change is the norm in this modern world of today might, in fact, express an insight sharpened by the struggle for a sententious tone. On the other hand, if it could be established that that assertion appeared on the page within 30 seconds after the essay was assigned, we might with greater confidence judge what kind of composing process generated it. It is such overt indicators of composing processes that we now survey briefly—start-up times, planning notes, thinking-aloud protocols, and revisions. The processes to which these overt indicators point are discussed in subsequent chapters.

Start-up Times

According to the knowledge-telling model, the time it should take to get started writing upon receipt of a writing assignment is the time it takes to retrieve a first item of content fitting requirements of the topic and genre. This would vary, of course, depending on the writer's familiarity with the topic and genre. Where these are very familiar, start-up time could be expected to be very fast indeed. A corollary is that start-up time should not vary with other requirements. According to the knowledge-transforming model, on the other hand, time to start writing should, in general, depend on goals set by the writer, the kinds of problems that have to be solved in advance, and the complexity of the plan constructed. Start-up times would thus be highly variable, but they should tend to increase as more time is available and, unless there is some requirement of condensation, should be greater for an anticipated long composition than for a short one.

Figure 1.3 (from Zbrodoff, 1984) shows how long people spent between the time they were given a simple story-writing assignment and the time they started to write. The top half of Figure 1.3 shows how people responded to time constraints, which varied from being allowed only 2.5 minutes for completing the story to being allowed 20 minutes. The bottom half of the figure shows comparable data for conditions in which there were no time constraints but where length was controlled instead, with required lengths ranging from 6 to 48 lines. It may be seen that grade 5 children behaved exactly as would be expected from the knowledge-telling model. Their start-up times were very brief—just a few seconds—and they did not vary with either the amount of time allowed or with the size of text they were to produce. Adults, on the other hand, showed the kinds of adaptations to be expected from the knowledge-transforming model. The more time they were allowed, the more time they spent before beginning to write; and when no time constraints were imposed they spent much more time than under even the most liberal time limits. Their start-up times also increased depending on the length of the story they were required to produce. It may be noted that the grade-10 students were more like fifth-graders than like adults in these respects, although there is some suggestion that they took longer to get started on longer stories.

Notemaking

The data just discussed deal with spans of time in which text planning of some kind is presumably going on, but the data give no evidence as to what sort of mental activity is taking place. In a study that will be reported at greater length in Chapter 8, we tried to bring mental activity more into the open by instructing people to plan a composition in advance of writing it, encouraging them to take notes but urging them not to write actual text. Figure 1.4 shows notes from a graduate student planning a story on an assigned topic. What we have here is best described as a worksheet. On it the writer enters ideas at several different levels of abstraction, evaluates, and builds a structure out of them. Figure 1.5 shows, by contrast, notes typical of a 10-year-old. Except for their telegraphic form, these notes are best described as constituting the first draft of a text. As further analysis in Chapter 8 will

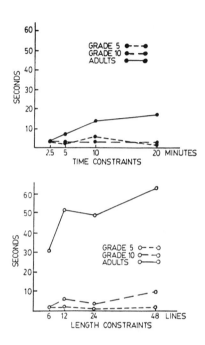

Figure 1.3. Time taken to start writing simple script-based stories on assigned topics (e.g., "Rick goes to a restaurant"). In Experiment 1 stories were written under different time constraints. In Experiment 2 they were written under constraints specifying the number of lines to be written (with unlimited time). From *Writing stories under time and length constraints* by N. J. Zbrodoff, 1984, unpublished doctoral dissertation, University of Toronto, Toronto. Reprinted by permission.

show, in fact, going from notes to final text is primarily a matter of editing in the case of younger students. For adults, on the other hand, going from notes to text involves going from a multi-level data structure, often set out in nonlinear form, to the creation of a linear text—a major transformation (cf. Beaugrande, 1984b).

These differences between younger and older writers are again congruent

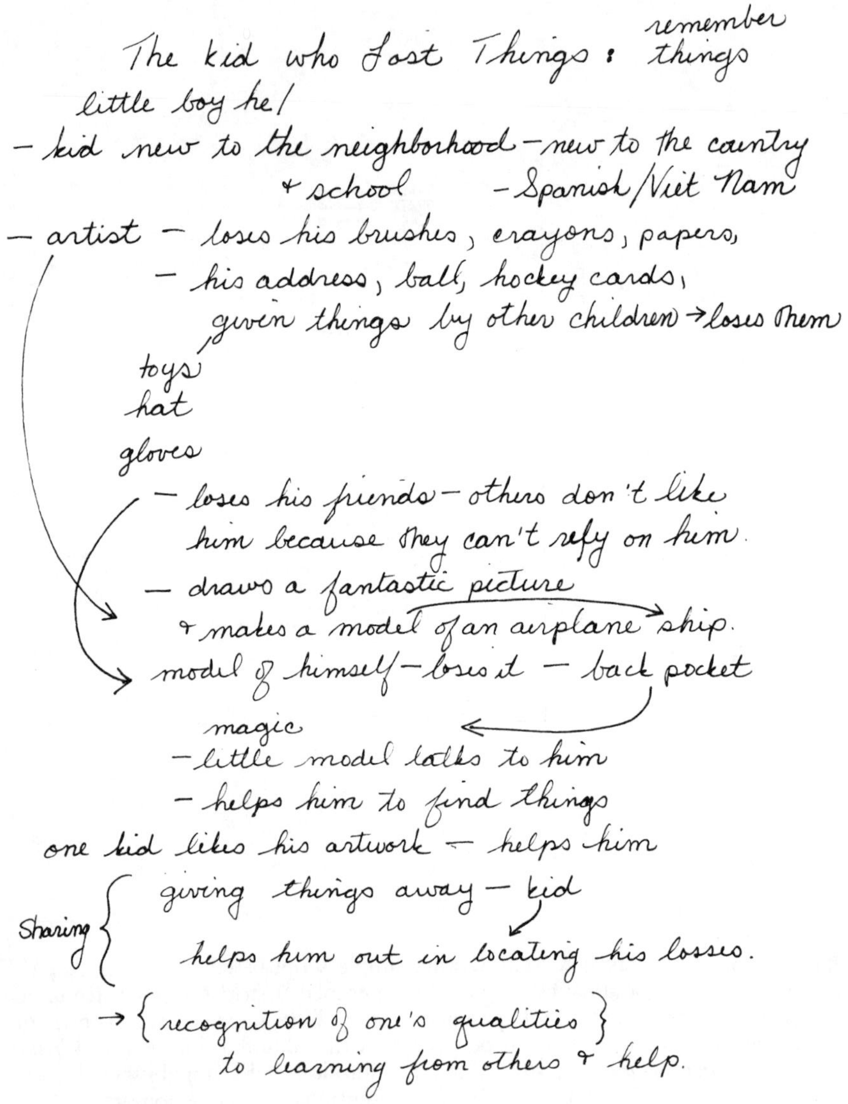

The kid who Lost Things : remember things

little boy he/

— kid new to the neighborhood — new to the country

       + school   — Spanish/Viet Nam

— artist — loses his brushes, crayons, papers,

     — his address, ball, hockey cards,

        given things by other children → loses them

toys

hat

gloves

    — loses his friends — others don't like

     him because they can't rely on him.

   — draws a fantastic picture

    + makes a model of an airplane ship.

  model of himself — loses it — back pocket

magic

   — little model talks to him

   — helps him to find things

one kid likes his artwork — helps him

Sharing { giving things away — kid

      helps him out in locating his losses.

→ { recognition of one's qualities }

       to learning from others + help.

Figure 1.4. Notes from a graduate student planning a story on the assigned topic, "The Kid Who Lost Things."

with the two models proposed. For novices, composing a text is a matter of generating a series of appropriate content items and writing them down. Instructions to plan rather than to write can affect the form of the output

The Kind how lost thing

There was a Kind named bob

He lost a bick

on street.

He can't see it

He is sad

He got home

His mother was mad

and what to his room bod did't have

supper

(the) in the morning he got it.

from a Big kind

the big kind (stole) stole it.

His mother was (happey) happle

the Big kind was punished from His

friends.

Figure 1.5. Notes from a grade-4 student planning a story on the assigned topic, "The Kid Who Lost Things."

(superficially) but cannot alter the process. This is what would be predicted if these young writers were following the knowledge-telling model. For more expert-like writers, however, composing is a complex goal-directed activity, significant parts of which do not involve the actual generation of text content or language. Instructions to plan rather than to write bring out evidences of these other activities in the form of nonverbal symbols (arrows, etc.), comments on ideas, and other types of notes not intended to form part of an eventual text.

Such operations on knowledge, only indirectly related to text generation, are suggested by T. S. Eliot in a response to questioning about his composing processes:

> That's one way in which my mind does seem to have worked throughout the years . . . doing things separately and then seeing the possibility of fusing them together, altering them, and making a kind of whole of them. (Cited in *Writers at Work*, 2nd series, 1963, p. 100.)

How such a process looks from the standpoint of knowledge telling is suggested by this sixth-grader's comment:

> Well, if he got all those ideas . . . well, first of all he wouldn't know what order to put them in. He could put them in a really bad order. And sometimes he might forget half of the information. . . . Then he starts writing the next paragraph on something else, then suddenly remembers something more about the [first thing]. . . . [That's happened to me] once or twice—very confusing for the reader who reads it.

From his own experience, this student concluded that it is best not to get involved with separate clusters of information that must then be fused together. Stick to one source:

> I think it's better if you're reading on somebody to get a book that is generally about him. So in one chapter or in one thing it would tell you everything.

Thinking-Aloud Protocols

Under normal circumstances, much of the planning that goes on in composition takes place during writing, not in advance of it (Hayes & Flower, 1980). Protocols obtained from people instructed to think aloud while they write provide a means of access to this kind of planning. The knowledge-telling model would suggest that what goes on mentally in the novice writer would bear a close resemblance to what appears on the page, and this is indeed what our protocol analyses of school-age writers have found (see Chapter 8). The knowledge-transforming model, on the other hand, would suggest that among more expert writers there should be a great deal of activity revealed in the thinking-aloud protocols that is not directly represented in the text. This is what our protocol analyses of graduate students show.

Figure 1.6 gives a gross quantitative indication of adult-child differences.

Darkened bars show the mean number of words in thinking-aloud protocols, plain bars the mean number of words in corresponding essays. At all ages writers say more than they write, but the difference for adults is proportionately much larger (Scardamalia, 1984).

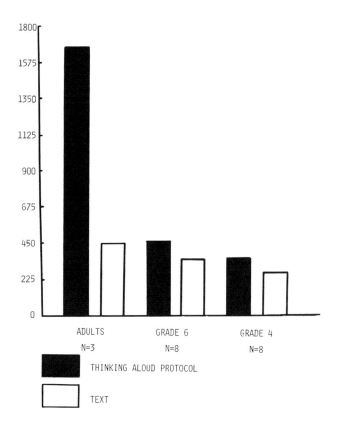

Figure 1.6. Mean number of words in thinking-aloud protocols of subjects planning compositions, compared to mean number of words in the resulting texts.

A look at the content of the protocols indicates that the adults are not simply being more verbose, but seem to be thinking about things that the younger writers do not consider. The following is a portion of an adult protocol. Material printed in boldface duplicates or paraphrases material that actually ends up in the story being written. The remainder, and in this case by far the bulk of the protocol, consists of provisional ideas, goal statements, comments, and problem-solving attempts, in relation to which the boldface statements are like tips of icebergs:

> ... Right now, he's isolated—and how I would ... If I have a connection made there—how I want to do that: Do I want an adult to intervene? Or do I want this to be that realistic? Or fairy tale-ish? Or ... because I can make it any way I want. Okay, maybe I ... weird!! Ah, let me see ... I know. **He makes this model of a ship, and on this ship he makes a little model of himself, and he loses it!** And this little model of himself happens to end up in his back pocket. Oh, why not? I can do anything I want with this story! Okay, so he just doesn't have any friends, and he's still losing things, and he doesn't know where he's put his ship and this little model he made of himself. But—magic!! The little model starts to talk to him, and helps him to find things! Let me see now ... I want to get some other kids involved, here. There's always one kid that shines through. **Okay, one kid likes his work, his art work, and, and, helps him. so, this kid who loses things and ends up giving—instead of losing things, he gives things away!** What a mixed-up story! Imagine, giving things away!! Okay, it's not too clear right now because there's kind of ... I have different directions—whether to go with the notion of this other child helping him out, or staying with the idea of some magic happening for him. Maybe I'll have both. You wanted a story? Once upon a time ... Okay. Not quite, not quite! I am just writing the title again, just to get a feel for it. "The kid who lost things." I think what I'm going to do here is have development of sharing that he gives, not everything away, but gives things away to this other kid. **This other kid, in return, without knowing it, helps him out in locating his losses. ...**

Here, by contrast, is the complete thinking-aloud protocol of a 10-year-old in the same study, coded in the same way. Except for a couple of procedural comments, the protocol consists entirely of content subsequently put into the story.

> **I could put him going to school and he probably loses a shoe. And then he's trying to find it and someone else finds it. And he goes home and tells his mother and his mother ... and then the person that finds it gives it back and the next day, and then the next day, the person that found it, so the boy says thank you to the person that found it. Then the next day he goes to school, he loses something else. And the**

teacher asks him what he lost and he says his short pants. He said his short pants. And they were in the washroom. And he goes home and brings them back. And then it's Saturday and school is over. And that's all. He goes back to school on Monday, he goes and plays, comes back in, he does his work, and he loses his gold ring and his mother says, "you lose everything." And he says it's true. And then he goes back to school and he never loses anything else. And his mother was happy because she doesn't want to buy him any more stuff. And they were happy from that day on. That's finished.

With a protocol like this one, it is fairly easy to reconstruct the composing process, using only the mechanisms posited by the knowledge-telling model. The first idea, "I could put him going to school," appears to be directly triggered by the narrative genre requirement of a setting. "And he probably loses a shoe" reflects the genre requirement of an "initiating event" (Stein & Glenn, 1979), combined with the assigned topic of the story (a kid who lost things). The next protocol statement suggests cuing from two more standard elements of story structure—the need for the protagonist to have a goal (finding the shoe) and the need for an obstacle to attainment of the goal (someone else's finding the shoe first). From that point on, it appears that much of the cuing of memory comes from items already generated, with continuing input from the genre schema, leading to a rambling string of ideas which nevertheless culminate in an appropriately formed story that sticks to the assigned topic. Although these processes are all detectable in the adult protocol as well, it would be impossible to account for the protocol on the basis of knowledge-telling mechanisms. A much more elaborate planning mechanism, involving goal setting and problem solving, would have to be posited—which is the sort of mechanism that we have tried to represent in the knowledge-transforming model.

The mental activities displayed by the adult and the child can both be regarded as planning, of course, and both are presumably directed toward attaining goals. But what the adult displays fits a definition of planning as working through a task at an abstract level in advance of working through it at a more concrete level (Anderson, 1983; Newell, 1980). The child's activity, on the other hand, might more precisely be labeled "rehearsal" (cf. Graves, 1975). It is working through the task at approximately the same level of concreteness as in the actual carrying out of the writing task.

Revising

The quotation from Aldous Huxley in an earlier section, about writing things many times over and all his thoughts being second thoughts, refers to a knowledge-transforming process that often reveals itself in substantive modifications of previously written text. Revision, indeed, seems to hold an almost hallowed place among professional writers (Murray, 1978). Student writers, on the other hand, are famous for their avoidance of revision and for confining it to a cosmetic level of little more than proofreading (National Assessment of Educational Progress, 1977; Nold, 1981).

A typical elementary school manuscript might well show no revisions at all. With certain kinds of support or instruction, however, elementary school children do begin to make revisions of some consequence (see Chapter 11, this volume, and Graves, 1979). Let us therefore look at the kinds of revisions made by a student who has had the benefit of such treatment. Figure 1.7 represents the original text by a sixth-grade student, plus the revisions she made to the text after a six-week program of instruction in ways of diagnosing and remedying text problems. (The instructional study from which this protocol is taken is described in the postscript to Chapter 11.) The student has made a number of stylistic improvements, but beyond that has made a major structural improvement through the addition of a topic sentence that ties together the rest of the text. With respect to the distinction between knowledge telling and knowledge transforming, however, what we must note is that even revisions of this comparatively high level represent alternative ways of saying the same thing or additions to, rather than transformations of, information. Through the process of revision, the student in question has produced a better composition and, as a consequence, a more compelling statement on the issue of children's television-watching. But there is little to suggest that these rhetorical operations led to reconsideration of the thoughts that informed the original composition.

C. Day Lewis summed up the knowledge-transforming function of writing in the aphorism, "We do not write in order to be understood; we write in order to understand" (quoted in Murray, 1978). The response of one of our articulate sixth-grade informants to this aphorism was:

> My main idea . . . is to make my ideas as clear to someone else—but only to someone else and not to me. . . . It's automatically going to be clear to me, especially if I put myself in someone else's shoes—because I wrote it.

Thus, from the perspective of the knowledge-telling model, knowledge is something one already has and that remains intact; writing is a matter of conveying a selection of this knowledge to someone else.

GRADE 6

DO YOU THINK THAT CHILDREN
SHOULD BE ABLE TO WATCH AS MUCH
TELEVISION AS THEY WOULD LIKE?

I THINK THE PARENTS SHOULD REMIND THEIR
CHILDREN NOT TO WATCH TO MUTCH T.V. But
I THINK THE CHILD SHOULD HAVE SOME
RESPONSIBILITY TO KNOW THAT THEY HAVE
WATCHED ENOUGH T.V. HE OR SHE CHOULD
BE ENVOLVED WITH OTHER ACTIVITIES TOO
SUCH AS SPORTS READING A GOOD BOOK OR
just PLAYING a game THEY SHOULD ALSO MAKE
TIME IN THEIR DAY TO DO THEIR HOMEWORK
OR PRACTICE THEIR MUSICAL INSTRUMENTS IF
THEY HAVE ONE AND TELEVISION SHOULDN'T
INTERFERE with it.

No I don't think that kids should be allowed to watch as
mutch T.V. as they want because every kid wants to watch
t.v. day in and day out.

Figure 1.7. Original text and revisions by a grade-6 student who had been through a six-week program of instruction in diagnosis and revision of texts. Original text is in upper case; revisions are in lower case, placed as they actually were by the student.

TESTING THE MODELS

The knowledge-telling and knowledge-transforming models fall somewhere in the middle among several types of models being used in cognitive research, and this raises questions about how one judges whether the models are valid, reasonable, a step in the right direction, or whatever. One type of model, often arising from work on artificial intelligence, amounts to an algorithm for executing a cognitive task (cf. Newell, 1980). Claims of merit for such models are generally based on demonstrations that the algorithm can actually be executed on a computer, producing something that bears a resemblance to observable human performance. The resemblance may be very crude and still be counted as evidence that the model is on the right track. For instance, a model of subtraction procedures intended to account for the kinds of systematic errors children make was able to account for only about half the "bugs" actually observed in children (Brown & Van Lehn, 1980). Yet the model is rightly regarded as a significant accomplishment, because it shows that a coherent set of rules can generate a substantial amount of what had previously appeared to be idiosyncratic error. The knowledge-telling model reflects a similar ambition of showing how writing behavior that has usually been attributed to deficiencies of skill or knowledge, faulty motivation, and the like, can be accounted for by a coherent procedure that runs according to reasonable rules. The model does, in fact, describe an algorithm; but the algorithm is nowhere near fully enough specified to be executed by machine, and so the possibility of validating it by showing that it can churn out something resembling student prose is not available. (Readers to whom this kind of talk is strange should be assured that there is no thought of reducing writing to something like long division, which would then be taught as a routine. Instead, the talk is about algorithms that represent partial theories of how a process works.)

Another type of model, and one of which there are already several examples in the literature of composing processes, is essentially descriptive. Such models categorize the kinds of mental processes that go on in writing and indicate something about how these processes are interrelated, but they stop short of suggesting algorithms by which composition is carried out. Examples are the models of writing proposed by Cooper and Matsuhashi (1983) and Beaugrande (1984b). Such models are often useful as frameworks for research and discussion. The knowledge-telling and knowledge-transforming models sketched in this chapter resemble these other models in that they characterize processes at a rather global level and do not specify procedures in detail, but their purpose is fundamentally different. The models we have presented are not intended to describe or to summarize current knowledge about the composing process. They attempt to explain phenomena by setting forth hypothetical systems that could generate these phenomena. Thus they come closer to what are generally recognized in science as theories. They are, for instance, falsifiable—that is, vulnerable to contrary evidence (Lakatos, 1970). We would expect any serious readers at this point in the book to have doubts and reservations about the validity of the two models, on the basis of facts which they feel to be inconsistent with what the models seem to imply. While we may hope that such doubts will be quieted as reading proceeds, it is worth noting at this time that such doubts would not occur if the models were merely descriptive.

The frequently-cited model of Hayes and Flower (1980) also occupies a middle ground between algorithmic and descriptive models, but in a different way from the models we have presented. Their model exists in two versions, representing different levels of detail. The more global version, shown in figure 1.8, is descriptive. This is the version most commonly cited, and true to its descriptive nature, it is mainly used as a framework for discussing the sorts of things that go on in composition. Figure 1.9 shows the portion of Hayes and Flowers' detailed model that deals with the generating process. It may be noted that it has considerable similarity to the model of the knowledge-telling process as shown inside the central box of Figure 1.1. Even though models like this are not specific enough to be executed, they are specific enough to raise genuine questions of whether they are true or not.

The research reported in this book is not intended as verification of the knowledge-telling and knowledge-transforming models. The research ranges

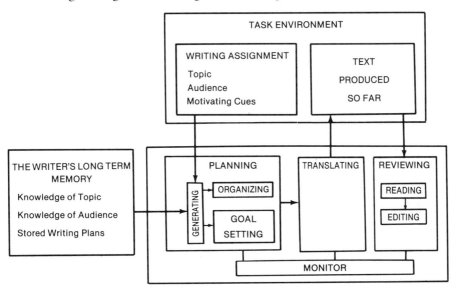

Figure 1.8. Structure of the writing model. From "Identifying the Organization of Writing Processes" by J. R. Hayes and L. S. Flower. In *Cognitive Processes in Writing* ed. by L. W. Gregg and E. R. Steinberg, 1980: Lawrence Erlbaum Associates.

GENERATING

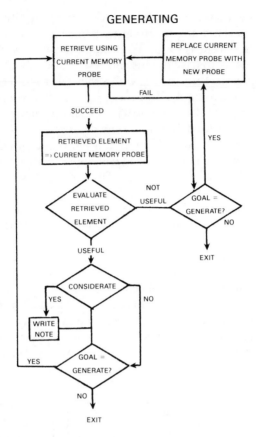

Figure 1.9. The structure of the GENERATING process. From "Identifying the Organization of Writing Processes" by J. R. Hayes and L. S. Flower. In *Cognitive Processes in Writing* ed. by L. W. Gregg and E. R. Steinberg, 1980: Lawrence Erlbaum Associates.

over many aspects of writing process and writing competence. The picture that emerges has much more to it than is covered by the models, but we believe it will become increasingly apparent as the findings unfold that something like the two models presented here is necessary in order to make sense of the picture. This will not constitute proof, of course, but it will, we hope, have the effect of raising criticism to a theoretically interesting level. That is, we hope that by the end readers who are critical of the models presented here will feel constrained to consider what other kind of model, or what revision of the existing models, would do a better job of making sense of the aggregate of findings.

CAUTIONARY NOTES

In this chapter we have set forth two different models showing how we believe people carry out written composition. We have then tried to apply these models and give them some provisional plausibility by discussing several observable differences between the composing behaviors of children we have studied (most of whom appear to be following the knowledge-telling model of composing) and university students (at least some of whom appear to be following the knowledge-transforming model). Concrete examples always introduce the risk of unintended generalization, however, and so we devote this concluding section to trying to head off several possible misunderstandings that could becloud not only what has been said so far but also what is to follow.

1.   Child versus adult competence. If one conclusion has emerged dramatically from the past decade of cognitive developmental research, it is that age differences in performance can have many sources and almost never lend themselves to straightforward interpretation in terms of intellectual competence. It is therefore important to be clear about what kinds of inferences we try to draw from the comparisons of younger and older writers that figure prominently in this book. As for what has been said so far, the matter is simple: We have not tried to say anything at all about child-versus-adult competence. The use of age comparisons has been purely incidental to the purpose of showing that there are distinct models of composing that have some correspondence to real behavior. It so happens that miscellaneous collections of elementary school students and of graduate students, when working under similar conditions, give fairly clear evidences of these contrasting models.

If we were to remain aloof from issues about the development of competence, there would be little likelihood of confusion arising from age comparisons: such comparisons would always be incidental. But the fact is that we are intensely interested in how the kind of composing process that graduate students exhibit gets established, whether what children show is an early version of the same model or whether it is qualitatively different, and what stands in the way of attaining expert-like competence. Such questions inevitably involve one in the perils of trying to identify age differences in competence among a tangle of confounding factors. One is going to make mistakes, and therefore needs working principles in order to minimize the damage done by mistakes. The following are the principles we have chosen to work by:

a.   Not to treat age (or more precisely, maturation) as an explanatory variable. Biological maturation may, in fact, have something to do with determining the complexity of intellectual processes children can sustain at different ages (see Chapters 5 and 6). But since this question is very much open, and since the kind of research currently possible on written composition is unlikely to contribute much to resolving the question, it has seemed advisable to adopt merely as a working assumption the position that all adult-child differences are due to learning experience.

b.   To try to explain differences rather than explaining them away. When older people display a higher type of performance on a task than younger people do, the difference can often be attributed to factors such as the older person's test-wiseness, interpretation of task instructions, motivation, or knowledge of relevant subject matter. It is also usually possible to show that by manipulating these factors one can reduce or even eliminate age differences (e.g., Chi, 1977). But if you show, for instance, that children produce more adult-like writing when their interest is high and when they are in a supportive environment, you have not really explained adult-child differences, you have only explained them away. For it remains that adults can write like adults even when their interest is low and when they receive no external support. A real explanation of adult-child differences must treat this differential dependence on situational factors as *part of what needs to be explained,* not as an easy way out of the explanatory muddle.

2.   Knowledge telling versus dumping memory. The computer memory dump (in which the contents of the computer's memory locations are written out seriatim) provides a convenient but *completely wrong* metaphor for the knowledge-telling process. We bring the matter up only because the metaphor is apparently very attractive to people who approach writing from an information processing standpoint. Human beings cannot list the contents of their memories—least of all young children, with their more limited memory-search procedures (see Chapter 3). There is a sort of "memory dump" task in the Stanford-Binet intelligence test, calling for children simply to say all the words they can think of. Children below the age of ten typically fail to reach the criterion of retrieving 28 words in one minute. Quite to the contrary of the memory dump metaphor, the knowledge-telling model is adapted to children's difficulties with memory search; it makes maximum use of external prompts, self-generated prompts, and the apparently powerful support of discourse schemas (story schemas, etc.) for memory retrieval.

3.   Good writing through knowledge telling. Much of the bad writing that one sees is explainable by the knowledge-telling model—writing that seems to lack purpose, plan, or consideration of the reader. It should also be recognized, however, that very good writing can arise from knowledge telling. If the writer has some distinctive content already organized and available in memory—and especially if this content has affect attached to it—then the knowledge-telling process may be sufficient to generate an organized, well-elaborated, and even eloquent composition. Virtually all of the procedures that are claimed to boost the quality of student writing may be understood as ways to achieve better results through the knowledge-telling process (Scardamalia & Bereiter, 1985b).

Even though knowledge telling relies on readily available material from memory, it is probably nevertheless the case that putting such material into words has a knowledge-transforming effect. Church (1961) has speculated on the value of such activity, which he called "thematization"—the processing of relatively raw experience into verbalized form. Thus the knowledge-transforming model cannot be claimed to have an absolute advantage over the knowledge-telling model either in terms of quality of writing or in terms of cognitive benefits to the writer. Why, then, make such an issue of the distinction between models? Answers to that question should emerge gradually from the chapters that follow. For the present, we may simply recall the initial discussion about the need to study both abilities that come naturally and abilities that come with difficulty and effort. The two models of composing appear to cover that range. It is from this standpoint irrelevant whether one model is judged "better" than the other. What matters is that both are models of significant human abilities, and that investigating their acquisition promises to show something about the different tracks that cognitive development can take.

4.   Models as idealizations. Do we really claim there are two models of composing? Why not three? Why not a continuum, running from relatively little strategic control over the composing process to a great deal? At a certain level of description it is no doubt true that every person who writes follows a different model (and, indeed, follows different models on different occasions). But models of the kind we have proposed are not intended to describe. They are more like representations of design concepts. They are intended to capture core ideas, which can be elaborated in different ways to correspond to real-world variability. Continuums are fine for describing the variability, but discrete models have an advantage for showing distinctions between design concepts.

As for there being two rather than three or more models, the possibilities for other models are open. At present we are studying talented writers of elementary-school age. We are interested in seeing whether their composing resembles that of experts, whether it resembles that of less talented students their own age, or whether it suggests some different model. The several quotations sprinkled through this chapter are from students in this study. They suggest a strong and even conscious adherence to the knowledge-telling model; but on the other hand these students show a degree of consideration of audience uncommon in writers their age. At this point we do not have enough information to say whether such talent is best accounted for by an elaboration of the basic knowledge-telling design or whether it calls for a distinct model. It has seemed to us that the idea that there are two distinct models of composing rather than one was radical enough that we should not be in a hurry to add still further models.

Chapter 2
An Integrative Schema
for Studying
the Composing Process

PREFACE

There seem to be three levels at which inquiry relevant to the composing process has gone on. One level consists of personal reflections, often by writers themselves (see, for instance, *Writers at Work,* 1963; a critique of this tradition is given in Bereiter, 1984). Another, carried out mainly by educational researchers, generally follows the empiricist conventions popular in all the behavioral sciences up until the 1970s, of defining quantifiable variables and testing statistical hypotheses about them. (An influential monograph, setting forth principles and topics for this kind of research on writing was Braddock, Lloyd-Jones, & Schoer, 1963.) And then, of course, there is the long tradition of literary scholarship, usually devoted to the close analysis of individual texts. In this chapter we define three additional levels of inquiry that are important to understanding the composing process—process description, theory-testing experimentation, and simulation. These are commonplace activities in cognitive research, but just beginning to be found in writing research. Our argument is not that these three kinds of inquiry should replace the earlier three. On the contrary, the argument is that all six are needed, with a proper understanding of the role of each.

It is not very common, either in psychology or in the study of writing, for a research program to move about between levels of inquiry. In psychology the typical way of studying a phenomenon seems to be to choose a certain level of analysis (for instance, the level of correlations between test variables or of differences in response latencies under task variations) and to pursue the resolution of problems describable at that level. Thus, a model colloquium will present a series of closely interlocked studies, often using a single basic method, each study moving a step closer to a satisfying theoretical denouement. In writing research the tendency has been either to do rather isolated studies that are linked to others only by topic or else to collect large bodies of data which are then described and discussed in a variety of ways over an extended series of reports. In either case, to the extent that there is integration of findings among levels of inquiry it takes place across research programs rather than within them.

In the research reported in this book, however, we have tried to combine inquiry at a variety of levels within a single research program. This has not been altogether a matter of preference. We have looked with admiration and envy at psychologists working in other areas, who have been able to carry out elegant series of experiments, systematically ruling out alternative hypotheses until some truth emerges with blazing clarity—a truth that then takes on added meaning when it is shown that the same truth has emerged from other elegant series of studies by other investigators, using different methodologies. Such a thing has been impossible in the field of research on the composing process. There has simply not been enough theoretically motivated research going on to permit more than the occasional fortunate discovery of a finding from one research program that helps clarify something found out in another. This has been particularly true of research involving the composing processes of children.

As a result, we faced the choice of either trying to nail down some particular theoretical result, the significance of which would remain uncertain because of the absence of collateral results, or trying to pursue promising ideas across a range of topics and types of inquiry, with the hope of achieving findings that would make some sense of the composing process as a whole. We chose the latter course, even though it meant leaving many a stone unturned and, instead of seeing whether particular empirical results could be replicated, seeing whether similar conclusions were supported by widely different kinds of investigation. The reader will have to judge from subsequent chapters whether this choice was a fortunate one. The present chapter is important, however, for making it clear what it means to take a multi-level approach to research on the composing process.

2 Research on the composing process is new and there is not much of it. It is not easy and there are, as yet, no magic keys to an understanding of it. Writing research needs to be varied without being unfocused, guided by theory without being dogmatic, progressive without being mindlessly trendy. To achieve such balance, it seems desirable for researchers to have conscious access to a scheme that allows them to conceive of their immediate activities within a larger pattern. In this chapter, we set forth such a scheme.

We conceive of research into the composing process as needing to go on at six interacting levels. These levels, briefly described in Table 2.1, will be discussed in detail in the body of this chapter. Although it is possible for individual researchers to devote their careers largely to inquiry at one level, we conceive of inquiry as a whole moving in a spiral course that starts at Level 1, moves upward and then returns to Level 1 to begin a new cycle—but with a heightened understanding acquired from the preceding cycle. The successive levels of inquiry are marked by movement that is (1) further and further away from the natural phenomena of writing that are observed in their full context and (2) closer and closer to the psychological system viewed as a theoretical construct. Continual return to lower levels is, therefore, in part demanded by the need to keep renewing contact with phenomenal reality.

It should be evident, although it cannot hurt to emphasize the point, that higher levels of inquiry are *not* seen to be in any way better than lower levels. Inquiry may be sophisticated or naive, superficial or profound, at any of the levels. Furthermore, understanding of the composing process does not emerge from inquiry at any particular level but rather through synthesizing knowledge gained in the course of spiraling through levels.

Why call them levels, then, the reader might ask, rather than something more neutral, such as phases, steps, or varieties? As we have already indicated, the levels are not merely sequential—in fact there is only a weak sequentiality to them—but they are ordered on a dimension of abstractness. The idea of

Table 2.1   Levels of Inquiry in Research on the Composing Process

Level	Characteristic Questions	Typical Methods
Level 1: Reflective inquiry	What is the nature of this phenomenon? What are the problems? What do the data mean?	Informal observation Introspection Literature review Discussion, argument, private reflection
Level 2: Empirical variable testing	Is this assumption correct? What is the relation between x and y?	Factorial analysis of variance Correlation analysis Surveys Coding of compositions
Level 3: Text analysis	What makes this text seem the way it does? What rules could the writer be following?	Error analysis Story grammar analysis Thematic analysis
Level 4: Process description	What is the writer thinking? What pattern or system is revealed in the writer's thoughts while composing?	Thinking aloud protocols Clinical-experimental interviews Retrospective reports Videotape recordings
Level 5: Theory-embedded experimentation	What is the nature of the cognitive system responsible for these observations? Which process model is right?	Experimental procedures tailored to questions Chronometry Interference
Level 6: Simulation	How does the cognitive mechanism work? What range of natural variations can the model account for? What remains to be accounted for?	Computer: simulation Simulation by intervention

levels has yet a stronger sense, however. It is possible for research to keep cycling between Levels 1 and 2, never going any higher. Indeed, the great bulk of educational research has tended to do this. We would argue that, although inquiry at Level 2 is not inherently inferior to inquiry at Level 4, a program of inquiry that never incorporates knowledge from levels higher than Level 2 is severely limited in comparison to one that incorporates Levels 1 through 4. In turn, such a program is limited in comparison to one that incorporates a level as high as Level 5. In this way, it is possible to compare research programs according to the highest level of inquiry they incorporate, but there is still no suggestion that the doing of Level 5 inquiry is in itself a more worthy intellectual endeavor than doing Level 2 or Level 3 inquiry.

THE SIX LEVELS OF INQUIRY

Level 1: Reflective Inquiry

Reflective inquiry does not involve seeking new information through empirical research. Instead, it involves reflection on the information one already has or that is available from ordinary experience. Reflective inquiry into the composing process has a long and honorable history, starting as far back as Aristotle's *Poetics*. Empirical scientists often disparage armchair analysis. Efforts to advance knowledge in fields like physics through purely reflective inquiry have, indeed, shown little accomplishment during two thousand years of earnest effort. With respect to the composing process, however, the reflective thinker has the benefit of access to an extremely important fund of information, the thinker's own experience as a writer. Many people who reflect on the composing process will also have had experience as teachers of writing, and all will have been exposed to numerous samples of the writing of others. Consequently, the armchair enquirer into the composing process is much better supplied with relevant knowledge than the typical armchair enquirer into astrophysics has been.

Some of the most influential contributions to our understanding of the process of writing and the process of learning to write have come from people who relied for material on their own experience as writers and teachers (e.g., Elbow, 1973; Moffett, 1968). In the present analysis, however, we are more interested in reflective analysis as part of a more comprehensive program of inquiry into the composing process. We see reflective inquiry as home base. It is the place from which other kinds of inquiry start; it is where inquiry keeps returning for fresh starts; it is where, finally, the knowledge gained through inquiry at other levels is consolidated into understanding. Thus we designate it as Level 1, not because it is the lowest (or the highest) type of inquiry, but because it is primary.

A sensitive discussion of the limitations of different kinds of Level 1 inquiry is provided by Emig (1971) as background to her ground-breaking venture to go beyond Level 1 in studying the composing process. We shall not dwell on those limitations here, leaving it to later discussion to argue the value of going to other levels of inquiry. It seems more important, at this point, to emphasize the significant role that Level 1 inquiry normally plays in empirical research. There is a caricature of empirical science frequently promulgated these days that depicts the empirical scientist as naively believing in objective truth and as disdaining intuition, introspection, everyday experience, common sense, ancient wisdom, and generalizations of any sort not based on statistical tests. This caricature is encouraged by the kinds of reports that appear in scientific journals. These reports seldom give any indication of the reflective thought that preceded or followed an investigation.

But that is a characteristic of scientific journalism, not a characteristic of scientific inquiry. If you listen to empirical scientists talking shop informally, you do not hear them talking much about details of procedure or statistical tests; much less do you hear them trying to thrust objective truths on one another. In our experience, the overwhelming question that dominates at least 70 percent of the serious conversation among researchers on human behavior is, what is it really? What is the real process that our data hint at and that our theoretical models crudely represent? This is Level 1 inquiry. It draws on knowledge and hunches of all sorts. Without it, empirical research can hardly move.

Level 2: Empirical Variable Testing

In the course of Level 1 inquiry, reflections inevitably make use of some premises that are testable matters of fact. In the course of reflecting on problems of writing instruction, for instance, premises like the following might come into play: the quality of student writing has declined in recent decades; students who read good literature write well; television watching encourages incoherent writing; many children do poorly because school writing assignments make them anxious. Although they are plausible, such premises could be factually wrong and, thus, could lead Level 1 inquiry astray. If one sets out to test such premises empirically, one has moved away from purely reflective inquiry to a different level, which we designate as Level 2.

Level 2 is called empirical variable testing because testing a premise empirically requires translating the premise into a statement about the relationship among observable variables. For instance, in order to test the premise that students who read good literature write well, one has to specify a procedure for measuring "writing well" (such as teacher ratings) and for "reads good literature" (such as score on a checklist of books read outside class). Defining such variables may not be easy, and the result may not be any less controversial than the original premise that the variables were designed to test.

Level-2 research, in fact, is continually beset by a chorus of objections that render every empirical finding questionable. The variables may be challenged as not adequately measuring the thing intended (some good writers will score low on your measure of good writing). The empirical relationships will be imperfect and thus reduce the force of the premise (not every student who reads good literature will be a good writer, no matter how you measure the variables). It will be impossible to be sure that the observed relationship would also be found under other conditions and among other kinds of students. It will be impossible to deny that the implied causal relationship (for instance, good reading causes good writing) could result from some other untested variable (for instance, a literate home environment that encourages both good reading and good writing).

If the results of empirical variable testing are so inherently dubious, one may ask, why do it? Level-2 inquiry, we believe, only makes sense as a supplement to Level-1 inquiry. It is not fair or reasonable to judge empirical variable testing against a standard of absolute certainty—to expect, for instance, that research on the relationship between good reading and good writing should finally yield us an answer that we can be as sure of as we are sure that two plus two make four. We should ask instead whether the research has given us a sounder factual basis for Level-1 reflection than we would have had without it—that is, whether the factual basis is sounder than we could achieve through informal observations, study of isolated cases, or commonsense assumptions. Not all Level-2 research passes this test, but some of it does.

It is too much to ask of any type of inquiry that it lead to error-free results, but a progressive form of inquiry should be capable of error reduction and that is where pure Level-1 inquiry fails. Level-2 inquiry, for all its limitations, does have the capacity, through a variety of experimental and analytical techniques, to diminish error. Therefore, it provides a supplement to—not replacement for—Level 1 inquiry.

A study by Scardamalia, Bereiter, and Woodruff (1980) will serve to illustrate on a small scale the role of Level-2 inquiry as supplementary to Level 1. Much advice to writers and much advice to teachers is premised on the belief that people write best about what they know best. This belief has a somewhat self-evident character about it in that, of necessity, people cannot write good pieces on topics about which they know nothing. Many of the commonplace beliefs that form the basis of Level-1 inquiry have this quasi-self-evident character—they are necessarily true in some sense or under some condition; and from this, their truth in general is assumed. But is the belief true across the relevant range of conditions? Is it true, for instance, across the range of topics about which a writer knows *something,* that the quality of composition increases according to the writer's familiarity with the topic?

The Scardamalia et al. (1980) study sought evidence bearing on this question. Elementary school children were interviewed to identify topics about which they claimed to know much or little. Then each child wrote two compositions, one on a high-familiarity topic and one on a low-familiarity topic. A variety of analyses failed to reveal any difference between compositions produced on the two kinds of topics. (A fuller treatment of this study is given in Chapter 3.) Most people to whom we have reported this finding have been reluctant to accept it. They have questioned the variables used in comparing the compositions. They have objected to our using the children's own nominations of familiar and unfamiliar topics (although we believe that if we had used experimenter-determined topics many of the same people would have objected to our not having left the children free to choose). They have questioned whether the same results would be obtained under different—for instance, more informal—task conditions. And they have suggested other variations of the experiment that would be needed to determine the generalizability of results.

These objections illustrate two points about Level 2 inquiry. First, the objections are quite legitimate and they illustrate the range of objections that can usually be brought against particular variable-testing studies. Second, the objections are at least partly motivated by an unwillingness to abandon a prior belief. If the study had shown that children produced markedly better compositions on more familiar topics, the study probably would not have provoked much criticism even though all the same criticisms would apply (along with the additional criticism that the study was only proving the obvious). This double standard, although troublesome at times, is on the whole quite sound. It reflects the fact that Level 2 findings are a supplement to, not a replacement for, Level 1 intuitions. One does not abandon an important belief grounded in common sense and ordinary experience simply because one empirical study has brought evidence against it.

On the other hand, a reasonable person will not ignore Level 2 results. At the very least, Level-2 findings that run against common knowledge should serve as signals that something is more complex than we had assumed. The Scardamalia et al. (1980) study, for instance, should at least provide a caution against assuming that a simple formula that relates greater topic familiarity to better expository writing holds universally. A good Level-2 study should, furthermore, establish its findings within a context that has some representative significance. Thus, the context in which Scardamalia et al. (1980) found the familiarity-quality equation to fail was not some bizarre situation never encountered in real life. It was well within the range of typical school writing contexts. To be sure, there may be other contexts within the typical range where the familiarity-quality equation does hold— but that remains to be established. Research that did establish it would add further increments to our knowledge about writing; it would not simply erase the previous finding.

Although Level 2 inquiry is a form of reality testing and looks for data that are representative of the real world, it can, nevertheless, be theoretically motivated. In the Scardamalia et al. (1980) study, for instance, we were not motivated by the question of whether children should be encouraged to write about what they know. We were motivated by an interest in children's difficulties with self-directed memory search. We suspected (in keeping with ideas underlying the knowledge-telling model described in Chapter 1) that children lacked effective procedures for self-sustained search of memory. If this were true, it should also be true that children would have trouble developing content even on subjects about which they knew a lot, provided the search had to be carried out deliberately. This conclusion seemed at variance with commonly accepted knowledge; therefore, a Level-2 study that would test children's memory-search capabilities in a realistic context was required. The proposed Levels of Inquiry scheme, it will be recalled, has a spiral structure. In early stages, Level 2 inquiry is likely to be motivated primarily by issues of belief or practicality; at later stages, it is likely to be motivated increasingly by theoretical considerations that impinge on ordinary world knowledge.

Until recently, Level-2 inquiry has been the dominant mode of research in education and the social sciences. Much ingenuity has gone into devising ways to overcome its inherent weaknesses: methods of statistical control for variables that cannot be controlled experimentally, multivariate methods that deal with the redundancy among measures, factorial designs that make it possible to examine the independent and joint effects of person and situation variables. All of these methods, however, add additional sources of indeterminacy that, in turn, call for even more empirical studies.

The ultimate threat to all Level-2 inquiry is combinatorial explosion. If one considers all the variables that might impinge on a simple empirical outcome and all of the separate combinations of these variables that might act in distinct ways, one quickly generates a staggering number of needed empirical observations and the possible outcomes grow to an unmanageable complexity (Cronbach, 1975). We could easily spend the rest of our careers running variations on a content-familiarity study and have nothing to show for our pains but conclusions so loaded down with conditions and exceptions as to be utterly worthless.

How can one escape this combinatorial explosion? The answer seems to lie in higher levels of inquiry. Instead of pressing further into studying the conditions under which content familiarity does and does not correlate with various characteristics of compositions, we can try instead (as will be illustrated in subsequent chapters) to find out how children actually use the content knowledge they have. How do they retrieve content from memory? How do they select what to include in their compositions? To what extent do they transform their knowledge to suit purposes of a composition as opposed to simply reporting knowledge as it is recalled? Note that such questions, while still questions about the relation between content knowledge and writing, reflect a different level of inquiry, a level that escapes the proliferation of empirical variables and their combinations because it is concerned with the structures and processes lying behind them.

Level 3: Text Analysis

Inquiry at Level 3 consists of trying to extract descriptive rules or principles by studying written texts. At the most general level, it embraces various analyses, for example, that of Halliday and Hasan (1976) aimed at uncovering a principle such as cohesion, which is applicable to all texts. It extends, however, to more specialized study too, such as that of Stein and Trabasso (1982) in which common structures found in children's narratives are used as a basis for inferring the mental schemata that children use in understanding and generating stories. A rather different kind of analysis, still within the same sphere of inquiry, is that of Shaughnessy (1977), which aimed at inferring the rules that basic writers follow in coping with spelling, punctuation, and standard English syntax.

Text-analysis of this rule-seeking sort has its analogues in other fields of study—in the work of anthropologists like Levi-Strauss (1963), for instance, who infer the kinship structures of tribal peoples or in the work of ethnomethodologists who infer the rules governing different kinds of social exchange, including conversation (e.g., Wooton, 1975). Not all analyses done on texts qualify as Level 3 analyses however. In fact, most of the research involving counting and measuring T-units and frequencies of various sentence and text features is straight Level 2 empirical variable testing, which happens to use variables drawn from written texts. Level 3 inquiry is not the study of empirical variables that happen to be derived from texts. Level 3 inquiry approaches texts as complex phenomena that exhibit internal lawfulness, and it aims to understand that lawfulness.[1]

There does not seem to be much text analysis going on that is related to understanding the composing process. Perhaps this is because writing researchers have assumed that, in analyzing texts, one is necessarily studying product and that to study process, one must do something else. Such a belief is forcefully dispelled, however, by the work of Beaugrande (1980; 1982a) who draws heavily on text analysis.

Although a text cannot directly reveal the composing process lying behind

---

[1]The distinction here is *not* the same as the distinction between sentence-level and text-level analysis even though, as a historical matter, most Level 2 research has used variables based on sentences or smaller units, whereas most Level 3 research has been concerned with text-level issues. It is quite possible to do Level 2 research using text-level variables—for instance, counting the number of cohesive ties. It is also possible to do Level 3 inquiry at the sentence level as illustrated by Beaugrande's (1980) inquiry into what causes certain kinds of sentence fragments to be frequently mistaken for complete sentences by student writers. The difference remains that of either treating texts as exhibiting phenomena that are to be explained (Level 3) or as a source of variables whose relationships to one another or to other variables are to be tested (Level 2).

it, it can provide indirect evidence. McCutchen and Perfetti (1982) used data on coherence relationships in children's texts to infer what features of a text children were holding in mind while retrieving text content. In a similar vein, in Chapter 6 we analyze texts to determine how many items of content children are holding in mind in formulating arguments. There is a direct link between written products and the composing process. Whatever lawfulness is found in a text must reflect lawful behavior on the part of the writer because the physical properties of the text impose no requirements of lawfulness. One could keep piling up sticks at random until one accidentally produced a structure that stood up. This pile of sticks would, then, exhibit a structure that had no necessary counterpart in one's own mind. But in writing, whatever lawfulness appears must have its counterpart in the mind of the writer (provided, of course, there has been no response from a reader). The counterpart may not be obvious and may not be inferable at all without supplementary information, but the product of writing is sure to remain an indispensable clue to process.

Level-3 inquiry does have significant limitations however. First, there appear always to be different rule systems that can be used to account for the same observed regularities in text. There are different story grammars (e.g., Beaugrande & Colby, 1979; Stein and Glenn, 1979), just as there are many different sentence grammars. There is no way of determining from text analysis which, if any, of these grammars actually represent knowledge as it exists in the mind of writers. Independent evidence of the psychological reality of particular rule structures must be sought (Stein & Trabasso, 1982). Second, Level 3 inquiry does not yield insight into the composing process as such. It yields insight into the knowledge structures that direct the composing process, and this is vital for understanding the process; but it remains to find out how this knowledge is brought into play during the actual course of composing. To overcome the limitations of Level 3 inquiry—to establish the psychological reality of rule structures and to discover how they function in the composing process—inquiry at still higher levels is required.

Level 4: Process Description

Whereas Level 3 inquiry is a search for lawfulness and pattern in written texts, Level 4 inquiry is a search for lawfulness and pattern in the writer's thoughts while composing. Level 4 thus brings the investigator into more immediate touch with the composing process.

Level 4 inquiry faces a dramatic methodological problem that tends to overshadow other problems associated with inquiry at this level. The problem is, of course, that the writer's thoughts are not normally accessible to observation. Hypnosis and truth serums are possible ways around this obstacle, but they have not, so far as we know, been exploited in writing research. The two main ways that have been used are the clinical-experimental interview (Piaget, 1929) and the thinking-aloud procedure (Ericsson & Simon, 1980). The origins of the former in work with young children and of the latter in work with adults are probably not accidental. It has proved possible to get at least some adults to verbalize copiously while they carry out mental tasks and thus to obtain a rich record of things passing through their minds relevant to the on-going process. It has proved much harder to get children to sustain this kind of verbalization. To do so usually requires repeated intervention by the investigator and some external structuring of the task. In doing these things one is shifting over to the clinical-experimental method. In collecting thinking-aloud protocols, the investigator interacts little with the writer; the investigator may not even be present. In the clinical-experimental interview, the investigator interacts with the writer and tries to structure a task in which such interaction will be natural, but the investigator tries, nevertheless, to engineer the exchange in such a way that all the thoughts come from the writer, not from the investigator. An example of clinical experimental methodology is the study of evaluation and revision processes presented in Chapter 11. Chapter 13 expands on this methodology in describing a variety of means to involve children as co-investigators of their mental processes.

It is important, however, not to confuse Level-4 inquiry with the methods that are normally used to conduct it. Thinking-aloud protocols, for instance, may be used simply as a source of variables for Level-2 inquiry, and they may also be used in inquiry above Level 4. The defining characteristic of Level-4 inquiry is its search for a description of the composing process. Because most of the process is covert, Level-4 researchers tend to get involved in mind-reading problems of some sort, but this is a secondary phenomenon. Level 4 researchers could limit their study to the observable part of composing behavior, obtaining a valid, although necessarily limited, description of the process (e.g., Stallard, 1974). Or they could choose to study the process of group composition, in which case much more of the process would be externalized in the form of conversation (an example is presented in Chapter 3, pp. 99–102). In any event, the Level-4 investigator's job does not end with collecting and transcribing protocols any more than the Level-3 investigator's job ends with obtaining written texts. The main job is the search for lawfulness in the protocols.

Level 4 inquiry is relatively new in writing research and, indeed, in language research generally. It has generated enthusiasms and objections that are both (we think) somewhat misdirected—because, again, they tend to focus on the method of data collection rather than on the inquiry itself. The common objections have to do with the inevitable violations of naturalism that occur when one tries to gain access to normally covert behavior. How do we know that what a writer thinks under the unnatural conditions of thinking aloud or the clinical-experimental interview is what the writer would think while composing naturally? The criticism parallels one that could be leveled against a naturalist whose account of the behavior of apes was based entirely on watching them in zoos.

These objections, however, fail to take into account the difference between testimony and data. Writers' verbal reports should not be taken as presenting a picture of the composing process that one judges to be true or false and rejects if it is false. Rather, they should be taken as data (Ericsson & Simon, 1980) that the investigator uses, often in conjunction with other data, in constructing a description of the inferred process. Verbal reports, like any other kind of data, may be misleading; the issue, however, is not whether they are perfect but whether they lead to better process descriptions than can be produced without such data. Ultimately it is the investigator's description, not the student's verbal report, that must be judged true or false.

Critics of thinking-aloud procedures frequently miss this point, but so do some enthusiasts, who seem to believe that thinking-aloud protocols offer direct insight into mental processes. A descriptive model of the composing process, such as that produced by Hayes and Flower (1980), is an intellectual construction based on inferred invariances in protocol data. It is not, like the naturalist's diary or sketchbook, simply a record of what was observed.

The fundamental limitations of Level-4 inquiry are similar to those of Level 3, but shifted to a different ground. There is a similar problem in establishing the psychological reality of the theoretical construction. Different models may be constructed that adequately describe patterns observed in protocol data. But what the actual organization of the composing process is within the mind of the writer is a question that cannot fully be answered through Level 4 inquiry. Instead, Level-4 inquiry produces possibilities, the testing of which requires inquiry at a higher level. This has been illustrated in Chapter 1 with respect to protocol evidence indicating qualitative differences between the composing processes of mature and immature writers. Taken by itself, this evidence could easily be explained away; but when related to theoretical models that have other kinds of support as well, the protocol evidence begins to be more persuasive.

The other fundamental limitation of Level-4 inquiry is that it describes only one layer of the composing process—an extremely important layer, to be sure, but one that still leaves much of what is most mysterious about composing untouched. The layer it describes is the layer of conscious thought. It describes the flow of attention during composing, but it does not reveal why attention shifts when it does and where it does. Part II of the present volume is largely devoted to basic processes in composition that are not accessible to consciousness and that therefore require study at levels other than Level 4.

In effect, thinking-aloud protocols and clinical-experimental protocols display the *products* of cognitive activities rather than the cognitive activity itself. Thus to a considerable extent, Level 4 inquiry, like that of Level 3, is a study of products. The differences are that at Level 4 the products are intermediate products, retained and further processed in the mind, rather than the final products that appear on the written page. This is an important difference, bringing us closer to, but not yet into, contact with the psychological system that generates composition.

Level 5: Theory-Embedded Experimentation

All levels of inquiry may be theory-guided in the sense that ideas, topics, or methods are inspired by some theory or other. The four levels of inquiry described previously, however, are all capable of thriving without theory. Although theory may often be invoked in interpreting results of inquiry at these lower levels, results can generally be understood and appreciated without a supporting theoretical context. In other words, inquiry at Levels 1 through 4 may proceed either bottom-up, by generalization from data, or top-down, by starting with a rational construction and testing it against data. The two remaining levels of inquiry, however, are ones that can only be entered top-down.

Level-5 research consists of testing a theoretical construction by testing its empirical implications. In a theoretically advanced field like physics, almost all empirical research is of this kind. For that reason, the lay person reading the procedures of an experiment in physics would seldom have any idea of the point of the experiment. With writing research, on the other hand, one expects to be able to infer purposes from procedures. This is normally the case with Level-2 research. As writing research becomes more sophisticated, however, we may expect studies to begin appearing that are incomprehensible except with reference to some theory or model out of which they are conceived.

We may perhaps best illustrate Level-5 inquiry by stepping aside from writing research to a related area where theory is better developed. Consider a study by Collins and Quillian (1969). Students were asked a variety of simple questions: Is a robin a bird? Is a robin an animal? Does a robin have wings? Does a robin have skin? The variable examined was the difference in time (measured in milliseconds) that it took students to answer these different questions. Notice that, without some further information, it would be impossible to figure out why the experiment was conducted. Even less would one be able to criticize the methodology—to argue that certain other questions should have been asked than the ones that were used, for instance. In fact, this experiment is of landmark significance because it provided evidence in support of a new model of memory organization. The model proposed a treelike structure. One implication of this model was that the time it would take to connect two items in memory (such as *robin* and *animal* would depend on the number of branches that needed to be traversed in getting from one item to the other. The questions were constructed so that they would hypothetically require different numbers of branches to make a connection; therefore, what was really at issue in the experiment was whether the theory was strong enough to predict the pattern of differences in the time required to answer the various questions.

Level-5 research cannot be reliably distinguished from Level-2 research by considering studies in isolation. The same methods may be used at either level, and sometimes the variables studied at Level 5 will have both theoretical and commonsense significance. A study reported in Chapter 4 illustrates the importance of considering purpose in determining the level of inquiry at which to interpret a study. The experiment had children producing compositions either by writing, by dictating into a recorder, or by slow dictation, which made use of a scribe who took dictation at each child's previously observed writing rate. The study up to this point is easily viewed as a Level-2 investigation of how mode of production affects composing. Although slow dictation is not a normal mode of production, it reflects an effort, common in both Level-2 and Level-5 research, to separate variables—in this case, to separate the variable of speed from the variable of oral-versus-written production.

Another feature of the experiment is less obviously accounted for, however. When children finished their compositions, the experimenter, through a series of prescribed prompts, urged them to keep going and to write or dictate more and more. People who approach this experiment as a Level-2 investigation find this manipulation ridiculous, of course. They see it as having no ecological validity (that is, it has no counterpart in real life) and as so absurd that children can only be expected to rebel or generate nonsense. But our purpose was not the Level-2 purpose of empirical variable testing. Our purpose, which is elaborated in the next chapter, was to investigate a theoretical notion about how the language-production system must change when it shifts from being dependent on conversational exchange to being capable of functioning autonomously. The experimental manipulation was designed to isolate one hypothesized aspect of conversational exchange (its activating function) from other functions. Because this isolation almost never occurs in nature, the experimental treatment was necessarily rather artificial. But no more realistic treatment—at least none we could think of—would have yielded the relevant information. (As it turned out, children did not rebel or generate nonsense and, as we try to show in Chapter 4, the results were theoretically interesting.) A point that bears repeating is that methods cannot be judged except in relation to purposes. This point becomes absolutely crucial in distinguishing between Level-2 and Level 5 inquiry.

Level 5 inquiry transcends many of the difficulties that plague Level-2 inquiry—the proliferation of variables, the endless succession of "yes buts" and "what ifs." The reason is that Level 5 inquiry is primarily concerned with developing and testing rational constructions rather than with accounting for data. Thus, Collins and Quillian (1969) were not trying to account for all the differences in response time between questions, they were interested in investigating a theory of memory organization; therefore, their interest in the observed phenomena extended only so far as it was relevant to the theoretical questions. Similarly, in our work comparing writing and dictation with prescribed prompts (Chapter 4), we have not been interested in identifying all the factors that affect fluency in writing; we were interested in exploring a theory about what keeps the language-production system going in writing as compared to conversation.

Level-5 research has its problems, but they are the problems of theoretical research in general. It is highly inferential, and it is often possible to keep patching up a weak theory so that it survives no matter what the research turns up. We shall not try to discuss these problems here because there is a vast literature on the subject (e.g., Lakatos & Musgrave, 1970). Instead we shall note one particular limitation that points the way to yet a higher level of inquiry. Level-5 experimentation is good for testing assumptions of theories or differences between theories. This is important in theory development at points where major decisions must be made. But Level-5 inquiry does not tell us how good a job, on the whole, a theory does—how well it explains or represents the composing process. For this we need a form of inquiry in which a theory may be made in some sense to run—to function in a way that will let us assess its overall fit to reality. That is the role of inquiry at Level 6.

Level 6: Simulation

Simulation by computer has proved to be a useful method of inquiry for gaining understanding of a variety of mental processes, such as problem solving (Newell & Simon, 1972), chess playing (Newell, Shaw, & Simon, 1963), and language comprehension (Reddy & Newell, 1974). On the one hand, computer simulation serves as a way of testing process theories originally constructed at other levels of inquiry. Gaps or flaws in the theory emerge as unprogrammable operations or as deviant outputs. On the other hand, computer simulation serves as a variety of inquiry in its own right. It permits the rapid exploration of variations that would be difficult to explore with live participants as well as the gradual development from a crude theory that accounts for only limited kinds or properties of behavior to a more elaborate theory that is able to account for more of the variety of actual human behavior.

At present there is only a limited scope for computer simulation in studying composition. This is because, with present-day artificial intelligence technology, computers fall too far short of human beings in the ability to produce language and to draw flexibly on large knowledge structures. Within these limitations, however, interesting work is going on. Meehan (1976) used computer generation of story plots to examine the world knowledge requirements of narrative production. McCutchen and Perfetti (1982) used simulated retrieval of content ideas to test hypotheses about the psychological bases of age differences in text coherence. Although these types of simulation cannot be said to model the *process* of composition, they do lead to a greatly enriched specification of the knowledge requirements of composition (Black, Wilkes-Gibb, & Gibb, 1982).

The idea of simulation is not limited, however, to simulation by machine. Role-playing, a frequently used therapeutic and educational technique, often involves one person simulating the behavior of another. It differs from ordinary acting in that novel, problematic situations are introduced and the role-player tries to behave as the designated person would behave. Thus it requires more than superficial imitation. It requires, in a sense, having a theory of the other person's behavior and operating according to that theory. The theory need not, of course, be understood in formal terms. It is usually tacit or implicit. Nevertheless it has the properties of a theory: it can be limited in scope or applicable to a variety of situations, it can yield confirmed or unconfirmed predictions, and it can be refined in the light of results.

Some teachers of writing apparently develop a keen enough understanding of how their students write that they can produce compositions indistinguishable from those of their students. (This indistinguishability criterion is often employed in computer simulation studies to test the adequacy of a theory.) The process the teacher uses to generate a composition that will pass for the work of a typical twelve-year-old is not necessarily the same process used by the typical twelve-year-old, but at some important level it must be functionally equivalent. Therefore, if we could understand one process, we should probably have made a significant advance toward understanding the other.

The trouble with simulation on the basis of tacit knowledge, however, is that the process used by the simulator is no more comprehensible than the process being simulated. Thus, although the person doing the simulation may have an excellent working theory of the composing process, the theory cannot be communicated to anyone else.

There is another approach to using human beings as simulators that is more overt and that can result in communicable knowledge. If, instead of trying to write like a twelve-year-old yourself, you design a procedure that will cause other adults to write like twelve-year-olds, you will, perhaps, have captured in the procedure some important principles that distinguish the composing processes of twelve-year-olds. If, in addition, you can use the same or a variant procedure to cause nine-year-olds to write like twelve-year-olds, you will even more surely have captured important insights into the development of the composing process.

The kind of simulation we have just described has recently started to be recognized as a potentially powerful method of inquiry (Brown & Campione, 1981; Butterfield, Siladi, & Belmont, 1980), but there are few examples of its deliberate use. One impressive example is the work of Case and his coworkers (Case, Kurland, & Goldberg, 1982) who tested a theory about the relation between speed of information processing and information-processing capacity. Studies were conducted to see whether by speeding people up or slowing them down to the rate of a target age-group, their short-term-memory performance would be raised or reduced to that of the target age-group. Simulation, it should be noted, is always partial or limited, and this is equally true whether one uses human beings or computers as the simulators. Just as the computer simulator does not expect the computer to watch television and exhibit sexual preferences, Case and his colleagues (1982) did not expect people to act in every way like the target age-group but only to resemble them in the particular way that was relevant to the theoretical inquiry. Similarly, when we apply this method of inquiry to writing, we do not expect the writing of one group to resemble in every particular the writing of another group (although this might be a long-range objective once a comprehensive theory has been developed). Instead, one seeks to achieve limited, predictable changes through interventions that are focused in a theoretically interesting way.

The authors have experimented with a variety of such simulations—not to boost the maturity of writing performance in a general way but instead to have particular effects that would show whether we were on the right track in our theorizing about development of the composing process. The most elaborate studies are described in Chapters 11 and 12; see also Scardamalia & Bereiter (1985b). In Chapter 11, a model is proposed for the mental processes that go on in revision. A simplified procedure is introduced to enable children to execute these processes. In keeping with expectations arising from the knowledge-telling model, the hypothesis is that children have the requisite competence to carry out the subprocesses in some fashion but that they lack an executive scheme for running the process as a whole.

As expected, establishing routines that paced them through knowledge-transforming operations led children who do not normally revise (except at the level of mechanics) to carry out the more mature process to significant effect. Self reports indicated that these young writers were starting to attend to and question the kinds of things that mature writers attend to and question in revision. This points up a particular advantage that simulation using human beings has over simulation using computers. In addition to producing outputs that can be compared to other outputs, human beings—even young and naive ones—can provide a wealth of intelligent commentary that helps the investigator to figure out what is going on.

Although this kind of simulation has begun to be recognized as valuable, it still lacks a name. The authors call it *simulation by intervention.* Like other kinds of simulation, it is a way of investigating one process by setting in motion a hypothetically similar process and comparing the outputs of the natural and the simulated process. Its special characteristic, however, is that the simulation is achieved by intervening in a natural process. This has a double-edged effect when contrasted to simulation by computer. On the one hand, simulation by intervention has greater scope because one does not have to understand or make strong assumptions about all the component processes to investigate one that is of particular interest. To simulate composition by computer, for instance, one must either build in a sentence-generating capability or else assume that sentence generation does not interact with the processes one is attempting to simulate. Neither of these is an attractive alternative. The choice can be avoided in simulation by intervention, however, by allowing sentence-generating capabilities to be as they are and to interact or not, as nature dictates, with the processes that one is attempting to simulate. On the other hand, simulation by intervention is more constrained in that the intervention, if it is to run, must be compatible with the student's actual psychological system, whereas in computer simulation the new program need only be compatible with the system architecture one has selected. Thus, simulation by intervention provides both more freedom to explore partly understood processes and more frequent and stringent reality testing.

Because simulation by intervention frequently involves instruction or some other kind of facilitation, it is easy to confuse it with theory-guided instructional research. Students whom we have tried to initiate into research at this level often fall into this trap, believing that Level 6 inquiry consists of designing an instructional procedure inspired by theoretical notions and then seeing how it works. Level-6 inquiry is not that simple. An instructional procedure can work even though based on a wrong theory, and it can fail to work even though the theory behind it is valid. (One would not wish, for instance, to see the validity of Piaget's theory judged by the success of educational programs purportedly based on it.) Level-6 inquiry in writing research is concerned with investigating the nature of different composing strategies or composing abilities by trying to simulate them, and it is only indirectly concerned with how well a particular intervention works. Nonetheless, Level-6 inquiry does offer the most promise of yielding knowledge that can be put to direct use in instructional design.

LEVELS OF INQUIRY IN RELATION TO CURRENT TRENDS

In this section we shall relate the Levels of Inquiry scheme to current trends in research methodology. Important changes are going on in approaches to research on human behavior. There is no dominant movement but rather a variety of new tendencies stimulated, we believe, by the collapse of empiricism. Empiricism, as practiced by social scientists in the English-speaking world, consists of research programs confined to Level-1 and Level-2 inquiry. Empiricist theorizing consists of trying to establish sets of lawfully related variables that will account for observed variations in behavior (Blalock, 1969). Reasons for the collapse of this once-dominant approach to research are too numerous and complex to be discussed here, but a number have already been suggested in our discussion of Level-2 inquiry.

We expect that eventually a new dominant approach will develop that incorporates inquiry corresponding to all six of the levels we discussed into a coherent, integrative program. In the meantime we have a number of more limited approaches used by researchers who emphasize inquiry at one particular level: for example, there are linguists and ethnomethodologists who emphasize Level 3, a number of cognitively oriented researchers who emphasize Level 4, and artificial intelligence researchers who emphasize Level 6.

A conspicuous development in the last decade has been the rise of holistic approaches to research, approaches that insist on viewing natural behavior in its full context and that seek to break down the rigid division between observer and observed (Mishler, 1979). These new approaches, bearing labels like phenomenological, ethnographic, hermeneutic, and qualitative, are too diverse to put all in one pigeonhole but there does not seem to be any fundamental reason why writing research employing these approaches cannot usefully be described within the Levels of Inquiry framework. At present, holistic methods appear to be used only at Levels 1, 2, 3, and 4. However, there are developments afoot in cognitive science that may provide the necessary theoretical tools for more phenomenological and contextualized inquiry at Levels 5 and 6 (Shaw & McIntyre, 1974; Shaw & Turvey, 1981).

Although holistic methods have much to offer in writing research, there is, on the other hand, a holistic ideology that poses an actual threat to writing research. The main feature of this ideology is opposition to any research (or instruction) that deals with less than the full act of writing carried out under natural conditions. One evident motive behind this ideology is to promote writing as a meaningful activity, but this laudable motive has gotten out of hand when it drives people to oppose any research procedure that they would not accept as an instructional procedure. It seems that advocates of this ideology make the same mistake that many researchers do. They confuse methods with purposes. To hold strictly to a holistic ideology would mean giving up any hope of understanding writing as a cognitive process. The Levels of Inquiry framework, we hope, will make it possible for concerned humanists of a holistic persuasion to see that various methodologies, ranging from naturalistic observation to esoteric laboratory procedures, can be combined into a coherent effort to understand how human minds actually accomplish the complete act of writing.

Chapter 3
From Conversation to Composition

PREFACE

The purpose of this chapter is to identify some of the hurdles that must be passed on the way to competence in written composition. The starting point of the present inquiry is to ask what anyone would have to learn in order to become a competent writer, given that the person already has normal conversational abilities and ability to read and produce written language. It might seem that in taking these abilities as given, we have chosen to ignore the most important bases of writing competence—the early acquisition of communication abilities (Bruner, 1983; Dickson, 1981) and early stages in the acquisition of literacy (Clay, 1975; Harste & Burke, 1980).

One reason for by-passing oral communication and the beginnings of literacy is, of course, that their significance is already recognized and heavily researched. These initial hurdles are, indeed, so dramatic, and failure to negotiate them is so catastrophic, that there is a tendency to ignore hurdles that lie beyond. Significant advances in reading research have come about through shifting attention away from the problems of initial reading acquisition and on to the question of what is involved in more advanced levels of

literacy (Spiro, Bruce, & Brewer, 1980). Far from producing a fragmentation of our knowledge about reading, this
shift in viewpoint and willingness to construct theories
about separate aspects of reading has led to more comprehensive and integrated theories than before (e.g., Lesgold
& Perfetti, 1978; van Dijk & Kintsch, 1983).

There is a somewhat deeper justification, however, for
looking beyond the early stages of competence in written
communication. The principal finding from the current
generation of research on early competence is that many of
the attributes that had been thought to distinguish mature
writers are found to be present in the very young. Prominent examples are audience awareness (Graves, 1983) and
knowledge of narrative structure (Stein & Trabasso, 1982).
One way of responding to such findings is to conjure up a
Platonic fantasy in which children are endowed at birth
with literary genius, only to have it stamped out by the
schools. Another response would be to re-examine our
assumptions about mature competence. Perhaps our ideas
about what it consists of have been superficial or off the
mark.

Competence, as Chomsky has long emphasized (e.g.,
Chomsky, 1964), is a tricky thing to determine. It cannot
be read directly off performance, even under optimum
conditions. It is, in fact, as we have already emphasized in
discussing models of competence in Chapter 1, a theoretical construction by the investigator. Like any theoretical
construction, it is in need of testing and modification in the
light of evidence and is susceptible to competition from
alternative constructions. The following chapter is an attempt
to identify elements of competence in writing that underly
observable differences between mature and immature writers.
It draws on a variety of experimental means of getting
behind observable performance. The findings on one hand
bear out those of research on younger children: Elementary
school children do, indeed, appear to have a great deal of
relevant knowledge and ability that is not apparent from
their ordinary performance. On the other hand, our findings suggest that there are abilities of fundamental importance that school-age students have yet to acquire.

3

Learning to write involves several obvious transitions that, on further investigation, appear to have major psychological implications. One is the transition from oral to graphic expression, which, according to Vygotsky (1978), is a major step in the development of symbolic thought. Another is the transition from face-to-face communication to communication with a remote audience, which, according to Olson (1977) and Goody and Watt (1963), is a critical step in the development of abstract logical reasoning. In this chapter we examine another transition involved in mastering written composition, one that entails a major transformation in the person's whole system for producing language. It is the transition from a language-production system dependent at every level on inputs from a conversational partner to a system capable of functioning autonomously.[2]

When people converse they help each other in numerous, mostly unintentional ways. They provide each other with a continual source of cues—cues to proceed, cues to stop, cues to elaborate, cues to shift topic, and a great variety of cues that stir memory. They serve as text grammarians for one another, raising questions when some needed element of a discourse has been omitted:

> "How did you happen to be hitch-hiking across South Dakota?"
> "But you still haven't told me where the money's going to come from."

They serve as auxiliary memory aids, helping each other stay on topic, keep a goal in mind, or recall a previous remark. A supportive partner provides encouragement, even help in finding a topic. Conversation is not always a collaborative effort, of course. People sometimes converse as adversaries or in asymmetrical relationships such as borrower and lender, direction-giver and direction-follower, or accuser and accused. Even then, however, they continue to provide supports to each other's language production: People who challenge your statements may not be helping you to win your point, but they are helping you to develop your argument.

In written composition supports are removed. This makes written composition not only a harder task than conversation, it makes it a radically

---

[2]We are indebted to David Bartholomae, who reviewed an earlier version of this chapter, for bringing home to us the need to draw a sharp distinction between *producing text autonomously* (which is what we are talking about) and *producing autonomous text* (which Olson, 1977, talked about). It is easy to get them confused, because they both have to do with a contrast between oral and written discourse. We are talking about how the language production system functions, while Olson was talking about the nature of the product issuing from the system. Although there is an affinity between the two notions, they are independent in the strict sense that the probability that one notion is right or wrong is unrelated to the probability that the other is right or wrong.

different kind of task. The magnitude of this difference becomes almost immediately obvious as soon as one compares speaking and writing at the level of continuous discourse. It has not been obvious to past generations of language specialists whose focus has been at the level of the sentence. As recently as 1974 a manifesto from the Conference on College Composition and Communication treated learning to write as primarily a matter of learning a peculiar variety of "prestige" dialect (Committee on CCCC Language Statement, 1974; cf. Farrell, 1978). Implicit in conventional school approaches has been the assumption that mastering written composition is a matter of incorporating new rules into an intact language production system— rules unique to the written medium, such as spelling and punctuation; rules of syntax and lexis related to the dialect properties of written language; and finally rules of form and content related to genres of written composition. We are proposing instead that the oral language production system cannot be carried over intact into written composition, that it must, in some way, be reconstructed to function autonomously instead of interactively.

Some language specialists sensitive to the problems of young children have recognized, at least implicitly, that the shift from conversation to composition is a radical one and they have tried to make it easier for children by providing intermediate mechanisms. For example, Graves (1978a) has developed a compromise between the conditions of conversation and those of composition that appears to be workable even with children in the first grade. Conferences between teacher and student provide a conversational means for developing topics and plans. Children present preliminary versions of their compositions to classmates who then follow up the topic with question-answer conversation, which helps the writer in preparing another draft.

In sections that follow, we examine research that suggests the kinds of things that a child must learn in the course of developing a system for generating discourse autonomously. Keeping language production going in the absence of a turn-taking partner is itself an accomplishment. Even more problematic is learning to activate and search appropriate memory stores in the absence of the continual flow of prompts that normally comes from conversation. At the level of structure, we see that a different kind of discourse schema must be developed for composition, one that contains internal criteria of completeness. Such schemata, our investigations suggest, may evolve from a process of "closing" the schemata used to structure conversations of different types.

While the written composition system must be adapted to the absence of conversational inputs, it must also be adapted to what is present in composition but not in conversation—namely the written text. Learning to act as a reader of one's own text and learning to overcome the saliency of what one has already written appear to be major steps in developing a language-production system that can operate flexibly with feedback from its own output.

The research to be reviewed reflects both theoretical and instructional concerns. The theoretical concerns center around evaluating and elaborating the central thesis of this chapter—that learning to write depends on revamping the language-production system so that it can function autonomously. The instructional concerns center around trying to understand what is difficult about this transformation and why. In order to make advances in teaching a subject like composition, it isn't enough to know what needs to be learned. One has to get to the heart of the difficulties people have in learning it. Cognitive research must accomplish this if it is to improve significantly on the instructional science of earlier years. Much of the detail in this chapter is concerned with exploring what it is that is so difficult for children in various aspects of the composing process.

This brings us to a broader purpose motivating our inquiry into writing development. To investigate the role of executive factors, we have devised a number of experimental techniques that take the general label of *procedural facilitation*. They are ways to ease the executive burden of writing in some particular respect, without providing any substantive help such as suggestions of content or form. We then observe how these procedures change children's compositions or composing behavior and also how they leave them unchanged. This is not a unique research strategy; consider, for instance, its use in studying memory development by getting younger children to adopt the rehearsal or elaboration strategies of older ones (Brown, 1978). We believe, however, that our research program is distinctive in having applied the procedural facilitation strategy to a variety of cognitive functions, all related to the same complex task. The result is a jigsaw puzzle of findings about executive control and knowledge problems, which the present paper fits together. Revamping the language-production system to make it function autonomously is the organizing idea that makes the pieces fit together. The picture itself, however, is one that we hope may be useful in understanding the growth of complexity in problem representation in a variety of cognitive activities such as comprehension, planning, and explanation. As we elaborate in Part IV, procedural facilitation also holds promise as a method of instruction. It is not a way of teaching new strategies and concepts, but is a way of setting more complex goal-directed processes in motion so that children can develop their own strategies for making use of conceptual knowledge they already have. It is thus a direct approach to facilitating cognitive development.

LEARNING TO GENERATE TEXT
WITHOUT A RESPONDENT

To begin our investigation into the development of composition, we want to look at those kinds of discourse that are most profoundly dependent on interaction with a conversational partner. For this we need to introduce a distinction between relatively open and relatively closed discourse schemata. Following a general schema-theoretic line (Rumelhart, 1980), we may assume that every sort of discourse production is directed by some schema that specifies types of things to be said and their relationships. An actual discourse "instantiates" the schema in force at the time—that is, provides particular instances of the kinds of things represented in the schema. Discourse schemata may be considered to be "open" or "closed" to the extent that their instantiation depends on social inputs.

Solitary written composition necessarily depends on closed discourse schemata, since there are no social inputs. All oral discourse, we assume, is open to some extent; even the recitation of a memorized verse would probably show some influence on intonation and pace as a result of audience response. Among the schemata for oral discourse, however, large differences in relative openness and closedness may be noted. A well developed narrative schema is relatively closed, in that it contains a strong system of internal requirements that must be met by the speaker (Stein & Glenn, 1979). Inputs from listeners may influence degree of elaboration and various aspects of delivery, but they are not likely to have much effect on the structure and principal content of the story as a whole. Another relatively closed schema, though not as closed as those for narrative, is the schema (or family of schemata) for giving directions and instructions. Although the listener is likely to play a more active role here than in narrative, the elements and their order in instruction-giving are largely determined by the speaker's own knowledge of the activity. The oral schema governing actual exposition, on the other hand, is more open. In telling someone about your job or your family background, for instance, there is not a coherent "plot" that must be run through, but there is instead a large fund of potentially usable information that will be drawn upon selectively in response to questions and other expressions of interest from listeners. In oral argument, a sophisticated schema will be very open. Most of its requirements will be conditional ones, depending on responses from other participants in the argument.

We should perhaps pause to caution the reader against attributing excess meaning to the terms "open" and "closed." "Open" does not imply anything much more profound than is suggested in the maxim that it takes two to tango. Thus, an oral argument schema is open in the sense that it cannot be instantiated without inputs from someone else. An opinion essay schema is closed precisely in the sense that it does not require the participation of someone else to instantiate it. "Closed" does not mean that the schema is a fixed structure whose slots a writer fills in while composing, that its elements are strictly ordered, that it is antagonistic to spontaneity or reflection, that it is insensitive to audience, or anything of that sort. The opinion-essay schema of a skillful, thoughtful writer would be extremely complex and flexible, would call for rich inputs from the writer's knowledge stores, would involve consideration of alternative opinions, and would, through its reflexive design, provide for development and change in the writer's own opinions as a part of the composing process. The point is that a closed schema, whether it be simple and linear or complex and recursive, constitutes a sufficient set of procedures for carrying a composition through to completion.

Written discourse schemata, to repeat, are closed. When children start learning to write, they already have in their repertoires a number of oral discourse schemata—some relatively open, some relatively closed. They now face the task of developing new, closed schemata that will direct written composition. A commonsense hypothesis is that they will try to adapt their existing oral discourse schemata to this function, and that this will be easiest to do for those schemata that are already relatively closed and hardest for those that are most open.

Testing this commonsense hypothesis runs into the difficulty of finding suitable indicators. It is not obvious how to judge whether children write better stories than they do arguments, or vice versa. There is, however, one usable indicator that at least has considerable suggestive value, and that is number of words produced. Number of words written on any given assignment is found to increase regularly with age (Harrell, 1957; Loban, 1976). We have always found number of words to correlate substantially with indicators of quality or maturity applied to writing (e.g., Bereiter & Scardamalia, 1978; Scardamalia & Bereiter, 1979). One would not expect this relationship to hold in the *beau monde,* of course, but it seems to be a robust empirical generalization about school-age children doing school-type writing tasks.

The hypothesis that children will have greater difficulty with relatively open than with relatively closed discourse schemata in composition leads, then, to the prediction that they will generally produce more words when writing in a closed schema. This prediction, while it may be highly plausible, is not self-evident. An open schema is indefinitely extendible whereas a closed schema is not, and so on purely formal grounds, one could be led to the opposite prediction.

Hidi and Hildyard (1983) have compared children's stories and opinion essays, in both oral and written modes of composition. Children in both grades three and five were found to produce significantly more words in the narratives, whether oral or written.[3] Combining data from the two grades, we find that in the oral mode, narratives averaged 127 words in length, compared to 54 words for opinion essays.[4] In the written mode, the respective lengths were 93 words vs. 32 words.

This very short length for written opinion essays is consistent with our observations in a dozen or more studies using similar writing tasks with similar students. The modal essay starts out, "I don't think boys and girls should play on the same teams because the boys are stronger and the girls might get hurt." Some children stop generating text at this point. Others go on to add something like, "Even if the boys try not to hurt the girls, they might because the boys want to win." Then they stop.

Judged as essays, such productions are far too short and undeveloped. But judged as conversational turns, they are about what one would expect in an argument or discussion. It would then be someone else's turn to respond to the opinion expressed. The idea that what children first produce in composition is a conversational turn can be extended to include their longer story productions as well. That is, stories, like other closed-schema productions, may be thought of as unusually long conversational turns. This idea has been developed by Sacks (1976), who notes conversational rules for gaining prior consent for such long turns.

The Hidi and Hildyard results point up another factor, besides the nature of the discourse schema, that affects the quantity of words produced; oral production significantly exceeds written production, and the difference is found in both genres. We shall examine this output-mode effect in detail in Chapter 4; at the moment we wish only to argue that this effect does not undermine the notion that children's compositions consist of conversational turns.

In normal conversation, the length of the turn a person will take can vary greatly depending on a host of factors, and so our problem in pursuing the notion that children start out writing compositions that are conversational turns is to decide when children have gone beyond single turns as opposed to simply taking longer turns. We don't know of any evidence on the matter, but we suppose people tend to take longer turns when they are fluent in the

[3]Given the number of studies to be discussed in this chapter, it would be tedious to report details of number and source of participants for each one. With few exceptions, every study involved 10 to 20 students per grade-by-condition cell. The participants were public school students from middle class or working class areas and had the high degree of ethnic diversity characteristic of Metropolitan Toronto.

[4]Hidi and Hildyard found a significant age effect, but age did not interact with other factors in their study nor in the other study to which their results will be compared. Since age trends are not germane to the point under discussion, all results have been collapsed over ages.

language being spoken than when they are not. Children of the ages studied by Hidi and Hildyard are certainly more fluent in speech than in writing, and this could account for the difference in quantity produced under the two conditions, even though in both media children are taking single turns.

Another kind of performance that might belie the conversational turn hypothesis is the extended "expressive" writing that children sometimes do about experiences or issues of great personal significance to them. Whenever we test large groups of children, we always find a few who seem to have a special feeling about the assigned topic, be it children choosing their bedtimes or animals being kept in zoos, and they deliver long, impassioned essays on the topic. We would grant that such productions amount to more than a conversational turn, but we would point out that the same kind of behavior does occur at times in conversation and that it does not show evidence there of using a closed discourse schema.

We refer to instances in which the speaker is in a high state of arousal and overrides the normal etiquette of conversation in order to give full expression to his or her thoughts and feelings. But, except with habitual ranters who make an art of it, one could not say that this sort of expression is guided by a closed discourse schema. The speaker is not being guided by the internal constraints of such a schema, but rather has thrown aside constraints in order to meet personal needs. The discourse ends, not when a schema has been instantiated but rather when the speaker has "run down"—that is, when the arousal motivating the production has been dissipated. We suspect that "expressive" writing is appealing to people (by no means only children) because it allows them to do freely what in conversation is often hampered by social restraints, such as the violation of conversational etiquette. While expressive writing undoubtedly has educational value, especially in developing written language fluency, it would be a mistake to suppose that expressive writing is a royal road to the acquisition of written composition schemata.

Because the variations that can occur within real conversational discourse are so great, it is not likely that one could set up crucial tests of the hypothesis that beginning writers are carrying conversational schemata over into written composition. We can show that available evidence is consistent with it. In such a case, confidence in the hypothesis must grow through converging evidence at more than one level of description (a requirement that we shall address in later sections) and through survival of the hypothesis under more detailed analysis of particular phenomena.

Research reported later in this chapter will attempt to identify conversation based strategies as they appear in content search, planning, and revision. Perhaps the most elementary evidence of children's dependence on conversational input comes, however, from observing the effects of prompting children to continue, that is, to take another conversational turn. An experiment detailed in Chapter 4 showed that with such "production signaling," as we call it, children greatly increased the amount of text they produced.

Eventually, we suppose, most kinds of composition come to be regulated by elaborate, closed discourse schemata. Continuing or ending a composition of any sort is then determined by internal criteria of completeness, as it is even for children composing narratives. But how are the open schemata of expository conversation to be developed into closed ones of composition? Surely it must be through experience in producing extended discourse autonomously, and coming to recognize and cope with the structural problems that arise. An important intermediate stage in learning would therefore seem to be one in which writers are able to keep themselves going so as to generate extended discourse within a schema that is still structured to depend on conversational inputs.

LEARNING ACTIVE SEARCH FOR CONTENT

By children's own reports, their main problems in generating text are problems of finding content, not of finding language to express it. As previously noted, contentless prompts that encourage children to tell more substantially increase the amount of text produced. Nevertheless, children reach a limit in the amount of content they generate—a limit seemingly well short of the amount of relevant knowledge they have in memory.

We have also experimented with suggestive prompts that nevertheless stop short of cuing specific content. These are prompts in the form of sentence openers, such as "I think...," "For example...," and "Even though...." Children from grades 4 through 8 consistently report that these sentence openers help them "think of things to write." The sentence openers appear to stimulate the children to search for new nodes in memory to meet the logical requirements of the sentence openers. When most successful, these searches have led children to shift to related but relevant major semantic nodes, as in this example (sentence openers the child selected from those provided are italicized):

> *One reason* I like winter is because of all the sports and games
> you can play in the snow. *A second reason* that I like winter is
> because when you come inside from playing in the snow, you
> can warm yourself up, with hot chocolate. *Not all* people
> think winter is so fun because of things like accidents with

cars, and slipping on the sidewalk. *Besides* just playing in the snow, I sometimes think it's fun to just watch the snowflakes fall. *But* when I don't think about it, winter is just another season.

When less successful, content searches have led children to trace further down from the node they were already working. The result, as shown in the next two examples, is greater detail (sometimes relevant, sometimes not), but not a broader development of the topic.

> *Even though* winter is the best time of year, I decide that children would enjoy winter. *Also* old people think that children who play in the snow can catch pneumonia. *The main point is* that teenagers think that when children are playing in the snow, it's silly. *The reason* that children who do like it enjoy playing in it. *For example* children who play in snow it can be dangerous. *Not all* decide to play in the snow.

> *I think* winter is the best time of year for some people and for others I think it is not. *But* sometimes kids think that it's the best time of year because they could shoot snowballs at people and they'd think that it was a joke but if the snowball had a rock in it the person could get badly hurt. *I think* that people should not even shoot snowballs because in winter people get hurt by snowballs or they have an accident by a kid who shot a snowball on the car window and the person who was driving it might have not been able to see and had an accident with another car. *That's why I* don't *think* winter is the best time of year for some people. *Not all* people like winter because people might be scared to drive a car because they're scared to have an accident.

Judged as finished texts, these examples are poor in coherence. But judged as first-draft material out of which a composition might be fashioned, they are rich in content by grade-four standards. Sometimes, however, prompts fail to help children tap new domains of content, as shown in the following:

> *Even though* a lot of people think that summer is the best time of year some say that winter is the best time of year. *But* some people say that when summer comes they think it is the best time of year but when winter comes they say it is the best time of year. *For example* I could have an argument with somebody that winter is the best time of year. *But* I think winter is the best time of year.

A commonsense hypothesis would be that the success of children's searches for content depends on how much they know. Such a view receives a good deal of indirect scientific support from research showing the effects of knowledge on comprehension (Spiro, 1977). Somewhat more direct evidence comes from Nelson and Gruendel (1979), who found that preschool children's abilities to converse coherently depend on shared world knowledge in the form of scripts. In understanding the writing problems of children, however, it seems that focus on the world-knowledge store will not lead to the heart of their difficulties.

All the evidence we know of indicates that children's main problem with content is in getting access to, and giving order to, the knowledge they have. In conversations with children, when we direct content searches and information retrieval with prompts such as the sentence openers cited previously, we invariably find children have relevant knowledge to fill each content node. Yet left to their own devices with lists of sentence openers they can select from, as was the case for the children who produced the texts presented above, their control over relevant content appears unstable.

The Scardamalia, Bereiter, and Woodruff study discussed briefly in Chapter 2 investigated the effects of children's reported familiarity with topics. Children in grades 4 and 6 were interviewed individually to determine topics they claimed to know a lot about (familiar topics) and topics they said they knew little about (unfamiliar topics). The first finding of note is that the children generally found this initial task to be difficult. The original intention to elicit five familiar and five unfamiliar topics from each student had to be abandoned because even after patient experimenter probing, many children were unable to come up with that many. The metaknowledge required here is not easy to account for (Brown, 1978). That is, it isn't obvious how we are able to say in a flash that we know quite a bit about x and not very much about y; but it seems that mature people can do this and that it is a very important ability in composition. It is important not only in choosing a topic but also in allocating space to subtopics and in planning strategies for reaching goals. As one veteran journalist put it, every feature-writer has to know how to "write around" his areas of ignorance.

The difficulty children had in naming familiar and unfamiliar topics casts some doubt on the rest of the study. Nonetheless, there are several indications that children had, on the average, identified topics that in fact varied along the familiar-unfamiliar dimension. They gave significantly more content for their familiar than for their unfamiliar topic when asked to plan what they would put in their composition, and when asked to itemize content relevant to the respective topics that they would *not* actually include in their compositions. But it was only at this preliminary planning stage that differences appeared in what children could do with familiar and unfamiliar topics. Compositions produced on the two kinds of topics were indistinguishable. Analyses on six different dimensions failed to reveal even a hint of difference.

These no-difference findings would evidently not have come as a surprise to the children themselves. When asked to evaluate their performance (in half the cases before writing, in half the cases after) they indicated they did not think they had done a better job with the topic they were more familiar with. The prevailing response was either that they were good writers who could write well on either topic (not many claimed this) or that they were not good writers and so they couldn't write well on either. Children do not, by the way, usually insist that nothing makes a difference except basic writing ability. In other studies, we have found them claiming that genre makes a difference—that they are better, for instance, at writing letters and stories than at writing essays. Their opinions on the effect of content familiarity, therefore, should perhaps be granted some validity as self-report.

The "plans" children produced were with few exceptions mere lists of content items, seemingly reported as they came to mind. While it is true that children were better able to list items *not* to include when the topic was a familiar one, this should not be taken as indicating some selection according to high-level rhetorical goals. Children found it very difficult to think of items about dogs, say, that they would not want to include in a composition about dogs. A third of all students could think of nothing they knew about either their familiar or their unfamiliar topic that they would not want to include. Many children in grade 4 responded with incredulity. They could not imagine thinking of something relevant to a topic and then not including it—a testimony to the magnitude of the content-search problem. When children did think of an item they would not include it was usually excludable either on the grounds of judged triviality (e.g., that dogs have claws, or that you use gloves in baseball) or on grounds of distastefulness (e.g., that dogs are bad or wild; that there is tripping, fighting, and high-sticking in hockey; that model racing-cars sometimes smash). Nothing was ever rejected on the grounds of not fitting with an overall plan.

Two distinct kinds of operations on long-term memory can be recognized for writing. The familiarity study indicates children have trouble with both of them. The first is a diffuse, topic-related search of memory directed by a question on the order of, "Let's see, what do I know about this?" The result of this search is not likely to be a complete inventory, but rather a list of major categories with some information concerning the extent of knowledge in each. This may properly be regarded as a *metamemorial* search. It does not directly yield content for use in writing, but instead yields knowledge about the availability of content. The other kind of operation is a top-down search, directed toward some goal such as proving a point, amusing the reader, or preparing an introductory lecture. For convenience, let us call these *metamemorial* and *goal-directed* searches.

Metamemorial search probably has more than an informational function. It probably has a priming or "tuning" function as well, so that in addition to giving the writer an awareness of what knowledge is available in memory, it also enhances the availability of that knowledge. For any complex writing task, the relevant knowledge is likely to be scattered among a variety of nodes. Unless the potentially useful nodes are brought up to a state of ready accessibility, goal-directed search is likely to fail.

Without a preliminary survey and activation of knowledge, one can expect the difficulties that are in fact typical of school children when they try expository writing: trouble finding a topic when required to do so, trouble finding a starting point (a beginning that the writer has enough information to follow up on), and running out of content even though a little gentle probing will turn up a great deal more usable knowledge.

The reason children evince little skill in metamemorial search would appear, again, to be that conversational experience produces little need for it. Socially sensitive adults may be aware occasionally of a desperate metamemorial search for a topic to fill a conversational void, but it is doubtful if children have much experience of this. Normal spontaneous conversation does not take up topics cold. The relevant memory nodes have already been activated either by something in the environment or by a process of conversational trials and probes—what Nelson and Gruendel (1979) call finding a "shared script." Moreover, the rules of topic shift (Reichman, 1978; Schank, 1977) ensure that the conversation will not take abrupt leaps to realms of knowledge not at least partially activated by the preceding conversation. In short, the question, "Let's see, what do I know about such-and-such?", is one that conversationalists need seldom ask themselves.

A common writing practice in schools is to carry out prewriting activities in advance of having children write on a topic (Harpin, 1976; Meckel, Squire, & Leonard, 1958). These activities may include showing a film or having some topical reading, but they almost invariably include class discussion and some form of listing of possible content items. These naturally evolved procedures for helping children write are a striking testimony to the universality of children's deficiencies in metamemorial search. What all teacher-directed prewriting activities have in common is that they take over the job of activating topically relevant memory nodes, doing for children what skilled writers need to be able to do for themselves.

In an effort to enable children to carry out metamemorial search for themselves, Robert Sandieson experimented with having children "brainstorm" by listing topical ideas in advance of writing. Although elementary-school children could make some use of this procedure, they found it laborious, and it seemed unlikely that they would persist with it voluntarily. One problem was that they had difficulty resisting text generation; although nominally listing items in any order, they were often in fact producing connected text, and so were dealing with all of its burdens from the start. Valerie Anderson devised an alternative procedure in which children, in advance of writing on a topic, listed all the relevant single words they could think of that might be used in their compositions. This approach was tested in a training study consisting of 12 one-hour sessions in which children practiced with a variety of expository and opinion topics (Anderson, Bereiter, & Smart, 1980). The results, as gauged from posttreatment compositions, were striking. Compared to control students, the experimental-group students wrote essays twice as long and used three times as many uncommon words. This may be taken to indicate more varied content. In an opinion essay, the experimental students offered an average of three arguments on the issue, as compared to two for the controls, and significantly more experimental-group students elaborated their arguments.

This experiment makes it evident that the kind of memory access needed for metamemorial search is within the capacity of elementary-school children (the children in the experiment were in sixth grade). What the children seem to lack is an executive routine for carrying it out.

While metamemorial search opens the possibility of goal-directed search, it does not, of course, ensure that it will take place. It may simply lead to a greater quantity of content relevant to the topic, but not specially selected for any purpose. This seems to have been the case in the experiment just reported. In ratings of overall quality, the compositions written by the experimental group were not significantly superior to those of the control group. Thus, although they produced more content in support of their arguments, their arguments do not appear to have been rendered more persuasive.

The experimental treatment was not aimed at helping children *plan* compositions. (We will get to studies of planning in subsequent sections.) Nevertheless, had the students been searching for content according to some criterion of persuasiveness—or even interestingness or significance—we should expect that improved access to memory should have given the experimental group a noticeable edge in quality as well. It seems that what children do instead is to find content first and then work it into their texts. Thus planning, in effect, starts *after* content has been found, not before.

School-age children obviously have a capacity for goal-directed memory search. Problem solving of all sorts depends on it. A child could not figure out how a mosquito and a sparrow are alike without it, and intelligence-test items calling for performance of this kind are typically passed by the age of seven or eight. In composition, however, where goals of memory search have to be constructed by the writer, the ability to draw content from memory according to goal-derived requirements appears much later.

An experiment by Bereiter & Scardamalia (1985) illustrates an elementary kind of goal-directed memory search that was found to occur spontaneously in students of age 16, but that could be induced experimentally, at least to an extent, in children as young as age 10. In this experiment, students were taught a game by means of a videotape, and their task was to write instructions for playing the game. With respect to its demands for memory search, this task was much simpler than the typical composition task in two ways: (1) Since the necessary knowledge had all just been acquired and formed a coherent package, there was no need for a metamemorial search to find and activate the knowledge store; (2) Leaving aside issues of presentation, the goal of writing an adequate set of instructions could be achieved simply by continuing to consult memory until all the facts about the game had been retrieved.

Students in grade 11 clearly met the memory search requirement. Of 23 ideas relevant to playing the game, they included an average of 20 in their instructions. Fourth-graders, however, included an average of fewer than eight ideas—in other words, about one-third of the total. In postexperimental interviews, it was determined that the fourth-graders did, in fact, remember the game rules quite well. However, to get them to give a full account of the rules it was again necessary to use prompts of the "tell me more" variety.

The spontaneous tendency of the fourth-graders was to recall high-order points and neglect subordinate ones unless questioned. This is very normal behavior and has been plausibly taken to reflect the hierarchical organization of memory schemata (Clements, 1979; Mandler & Johnson, 1977; Meyer, 1977). But it is not an appropriate memory-search strategy for composing instructions. Such a task requires not only accessing high-order nodes, but also working down the branches leading from those nodes to track down all information relevant to performing the activity.

How might children learn to do this without having to be prompted or told? An experimental treatment used in the Bereiter & Scardamalia study (1985) tested the effect of sensitizing children to the nature of the communication problem they faced. Whereas control-group children viewed the instructional videotape twice, experimental group children viewed it once and then were shown another tape portraying an inept attempt at instruction— vague, incomplete, or misleading instructions leading to a succession of blunders. This "sensitization" videotape never modeled correct instructions but only provided evidence of the pitfalls that poor instruction could lead to. Fourth-graders who viewed this videotape produced 50% more items of task information in their compositions than did control students. (The experimental treatment increased idea output of students up through grade 9 as well, though not at grade 11, where control students were already at ceiling.)

It should be emphasized, however, that the search task in this experiment was an extremely simple one, requiring only that the writer press on to an exhaustive search of a limited and clearly identifiable knowledge domain.

The kind of memory search required to do a good job on even the simplest essay assignments is bound to be far more complex, involving scattered knowledge stores and the meeting of internal constraints—searching for knowledge to illustrate x, to prove y, to explain z, and so on.

Memory search of these more sophisticated kinds obviously demands high-level guidance from problem analysis, goal formulation, and planning. We should not be too quick to conclude, however, that only these higher-level processes warrant instructional attention. If sophisticated memory search depends on having a plan, so does having a feasible plan depend on memory search—particularly on metamemorial search that ascertains what knowledge resources are available. The two abilities we have examined in this section—the ability to conduct metamemorial search and the ability to conduct exhaustive search of a small domain—are both abilities that elementary-school children seem not to practice, but which they can, with a little help, bring into use. It seems reasonable to suppose that if children learned how to gain more ready access to the stores of world knowledge that they have available for use in writing, they would be more receptive to instruction relating to selecting and organizing knowledge to meet composition goals. An instructional study to be reported in Chapter 12 found, in fact, that it was not until children were able to generate more content than they could use that they began selecting content in the light of goals. It thus appears that outgrowing knowledge-telling may depend on developing memory-search strategies that are so effective that they give the knowledge-telling process more material than it can handle.

SHIFTING FROM LOCAL TO WHOLE-TEXT PLANNING

One of the most obvious differences between composition and oral communication is the extent of planning that composition permits and sometimes requires. In conversation, one may have a global intention that influences conversational moves over a long series—for instance, the intention to convince someone of something. But this intention cannot be realized through an elaborate plan. Adherence to such a plan would be self-defeating, in fact, for it would not permit sufficient adaptation to moves made by the conversational partner.

Expert writing, on the other hand, is characterized by abundant planning—not only in advance of writing, but also during writing, as plans are revised and further elaborated in response to "discoveries" occurring in the course of composition (Hayes & Flower, 1980). Our investigations of children thinking aloud while they compose (discussed in Chapter 8) reveal a much more limited kind of planning. The planning that appears in children's protocols is of a local sort—planning or evaluating a small unit of discourse, taking into account only the immediate context or the general topic.

In brief, the planning children do is of the sort people do in conversation. It is forward-looking, concerned with the question, "What shall I say next?" It lacks the *attention to the whole,* and the backward- and the forward-looking analyses that are the hallmarks of compositional planning. In thinking-aloud protocols, elementary-school children show virtually none of the explicit planning found in the protocols of mature writers. What they mainly do is just generate text. This could be an illusion created by the methodology, however. Children may not be able to reveal as much of their thought while composing as adults do. Accordingly, we tried a more structured approach to finding out how children make local decisions in composing.

To investigate the local decisions children make in composing, Scardamalia and Bracewell (1979) asked students to write using sentence openers from a pre-established list, as in studies mentioned earlier in this chapter. At each sentence break in the composition, however, the writer was instructed to choose two openers and use them to compose alternative next sentences. Since the different openers pointed to different text functions ("For example . . . ," "Another reason . . . ," etc.), it was reasonable to expect that the alternatives constructed would not be mere stylistic variations, but would represent different directions or strategies for developing the text. We were interested, therefore, in the reasons children would give for choosing between alternatives— whether these reasons would show a consideration of what the choice was committing them to, its implications for the overall development of the composition, or whether the reasons would reveal only short-sighted considerations.

As it turned out, most of the alternatives generated by children in grades 4 through 8 were, in spite of the divergent force of the sentence openers, merely different ways of presenting the same idea. We take this as further evidence of a knowledge-telling strategy of composition, in which the predominant task is to think of a next item of content. As to reasons, the prevailing basis for choice was the judged merits of the two sentences, without any regard even to the local context. One sentence was preferred to another because it was more truthful, because it sounded better, or because its competitor had some perceived flaw. But there was not a single indication of a child considering the commitments implied by a choice or the value that a sentence might have in reaching a goal or filling out some plan.

These negative findings, though striking, are not definitive about children's competence for high-level planning in composition. They serve mainly as background for a program of facilitative intervention studies. This chapter will deal with two of the approaches we have taken to facilitate higher-level, goal-directed planning in children's composition. Further studies are reported in Chapter 12.

> **1.** Ending sentences. Instead of giving children topics or beginnings, we give them final sentenes that they must build their compositions toward. While this is not the kind of goal that writers normally plan for, it is a goal that requires means-end planning of a sort. Accordingly, it serves as a way of exploring what it takes to set means-end planning in motion and how children handle it.
>
> **2.** Abstract planning elements. Here the concern is with hooking local planning up to higher-level knowledge. Instead of thinking "What shall I say next?", can children ask themselves "*What kind of thing* shall I say next?" Before composing each sentence, the child chooses from a set of abstract text elements such as *reason, example, reason on the other side,* and *conclusion*—and then composes the next sentence in accord with this choice. This procedure is intended not only to cue a higher level of planning, but also to provide a simple executive routine for switching between text generation and planning.

Research Using Ending Sentences

Let us first consider some results with ending sentences. With certain appropriately problematic story endings, we have been able to provoke planning in children that begins to have the flavor of the adult planning that Flower and Hayes (1980a) report. Here is a reconstruction[5] of a dialogue among four sixth-graders who were given the task of composing a story that ended with the sentence, "And so, after considering the reasons for it and the reasons against it, the duke decided to rent his castle to the vampire after all, in spite of the rumor he had heard."[6]

The children quickly recognized that they needed more than one reason for and more than one reason against renting the castle to the vampire. Brian suggested, as one reason for it, that the duke needed money. Marilyn added:

---

[5]The discussion was not taped, the occasion for it having arisen unexpectedly. It is here reconstructed as accurately as the one of us who was present (M.S.) could recall it.

[6]From Osgood, C. E., & Bock, J. K.: Salience and sentencing: Some production principles. In Sheldon Rosenberg (Ed.), Sentence production: Developments in research and theory. Hillsdale, NJ: Lawrence Erlbaum Associates, 1977, pg. 133.

"Yeah, he had this big castle that cost a lot to heat. So that's why he wanted to rent the castle."

Kay then asked what a second reason for wanting to rent the castle could be.

> ANGELO: We already have two reasons. One, the duke needs money. Two, the duke's castle is very large and it's expensive to heat.
>
> KAY: That's just saying *why* the duke needs money. It's not another reason for renting the castle.
>
> ANGELO: He could have hundreds of reasons for needing money. One happens to be that he has a big expensive castle.
>
> KAY: See, you said that's one reason. We need another reason.

At this point, Marilyn interceded to complain that they were wasting too much time, when they hadn't even gotten to the "hard stuff" yet. Angelo agreed and proposed they switch to reasons why the duke wouldn't want to rent the castle. Brian suggested as an obvious reason, that vampires suck blood out of women at night, and "the duke doesn't want a bunch of bloodless women hanging around his castle."

The others murmured assent to this idea, except for Angelo, who objected: "This isn't gonna work. We've got to end up with the duke deciding he will rent the castle. If we make the reasons against it too good, it won't make any sense for the duke to do it."

Daunted by this criticism, the children decided to have the vampire be harmless but rich. In agreeing on this point, they abandoned altogether the search for reasons against renting the castle. Later they turned to the problem of the rumor mentioned in the ending sentence.

> BRIAN: Let's just say the vampire is supposed to be a thief. So he's probably just trying to trick the duke and he really won't pay him after all.
>
> ANGELO: Wait a second. Then why would the duke be so dumb as to decide to rent the castle?
>
> KAY: Yeah. This whole story is getting kinda dumb.
>
> ANGELO: All we've come up with after all this time is a poor duke and a rich vampire. Dukes aren't even supposed to be poor. We should at least work out something neat about how he lost his money.
>
> MARILYN: And how did the vampire get so rich?
>
> BRIAN: What difference does it make? Nobody's going to think about all these things we're worrying about. They'll just read the story and never notice.
>
> KAY: Well, I don't think our story is very good. We just have one

person who is rich and one who is poor, and nothing very exciting happening.

ANGELO: What if we work out something about the duke is poor because of something the vampire did.

MARILYN: Yeah. Then we could have the duke rent the castle to him to try to trick him somehow.

With this appealing idea, the children essentially started planning over again from the beginning. By the end of the 40-minute session, they were still not ready to begin writing and in fact had not yet settled what the "reasons for" and "reasons against" were, Brian pointing out at the end of the period that they had been farther ahead 15 minutes earlier.

This protocol was chosen partly because it shows some of the highest levels of planning we have observed in elementary-school children (the group interaction undoubtedly helped) and also because it points up a troublesome uncertainty about just what kind of problem solving is induced by a task of this sort.

At the outset, the children are wrestling with a world-knowledge problem. The problem may be stated explicitly as, *Think of two or more reasons why a duke might wish to rent his castle to a vampire.* Although the question is derived by inference from the ending sentence, it is treated at first without reference to the intended story. That is, the children act just as if they had simply been given the problem as stated. Thus, it is legitimate to ask whether their thinking has anything to do with planning a composition. Much of the thinking that we find to be elicited by ending sentences is on problems of this kind. We call them "armless violinist" problems, referring to the imaginary assignment to write a story about an armless violinist. The problem that immediately comes to mind is how an armless person could play the violin. Solving this is solving a physical problem. True, the problem needs to be solved before one can proceed to write a story about an armless violinist, and the solution may suggest the point of the story one eventually writes—but the problem itself is not a literary or rhetorical problem.

The nature of the children's problem solving takes a sudden turn when Angelo says, "This isn't gonna work," and points out that if the reasons against renting the castle to a vampire are too strong, it will be impossible to construct a plausible story that ends with his renting the castle to the vampire after all. This is a problem rooted in the internal constraints of the story, not in a world of dukes and vampires. From that point on, the children begin considering everything in the light of the story. Solutions to duke/vampire problems may now be rejected, not because they are implausible, but because they make for a "dumb" story. Brian rejects one problem out of hand because he thinks it will not occur to readers to wonder about it. Finally, the children shift their attention to planning the story around an idea that is not required by the constraints of the ending sentence at all—the idea of the vampire's being responsible for the duke's poverty. The virtue of this idea, which seems to have been appreciated by all the children, is that it not only meets constraints imposed by the ending sentence but also serves as the basis for an interesting story. This would seem to mark a shift into a knowledge-transforming mode of composing (see Chapter 1). Instead of merely generating content and judging it for appropriateness to the story, they moved back and forth between content considerations and rhetorical considerations until they had achieved a result that satisfied both kinds of concerns.

With the protocols of individual children up through grade 8, however, we seldom find unambiguous evidence that they are considering text problems in their planning. It is quite possible that all they do is to deal with the world-knowledge problems implied in the sentence endings. (Why would a duke be renting out his castle? Why would a woman risk going to a laundromat at midnight?, etc.) While the solutions provide them with material to write about, this may be an incidental consequence of the way the task is designed and may not reflect actual text planning on their part.

Even if this is true, however, the kind of problem solving set in motion by ending sentences should not be written off as inconsequential for writing. Solving world-knowledge problems arising in the course of composition may be an important, concrete step on the way to handling the more abstract structural, semantic, and stylistic problems that mature writers encounter. A study by Hildyard and Hidi (1980) suggests that at least the recognition of world-knowledge problems in writing has some rhetorical relevance.

Hildyard and Hidi asked children to write stories using a setting taken from Stein (1979): "Once there was fox who was mean and greedy and never thought of sharing anything. . . . The fox decided to catch a fish so that he could give it to the bear for dinner." In one condition, the two sentences were presented as the beginning of the story and the task was to complete the story. In the other condition, the first sentence was presented at the beginning and the second at the end, the task being to interpolate a story connecting the two statements. Table 3.1 shows the number of children in grades 3 and 5 who resolved and failed to resolve the inconsistency implied by the two sentences. Overall, children were about twice as likely to resolve the inconsistency in the interpolated condition.

From our reading of the compositions produced in this study, it appears the children were treating the problem as a world-knowledge problem—a problem in psychology, as it were, that could be solved by imagining, for instance, some condition of threat or obligation that could cause the selfish fox to act out of character. There was little indication of what we saw in the group-planning session of sixth-graders—little indication that children tried to find a solution to the problem that would have good narrative possibilities. Instead, the children apparently took whatever explanation occurred to them, planted it in the space between beginning and end, and thus produced a structurally adequate, but not very interesting, story.

It remains significant, however, that children tended not to do even this if the inconsistent information was presented to them as a story beginning. Clearly, simply reading the two sentences together failed for many children to alert them to a problem that needed solving. When they had to join the inconsistent items of information by means of a story, almost all children came to grips with the inconsistency. The condition in which the inconsistent information was given at the beginning allowed children to use their familiar forward-acting strategies for generating content. In this condition, half of the children simply ignored the first item of information (about the fox's greediness) and spun their story from the second item only.

One interpretation of the Hildyard and Hidi results is that, whereas the beginning sentence condition activated only the forward-acting strategy, the interpolated condition set two strategies in motion. One involved the straightforward development of the greedy-fox theme. The other was a means-end development concerned with devising a story that ended with the fox's decision to catch a fish for the bear. The incompatibility of these two lines of story development, then, gave rise to the world-knowledge problem concerning the fox's motivation, rather than the world-knowledge problem being the source of the story. Alternatively, one could argue that the forward-acting strategy followed (especially by the younger children) in the beginning-sentence condition, made it unnecessary for children to process the first item of information, since they could continue the story without it. By either interpretation, however, it is seen that the kind of thinking set in motion by an ending sentence is much closer to compositional planning than is the approach children carry over from conversation.

Table 3.1 Number of Children Who Resolved and Failed to Resolve Inconsistencies When Two Statements of Inconsistent Information Were Presented

Grade	Inconsistent Information Presented as Story Beginning		Inconsistent Information to be Connected by Interpolated Text	
	Conflict Resolved	Conflict not Resolved	Conflict Resolved	Conflict not Resolved
Three	3	7	7	3
Five	9	7	15	1
Total	12	14	22	4

Note: Adapted from "Resolving Conflict in Narratives," by A. Hilyard and S. Hidi, paper presented at the meeting of the American Educational Research Association, Boston, 1980. Copyright 1980 by A. Hilyard and S. Hidi. Reprinted by permission.

Jacqueline Tetroe of our research group has been experimenting with a variety of ending sentences, in other narrative and expository genres, and has been collecting thinking-aloud protocols in connection with some of them. It appears (Tetroe, 1981; Tetroe, Bereiter, & Scardamalia, 1981) that there are two main strategies children use for shaping a composition toward a given ending. The first is a serial strategy that deals with elements of the ending sentence one at a time. The second is a simultaneous strategy, in which decisions are made in light of all the constraints (or as many of them as the child can keep in mind).

In using the serial strategy, the child resolves one problem raised by the ending sentence (for instance, why the duke wants to rent his castle) and then starts planning the narrative with that as a starting point. Then the child attends to another problem (such as how the vampire arises as a prospective tenant) and advances the story further on the basis of this resolution. If all goes well, the child takes care of all the constraints implied in the ending sentence and has a complete story by the time the last constraint is dealt with.

This strategy reminds us of that of a talented carpenter we know who prefers not to plan much in advance but to start in and trust to his cleverness and skill to make everything work out right in the end. He is, in fact, very adroit with what he calls "finishing problems," such as what to do when the cabinets he is building across one wall meet (or just fail to meet) the shelves he is building across another. He prefers this serial strategy because it is easier (that is, avoids the burden of considering a number of variables at once), because sometimes problems take care of themselves and don't need to be solved, and because it "makes life more interesting." All of these considerations apply to writing and suggest that a serial strategy may be the method of choice for some people who develop into skilled writers.

The simultaneous strategy, because it requires attending simultaneously to several constraints, places much higher demands on working-memory capacity. Nevertheless, there are elementary children who use it spontaneously. Tetroe found, moreover, that some children who used the serial strategy had the simultaneous strategy available to them and would use it if prompted to do so.

Tetroe also investigated the influence of the task on choice of strategy. Children tend to side-step means-end planning if the ending sentence imposes too few constraints. A sentence like "The captain of the space ship said they'd never go back to that planet again" is apparently taken simply as a cue to write a space travel story. It is not necessary to think about the sentence again until near the end, at which point there is a minor "finishing problem" to deal with in getting a cohesive link between the text and the ending sentence. But the sentence can serve as a reasonable ending to almost any space adventure a child might compose. Thus, it offers no reason for children to plan ahead.

Research with Abstract Planning Elements

Let us turn now to the second type of planning research, that involving abstract structural elements such as reasons and examples in argument, settings and events in narrative. Our concern here is with the hookup between high-level knowledge and local decisions. The research we have cited so far in this section may seem to be inconsistent with research on children's story grammars (Mandler & Johnson, 1977; Rumelhart, 1975; Stein & Glenn, 1979; Stein & Trabasso, 1982). Story-grammar research indicates that by the time children enter school they already have well developed structural schemata that permit them to comprehend and generate stories. In the remainder of this section, we examine questions about children's structural knowledge of discourse as it applies to writing. Is their knowledge limited to stories or do they have structural schemata for other genres as well? Can they use this knowledge consciously in planning or is it a kind of tacit knowledge that influences performance without itself being susceptible to manipulation? Finally, we will take up the problem of reconciling evidence of structural discourse knowledge with our thesis that children's language-production systems are bound to the open schemata of turn-taking conversation.

A series of studies has investigated children's knowledge of discourse structure and its availability for use in planning compositions. We wanted to know if children have structural knowledge of anything besides stories, whether this knowledge is accessible to consciousness, and whether they can make use of it in planning. The answer to all three questions turns out to be Yes, with the important reservation that children do not appear to access and use this knowledge spontaneously.

To get a preliminary indication of children's consciously accessible knowledge, Turkish (Bereiter, Scardamalia, & Turkish, 1980) interviewed children of ages 10 to 12. The children were questioned about the kinds of elements they thought belonged in texts of three genres—narrative, argument, and directions (how to get somewhere). To elicit this information, the experimenter showed the interviewee a sheet of paper and explained that on it was a story, for instance, that the experimenter had written. The interviewee was not allowed to examine the text, but was asked to speculate on what *kinds* of things must be on it to make a good story, a persuasive argument, or a good set of instructions. If, as was common, the child guessed at concrete items of content, a series of prescribed prompts was used to lead the child to formulate an abstract characterization of the type of content indicated.

The questioning also proceeded spatially—what kind of thing would likely be at the top of the page, next after that, in the middle of the page, and so on. Table 3.2 shows a tally of the frequency with which various kinds of text items were named. This table shows our own categorization of discourse elements in the three genres, based on analysis of both children's compositions and interview responses. For narrative, a classification of responses according to the story grammar of Stein & Glenn (1979) is also shown. A month or more later in the school year, as part of their normal school work, students wrote in each of the three genres on which they had been questioned. The resulting texts were parsed using the same schemes as for the interview responses. Table 3.2 also shows the frequency with which the various discourse elements appeared in pupil texts.

While in every genre children on the average used more different discourse elements than they named, in the aggregate they named all the elements they used. This suggests that children have, potentially at least, conscious access to their discourse-grammar knowledge. Such access is quite astonishing if one considers how little access children have to their sentence-grammar knowledge, as evinced by the time-honored difficulty of teaching formal grammar in school.

The nature of this consciously accessible knowledge is not clear. It is not knowledge that children can read out of a memory store, like the names of their siblings. It usually took quite a bit of coaxing before they tuned in to the level of abstraction we had in mind, and even then there was quite a bit of straining and occasional backsliding to the concrete level. In some sense, clearly, the knowledge was being constructed on the spot—but what it was being constructed from is the mystery. The mystery is darkened somewhat by the fact that there is no apparent intra-individual consistency in the naming and use of text elements. In the aggregate, as Table 3.2 shows, the frequency with which various discourse elements are named is correlated with the frequency of their use—i.e., the most frequently named are also the most frequently used, etc. But students are not consistent across genres or between naming and using. The number of elements a student names is not correlated with the number he or she uses, nor is there any correlation between the number named in one genre and in another, nor even between the number used in one genre and in another.

The question of whether this consciously accessible discourse knowledge has any functional significance was pursued in a study by Paris, Scardamalia, and Bereiter (1980). One aspect of the study investigated whether there is a natural order of discourse grammar elements. Students were asked to arrange elements of an opinion essay (with slight variation, the same elements as shown for that genre in Table 3.2) as they would if they were actually going

Table 3.2   Frequency with Which Discourse Elements Were Named and Actually Used in Writing in Three Genres by Elementary School Students

Discourse Element	Frequency Naming	Use	Discourse Element	Frequency Naming	Use
Narrative (N = 31)[a]			Opinion Essay (N = 32)		
Major Setting	21	30	Statement of Belief	25	27
Minor Setting	15	30	Reason for	23	25
Initiating Event	9	25	Elaboration	0	19
Internal Response	4	18	Example	5	17
Internal Plan	0	6	Repetition	0	2
Attempt	3	24	Statement on Other Side	4	7
Direct Consequence	2	25	Reason Against	7	21
Reaction	1	12	Conclusion	10	7
Total	55	170	General Statement	4	5
			Personal Statement	3	9
			Total	81	139
Narrative (N = 31)			Direction (N = 32)		
Setting	11	25	Orientation	7	18
Intro. to Character	19	29	Destination	18	12
Description of Character	12	18	Duration	6	0
Plot Action	21	19	Distance	5	0
Motives	4	14	Route	21	30
Direct Consequence	2	21	Landmark	2	27
Resolution	4	15	Transportation	11	0
High Point	3	17	Directional Referencing	20	29
Dialogue	2	7	Description of Place	1	5
Moral	0	0	Location of Place	12	28
Role	1	7	Arrival at Place	13	13
Cause	3	5	Complications	5	3
Initiating Action	9	25	Total	121	165
Time Reference	6	11			
Scenery	2	5			
Feelings	5	15			
Total	104	233			

[a]These categories are from Stein and Glenn, 1979.

to write an essay. The modal order of these abstract elements was the same order observed in compositions by children of the same ages in other studies. Later, students were required to write two opinion essays following specified orders of discourse elements. One order was the conventional one found in children's essays, the other an order not found there, although it was an order a mature writer might use. According to several indicators, children had more difficulty following the unconventional order—they took longer to get started and deviated more from the prescribed plan. These data we take as support for the psychological reality of the discourse-grammar knowledge that children report. This knowledge is not just representational, but seems to have operational significance.

From the two studies just summarized, we conclude that children do have structural knowledge of genres other than narrative and that this knowledge potentially could be put to conscious use by them in planning, but there are no indications that they actually do use it consciously. It must function as implicit knowledge, like their knowledge of sentence grammar, shaping production but having no role in conscious planning. This might be part of the reason children's composition planning is concentrated at the local level and shows little articulation with higher-level intentions. Further experimental evidence reported in Scardamalia and Paris (1985) and summarized in Chapter 14 confirms young writers' limited access to high-level mental representations of their texts and also their tendency not to make connections between levels.

What would it take to get children to make more deliberate use of their tacit structural knowledge? In the Paris et al. study, some children expressed the belief that just having learned to recognize structural elements had given them a new power in planning compositions. Their writing performance did not support this optimism, however. Beyond gaining access to structural knowledge, it seemed that children would need an executive procedure for bringing the knowledge into play.

In a training study by Bereiter, Scardamalia, Anderson, & Smart (1980), children received practice in using a simple executive routine for switching between text generation and making choices at the level of structural elements of discourse. They were supplied with lists of discourse elements like those listed in Table 3.2, translated into imperatives—e.g., "reason" became "give a reason for an opinion" and "elaboration" became "tell more about the reason." The routine was simply to choose one of these directives, write a sentence fulfilling it, choose a next directive, write a sentence fulfilling it, and so on. No principles of ordering the elements were taught, and children were discouraged from ordering them in advance. Instead, they were encouraged to consider, at each point in the composition, which element was most appropriate according to their own criteria.

The effect of this training was assessed by comparing posttest compositions by the experimental group of sixth graders with those of a comparable group in the same school. These compositions were written without structural element lists at hand, and thus they represented a test of transfer to a more typical school-writing condition. On the post-test essay, the experimental group significantly exceeded the control group in both the total number and in the number of different types of discourse elements used. There was no significant effect, however, on overall judged quality or on quantity written.

These results suggest that training in the conscious use of structural elements may have had an effect on composition planning. The use of a greater variety of structural elements cannot be explained simply on the ground that children were exposed to a variety of them in their training. Unless one is prepared to argue that a few sessions of practice is enough for new structural elements to be assimilated into an unconscious language-production system, it must be acknowledged that the experimental-group children were making some conscious decisions to use these elements. And that is all that could be expected from the intervention, since the training did not include anything to help children make these decisions wisely or to enhance their ability to carry the decisions out.

We now turn to a more basic question: How can the appearance of structural knowledge of prose discourse be explained in a language-production system supposed to be geared to conversation? This is a speculative issue, but we believe present evidence favors different answers for different genres. Children's discourse knowledge, we suspect, is quite heterogeneous, and this heterogeneity reflects both differences in the ways kinds of knowledge are stored in the mind, and differences in learning experiences with various genres. For narrative discourse, it seems reasonable to accept the accumulated evidence that children have a well developed closed schema for it that corresponds reasonably well with mature ideas of what constitutes a story and what are its necessary elements (Stein & Trabasso, 1982). The learned aspects of such a schema could be accounted for by children's frequent exposure to narrative in several media, including conversation.

In the genre of argument and expressions of opinion, children display a knowledge of rhetorical elements, but this knowledge does not necessarily constitute a schema corresponding to the literary genre of the opinion essay. It seems more reasonable to suppose that the knowledge children draw on when they contend with an opinion essay is a knowledge of the moves and countermoves used in conversational attempts at persuasion. The same elements will be there as in the literary genre, but they will be organized in an open schema, adapted to the give and take of social interaction. The opinion-essay schema would be acquired, then, not primarily through exposure to examples but through the gradual closing of the conversational schema through experience in composition (helped along, of course, by whatever exposure a child may have to models). (cf. Hidi & Klaiman, 1984).

The other genre we have studied, direction giving, may point to yet another source of children's discourse plans. In the interview study of children's genre knowledge discussed above, the results for instruction writing were different from those for the other two genres. The correlation between frequency of naming and frequency of use was substantially less. Moreover, in a replication study, the frequency with which various elements of narrative and opinion essay were named was highly correlated with the frequency found in the original study, but a much lower correlation was found in the case of instruction writing. We suspect that the greater variability of response in this genre may indicate that children are not drawing on discourse knowledge at all in this case. Rather, they may simply be consulting their stores of "how to get places" knowledge and abstracting the general kinds of things they need to know in order to get somewhere—what direction to go, what means of transportation to use, what to look for, etc. The schema, in other words, is a schema for representing procedural knowledge and does not have anything special to do with discourse. The same schema would be involved whether one was acquiring the procedural knowledge from discourse or from observation. Much of children's and novices' expository writing may receive its only structuring from the structure that the knowledge has in the writer's own mind. This leads to the "knowledge-telling" strategy of composition described in Chapter 1, a simple, serviceable strategy that, however, lacks planful pursuit of rhetorical goals. The development of a genuine discourse schema for informative writing may be quite rare.

To summarize the preceding argument, we are cautioning the reader against any simple view that planfulness in writing develops from the gradual assimilation, through exposure to written genres, of discourse schemata. Children's composition is probably regulated by various sorts of structural knowledge obtained in various ways, and the evolution of schemata specifically tailored to composition is probably a messy and highly variable process about which little is presently understood.

LEARNING TO GO BEYOND THE TEXT AS WRITTEN

One of the main things that outwardly distinguishes composition from conversation is revision. It also sharply distinguishes expert from novice, being but little developed in young writers (National Assessment of Educational Progress, 1977) while for good writers it has an importance immortalized in the old saw that there is no such thing as good writing, only good rewriting. But revision is a term used to describe what happens to a text, and it covers such a multitude of things that might be going on inside the writer's head that it is not a very useful concept in cognitive analysis. A particular failure of revision could result, for instance, from the writer's inability to diagnose a fault in the original text or the writer's inability to solve the problem diagnosed.

If we look at writing from the inside, that is, from the point of view of the cognitive system, we see immediately that revision requires a language-production system capable of operating iteratively, using its own outputs as inputs. Although in conversation people do listen to themselves talk and occasionally amend their utterances, a highly developed iterative system is out of the question because of the transitory nature of the auditory signal and because of the turn-taking conventions of dialogue, which require responding to what the other person says rather than to what oneself has said previously.

In this section we examine two elementary requirements of an iterative language-production system. The first is an executive mechanism for switching between the forward process of text generation and the backward process of evaluation. We assume, in this regard, that feedback from the written output is not automatic, but that an active (resource-demanding) directing of attention is required. There is empirical support for this assumption in the finding that skilled writers do, in fact, look back more and pause longer in apparent evaluation of what they have done (Stallard, 1974).

The other requirement is best described as a capacity. If the text you have just written re-enters your language-production system as feedback, what is to prevent it from coming back out unchanged from the way it was before? As we shall see, that actually happens with children, even when their evaluation is that something needs changing. The already existing text constitutes a highly salient stimulus that must be attended to, but not attended to exclusively, if revision is to occur. This problem of attending to, but not being dominated by, a salient stimulus is a common one in children's performance of logical tasks (Case, 1975; Odom & Mumbauer, 1971; Pascual-Leone, Goodman, Ammon, & Subelman, 1979). Scardamalia (1973, 1975) has shown that stimulus-saliency effects depend on information-processing load. Irrelevant stimulus characteristics that are overcome when the task is within processing capacity come to bias performance when the processing load is beyond capacity. In writing, we have a natural situation in which what is most salient (the text already sitting there) will usurp attention that ought to be directed elsewhere (for instance, to generating alternative language or to searching memory for different content).

Executive Problems in Evaluating One's Own Writing

Novice writing often appears egocentric. Flower (1979) calls it "writer-based," being structured according to the writer's memory or experience rather than according to the process the reader will go through in comprehending it. A natural conclusion from their symptoms has been that young writers lack the capacity to take the reader's point of view—that they cannot "decenter" or "distance" themselves from what they have written. Such a condition would also explain their inability to revise: Since they know what their texts mean, they cannot imagine anyone failing to understand. Some doubt was cast on this explanation by early studies in which we manipulated "psychological distance" from the text (Bracewell, Bereiter, & Scardamalia, 1979). Waiting a week to revise had no effect. Revising someone else's composition instead of one's own led to spotting more spelling errors and the like, but it had little other effect.

The knowledge-telling model (Chapter 1) would suggest, however, that the problem might not be that children lack ability to evaluate, but that their writing process lacks the feedback capabilities necessary for evaluation to function effectively. In the external feedback system that regulates conversation, evaluation is triggered by signals from the conversational partner—signs of incomprehension, disbelief, boredom, etc. In writing, nothing happens to trigger evaluation. Furthermore, if children do stop to evaluate, they have the problem of switching back to generation without having lost track of where they were in that process. In other words, there is an executive control problem that could perhaps be severe enough to mask children's abilities to evaluate and revise.

In a study reported in detail in Chapter 11 a procedural facilitation was used to provide a simple, externalized executive routine for switching between evaluation and generation. Thirty children at each of grades 4, 6, and 8 were involved, and they were unanimous in declaring that the procedure got them to do something they did not normally do, which was to evaluate their writing closely and try to do something about it. Thus, from the children's standpoint, the procedure set in motion an evaluative process that did not occur—or that they were at least not aware of—in their ordinary composing behavior.

It is clear that executive control of internal feedback is not the only thing that stands in the way of children's making effective revisions. They have trouble with both diagnosis and remediation, although they seem to be good at recognizing symptoms. But it is little wonder that diagnostic and remedial skills should be undeveloped. It is hard to see how they could develop except through the functioning of an internal feedback system—through extensive experience of noting that something is not right, trying to do something about it, and noting whether or not the effort succeeds. From present evidence, it appears that children do not get such experience, and that in order for them to get it, they may need help putting an internal feedback system into operation.

The importance of such a feedback system, it must be emphasized, is not just for polishing up the style of sentences. It is vital for revisions from the lowest to highest levels, and for the revision that takes place as one composes original drafts as well as for the revision that takes place afterward. Neither does its importance lie only in enhancing the communicability of the text. A feedback loop is essential to the dialectical processes of planning that support "epistemic writing" (Bereiter, 1980), in which composition serves to advance the writer's own understanding. Experiments concerned with teaching such planning and revision strategies are reported in the postscript to Chapter 11 and in Chapter 12.

Overcoming the Written Word

When children are found unable to revise their texts for the better, the most obvious explanation is that they lack know-how—that they simply don't have in their repertoires the better expression, the better example, the better arrangement, or whatever it is that the expert writer would draw forth under the circumstance. This may be true. Our purpose in studying executive control problems is not to advance them as an alternative to explanations in terms of knowledge, but rather to gain an understanding of underlying systemic factors that impede the acquisition of know-how. The expert's repertoire of alternatives was acquired, we assume, through a reciprocal process of receptive learning and experimentation, i.e., in working to construct alternatives, the future expert became alert to alternatives used by other writers. Models absorbed from reading or instruction, in turn, encouraged the future expert to experiment with a wider range of possibilities. When we turn from this ideal picture to the struggling school child, we find not only someone who has not yet acquired the repertoire, but someone who has not yet acquired the mobility of executive procedures that will lead to rapid growth in repertoire.

A sense of children's difficulties in generating alternatives can be gained by looking closely at revisions produced by children. A detailed analysis is presented in Chapter 11. Here we note simply that there was not a single instance from the work of 90 children of a child scrapping a sentence and successfully producing a new one that was markedly different from the original. This seems to be too much to attribute solely to lack of a repertoire of alternatives. Children are simply not that deficient in linguistic resources (Loban, 1976). Some additional difficulty must be present. That difficulty, we suggest, is similar to the one one might encounter in trying to whistle *Men of Harlech* while a band is playing *Loch Lomond*. It is the problem of resisting the other language present in the environment.

A series of studies by Bracewell and Scardamalia (1979) and Bracewell (1980) document the difficulties children have in manipulating language form in the presence of a competing language form. In these studies, students were given information in sentence or matrix form and their task was to formulate it in sentences of specified forms. Table 3.3 gives an example of one such task. The general procedure for conveying to students what form of sentence they were to produce was to model for them the construction of sentences of that form. Thus, the task related to the example shown in Table 3.3 was to produce a sentence like "The yellow bird is in the cage under the table in the room." In modeling this task, identically structured material of different content would be used, leading, for instance, to "The happy hamster is in the nest on the shelf in the kitchen."

The main finding from these studies was that the difficulty for children in producing sentences of the required form was significantly affected by the form in which the information was presented to them. In the example, for instance, it took more modeling trials for children to encode information into a complex sentence when that information was originally presented in a sentence form than when it was given in matrix form. In other experiments, a similar effect was found when the task was to go from an integrated sentence to an unintegrated set of simple sentences (the reverse of the task shown).

In response to heavy attention demands of sentence revision, children seem to adopt a "least effort" strategy: change first what is easiest to change. When the content is hard to change, as in an opinion essay, then the first choice seems to be small word and phrase substitutions, followed by elaborations and deletions. In a series of studies by Scardamalia and Baird (1980), where the job was to produce more interesting sentences, without regard to the message conveyed, a somewhat different but compatible order of choices emerged. When no restrictions were placed on efforts to make a sentence more interesting, the prevailing strategy was to shift topics. This avoided any need to deal with the previous sentence at all. If required to retain the same topic, children shifted to a strategy of elaboration—simply adding information to the previous sentence. Again, this is a strategy of relatively low attention demand. If they are required to retain the topic and are severely

Table 3-3   Sentence Information in Two Formats

Sentence Format	Table Format		
	What	Relation	What
The bird is in the cage.	bird	in	cage
The cage is under the table.	cage	under	table
The table is in the room.	table	in	room
The bird is yellow.	bird	is	yellow

Note: Adapted from "The Ability of Primary School Students to Manipulate Language Form When Writing," paper presented at the annual meeting of the American Educational Research Association, Boston, 1980. Copyright 1980 by R.J. Bracewell. Reprinted by permission.

restricted in the number of words they may reuse from the previous sentence, children finally begin shifting to changes in the sentence plan. This was done with some success by children in grade 6, whereas the sentencing skills of fourth-graders seemed to falter before this challenge.

It appears, then, that children, when barred from easier ways of varying their rhetorical strategy, will finally resort to radical restructuring of their language. The linguistic alternatives are not, of course, invented on the spot. Presumably children have been learning alternative language forms all along through their normal experience, but not exerting deliberate choice among options. They have not been making strategic use of these linguistic resources in the conscious pursuit of goals.

We thus observe the same condition here as we did with knowledge of structural elements of discourse and with knowledge of content (world knowledge). Children have funds of relevant knowledge that influence their language production through unconscious means. In order to make purposeful, planful use of these resources, children need to accomplish two things (not necessarily in the order given):

> **1.** They need to gain conscious access to these knowledge resources. Conscious access seems to play a larger role in revision than in original composition. If the only alternatives available for use are those that come spontaneously to mind, then revision has little chance. The original version of the text, because it is perceptually present, has a direct claim on conscious attention. Unless the writer can deliberately bring alternatives to mind, the original text will win for lack of competition.
>
> **2.** They need an executive procedure for bringing this knowledge into use at the right times and in the proper relation to other resource demands of the task. This executive procedure must be able to switch attention from one subtask to another without disrupting progress. It must also keep the attentional burden under control without losing hold of essential elements.

Success in overcoming the existing text probably comes through a combination of these two accomplishments. Gaining conscious access to linguistic resources entails having knowledge coded in ways that make it accessible—which would mean having it coded in some hierarchical way (Loftus, 1977). Deliberate search for an alternative to an existing expression would not typically consist of searching memory for an already formed expression to use in its place. Rather, the existing expression would be encoded at a more abstract level, as an instance of such-and-such, and the search would go on among alternatives at this more abstract level. If a promising alternative was found, it would then be instantiated in actual language that could replace the original. By carrying out comparison at an abstract level and then generating actual alternative language top-down from this abstract level, the stimulus saliency of the existing text loses much of its force; much of the crucial work is done without having to attend to particular properties of the already written expression.

But this whole maneuver requires both accessibly coded knowledge and an executive procedure that will switch from one level of analysis to another, so that attention does not remain fixed on what is perceptually present. The novice writer, handicapped both in the accessibility of knowledge and in the executive capabilities for attending to it, has to depend on generating new language spontaneously. In this process, the one element in the field of attention most likely to trigger generation of a piece of language suitable to the context is the already existing item of text. This is true whether the text was just written or written a week ago, and whether it was written by the writer or someone else (Bracewell et al., 1979).

While we have been discussing the problem with reference to alternative ways of expressing an idea, the same considerations apply to higher levels—to alternative ideas, organizations, and rhetorical strategies. In all cases, it would seem that the ability to transcend one's original choices depends on having access to classes of alternatives. This does not mean that the composing process as a whole must become one of rational decision-making. That would be impossible, not to mention undesirable. One need only read the verbal protocols of expert writers as they compose to appreciate that what they are doing consciously is only a small part of the process, and that most of the deciding and generating is done spontaneously, with only the result appearing in consciousness.[7] But the ability to seek out alternatives deliberately appears to be essential if writers are to go beyond their first impulses and productions.

[7]The protocols of writers thinking aloud have been variously compared to a window on the composing process and to the occasionally surfacing portions of an underwater monster. We prefer a different metaphor. When you read the protocol of an expert composing aloud, you are watching a conductor under the spotlight in a darkened opera house. You do not see the orchestra performing in the shadows, and so, if you were very naive about such things, you might imagine that the music was issuing from the conductor's baton.

SUMMARY:
COMPOSITION AND GROWTH

Keenan, Schieffelin, & Platt (1976) have presented a plausible account of how the very young child relies on conversational interchange to develop a single proposition. The child first notices something, then produces an utterance aimed at getting the hearer to notice it, and the hearer responds with some indication of having noticed it. This establishes the topic of the proposition, upon which a comment may then be made. By the time children enter school, they have learned how to develop complete propositions autonomously, presenting the topic-plus-comment package as a single utterance.

Children entering school, however, are still for the most part dependent on conversational interchange to develop text—to develop, for instance, an extended set of comments on a single topic. The preceding sections of this chapter have been devoted to an exploration of what is involved in learning to develop text autonomously. Our focus has been on the functioning of the language-production system as a whole, reflecting the conviction that the major problems in composing lie in the organization of the system.

The lowest-order capability that must be acquired is simply to go on generating text without signals to continue. Another capability of fairly low order that is, however, essential to make higher-order planning possible, is the ability to activate relevant nodes of semantic memory in advance of writing. Teaching children a subroutine for doing this appears to increase their ability to generate content. Less easily acquired, however, is the ability, without probing from others, to trace down branches of semantic memory until all the content needed to convey a message has been extracted.

Writing involves planning not only at the clause level, but also at the level of units too large to be mentally constructed verbatim. It also requires repeatedly viewing the text from the position of reader rather than writer. These operations all require a central executive system like that represented in the knowledge-transforming model (Chapter 1), which can switch attention back and forth between levels and modes without losing hold of the process as a whole. We find that when tasks are structured, or executive routines are provided to facilitate this switching, children exhibit competence that is masked by their normal performance.

Our account of the development of ability to compose was not intended to cover all the kinds of learning that contribute to making a competent writer. We have not talked about general language development that continues in the school years through oral experience, sometimes augmented to a significant degree by reading. Nor have we talked about general growth of world knowledge, which surely interacts with composition skills and does not just provide a library for the composing process to draw upon.

Closer to the front, we have not dealt with those kinds of learnings specific to use of the written medium—the mechanics of handwriting, spelling, punctuation, and the like; the distinctive dialect properties of written English that set it apart from spoken dialects; and the forms of written discourse—the business letter, the familiar essay, etc.—and the stylistic requirements of each. These matters, it will be noted, account for the whole of writing instruction as it is conventionally carried out. We have no thought of minimizing the importance of these aspects of writing ability nor the difficulties of teaching them. What we have been at pains to show, however, is that there is a vast range of learnings, absolutely critical to being able to compose, which remain untouched by the traditional syllabus.

Two general sorts of objections might be raised to the approach we have taken in our analysis. One objection might be that we have throughout treated the oral mode as something to be transcended whereas many a teacher could testify to efforts well spent in the opposite direction—to getting students to write more like the way they speak. The issues here are not really grounds for controversy. A major reason for encouraging "orality" is that students trying to master a written dialect often seize first on its most awkward aspects and need to be brought back to trusting their "ear" for the spoken language. Another reason is to enable students to produce first drafts of compositions with as little interference as possible from concerns about surface features of the language. We have said nothing to oppose these strategies. In fact, we have said nothing about oral versus written language at all. What we have talked about children "transcending" is not oral language but dependence on a conversational partner.

Another and deeper sort of objection might be that, in our approach, we have ignored the meaning of composition to the student. Why is the student trying to compose in the first place—merely to produce a piece of work to please the teacher? The idea of the meaning of the task to the student is an important one and the main problem is to find the right place for this idea among others in an understanding of the composing process. There is a temptation, yielded to by some language-arts specialists, to assign the idea such a high place that it drives out all others, seeming to explain everything, but instead rendering everything unexplainable. One elementary point needed for perspective is that all the abilities we have been discussing are ones that skilled writers can demonstrate on demand, whether a given task has intrinsic worth to them or not. When children show a conditional competence—when they show, for instance, that they can produce abundant and coherent material on the topic of great current interest to them but not on a neutral topic—we must not rest content with saying this shows writing tasks must be meaningful if children are to do their best. We must seek to find out what is different about the competence of skilled writers that allows them easily to produce abundant and coherent content, and what is different about the way content on a meaningful topic is brought forth in children's minds from the way in which less interesting material is activated. To the extent that our work provides clues for answering this kind of question, it is a step in the direction of understanding meaningfulness in writing.

In a broader sense, "meaningfulness" of the composition task may be thought of as the driving force behind the developmental process we have been describing. Writing can be meaningful to the writer at many different levels, from the mere urge to tell, which motivates the relating of personal experiences, to the desire to work out ideas through composition that are too complex to work out by other means. Composition does not get easier as one moves to higher and higher levels of ability. Instead, one keeps tackling harder and harder problems. It is difficult to see why development toward more complex levels of composition would occur, why people would not just go on relating personal experiences with greater and greater facility, were it not for the urge toward higher levels of meaningfulness. "The whole duty of a writer is to please and satisfy himself," say Strunk and White (1959, p. 70). Surely no effort to teach composition would be successful that barred students from the continual opportunity to discover higher levels of personal satisfaction in writing.

The children who took part in our studies had been exposed to the normal varieties of school writing experiences—writing on assigned topics, writing on whatever they pleased—usually with response only from the teacher, sometimes with other kinds of feedback, or none at all. The announcement that they would be expected to write something was often met by groans and a scramble for a pencil with a good eraser. In short, they often acted in ways to suggest that writing for them was not a highly valued and meaningful school activity. Yet as soon as we provided them with a procedure that allowed them to get hold of some elusive part of the composing process, they were almost invariably excited by what it enabled them to do, intensely interested in the process, and eager to talk about it (see Chapter 13). This repeated experience, with a variety of experimental procedures, impresses us with the thought that composition itself, as a process, is intrinsically meaningful to children, over and above the meaning that inheres in the language produced. They find the process to be an important one and are eager to master it, given some method for doing so. This suggests that the improvement of writing abilities may not require a cultural revolution or an overhaul of our education system; rather, significant gains could be made by finding ways to give children needed handles on the cognitive processes of composing. We return to this issue in Part IV of this book.

Part II
Basic Cognitive Factors
in Composition

One of the great accomplishments of contemporary research on reading has been its progress in understanding how lower-level parts of the reading process interact with higher-level parts. What "lower" and "higher" mean will vary with the theory, but in general higher-level parts of a process depend on the lower-level parts, exert some measure of control over them, and are more closely associated with the goal of an activity. Lower-level parts of the reading process include word recognition and (possibly) sounding out words or forming some acoustic representation of them. Higher-level parts include expectations based on prior knowledge, objectives (what one is trying to find out, for instance), and strategies. It will be evident, by analogy, that most of what we have had to say about writing so far has dealt with higher-level parts of the process.

Complete theories of a complex process must, of course, deal with lower- as well as higher-level parts of the process. First approximations to such theories tend to posit sequential stages. In reading, the theory of LaBerge and Samuels (1974) played such a role, proposing that an act of reading progressed from a visual stage to a phonological stage and finally to a semantic stage in which information picked up at lower stages was related to stored knowledge. Such a theory was easily assailed by evidence that stored knowledge could affect the speed of visual word recognition, thus requiring that the theory be amended to include processes working in both directions (Samuels & Eisenberg, 1981). The nut of the theoretical problem is to explain how processes at one level affect those at another, and it is on this matter that interesting progress has been made.

One illustration will have to suffice. It comes from the work of Perfetti and his colleagues on the role of context in speed of word recognition (Perfetti & Roth, 1981). Comparing good and poor readers, they found evidence of alternate routes to word recognition. Paradoxically, it was the poor readers who showed evidence of making most use of higher-level processes in word recognition, their speed being the most influenced by familiarity or predictability. Good readers, on the other hand, relied more on rapid, automatic processes of word recognition. The paradox vanishes, of course, when one sees the situation as one in which good readers are free to use their higher-level processes for dealing with the meaning of the text, while poor readers are forced to devote these processes to figuring out what the words are. The problem, then, is one of how mental resources are allocated to parts of the reading task. A similar problem will occupy us in the chapters that follow.

Research relating higher- and lower-level parts of the writing process has been close to nonexistent. There are bodies of research on lower-level processes such as handwriting (Thomassen & Teulings, 1983) and spelling (Beaugrande, 1984b, 214–232; Frith, 1980). And, as the preceding chapters have already indicated, higher-level processes in writing are being actively investigated. Beaugrande (1984b) has extensively reviewed research related to all levels of the writing process and suggested a number of integrative ideas. But research comparable to that of Perfetti and others on reading, which actually explores functional relationships between processes at different levels, has been lacking.

It is important to distinguish research that relates low-level and high-level processes from research that makes use of low-level indicators of high-level processes. In reading research, gaze duration has proved to be an illuminating phenomenon to study, but it has been illuminating primarily as an indicator of the extent of central processing that is going on at different points in reading (Just & Carpenter, 1980). The same has been true of the study of pause time during writing (Van Bruggen, 1946). Pauses are best thought of, not as low-level parts of the writing process but as observable pointers to high-level processes (Matsuhashi, 1982).

The research discussed in the next three chapters centers around one way in which low-level and high-level processes may interact. They may compete for mental resources. The underlying idea here, a commonplace of cognitive psychology, is that people can pay active attention to only a limited number of things at once. If low-level processes such as spelling and punctuation require a good deal of active attention, as they may for novices, then less attention should be available for higher-level processes; correspondingly, as low-level processes become automatic with practice, they should require less attention and thus free it for higher concerns. On the other hand, certain kinds of high-level abilities may be expected to reduce the load on mental resources. These would include (1) efficient ways of representing information so that large units of it can be handled as single chunks (Miller, 1956), and (2) efficient executive procedures that make it possible to attend to parts of the task one at a time, thus reducing the number of things that need attention simultaneously.

These considerations make a strong a priori case for supposing that inexperienced writers should be severely hampered by attentional demands and scarcely able to cope. But cope they obviously do. And so the challenge to research has been to find out how they cope with such a complex task, under the combined handicaps of low-level activities that require inordinate amounts of attention and unsophisticated high-level procedures. As Chapter 1 indicated, the knowledge-telling strategy serves as an answer to this question—an answer that amounts to saying that for many people writing is not nearly so complex a task as one might suppose by viewing it in terms of all the problems that sophisticated writers contend with. The three chapters that follow provide more detailed examination of some of the ways in which young writers are able to keep the cognitive demands of writing within limits that they can handle.

Chapter 4
The Role
of Production Factors
in Writing Ability

PREFACE

This chapter investigates the role of three basic factors in children's written text production. The first is short-term memory loss due to slow rate of writing. The second is interference from the mechanical demands of writing (penmanship, spelling, etc.). The third factor is one suggested by the analyses in the preceding chapter. It is disruption of discourse production due to the lack of external cuing of the kind provided in conversation. Although some evidence of effect is adduced for all three of these factors, the current indications are that the first two factors are less potent than might have been assumed, while the third has been underestimated.

 Most cognitive research on writing, including the bulk of our own, focuses on what Sternberg (1980), in his componential theory of intelligence, calls *metacomponents*. These are components of performance having to do with goals, plans, strategies, task-related knowledge, and the like. It is easy to see why these components should receive the main attention of people trying to understand composition. Writing, as we experience it, consists largely of the interplay of these metacomponents, and it is this interplay which is captured through thinking-aloud protocols (e.g., Hayes & Flower, 1980) and through clinical-experimental interactions of the sort reported throughout this book.

There is a whole other range of mental activity involved in writing, however, that is but little accessible to consciousness and that has been little investigated. It involves what Sternberg calls *performance components*. (In the context of language production, we shall refer to these as *production factors*.) Performance components, according to Sternberg, are processes used in the actual carrying out of decisions arrived at through action of the meta-components. Among these processes are recognizing, relating, and, of course, overt responding, as in directing the motor activities of handwriting. When we listen to people thinking aloud as they write, we find indications that these processes are occurring, but we do not witness the process.

Here is a typical bit of thinking aloud during composition (drawn from Emig, 1971):

> Now the problem is how to start. I could say that I walked into the living room one evening after work and there it was sitting in the middle of the living room. Or else, I could say something like, it's going to sound like a third grade intro-duction, but something about, "Can you imagine our surprize when we received a three foot by three foot cardboard packing thing in the mail?" That's not too good a start ... [p. 131]

The writer poses a problem and then immediately produces a possible solution. The idea for a beginning of the composition seems to come out of nowhere; the protocol gives us no clue to the process of memory search and construction by which the idea was produced. The writer then proposes an alternative idea for a beginning. This suggests that some evaluation has taken place, which has found the first idea wanting, but again there is no indica-tion of an evaluation process going on. The second idea, however, appears to have been classified and evaluated even before it was expressed.

Clearly much of the interesting work of composition goes on in between the points that are mentioned in thinking-aloud protocols. It consists of mental acts of short duration—comparisons, memory searches, inferences, etc.—of which only the major outcomes rise to consciousness. Yet it would seem that much of the success or failure of writing must depend on these processes. At the conscious level, success might depend on thinking of the right idea. But whether or not one thinks of the right idea and thinks of it at the right time might depend on a variety of undetected production factors—on the speed at which memory is searched, on the length of time information is held in short-term memory and the speed with which it is placed in more permanent storage, on the number and nature of competing demands for attention and on the efficiency with which one can program the switching of attention among competing demands, and a host of other factors of this sort.

A theory that explains the composing process will need to encompass both metacomponents and production factors—both properties of the writer's knowledge and properties of the writer's psychological system that constrain the use of that knowledge. This is particularly true if we want a theory that accounts for what happens in learning to write—as compared to a theory that only accounts for performance as it is observed in discrete time frames. If one considers only metacomponents, then it is not clear why novice writers cannot be turned into experts simply by tutoring them in the knowledge expert writers have. To some extent, of course, this can be done, and it should become increasingly feasible as we develop a better understanding of the procedural knowledge that guides expert performance. But still there are limits on what young writers are ready to learn, and these limits would appear to have much to do with production factors. Children's ability to incorporate new principles and procedures into their composing processes must surely depend in part on what they are able to hold in mind while writing, and this will depend on such underlying factors as how much they can retain in short-term memory for how long, how many things are competing for attention while they write, and how efficiently they can distribute attention to these demands.

Our goal in this chapter is a relatively modest one, stopping short of any attempt to formulate a model that embraces both metacomponents and production factors in an integrated picture of the composing process. We believe the research base is far too weak for that. A strong research base is needed as soon as one tries to venture theoretically beyond conscious levels of the composing process because inferences are necessarily based on very indirect evidence, and one no longer has one's own tacit knowledge of the composing process to use as a tempering influence on speculation.

Our aim in this chapter is to develop and test a few preliminary ideas about ways in which the conditions of text production may influence cognitive processes in composition. Manipulating conditions of text production while keeping the writing task the same is one obvious way of investigating production factors, because in keeping the task the same one presumably holds constant the effect of a wide range of metacomponents (those having to do with rhetorical and world knowledge) and thus may with greater confidence attribute observed effects on writing to the action of production factors. As we shall see, however, the separation of effects is never clean. Consequently, in order to make progress in the interpretation of findings, it is necessary from the outset to rely on psychological intuitions that run in advance of the experimental findings, and which the experimental findings serve mainly to strengthen or weaken.

Let us, accordingly, begin with an intuitive consideration of the act of writing so as to get an idea of the range of production factors that might be relevant to it. To start with a concrete example, consider a normal third-grade class engaged in a writing assignment. Almost all the children will write very slowly and many with obvious labor, some more drawing than writing the letters. There is likely to be audible sounding of words or at any rate lip movement as the children write (Simon, 1973). Even without direct evidence it seems reasonable to infer two things: (a) that handwriting is taking up considerable attention, which accordingly must be taken away from other aspects of the writing task such as content planning (Graves, 1978b); and (b) that the slow rate of production must create problems of remembering—not only problems in remembering immediately forthcoming words but also problems in remembering higher-level plans and intentions.

In more mature writers, of course, handwriting is fluent and automatic enough that production problems associated with it should be greatly reduced. But writing remains a complex activity in which many different processes must compete for limited attentional capacity and it remains slow enough that writers will frequently be heard to complain that they cannot keep up with their thoughts. It seems reasonable to suppose, therefore, that how well a person writes will continue to depend not only on what conceptual and procedural knowledge the person has available but also on how successfully the operations involved in using it are coordinated.

Research on speech production has revealed the elaborate orchestration of mental functions that must go on in this apparently effortless activity. (See for instance the two chapters devoted to this topic in Clark and Clark, 1977.) While part of the cognitive system is concerned with articulation and coordinating speech with gestures and eye contact, another part is occupied with planning ahead. These processes use some of the same resources, however, so that finely organized time sharing is required, and even at that the system is frequently overtaxed, with the result that speech is filled with errors and unplanned pauses (Butterworth & Goldman-Eisler, 1979).

Written language production differs from conversational speech production in several ways that should make production factors less problematic. Writing is less time-constrained and there is not the immediate social situation that requires monitoring. (Butterworth and Goldman-Eisler, 1979, note, for instance, that during planning phases of speech production the speaker is vulnerable to interruption and will therefore often break eye contact with listeners so as to keep the floor.) The absence of incoming social stimuli may also, however, create serious problems.

A key factor in fluent language production seems to be temporal organization of subprocesses. By this we mean the fine-grain (small fractions of a second) distribution of time among various levels of planning so that language production both proceeds steadily and maintains purposefulness and high-level organization. By the time children begin learning to write, they already speak fluently and coherently enough that it seems that the major temporal organization of language-production processes must already have been achieved. This organization has developed through conversational experience, however. It would be reasonable to expect, therefore, that the programing of production factors would be keyed to conversational events. As discussed in the previous chapter, there is substantial evidence that metacomponents of the composing process still bear the stamp of conversational circumstances in young writers. It therefore seems worth investigating the possibility that some of the difficulty children have in writing production has a more profound basis than the slow and demanding qualities of handwriting, that it reflects breakdown in the organization of subprocesses when language production must go on in the absence of signals from the conversational milieu.

To get a concrete sense of what such a breakdown of organization could be like, readers who are touch-typists might try the following experiment. Put your fingers on a table top and try to go through the motions of typing a simple sentence such as, "When in Rome, do as the Romans do." In informal tests, we find that proficient typists are at least slowed down and are sometimes immobilized by this task. Evidently then, typists are dependent on reactions of the keyboard for organization of the typing process. In this instance we have a kind of behavior that would seem to proceed entirely from the inside out, and yet we find that for some people at least its organization depends on response of the passive instrument to which it is directed. In conversation, we deal with reciprocal action rather than passive response, and so we may expect that the organization of processes will depend even more on feedback, as it does in such other reciprocal activities as tennis and dancing. (See Schmidt, 1975, on the interaction of feedback with internal programing in skilled performance.)

This intuitive analysis of the act of writing depicts it as a complex, internally regulated process characterized by slow and attention-demanding output. The analysis has suggested three production difficulties that we shall explore further in this chapter: (a) short-term memory loss, to which slow rate of production could be a contributing cause; (b) interference from mechanical demands of the written medium that compete for mental resources with the higher-level demands of content planning and the like; and (c) general discoordination of language production resulting from the lack of external signals.

In the following section we shall review the little available evidence bearing on these three possibilities. Then we shall report in detail an experiment that examines all three at once. In a final discussion we shall press toward a more integrated view of production factors and their relation to metacomponents in writing.

SHORT-TERM MEMORY LOSS
DUE TO SLOW WRITING RATE

The most obvious place to look for an effect of production factors on written composition is at the interface between the mental process of language generation and the physical process of transcription. Models of language production generally place at this interface a buffer, a short-term memory store, that holds language already composed while it awaits translation into physical speaking or writing responses (e.g., Fodor, Bever, & Garrett, 1974). Such temporary storage is a necessity, even if we imagine the slowest of planners. Even someone who planned only a single word ahead would need to hold that word in mind long enough to write it. But no one could produce coherent language without planning farther ahead than that, and so somehow the products of planning must be held in mind while transcription goes on.

In writing, because of its slowness, the products of planning must often be held in mind for some seconds, an appreciable period of time by short-term memory standards. This raises the possibility that "forgetting what one was going to say" may be a more significant factor in writing than in speaking. Some relevant data on memory loss in writing comes from a study by Bereiter, Fine, and Gartshore (1979).

This was an exploratory study, using a very simple methodology. Students wrote, in the presence of an experimenter, on any subject of their choice. At irregular intervals the experimenter would halt the writing process by suddenly placing a screen over the writing paper. Students were then to report any words they had already formed in their minds, but they were urged not to make up any new material. After each forecast, the screen was removed and subjects resumed writing where they had left off. After a paragraph was completed, the students were asked to repeat from memory, as exactly as they could, the paragraph they had just written. The forecasting part of the experiment was explained to students in advance, but they were not forewarned of the recall task. The study was conducted on 14 children in fourth grade and 14 in sixth grade (mean ages approximately 10 and 12 years).

The experimental procedure made it possible to compare at certain points in each composition (a) what students reportedly intended to write; (b) what they actually did write; and (c) what they remembered having written.

The number of words per forecast—that is, the number of words children supposedly already had formed in their minds in advance of the last word they had written—averaged five to six. There was great variability, however, the forecast tending to run to the end of a clause regardless of the number of words that took. (Compare Fodor et al., 1974, on the clause as the basic unit of planning in speech production.) When we count only words spoken before the first pause of a second or longer, however, the mean is two words less, and the forecasts no longer regularly run to the ends of clauses. The rationale for this stricter count is that pauses of a second or longer are typically assumed to be planning pauses (Matsuhashi, 1982), and therefore suggest that the child has started fabricating new material rather than reporting language already held in short-term storage.

Regardless of which criterion is used, however, the outstanding finding is that what children say they will write they by and large do write. The average number of discrepancies between forecasts and actual writing was .5 per forecast. Thus, for about half of the forecasts children subsequently wrote exactly the words they had claimed to have in mind. Furthermore, of the discrepancies, 78% were stylistic variations that carried the same meaning in writing as in the forecast. (More about these variations presently.)

In 17% of the discrepancies, however, significant words uttered in the forecast failed to appear in writing. In about half of these cases the result was a syntactic anomaly—for instance, the forecasted phrase *on the way to school* was written *on the to school.* Lapses of this kind clearly indicate language getting lost somewhere between its storage in an output buffer and its translation into handwriting movements. But, just as clearly, these lapses cannot be described as "forgetting what one was going to say." For one thing, the lapses were almost invariably repaired on recall: in the case of *on the to school,* for example, the author not only intended to write *on the way* but claimed later to have written it.

Lapses of this kind are common in first-draft writing by experienced writers (Hotopf, 1980). They probably represent a lack of monitoring of the written output, the result of devoting conscious attention entirely to planning ahead, while leaving the process of transcription to run "on automatic." If this is what children are doing as well, then it is a sign that temporal organization of the writing process is already well advanced for them, making it possible for them to carry on planning and transcribing operations in parallel.

Such a speculation gains interest when related to the developmental observations of Simon (1973). Simon observed that primary-grade children tended to dictate to themselves, mouthing each letter or syllable as they wrote it. This activity would bespeak a heavy investment of conscious attention in the process of transcription, making it unlikely that any planning ahead could occur while the child was transcribing. This simultaneous mouthing of the words was observed to give way after the first couple of years, however, to the practice of mouthing a string of words and then writing them. This latter practice would clear the way for planning while transcribing.

Simon's findings were replicated and extended somewhat by a study conducted in our laboratory by Gartshore. Mouthing of individual letters and words during transcription was found to be common in children in second and third grades but virtually to disappear by fourth grade. On the other hand, mouthing of language during pauses in writing was almost nonexistent in second and third grades but was shown by half the children in fourth grade. Moreover, at fourth grade the rated quality of compositions was positively correlated with the frequency of subvocalization during pauses. This correlation lends further support to the notion that parallel planning and transcribing processes come into play around fourth grade and that they significantly enhance composing ability.

The existence of such parallel or overlapping processes means that we cannot look for a simple connection between production rate and short-term memory or other production factors. A variety of mental activities may be going on while the writer's pencil is in motion. Some of these may interfere with retention of language in the buffer and its translation into writing, others may have no such effect, and still others might provide rehearsal of buffer contents, thus reducing the effects of delay in transcription. It remains, however, a question of some interest whether, on the whole and for whatever reasons, loss of information from short-term storage may be a significant factor in written language production. The previously cited study of discrepancies between what children say they are about to write and what they do write provides evidence that short-term memory losses may be significant, at least for elementary school children.

Seventeen percent of the discrepancies between forecasts and actual written text involved some information loss whereas only 5% involved some information gain (usually in the form of an inserted word not present in the forecast). When lapses of the kind mentioned previously, resulting in linguistic anomalies, are eliminated, there are still twice as many information losses as information gains. The typical result of these losses was reduced richness of detail. For instance, a reference to *the purple martians* appeared in writing simply as *the martians*. The data would suggest that in perhaps 1 out of 10 sentence constituents written by elementary-school children there is some loss of content due to short-term memory loss. This would be an upper-bound estimate, since it does not take account of the possibility that some deletions may be intentional—that the child might have decided against representing the Martians as *purple,* for instance. The results thus suggest that short-term memory loss is at most an appreciable, but not a predominant, factor influencing the content of children's writing.

But does this short-term memory loss have anything to do with slow rate of production? The forecasting study has no evidence to offer on this question. Between the forecast and the appearance of the written language, not only did time elapse but also the child had to contend with whatever difficulties might have arisen in transcription—spelling problems, for instance. And so memory losses could as well be attributed to interference from other attention demands as to the lapse of time between input to the buffer and output. Isolation of the effects of rate would require an experimental situation in which production rate varied while mechanical demands of the output medium remained constant. In an experiment to be reported later, we tried to isolate rate in this way.

The evidence considered in this section serves mainly to remind us that even in fairly young children the process of writing is organized with sufficient complexity that single production factors can only be understood in relation to the process as a whole. Studies of speech production suggest that output rate presents different kinds of problems at different stages in discourse production. At an early stage of expressing a unit of discourse, when time is needed for assembling content and language, speakers may find that the output rate forced on them by the press of conversation is too fast for their needs (Clark & Clark, 1977). Once the unit has been mentally constructed, however, speakers will tend to speed up output so as to "clear the decks" for construction of the next unit—that is, free up short-term memory capacity for use in storing the products of advance planning. The kinds of memory loss that might occur would seem to differ, depending on what stage the speaker was in, and might be caused by excessive output speed in one case and excessive slowness in the other. In writing, where there is usually no social press to maintain a high rate of output, slow rate of output might be beneficial or at least harmless during the extensive constructive phases of composition and be detrimental only during those periods when clearing the decks is called for. If this is true, then an understanding of the relation between production rate and short-term memory loss will depend both on more sophisticated methodology than is currently available and on more fine-grained models of the composing process.

INTERFERENCE FROM MECHANICAL REQUIREMENTS OF WRITTEN LANGUAGE

Although ideas about production factors tend to be esoteric, there is one such idea that seems already to be firmly established in conventional wisdom. This is the idea that having to attend to low-level considerations such as spelling and punctuation interferes with attention to higher-level concerns of composition. Some teachers operate on this idea by urging their students to pay no attention to correctness, at least until after a first draft has been produced. Others take the approach of stressing early mastery of these mechanical aspects of writing so that they need no longer demand much attention. The policies are different, but the underlying psychological premise is the same, that the writer has a limited amount of attention to allocate and that whatever is taken up with the mechanical[8] demands of written language must be taken away from something else.

This premise cannot be accepted in so simple a form, however. We must ask what gets interfered with and when. Although language production is often a rapid process, the development of an utterance through stages of intention to choice of syntactic frame to construction of constituents to overt output covers a time span that is not trivial in the time scale of cognitive operations. What gets interfered with when a writer is caught up by a spelling problem is the other cognitive activity going on at that moment. If the meaning of the sentence being written has already been fully constructed in the writer's mind, then *ipso facto* attention to a spelling problem cannot interfere with construction of *that* unit of meaning—although it could interfere with construction of some other unit of meaning—if the writer was thinking about it at the time. Thus we must consider possible interference in relation to the temporal unfolding of the composing process, which, as we have already noted, is greatly complicated by the existence of parallel or overlapping mental activities. We must furthermore take account of the possibilities of time sharing. In an unhurried activity such as writing, it seems likely that a writer with a well-developed executive system for sharing time among different activities could tolerate all sorts of additional attentional burdens without reducing the total amount of attention devoted to any one of them. Additional burdens would simply call for filling in spare time-slots or extending total time (cf. Spelke, Hirst, & Neisser, 1976).

In the forecasting study (Bereiter et al., 1979), discussed in the preceding section, we have indicated that the small amounts of information loss observed between forecasts and actual writing might reflect interference from the attentional demands of mechanics. This would not show interference with higher-level composing processes, however, simply interference with short-term storage of language already composed. Consequently we would expect this type of interference to have only minor effects on the composing process. We also noted evidence of a different kind of interference resulting in syntactic anomalies. But this phenomenon seemed attributable to *high-level* processes interfering with *low-level* ones—the very opposite of the phenomenon we are concerned with here.

We have not yet, however, considered the 78% of discrepancies found in

---

[8]By mechanics of writing we do not mean merely handwriting or other means of transcription. Mechanics also includes spelling, capitalization, punctuation (for the most part), hyphenation, indentation, etc. In short, mechanics comprises all those parts of the writing task that are avoided when one dictates.

that study between forecasts and actual writing that did not involve meaning changes or errors but simply stylistic variations. The nature of these discrepancies might offer a clue as to the kinds of language processing going on very late in the production process and, hence, the kinds of language processing that would be susceptible to interference from mechanical demands of writing that also apply to that late stage.

We have not been able to discover any significant regularities in the nature of these stylistic variations, but there was a tendency for the written versions to differ from the forecasted versions in the direction of greater formality, suggesting that at a late stage in production children may have been editing their language according to understood requirements of the written medium. The failure to find a consistent tendency in this direction might reflect inconsistencies in children's knowledge of written English conventions.

Whatever the nature of these stylistic variations, their frequency has interesting implications for theories of written language production. It adds support to suggestions that what is stored in the output buffer waiting to be translated into script is not fully formed language, but rather some more general kinds of syntactic and semantic choices, with more detailed choices remaining to be made "at the point of utterance," as Britton (1978) puts it. Krashen (1977) has proposed a model that accords with our observations that "shaping at the point of utterance" seems to take the form of shaping in the direction of written English. According to Krashen's Monitor model, language is generated according to an unconscious rule system acquired through natural language experience. Conscious, "learned" rules have no generative capability. Instead, they have their effect through a Monitor, which applies to language after it is generated but before it is uttered and edits it according to the learned rules. What we might therefore be observing in the discrepancies between forecasts and actual written text is the difference between relatively unmonitored spoken language as spontaneously generated and language as it has been altered by action of the Monitor. Indeed, our instructions to children to tell us only the language they already had in their minds and not to make up any new language might have had the effect of getting them to bypass the Monitor, much like the psychoanalyst's instructions to freely associate.

Krashen's Monitor model is interesting when applied to writing (it has mainly been applied to second-language learning). Writing appears as an activity in which the Monitor plays an unusually large role, compared to most oral language activities—an essential role, in that so many writing conventions must be applied consciously at first, but a role that could be severely constraining on children's generative capabilities.

Unfortunately, Krashen's model has not been elaborated or tested sufficiently to show whether it can serve as a viable model of language production. What kind of mechanism would enable the Monitor to edit language even though it could not generate it? Such a mechanism is certainly conceivable, inasmuch as there is computer software than can perform fairly sophisticated monitoring functions even though it cannot generate a sentence from scratch (Frase, 1980). But it is not obvious how the editing and generating functions could be so sharply divided within a human information processing system.

Whether or not there is a distinct phase during which output editing occurs, the notion of gradual refinements from global to specific features is common to most views of language production (Clark & Clark, 1977; Luria, 1976; Vygotsky, 1962). Thus, in keeping with the ideas underlying Krashen's Monitor model, we may suppose that much of a writer's knowledge about written language style and about conventions of punctuation, spelling, capitalization, and the like will be applied at a very late stage in language production.

On the basis of these theoretical considerations, it seems that we must reject the commonplace idea that attention to how written language is to be spelled or punctuated will interfere with its content. If concerns about mechanics only enter after the original intention has already been shaped into propositions, then it is too late for them to interfere with the construction of meaning. The meaning of the sentence in question will already have been constructed.

There remain, however, three ways in which attention to low-level aspects of writing could interfere with the higher-level metacomponents.

1. It could lead to forgetting high-level decisions already made. In the preceding section we considered only forgetting of material that was already at an advanced stage of shaping into utterance. We did not consider and have no direct evidence bearing on the possibility of forgetting less-developed intentions and meanings—for instance, concentrating on details of expression and in the process forgetting what purpose a sentence was intended to serve. We have introspective reason to believe that this occurs, from everyday experience. Consider, for instance, pausing to consult a dictionary and finding, on return to writing, that although we can recall the rest of the interrupted sentence, we have forgotten what it was supposed to be leading up to. As we shall consider further toward the end of this chapter, this effect will depend on how intentions are represented in the writer's memory. We shall also consider the possibility that having to reconstruct intentions periodically may be an aid rather than a hindrance to planful writing.

2. Concern with mechanics could interfere with high-level planning of the *next* unit of discourse. This could happen if people are simultaneously expressing one unit and planning another, and we

have already noted indications that even children as young as 10 years old do this. The result of this kind of interference would be that whereas individual sentences are well expressed, overall coherence and the complexity of content integration suffer. Thus evidence on the low level of content integration in children's writing (see Chapter 5) could be taken to suggest interference of this sort.

3. Finally, attention to problems of mechanics could interfere with consideration of intentionality *at the point of utterance.*

This last possibility has interesting implications, but it is one for which systematic evidence is entirely lacking. Bracewell (personal communication) has observed that skilled writers make, as they go along, small changes in wording that seem to an observer to have no point to them. One word or phrase is replaced by another that has no discernible semantic or stylistic claim to preference. Leaving aside the possibility that the writer has more refined sensibilities than the observer, we may speculate that the writer makes such changes in order to make the expression more closely fit his or her intentions. Having no independent knowledge of those intentions, the observer cannot judge one expression to be more appropriate than the other, as the writer can. But, considering that the writer has already written one thing and then changed it to another, it seems that this very precise fitting of expression to intention goes on into the very latest stage of written language production. Consequently, if this stage is being occupied with concerns about spelling, capitalization, or even penmanship, there will be little opportunity for this fine fitting to occur.

Although effects on text due to the production factors just discussed might be variable, they should account for some variance in global impressionistic judgments of text quality. The most obvious way to isolate variance due to the mechanical demands of writing is to compare oral and written text production. The control is imperfect, because speaking and writing also differ in other characteristics, for instance, rate; however, the comparison may at least provide suggestive findings. Note that comparing oral and written text production is not the same as comparing writing with speaking in the normal sense. It is comparing two ways of producing what is eventually to become a written text. (Blass and Siegman, 1975, provide an interesting example of the opposite kind of study, one that compares oral and written modes of conversational interaction.) In the oral mode of production— that is, in dictation—the author generates language but need not be concerned at the time with such low-level requirements of writing as spelling, penmanship or typing, punctuation, and capitalization. Although speech production has its own requirements, we assume that speech articulation is highly learned and automatized (as might not be the case if, for instance, one were speaking in a foreign language).

Gould (1980) has done extensive comparisons of writing and dictating, using adults who were either novices or experts at the latter. One of his initial hypotheses was similar to the ones being considered here—that dictating might produce superior compositions because of less interference and forgetting. In a long series of experiments, however, quality differences have failed to appear. But with capable adults producing business correspondence it could be that the low-level parts of writing production are so well learned that there is no interference to be removed. Although dictating was found to be somewhat faster than writing (20–65%), it was not enough faster that time alone could have much effect on memory.

With children, however, interference and/or speed factors might be considerably more important. A study by Scardamalia and Bereiter (1979) investigated these factors in children (grades four and six) and furthermore introduced an experimental procedure for separating the effects of mechanical interference from the effects of rate. This was done by introducing a third production mode, in addition to writing and normal dictation. In this third mode, called *slow dictation,* the children dictated to an experimenter who transcribed according to each child's previously determined writing rate. Thus it was possible to isolate the effects of mechanical interference by comparing writing with slow dictation, since they were equivalent in speed; it was correspondingly possible to isolate the effects of speed by comparing slow dictation with normal dictation, since these were alike in their mechanical demands but differed substantially in speed (normal dictation being in fact about five times faster than slow dictation and writing).

Results suggested that mechanical demands and rate were additive in their effects on quantity of production. Children produced 86% more words in slow dictation than in writing and 163% more in normal dictation than in writing. With respect to quality, however, the differences were small. There was a tendency, significant at the .06 level, for ratings on quality of presentation to differ in this order: writing (lowest), normal dictation, slow dictation (highest). Results suggested, therefore, that freeing children from concerns about written language mechanics improved the quality of their writing, but that a more rapid rate of production was not an aid to quality.

This study indicated that the low-level requirements of writing do make a difference to children. Take away those requirements and children produce considerably more and do it a great deal faster. The quality ratings, however, indicated that mechanical demands of writing had only a weak effect if any on higher-level components of the writing process. As in Gould's studies with adults, the most striking result of this study with children was the similarity of products from different modes of production.

Hidi and Hildyard (1983) have compared oral and written composition in two genres, opinion essay and narrative, using children in grades three and five. Their results are generally compatible with those obtained by us when we compared writing with normal dictation: Students produced significantly more in the oral mode, but quality did not differ. Hidi and Hildyard assessed quality both on the basis of cohesion at the sentence-to-sentence level and on the basis of being well formed at the level of text structure.

DISCOORDINATION RESULTING FROM LACK OF EXTERNAL SIGNALS

The discussion so far has presupposed a model of the composing process that consists of a number of subprocesses governed by an executive system (or monitor, as it is called in the Hayes and Flower [1980] model). The production difficulties considered so far all have to do with one subprocess impinging on another—with motor-output delays impinging on retention of language in short-term storage, with attention to mechanics interfering with planning, etc. In every case we have had to allow that the effect of these production factors will depend on how the system as a whole functions—on how well it can share time among competing attentional demands, for instance. In other words, the way in which one subprocess impinges on another will depend on the executive system, which regulates or orchestrates the subprocesses.

We turn now to a different and potentially much more significant class of production factors. These are ones that impinge on the executive system itself, influencing how reliably it functions and what capacity it has to cope with demands such as we have considered previously. The most fundamental of these factors is one that we shall not deal with at this point, although it serves as background to much of our analysis. This is the limitation imposed on executive functioning by the capacity of working memory, the same limitation that affects subprocesses. As Brown and Campione (1981) put it, "The executive competes for workspace with the subroutines it controls." It is probably this factor more than any other that limits the novice's ability to profit from being taught the strategies of the expert. Because the novice's subprocesses are not fully mastered and therefore require large amounts of attention, the novice has little spare capacity to be used for implementing more sophisticated executive procedures.

This is a general problem, however, affecting the acquisition of executive procedures in all areas of intellectual functioning (Case, 1985b). In this section we want to focus on a factor specific to executive functioning in writing. The factor has been referred to in the introduction as discoordination of language production resulting from the lack of external signals. We assume that the child develops an executive system to control everyday speech production and that, in learning to write, the child does not construct a whole new executive system but instead tries to adapt the existing one to the new requirements. But the existing system is an interactive one, designed to respond to signals from the external environment, specifically signals from conversational partners. Without such inputs, it has trouble functioning, much as we have noted that typists have trouble functioning without a keyboard to provide cues for programming their motor output.

In order to understand the child's predicament from the standpoint of production factors, we must rather ruthlessly abstract elements from the social situation. For conversation is a very complex social activity that impinges on the individual's language production system in a number of ways. In so far as conversation provides meanings to which the individual responds, it is implicated in the metacomponents of language production. Meanings (broadly conceived, so as to include those of both linguistic and paralinguistic origin) are of course the main elements of conversation; and no doubt the main strand in the story of how children acquire literacy is the story dealt with in the preceding chapter, of how they learn to produce meaningful discourse without the dialectical exchange of meanings that occurs in conversation. But there is more to conversation than meaning, and it is this remainder that we need to examine if we are to understand the workings of the executive system in writing rather than understanding only the content it works on.

In the present discussion and in the experiment reported thereafter, we focus on what is perhaps the most elemental feature of conversation from the standpoint of executive system functioning. This is *production signaling*—that is, signaling that simply activates the executive system to produce another unit of language. In conversation, we assume, the executive system is attuned to such signals; it normally responds to them when they are presented and does not respond without such signals, since to do otherwise is to violate conversational etiquette. In composition, however, there is usually neither a partner nor anything else in the environment to provide production signals. Therefore, in order to produce continuous discourse, the language production system must somehow provide its own means of sustaining production.

In the experiment to be reported in the next section we introduced a simple form of production signaling as an experimental variable. Although the signaling was done by social means, through words spoken by the experimenter, the intent was *not* to duplicate the social situation of conversation but rather to abstract from conversation this sole element of production signaling without the meaning elements that normally accompany it. When we undertook the experiment we had few expectations other than that external production cueing would increase the quantity of text produced. It did that, but it also had such a variety of other striking effects as to make us believe that the production factors most urgently in need of further study are those that impinge directly on functioning of the executive system.

An Experiment Investigating Production Mode and Production Signaling

In the preceding sections we have considered three production factors that might have a significant effect on the ability of people, especially children, to realize their intentions in writing. Some evidence was found of short-term memory loss in writing, but it was not possible to tell whether this was due to the slow rate of children's writing or to interference from the mechanics of writing. This second factor, interference from the mechanical requirements of written language, was found to have a significant effect on quantity of text produced, both in children and adults, but far more so in children. There was little indication that this factor had any influence on the quality of writing at any age, although the possibility remains that interference from mechanical requirements might have a long-term effect on writing development through its effect on the allocation of attention at critical points in the writing act. For the third factor, discoordination resulting from lack of signals, it is possible to build a strong circumstantial case that this factor is a major impediment to children's writing and interferes with their developing adequate executive structures to direct the composing process. However, direct evidence is lacking.

In addition to the shortcomings just noted, there are two other shortcomings that characterize research to date. Production factors have generally been studied in isolation, so that little is known of their interaction, and their effects have generally been measured only in global ways. Thus, for instance, although we have evidence that written and dictated compositions do not differ much in overall judged quality, we do not know if they differ in the stylistic and structural means by which quality is achieved. The study to be reported here is a step toward remedying these two shortcomings and also toward remedying the lack of any direct evidence bearing on the third production factor noted previously.

The present study used an elaborated and refined version of the procedure previously described for the Scardamalia and Bereiter (1979) study comparing writing, normal dictation, and slow dictation. Like its predecessor, the study was run on children in grades four and six, 24 of each. Each child produced three compositions, one using each of the three production modes, and each on a different one of the following opinion essay topics:

Is it better to be an only child or to have brothers and sisters?
Should children be allowed to choose what subjects they study in
school?
Should boys and girls play sports together?

The assignment of topics to conditions was counterbalanced so that each
topic-condition pairing occurred with equal frequency. Order of condition
was counterbalanced, with the limitation that students always composed in
the writing mode before they composed in the slow dictation mode. The
reason for having all students compose in the writing mode first was that
their writing rate was used to determine the rate at which the experimenter
transcribed in the slow dictation condition.[9] All sessions were conducted
individually. In the writing session the children were asked simply to write
as much as they could on the given topic. In normal dictation the instructions were similar except that the children were told to speak their composition into a tape recorder and were told that "some people at OISE" would
type the composition from the tape. The following instructions indicate
how the slow dictation condition was handled:

Remember what we did before? Well, today we're going to do
something a little different. I'm going to give you another
question to talk about, and you are to say as much as you can
about it, just like before. Only this time you don't have to
write it. You just say what you think, and I will write it for
you. But, when I write, I will write at the same speed you did
when you wrote the other day. The stop-watch is here in front
of me so I know that I am writing at the same speed you did.
It is not to time you, but to time me. Now, here is an example
of how you wrote the other day. You wrote the words
_____. Now, I'm going to write those words at the
same speed you did, so you watch how fast I write (demonstrate
example). There, that's how fast I'll be writing when you tell

[9]This was done by dividing total time by total words in the written composition. In slow
dictation the experimenter then paced himself so as to average the same number of seconds per
word in total elapsed time. Thus what was controlled was composing rate, which included both
pauses and transcribing time, rather than transcribing rate alone. Composing rate was, with few
exceptions, so close to transcription rate that transcribers could not adjust speed of transcription precisely enough to differentiate between the two rates. Data were analyzed separately for
the few children whose rates were different enough that transcribers could have in fact adjusted
their speeds to accommodate the differences, but such reanalyses had no significant effects on
results. Adequacy of the experimental procedure was judged by comparing logarithms of time
per word. The mean rates for writing and slow dictation were almost identical and the
correlation between the two, calculated over all students, was about .75.

me what to write. We'll need a bit of practice before you get the new topic, so you talk about the topic (*specify*) that you wrote about the other day, and I'll write what you say. Don't try to say exactly what you wrote from memory, just tell me what you think about the topic.

Several differences in procedure from the original Scardamalia and Bereiter (1979) experiment were introduced in order to overcome the unusually low quantity of text produced by children in the first experiment. Whereas in the first study children produced all three compositions in one session, in the present study they produced them in separate sessions spaced a day apart. Furthermore, in the present study children in all conditions were instructed to write or say as much as they could on the assigned topic, whereas no such urging was given in the earlier study. These efforts were apparently successful, since children produced about three times as many words in each condition as comparable children did in the first experiment.

Other changes in procedure reflected an increased sensitivity to the possible importance of subtle social inputs to the composing process. In the two dictation conditions, as in the writing condition, the experimenter sat beside students while they were dictating and avoided eye contact with them, whereas in the earlier experiment (and we suspect in other experiments comparing speaking with writing) no such controls were imposed and the experimenter may well have responded to the speaker through expressions and nods, thus unintentionally introducing conversational elements into the experimental conditions.

The major distinguishing characteristic of the present experiment, however, was the addition of a further experimental intervention. At the point when the child had apparently finished his or her composition, the experimenter introduced the first of three contentless "production signals" intended to encourage the child to continue speaking or writing:

SIGNAL 1: *You're doing fine. Now I know this is a bit tough, but can you say (write) some more about this?*

After each of the next two cessations of production yet another signal was offered:

SIGNAL 2: *That's fine. This is hard to do, but now can you say (write) even more?* If children asked if they could say the same thing again, the experimenter responded, *Try to say even more than you've already said.*

SIGNAL 3: *Do you think you could say (write) 10 more sentences about this?* If the child responded negatively, the experimenter said, *What about 5 more?* If the response was still negative, the experimenter said, *Then try just two more sentences.*

The experimenter tried to give the cues in an encouraging and not belittling manner.

The purpose of introducing these production signals was to get some more direct information than has previously been available on the extent to which children's language production depends on external inputs. Most normal kinds of conversational response include both content-relevant and contentless elements. The response, *Is that so?*, for instance, not only provides the speaker with a signal to continue speaking but it also calls on the speaker to provide warrant or confirmation for an assertion just made. If inputs of this kind are found to aid language production, there is no way to determine whether they have their effect at the level of production factors or at the level of metacomponents. It is impossible, that is, to separate the extent to which such inputs directly help the language production system to keep going from the extent to which they provide information useful in planning the next utterance.

We wanted to provide inputs of a kind to which children would already be used to responding and that would seem natural to them in the situation. We did not, therefore, want to resort to lights that would flash on to signal "write more" or anything of that sort. But on the other hand we wanted, for purposes of comparability across conditions, inputs that could be standardized and that would not carry any suggestions as to content. Of particular interest was the extent to which production cuing might serve to eliminate some of the previously observed differences between oral and written modes of composition.

Results

In the analyses that follow, each composition is treated as providing three different text bases:

> **1.** The standard portion. This is the portion of text produced before administration of the first production signal. It is called the standard portion because it constitutes what under normal test conditions would have been the complete composition.
>
> **2.** The signaled portion. This is the additional portion of text produced in response to the prescribed series of production signals.
>
> **3.** The extended composition. This is the combined standard portion and signaled portion, treated as a single text.

The first results to be reported will be those that permit comparison to the findings of other research—namely, results in terms of numbers of words produced and global quality ratings. Table 4.1 summarizes these results for the standard portion and for the extended composition. Results for the standard portion of text provide results similar in profile to those obtained in the earlier study (Scardamalia & Bereiter, 1979). Even though in the present study children produced far more words in every condition than in the previous study, the relative differences are the same: Children produce most in normal dictation, least in writing, and an intermediate amount with slow dictation, suggesting again an additivity of the effects of production rate and of the oral-versus-written difference. When production signaling is added, however, normal dictation retains its large quantitative advantage but the difference between writing and slow dictation largely disappears. Overall, however, the effect of production signaling is quite pronounced. In both the writing and the normal dictation conditions it resulted in a doubling of the total quantity of words produced.

The quality ratings are ratings on a five-point scale of quality of presentation, taking into account clarity and cohesion. Ratings are the average of two independent ratings. The standard portions of compositions were rated in separate batches from the extended compositions, so that the part compositions were never compared directly to the wholes. It should be kept in mind, however, that the standard portions are whole compositions in the ordinary sense, even though they subsequently form parts of larger compositions. Quality ratings of the standard portions do not show any significant differences between production modes, although there is a significant grade difference ($F(1,44) = 11.42$, $p = .002$). The tendency, however, is similar to that in the earlier study in showing the written compositions to be rated lowest. Ratings of the total compositions show a distinctly different profile, and this time the difference between production modes is statistically different ($F(2,88) = 4.32$, $p = .016$). In both grades now the written compositions are rated highest. When the standard portions are compared to the extended compositions, it is seen that for written compositions the material added after signaling raises the judged quality whereas for the dictated compositions the added material lowers total quality.

Table 4.1 Mean Word Counts and Quality Ratings for Compositions Produced in Three Modes

Production mode	Number of words				Quality Rating			
	Standard portion		Extended composition		Standard portion		Extended composition	
	Grade 4	Grade 6	Grade 4	Grade 6	Grade 4	Grade 6	Grade 4	Grade 6
Writing	57	90	112	194	2.45	2.97	2.78	3.10
Normal Dictation	97	143	167	336	2.54	3.19	2.52	2.73
Slow Dictation	72	108	119	193	2.54	3.06	2.43	2.84

Note: N = 23 in each grade.

Apparently production signaling has a more positive effect on writing than it does on normal or slow dictation. Before speculating on the possible causes of this effect, we need to look more closely at its nature. What do children do differently in the writing condition from what they do in the dictating conditions? In the next section of results we look for clues to this through analysis of the compositions.

Coherence Analysis   At the level of observable behavior, the preceding results could be interpreted as showing that in writing children stop too soon, whereas this is not true when they dictate. Thus, when children are prompted to continue producing, their written compositions improve whereas their dictated ones decline—possibly because in dictation they have already said all they have to say and therefore start repeating themselves or going off topic. In the analyses that follow, these latter conjectures are tested. More generally, the analyses are concerned with what determines when children normally end a composition and what happens when they continue generating text beyond that point.

Clearly, such analyses must deal with content and structure. The analyses to be reported here progressed through three stages: first, a parsing of the texts into functional units and a classification of these according to their text grammar functions; second, an analysis of the distribution of these functional units without regard to their structural relationships; and, third, an analysis of sequences of these functional units in terms of coherence. Although the methods employed have numerous roots in other work on text analysis, they are sufficiently novel and sufficiently critical to the conclusions that follow that the methods will be explained in some detail.

Parsing and Classification of Text Units   The parsing scheme for opinion essays generally follows Toulmin's analysis of arguments as consisting of premises and warrant for premises (cf. Kneupper, 1978). Table 4.2 shows the scheme as it was applied in this study. The main categories are premises enunciating one side or other of an issue, reasons providing warrant for these premises, and conclusions. A particular text element is classified as either an initial statement of one of these or as an elaboration on it. The scheme obviously does not capture all the complexities of argument structure. For instance, elaborations on elaborations are here simply treated as further elaborations on an initial statement, and there is no way of representing arguments embedded within arguments. The lack of such refinements may be justified for present purposes on grounds (a) that the analyses to be performed would not be likely to benefit from more elaborate parsing and (b) that rater reliability was found to decline sharply when the level of analysis was finer than the one used here.

Texts were segmented into minimal parsable units—that is, into the smallest units that could constitute separate entries into the matrix illustrated in Table 4.2. For instance, if the first sentence of a text read *Children should not*

Table 4.2   Schema For Classifying Opinion Essay Text Function Units

	Original position					Contrasting position				
	Initial statement	Elaborations				Initial statement	Elaborations			
		1	2	3	–		1	2	3	–
Premise										
Warrant										
Reason 1										
Reason 2										
Reason 3										
. . .										
. . .										
. . .										
Conclusion										
Nonfunctional units										

eat junk food because it is bad for their health, then *Children should not eat junk food* would be treated as a unit, since it can be classified as the initial statement of a premise. Accordingly, a number 1 would be so entered in the matrix. *Because it is bad for their health* would be treated as the second unit and entered in the matrix as the initial statement of reason 1, since it provides a warrant for the premise stated in the first unit. Potentially parsable idea units that, however, did not appear to play any role as premises relevant to the topic, as warrant, or as conclusion, were entered in the "nonfunctional" category. The nonfunctional category included material that was tangential to the argument being presented or that repeated, with no discernible rhetorical purpose, statements already made. The nonfunctional category did *not* include units that might be judged nonfunctional on quality grounds—unconvincing reasons, for instance. Units clearly intended to serve a function in the argument were classified according to that function regardless of how well or poorly they served it. Hence the parsing of texts was as much as possible descriptive, not evaluative.

Distribution of Text Function Units   The frequencies with which major categories of text units were used are presented in Table 4.3, which shows in each case the frequency of units in text produced before the first production signal (the standard portion) and the frequency in text produced after signaling began. Two main findings emerge from these data:

> **1.**   In normal dictation children produce more of every kind of text unit than they do in either slow dictation or writing. This is true both before and after production signaling. These results parallel the results for number of words produced. These differences between produc-

Table 4.3   Frequency of Test Function Units before and after Production Signaling (N = 46)

	Production Mode					
	Writing		Normal dictation		Slow dictation	
	Before Signaling	After Signaling	Before Signaling	After Signaling	Before Signaling	After Signaling
Total units	4.70	4.15	7.04	6.77	6.00	3.27
Reasons	1.81	.77	2.36	1.04	2.09	.50
Elaborations	1.43	1.75	2.13	2.43	1.52	1.18
Nonfunctional units	.31	1.20	1.13	2.75	.90	1.27
Reasons per unit	.37	.19	.37	.20	.34	.14
Elaborations per Unit	.24	.42	.26	.35	.21	.42
Nonfunctional units Per unit	.06	.25	.10	.30	.12	.31

tion modes vanish, however, when the *proportion* of text units falling into the various categories is considered. Analyses of variance showed a significant production mode effect ($p < .05$) for all three categories of elements, reasons, elaborations, and nonfunctional units; but when the ratios of each of these to total number of units were analyzed, no significant production mode differences were found.

2.   These ratios did, however, differ significantly between the standard and signaled portions. Reasons per unit, elaborations per unit, and nonfunctional units per unit all differed at beyond the .001 level of significance between portions. Reasons were twice as frequent in the standard portion, elaborations and nonfunctional units were twice as frequent in the signaled portion. In the standard portions, reasons are the most frequently used text unit, accounting for 36% of all units. After production signals are introduced, elaborations become the most frequently used unit, accounting for 59% of the total. Nonfunctional units, which constitute only 10% of units before signaling, account for more than a fourth of the units produced afterward.

These findings give us an idea of how children respond to calls for further text production after they have reached the normal end of composing. They add more material mainly by elaborating on points made previously. The distribution analyses do not, however, give us any clue as to why the judged quality of written compositions is increased by these additions while that of dictated compositions is diminished. Such clues might have appeared in analyses of variance as an interaction between production mode and signaling condition, but no significant interactions of this kind were obtained. Consequently, in the next section we look not to the frequency of text function units but to their interrelationships for clues to quality changes.

Coherence Evaluation. Following Widdowson (1978), we here treat *coherence* as the tying together of meanings in text and distinguish it from *cohesion* (Halliday & Hasan, 1976), which refers to linguistic means by which coherence is displayed in surface structure. Several investigators have used cohesion as an index of development in children's ability to compose text (Bamberg, 1980; Bracewell, Fine, & Ezergaile, 1980; Rentel & King, 1983). An underlying expectation, of course, is that where there is cohesion there is also coherence, but this is not necessarily true, and in children's efforts to present reasoned arguments exceptions are not uncommon.

Consider the following sentences, which open a fourth-grader's composition:

> I think they should because sports are for girls and boys and there is no difference between girls and boys. The girls might not be good in sports, so that's why the boys don't like the girls to play.

There are ample cohesive links between the two sentences, but the concatenation of ideas is incoherent. The second sentence seems to be an elaboration on the reason offered in the first sentence but in fact it is not, and it even contradicts the first sentence. Subsequent text might, of course, provide a linking idea that would restore coherence, although in the actual case it did not. The point is that the network of ideas and not the use of cohesive devices determines coherence. Cohesion provides help in discovering the network if one exists.

Furthermore, especially with unsophisticated writers, coherence can exist even with marked failures of cohesion. The fragment of text quoted previously affords an illustration of this as well. *I think they should because...* shows two faults in cohesion, the unreferenced pronoun *they* and the ellipsis, *should...*, without previous occurrence of the omitted verb. Nevertheless the meaning is clear. The reader does not, as is the case with real incoherence, have to guess at communicative intent.

The present analysis is built around the idea of a *coherent string*. A coherent string is a sequence of text function units that contains no nonfunctional units and no incoherent orderings of units. Coherence is inherently relative—relative to the amount of speculation that the reader is prepared to apply to the text. Almost any two propositions can be rendered coherent by the addition of unstated ideas. In the text fragment we have been considering, for instance, it is possible to achieve a coherent reading of the two sentences by assuming that what the writer means by *no difference* between girls and boys is "no difference in basic needs and dispositions." But nowhere in the text does the writer suggest that this is what is meant.

The standard of coherence set in the present study was fairly conservative. There had to be some definite warrant within the text for coherence-creating inferences. Thus, in the example cited, the second sentence was scored as a break in the coherent string, because there was no warrant anywhere in the text for inferences that would establish a logical connection between it and the preceding sentence.

A coherent ordering of units was one that followed the main pattern of premise followed by reasons, with elaborations incorporated in either of the following ways: (a) in series immediately following the initial statements to which they are related (for instance: premise, elaboration on premise, reason 1, elaborations of reason 1, reason 2, elaborations of reason 2); or (b) in parallel with the initial statements on which they elaborated (for instance: reason 1, reason 2, reason 3, elaboration on reason 1, elaboration on reason 2, elaboration on reason 3). Any departure from these patterns was treated as a break in the coherent string. For instance, the sequence—premise, reason 1, reason 2, elaboration on reason 1, reason 3—was scored as having a break in coherence after reason 2.

Arguments on an opposing side could be introduced provided they consisted of at least a premise and a reason. Introducing an opposing premise with no support or a contrary reason with no explicit premise were both scored as incoherent. Any nonfunctional unit constituted a break in coherence. This follows almost by definition, since to be scored as nonfunctional a text unit had to have no discernible function in developing the argument.

Two dependent variables were analyzed: (a) the length of the longest coherent string in each composition, as measured by number of text units it contained; and (b) the location of the end of the first coherent string—whether before, at, or after the point at which the writer ended the standard portion of the composition. Length of longest string was regarded as a general index of coherence that would have special relevance to the study of production factors, since it would be sensitive to various kinds of interference and breakdowns in processing. The "end of first string" variable was of particular interest for what it might show about the effects of production signaling: Would such signaling disrupt coherence, would it lead to extending coherent strings, or would coherence already have been broken before signaling began?

Results are presented in Tables 4.4 and 4.5. An analysis of variance on length of longest string showed that the only significant effect was an interaction between grade level and production mode ($F(2,88) = 3.79, p < .05$). As Table 4.4 indicates, fourth-grade children produced their longest strings in normal dictation, whereas sixth-grade children produced theirs in writing. Slow dictation yielded the shortest strings in both grades. The crossover between grades is sufficiently pronounced that by grade six children were actually showing weaker performance in normal dictation than the fourth-grade children. This suggests that developmental changes in language production are going on that not only improve writing but that make speaking a less satisfactory means of generating extended coherent text.

The second dependent variable was quantified as a *continuity index* by assigning a score of + 1 to initial coherent strings that extended past the onset of production signaling, 0 to coherent strings that ended precisely at the onset of signaling, and − 1 to coherent strings that ended before that point. Mean continuity indices, shown in Table 4.5, indicate that children at both grades four and six tend to continue the first coherent string beyond the onset of production signaling when they are writing but that when they are dictating the coherent string tends to have been broken before they get to that point, that is before they get to the normal ending points of their compositions. In an analysis of variance on the continuity index, a significant effect for production mode was the only one to emerge ($F(2,88) = 4.63, p < .025$). This finding is the first to offer a clue as to what lay behind the increase in rated quality of written compositions after production signaling compared to the decrease in rated quality of dictated compositions. Evidently signaling to produce more led children in writing to extend coherent strings whereas in the dictated compositions the initial coherent string was usually already ended.

Table 4.4 Mean Length of Longest Coherent String of Text Elements

Grade	N	Writing	Normal dictation	Slow dictation
			Production mode	
4	23	4.13	5.22	3.78
6	23	6.26	4.61	4.52

Table 4.5 Mean Continuity Index[a]

Grade	N	Writing	Normal dictation	Slow dictation
			Production mode	
4	23	.26	− .17	− .17
6	23	.17	− .39	− .35

[a]Continuity index = +1 if the initial coherent string ended after production signaling began; 0 if it ended at the point signaling began; and − 1 if it ended before signaling began.

Discussion

In this section we shall briefly reassess, in light of the experiment just reported, earlier speculations about the role of production factors in writing. Following that we shall offer some more general ideas about how a theory of the writing process might incorporate both production factors and metacomponents.

Short-Term Memory Loss Due to Slow Rate of Production   From the previous research, the only evidence pointing to short-term memory loss was the Bereiter et al. (1979) study showing information loss between forecasted and written text. However, as noted previously, such loss might be accounted for by interference from the mechanical demands of writing. In the present study the slow dictation condition was introduced to permit separation of effects due to speed of production and those due to interference from low-level demands of writing. Inquiry into effects of speed alone are best addressed through comparison of normal and slow dictation, since in this comparison mechanical demands of the medium are held constant.

Results show that speed of production has a substantial positive effect on quantity produced. Furthermore, differences in quantity are not reduced by urging children to continue beyond their normal stopping point. The additional text added in response to production cuing, in fact, increases the disparity in quantity between normal and slow dictation modes.

Turning to questions of quality, we see that speed of production, and the increased quantity that goes along with it, do not lead to texts of higher rated quality. In both the present study and in Scardamalia and Bereiter (1979), differences in quality ratings due to dictation speed were small and inconsistent. In analyses of coherence, fast and slow dictation emerged as similar; wherever differences appeared they were between writing and dictation, not between the two speeds of dictation.

Consistent now over two experiments we have the factor of production speed favoring quantity but showing no corresponding advantage when it comes to quality. These results do not support the hypothesis that loss from short-term memory is aggravated by the slow rate of output in writing. The present research does not, of course, address this hypothesis directly, but then neither does any previous research. If the slower output condition had led to substantially greater loss of intended content, we should have expected this to be reflected in lower quality ratings. If slower output had led to forgetting of high-level intentions and plans, we should have expected this to be reflected in lower scores on coherence variables or in a greater relative frequency of nonfunctional text units. None of this was found either.

The possibility remains that effects of output rate on memory loss occurred but were too slight to be detected by the variables assessed. It is also possible that they occurred but were offset by other variables that favored slow dictation. Clearly output rate has an effect on language production, but in the absence of positive evidence we are left with little ground for supposing that this effect can be accounted for by loss of material from short-term storage. What might account for the effect is a question we shall take up further in a later section.

Interference from the Mechanical Demands of Writing   This factor was assessed fairly directly in the present study, in the comparison between writing and slow dictation, where production rate was held constant and where the mechanical demands of writing (handwriting, spelling, etc.) were eliminated in the dictation mode. The results here do not lend themselves to a simple interference interpretation. There does seem to be interference, over and above that produced by a slow output rate, which prevents children from producing as much text when they are writing as when they are dictating slowly. However, differences that did exist in quantity of output between writing and slow dictation were eliminated by production signaling. (Recall that such signaling did *not* serve to eliminate differences between normal and slow dictation.)

Findings for quality mirrored those for quantity: Quality of texts produced before signaling favored the slow dictation mode, as it did in a previous study (Scardamalia & Bereiter, 1979). The difference, though not statistically significant in either study, was in the same direction in both grades in both studies. Thus, having held up through four replications, the difference in favor of slow dictation appears to be reliable. But when production cueing was added, the difference was reversed. This suggests that quality of the written compositions was limited by their low quantity. It therefore appears that children are not producing discourse of inferior quality when they are writing, they are simply producing less of it. Accordingly, when they can manage to get the quantity of their output up to what it is in the slow dictation condition, the disadvantage due to the written medium disappears. The present study indicates, in fact, that writing is the superior medium for producing coherent and well-expressed compositions.

Overall, interference due to mechanical demands of writing appears to be a factor, but it seems to affect quantity of text produced, not quality of written products, as might be expected. Thus its effect would seem to be on the child's ability to sustain production and to carry on planning. This is a matter we shall take up in greater detail later.

Discoordination Resulting from Lack of External Signals   Results of the present study suggest that this is a very potent factor influencing text production in school-age children. The administration of contentless production signals, after children had ostensibly written or dictated all they could, led to their going on to produce about as much additional text as they had produced up to the point signaling began. Although the resulting extensions of text contained an increased proportion of nonfunctional text units, including repetitions, more than 70% of the material added was functional, consisting mainly of elaborations and additional support for opinions.

Production signaling was found to interact with other production factors. It enhanced the judged quality of writing but lowered the quality of texts produced by dictation. A possible basis for this interaction was found in the analysis of coherence. After signaling, children in the writing condition tended to continue a structurally coherent string of text units, whereas in dictation they did not. We shall consider in the next section what this might mean in terms of cognitive processes.

Production Factors as They Relate to Planning   In this final section we shall try to present an organized set of ideas that make provisional sense of the research reported and cited in this chapter. The key idea in this discussion, which we will return to in the final chapter of this book, is that the production factors we have been examining affect performance through their influence on mental representation of text.

In order to construct coherent extended discourse, the writer or speaker must build progressively on the text already produced. In writing, this is true in the concrete sense that the writer keeps adding lines to the lines already written. But in oral composition there is no concrete text to build on, and even in writing people are able to construct coherent text without being able to see what they have written (Gould, 1980). From a psychological standpoint what counts in composition is the mental representation of text. The physical text, when there is one, is important only in so far as it influences the mental representation.

The following postulates serve as the basis for the subsequent interpretation of experimental results:

1. *There is no single mental representation of a text. Instead, there are a number of possible representations corresponding to the different kinds of text processing that a writer may engage in.* The key idea here is that the text is not represented in memory as a single more-or-less accurate copy of the actual text. Rather, we assume that when writers are engaged in high-level planning they draw on a representation that consists of goals, central ideas, structural decisions, and the like. When they are dealing with problems of *development* (see Beaugrande, 1982a) they may draw on this same high-level representation, but in addition on a more detailed representation of content (cf. Kintsch & van Dijk, 1978). When they are working at the level of generating actual language, they will need a representation that contains at least a substantial amount of verbatim record in order for them to keep anaphoric reference under control and to avoid unpleasant lexical repetitions.

2. *In general, these representations are not automatically formed and*

stored, ready for immediate recall. Instead, they have to be constructed or reconstructed every time they are needed. We assume in this discussion a multilevel interacting model of composing, such as that presented by Beaugrande (1982a), with different mental representations corresponding (though not necessarily in a one-to-one fashion) to the different parallel stages of processing. One view of mental representations might accordingly be that they are simply the continuously up-dated traces of mental activity at the different levels. We reject this hypothesis because it implies either very chaotic and overly detailed representations or else a great deal of mental effort continually going into revising and consolidating representations at every level. It seems more plausible to adopt a constructive view of memory (e.g., Minsky, 1980). According to this view, there would be no fixed types of mental representations. Instead, representations are constructed for purposes of the moment, using retrieved information of quite variable kinds. A given set of conditions could give rise to various representations of the same general type and a given representation could have been constructed from more than one body of retrieved information.

3. *Constructive mental effort is required in going from lower to higher levels of text representation. The lower the level of representation that a writer is presently attending to, the greater the amount of constructive activity required to reach a given higher level.* High and low here refer to levels of inclusiveness; no preferential distinction is implied. Since one meaning subsumes a variety of possible expressions, meaning representation is at a higher level than lexical representation; one word may subsume a number of possible spellings, etc. This postulate says that if you are currently dealing with a very low-level representation of your text—worrying about a doubtful spelling, for instance—and you need to switch to a high level, such as a representation of the overall plan for a text segment, this will require more mental work than if you had already been working with a higher level of representation— say a representation at the level of content units. The rationale for this postulate is simply that when one is constructing a representation at a neighboring level, much of the relevant information will already be activated. In jumping from a very low to a high level of representation, on the other hand, one is more likely to start cold with the question, *Now, where was I?*

4. *Mental representations of text may vary from vague and fragmentary to sharply delineated and detailed.* Completeness of the representation will depend on a number of factors including (a) the level of sophistication of the writer, especially as sophistication entails having a repertoire of general plans or genre schemes (Bereiter, 1980) to structure text representations; (b) how frequently the writer has previously reconstructed this representation, assuming that representations will get increasingly rich as they are repeatedly reconstructed; and (c) the needs of the moment. A minimal representation may suffice if all the writer wants to do is test whether some new idea fits the plan; a much fuller representation may be needed if the writer lacks an idea for what to write next and must deliberately generate one appropriate to an overall plan. The fullness with which content is represented will vary considerably depending on whether one is sketching ideas for a naive audience or working on a presentation that must withstand expert scrutiny.

Armed with these postulates, let us now interpret what went on in the experimental comparison of writing, normal dictation, and slow dictation. In normal dictation, as far as we can tell from protocols of children composing aloud, attention is mainly concentrated on representations involving items of content and syntactic plans (Scardamalia, Bereiter, Woodruff, Burtis, & Turkish, 1981; Tetroe et al., 1981). We assume that children edit their spoken language but little, so that there is not much attention to the verbatim level, and in dictation there is of course no graphic representation. Since children are mostly switching between neighboring levels of representation (individual items of content and syntactic plans), very little reconstructive activity has to go into representation. Such references as need to be made to the top-level representation require only minimal development of that representation, one that is easily reconstructed as needed. The result is easy, rapid composition, with the maximum opportunity for one item of content to suggest another one, producing an abundance of topically relevant content.

Slow dictation would be similar to normal dictation, except that the frequent pausing to wait for the scribe to catch up should lead to more constructive activity at the verbatim and syntactic plan levels—rehearsing previously planned language or revising and adding to the language within constraints of the syntactic plan. This should result in more carefully planned language than normal dictation, but at the expense of greater difficulty in returning to constructive activity at the content level. Thus the amount of content generated should be less than in normal dictation.

With writing we add the further element of attention to the graphic level of representation. When attention is focused at this level, memory for meaning and structure tends to get lost. Among children with very undeveloped writing skills, meaning and structure may stay lost, with the result that writing is fragmentary and often incomprehensible. But most children of the ages we have studied (10 years and older) seem able to maintain a degree of coherence even when composing in relatively unfamiliar genres such as argument or factual exposition. In order to do this, while also devoting attention to problems at the graphic level, it would seem that they must engage in considerable reconstructive activity of the "Now where was I?" variety. This continually having to reconstruct content units is a serious enough impediment to fluent production that it results in shorter compositions than are produced orally, either by slow or normal dictation, but it pays a dividend. Ordinarily, it seems, this dividend remains unrealized for children, but in our experiment it was brought to realization through production signaling.

Production signaling, it will be recalled, was introduced only after children claimed to have dictated or written all they could. At that point, the child's top-level mental representation should be that of a completed text. An opinion has been stated and reasons in support of it have been presented. In being urged to go on, the child is in effect being urged to treat this representation no longer as the representation of a whole text but rather as the representation of a text segment forming the first part of a larger whole. What is being forced on children is something we assume they do not normally face, although it is similar to what more mature writers face continually in all but very brief compositions. The children are faced with a major text juncture, one that requires a focus on higher levels of representation.

This is where the extra mental work done by children in the writing condition pays off. The work of repeatedly reconstructing content units and higher-level text representations should, as we indicated in the fourth postulate, lead to more sharply delineated and detailed mental representations of text. Thus, when faced with a major text juncture, children in the writing condition can more readily reconstruct representations that are sufficiently complete that they can build on them or use them as guides for generating coherently related new material. By contrast, in oral composition children have had to do little reconstructive activity at higher levels, because their attention has been occupied most of the time with items of content. Consequently, they have less often had to face the "Where was I?" problem. When unexpectedly faced with a major text juncture, they are less able to construct a text representation suitable for planning a coherent continuation. This is because their top-level representations, though sufficient for testing the adequacy of content units thought of spontaneously, are too vague to serve a useful generative function.

What happens, we suspect, is something like this. Suppose the child has been composing an essay on the evils of junk food and claims such food causes acne and tooth decay. Now, under the instigation of production cuing, the child tries to extend the essay, and so tries to recall what has been said so far. A vague representation might capture only the topics—acne and tooth decay. With only this much information to go on, the child might digress about acne or tooth decay or might generate an additional topic of the same class. The result would be something more or less connected with the previous text, but something that might not rate very high in coherence or be judged to raise the overall quality of the text. This, then, is what we conjecture tended to go on in the two dictation conditions.

In writing, however, the child, having already had to reconstruct the content units, might be able at the text juncture to reconstruct a more complete representation. The gist might be something like this: *I said junk food was bad because it causes acne and I said it was bad because it causes tooth decay.* With this more complete representation, the child is in less danger of generating an incoherent or irrelevant continuation and is in a better position to invent a reasonable continuation—to add a parallel reason or an appropriate elaboration. This is because the representation includes not only items of content but also information as to the purpose and organization of the content.[10]

These hypotheses about differences between writing and dictation only apply, it should be noted, to writers who do little intentional manipulation of higher-level text representations—in short, to knowledge-tellers. As evidence discussed in Chapter 14 and in Scardamalia & Paris (1985) indicates, more mature writers make use of a variety of interconnected representations of their texts. In particular, they make use of representations of intentions and main ideas to serve planning needs. It is therefore not surprising, as Gould (1980) found with skilled business writers, that the medium of production had little effect on composition.

CONCLUSION

From the standpoint of understanding the composing process as a whole, the present view has much to recommend it over a view that treats production factors merely as variables that must somehow be taken into account in

---

[10]In interpreting the changes that take place after production signaling, we must not neglect the possible role that availability of the written text may have had in boosting performance in the writing condition. We did not collect data of rereadings and so we cannot judge the extent to which children in the writing condition may have used their actual texts as an aid in reconstructing a high-level plan at the onset of production signaling. Our impression, based on one-to-one work with scores of children, is that they almost never consult text for this purpose. Observations by Gould (1980) on adult writers support this impression. Hayes-Roth and Walker (1979) found, furthermore, that students were better able to synthesize information drawn from memory than information available in text.

computing the relationships between metacomponents and performance. Instead of viewing composing as a process in which mental products are created, held in buffers awaiting use, and occasionally lost through decay or interference, we view it as a process in which mental representations are continually being reconstituted. This gives the three production factors that we considered at the beginning of this chapter a different import. The important production factor is not memory loss but rather reconstructive activity that influences the writer's ability to plan at all levels of composition from the lowest levels of mechanics to the highest levels of rhetorical intent. We no longer view attention to mechanics as interfering with higher-level processes. Rather, it creates the need for a greater amount of reconstructive activity at higher levels of text representation, and this can have benefits as well as disadvantages as far as the production of extended discourse is concerned—benefits in terms of coherence, disadvantages in terms of ease with which content can be generated.

Another factor, discoordination of executive functioning due to lack of external signals, takes on even greater potential significance in the current view. Composition begins to appear very much like the job of the proverbial one-armed paperhanger. Mental effort at a number of levels is continuously required, and there is not some neat high-level plan sitting there and quietly directing activities. The demands for skillful internally regulated coordination of activities are so severe that we find it remarkable children as young as 10 years are able to function in composition as well as they do. Explaining how this is possible was a major impetus for creation of the knowledge-telling model described in Chapter 1. Although that model shows how a simplified procedure could reduce the mental effort involved in content generation, it does not deal with how the writing process as a whole is coordinated. The present study begins to suggest where some of the major demands on the information-processing system occur and the kinds of time-sharing that must go on in order for the writing process to proceed.

In concluding, we should like to mention one practical suggestion that emerges from the research reported here. Our analysis suggests that in school-age children oral and written composition differ in the extent to which they bring various kinds of mental representations of text into play. Oral composition fosters the mental representation of content units and syntactic plans, whereas writing fosters the active reconstruction of higher level representations in order to achieve coherence. Both are important, and so it would seem that both ought to have a place in school language arts curricula. Writing already does, of course, but oral composition does not. We are referring here specifically to oral composition, not to oral activities such as discussion and conversation, which have educational values of their own and which are common at least in some schools. Oral composition is, like written composition, the sustained and solitary production of a self-contained text. Extemporaneous speaking (planned but not scripted) would qualify, as would dictating texts, one child to another, and producing audiotaped compositions for listening. Such oral composition as does exist in schools seems to be reserved for children who are not yet literate enough to produce written compositions (except where extemporaneous speaking reappears as a specialty in college speech courses). It seems likely that oral composition would be beneficial throughout the school years for fostering fluency of content generation and spontaneity of expression.

Chapter 5
Information Processing Load of Written Composition

PREFACE

In the preceding chapter the point was made that listing the many demands on a writer's attention (spelling, punctuation, word choice, purpose, organization, reader characteristics, and so on) misrepresents the difficulty of the task. What count are the demands that compete for attention *simultaneously*. A process may consist of many parts and yet be simple to carry out, provided those parts can be dealt with one by one. What makes a process *complex* is the interdependency of components, which requires that a number of elements be coordinated or taken into account jointly. The question raised in the present chapter is, How complex is composition really? We do not presume to give a decisive answer to the question, but we do try to show that more can be said on the matter than might at first seem likely.

One of the important accomplishments of modern cognitive psychology has been to put the vague notion of complexity on a solid enough basis that it can be researched. George Miller (1956) is generally credited with the seminal contribution, through his observation that over a surprising range of activities the number of items, variables, or whatever that people are able to handle simultaneously turns out to be approximately seven. At present almost all theories of higher mental processes incorporate some notion of a limited-capacity central processor. Limited capacity means that at any given moment only a limited number (current estimates are fewer than seven) of mental objects are available to be operated upon. This greatly limits the capacity of the human mind to solve multi-faceted problems, to synthesize large bodies of information, or to make decisions that take account of very many variables. Obviously, this central capacity limitation should be crucial in writing, where complex problems must be solved, where a large number of ideas need to be coordinated, and where decisions need to take account of a variety of factors.

An effort to understand basic factors in writing competence accordingly requires an attempt to discover the extent to which limitations of human information processing capacity limit the strategies available to writers and the results writers can achieve with those strategies. Of particular interest is the effect that capacity limitations have on young or beginning writers. Could it be that for some writers knowledge telling is the only strategy that can operate within the capacity they have available for generating text content? In the present chapter questions concerning the information processing demand of composition are addressed at a fairly abstract and technical level. Then in Chapter 6 we turn to a more concrete examination of how processing limitations are reflected in the content of children's texts.

5 Investigators into the psychology of text composition frequently remark that the information-processing demands of the activity appear to be very high. Beaugrande (1981) refers to "the impression that can be obtained from large stores of empirical evidence, namely: that *discourse production routinely operates near the threshold of* OVERLOADING [p. 2]." We agree, certainly, that this is the impression supported by the bulk of empirical observations. On the other hand, in experimental research on written composition we have repeatedly come upon observations that give a somewhat different impression. The purpose in this chapter is to subject the hypothesis of high information-processing load to critical scrutiny in the light of evidence and theory. How heavy is the processing load in text composition, and what are the implications of processing load for the development of competence in composition?

A degree of definiteness about processing load is important for theoretical progress. It isn't enough simply to acknowledge that there is a processing load and that difficulties in performance may arise from it. At the very least we need some way of judging whether the processing capacity imputed to humans by a theory is of the right order of magnitude.

More definite knowledge about processing load is also important for instructional planning (cf. Case, 1985a). Composition can be handled by a variety of strategies differing in complexity. In designing composition instruction a major decision is the level of strategy complexity to teach. Should one press for a complex strategy that will involve students in coordinating more variables than they do already, or should one aim for a simplified strategy that will reduce an already too complex task to one that is within their processing capacity? The fact that educators usually make such choices intuitively and without conscious attention to the issue of processing load does not make the choice any less crucial. A wrong choice could lead to promoting strategies that students are incapable of applying or that impede rather than aid skill development.

THE INADEQUACY
OF INFORMAL EVIDENCE

There seem to be three main bases—all of an informal or suggestive nature— for belief in the high processing demands of discourse production. The first is the quality of speech output, which Chomsky (1967) described as consisting to a substantial degree of "false starts, disconnected phrases, and other deviations from idealized competence [p. 441]." These characteristics, together with the misfirings that show up as systematic speech errors (Fromkin, 1971), suggest a language production system that is barely coping. They do not, however, necessarily point to an inherent overload problem in text composition. In the first place, these phenomena suggest that overload is associated with the need to keep up with the pace of social speech. In writing or dictation, where pauses are unrestricted and normally take up 2/3 of the time (Gould, 1980), the processing load difficulties associated with rate should not occur. Although according to Hotopf (1980), "slips of the pen" occur, these do not necessarily reflect processing load (Hotopf, 1980). Omitted function words, for instance, may indicate automatization of the transcribing process (see Chapter 4). People will make errors in lengthy arithmetic calculations as well, yet the standard arithmetic algorithms are well designed to minimize processing load. Clearly, if we are to infer processing load from pause and error data, we must come equipped with sufficiently sophisticated theory and techniques to sort out competing hypotheses.

A second basis is direct experience of processing load. People who approach writing seriously generally agree that it is very taxing mental work, and they will report experiencing difficulty in keeping cognitive control over all the content and constraints. We do not doubt the validity of such subjective reports. Even children give what appear to be accurate reports on variations in their mental effort (see Osherson, 1975). We must, however, distinguish between isolated moments of peak processing demand and a continuously high processing load. What writers experience as the high processing load of text composition may be only occasional, though memorable, instances when a particularly complex problem had to be solved. On the other hand, occasional overloads in composition could be critical, if they mean the failure of efforts to achieve overall syntheses or optimum solutions to problems and a consequent downsliding to more simplistic strategies. To sort this issue out, we need to examine the composition process in ways that will permit us to evaluate the processing load of critical moves.

The third basis is simply the list of things that must be taken into account in composition, ranging across the whole spectrum from fine points of style to deep matters of truth and authenticity in content. Contemporary views about the architecture of the text-production system almost universally recognize the interdependence of decisions made across this spectrum. This interdependence implies that in executing a particular subprocess the products of other subprocesses must be mentally available, which in turn implies a big task for working memory. This argument is a particularly compelling one because it seems to follow directly from well-accepted assumptions about the composition process. The trouble with the argument is that if carried far enough it can easily lead to the conclusion that text composition is impossible (cf. Elbow, 1973)—that the processing load is not only high but far too high for a cognitive system that tends to break down when asked to multiply three-digit numbers mentally. (This task is comparable, because products of previous operations must be stored mentally while other operations are being executed.) But language processing is generally like that; it seems to demand more intellectual resources than it is plausible to believe are available, especially in the very young. If Chomsky's innateness and modularity hypotheses, which are partly motivated by these considerations, are correct (Chomsky, 1980), then it may simply be that we are a great deal smarter in language than we are in other things and that, consequently, ordinary parameters of processing load do not apply. Before we can accept the *laundry list* argument for high processing load in composition, therefore, we need to determine whether language performance behaves the way other kinds of performance do with regard to the quantitative aspect of processing demand.

The preceding reflections serve mainly as cautions against a facile treatment of the processing-load problem. No arguments were actually brought against the hypothesis that composition entails a severe information-processing load. Let us turn, therefore, to experiences that have led us to raise questions about the hypothesis.

When we first began experimental research on writing in 1976, one of the few things we were confident about was the high processing load of composition. We were so confident of this assumption, in fact, that it formed the basis of what was intended to be one of our major research approaches. It was reasoned that if writers are working at or near their information-processing capacity limits, then it should be relatively easy to degrade their performance or possibly break it down entirely by putting additional burdens on working memory. Therefore, it seemed, a useful experimental methodology could be built around testing to see what kinds of interventions disrupt writing performance and in what ways they disrupt it—a sort of Luria-without-lesions approach to mapping the cognitive system. The methodology was also expected to be illuminating with respect to the developmental psychology of writing. Children fairly new to literacy might be expected to have fragile systems of production that would be vulnerable to interventions to which more mature writers would have means of accommodating.

The first ventures centered around the use of *blind* writing, a method suggested by Britton, Burgess, Martin, McLeod, and Rosen (1975). The student writes with an inkless pen—carbon paper or some other device being used to obtain a record of the composition.[11] This intervention seemed promising because it left the composing process largely unmolested but added an additional burden on short-term memory because of the need to carry information in memory that would normally be available from the visible text. After eight pilot studies, the procedure was abandoned. With students ranging in age from 10 years to adult and with a variety of easy to difficult writing tasks, significant disruption of writing performance was never produced.[12] Both Gould's studies

---

[11]Much of this research was done by R. J. Bracewell.

[12]J. Gould was also doing research on blind writing at about the same time using adults composing business letters. He reported the same finding of no measurable effect (Gould, 1978). The finding that having text hidden from view does not disrupt writing and sometimes facilitates it has since been so well established that there is even a word processor available for school use that blocks out the screen while students are writing their first drafts.

and ours involved short compositions. (Naturally, if composition goes on long enough, a point will be reached where inability to review the previous text will cause problems, but these would be problems of long-term storage and retrieval and relevant to a different set of issues from those being considered here.) There were a few interesting hints of style variables that might depend on visual monitoring, but they are not germane to the processing-load issue, and furthermore, they were observed only in the most skilled writers. Children, on the other hand, seemed to be unbothered by blind writing and sometimes even found it facilitating. It is possible, in fact, that blind writing had the opposite effect for children to that intended: By giving them less to worry about at the graphic level it may actually have reduced processing load.

But children's writing performance seemed to be invulnerable to other sorts of interference as well. Doing mental arithmetic between sentences had no measurable effect. In one experiment (Scardamalia & Bracewell, 1979) children were required after each sentence to compose a pair of alternative next sentences and then to choose one. This forced divergent production led to compositions that may have been somewhat below par in coherence, but doubling the sentence production burden did not produce anything resembling a breakdown in performance.[13]

In a dozen or more other studies summarized in Chapter 3, children have shown themselves invulnerable to or even to thrive on different kinds of interruptions and additional tasks. In one instance, however, an unequivocal decrement in performance was observed. That instance is instructive as to the amount of additional processing burden that must be imposed on children before they begin to show evidence of overload.

What appears to have been an information-processing overload occurred when 14-year-old students for the first time composed opinion essays on a computer, using an interactive program that led them after each sentence through a branching sequence of questions designed to induce means-end planning of the next sentence (Woodruff, Bereiter, & Scardamalia, 1981). The decrement did not occur if students had one prior experience of composing on the computer without the questioning program. Thus a significant degrading of performance apparently required the combination

---

[13]The *whole* burden of composing was not doubled, of course. Doubling would be achieved by having people compose distinct essays in parallel, a task we have never tried but that might be worth exploring. But the burden in certain phases of the composing process should have been greatly increased, and this should have led to breakdown if the processing load during those phases was already near capacity.

of (1) a novel production mode—composing on a computer,[14] and (2) a highly intrusive intervention that presented students with taxing questions and suggestions at each sentence juncture. Neither factor alone produced a measurable decrement.

It appears, then, that writers can experience a disruption of performance because of information-processing overload, given a sufficient concentration of novel demands to contend with. But it also appears that during normal composition, writers—including young and not particularly proficient ones—are not operating near the threshold of overload.

The reasons cited for doubting the high processing load of writing are, of course, as informal and impressionistic as the reasons for believing in it. On the basis of informal evidence, then, it is possible to believe almost anything one wishes about the processing load of writing. Before drawing on more formal evidence we must state more definitely what is meant by information-processing load.

INFORMATION–PROCESSING DEMAND AND COMPLEXITY

Information-processing demand and information-processing capacity are manifestly quantitative concepts, and unless they can be quantified at some level, they are of little value. Psychologists have for the most part confined themselves to quantifying these concepts at the ordinal level—for example, task A has a greater processing demand than task B. Although even this level of quantification is a challenge when it comes to text composition, it will help clarify concepts if we direct our attention first to tasks in which a high level of quantification has been achieved.

In the ensuing discussion we equate information-processing demand with load on working memory. Information-processing demand, accordingly, depends on the amount of information—task constraints, data, etc.—that must be held in immediate memory while carrying out a mental

[14]The students had used computers before and were familiar with screen editing functions, but their experience had been mainly with games and with computer-assisted mathematics instruction so that they had little if any experience with the computer as a mode of producing written language.

operation.[15] This processing load will, of course, vary from moment to moment in the course of executing a task. When we speak of the processing demand of a *task*, we refer to the working-memory load imposed by the most demanding step in task execution.

For a variety of mental tasks it has been found profitable to quantify information-processing demand up to the level of an absolute scale—that is, to quantify it in terms of countable units of information (Bereiter & Scardamalia, 1979; Case, 1974; Pascual-Leone, 1970; Pascual-Leone & Smith, 1969; Scardamalia, 1973, 1975, 1977). Tasks that have lent themselves best to this kind of quantification have been ones that involve a set of more or less equivalent elements that can be varied in number without altering the structure of the task. The most familiar task of this kind is backward digit span, where processing load may be increased by increasing the number of digits that must be repeated in reverse order. Other tasks having similar properties are (1) Generating all possible combinations of stimulus features, in which load is increased by increasing the number of stimulus dimensions (Scardamalia, 1977); and (2) Raven's Progressive Matrices, in which for a given matrix type the processing demand increases with the number of dimensions that must be taken into account (Bereiter & Scardamalia, 1979).

On tasks of this kind, people tend to have an absolute level of performance that is constant across tasks. Thus, for instance, the person who can reverse four digits but not five tends also to be able to produce combinations of four stimulus dimensions but not five (Scardamalia, 1977), whereas the person who can reverse five digits can also produce combinations of five dimensions and so on. The appearance of such constancy across tasks, noted first by Miller (1956), supports the notion that a person can hold a fixed number of *chunks* of information available for immediate use and that, correspondingly, the information-processing demand of a task can be specified by the number of such chunks that must be kept simultaneously available in order to execute the task (Bachelder & Denny, 1977a, 1977b; Case, 1974; Pascual-Leone & Goodman, 1979).

Most mental tasks of ordinary life do not lend themselves to straightforward manipulation of information-processing demand. Usually, the elements that must be handled in working memory are not equivalent, and adding or removing one changes the nature of the task. Furthermore, it is

---

[15]There are other aspects of information-processing load, most notably time pressure. We will not consider time pressure here, however, because it is not normally a factor in text comprehension or production. Furthermore, where time is a factor people probably respond to it by changing strategy rather than by carrying out the same process under greater load (Just & Carpenter, 1984).

often not obvious what will constitute a chunk. In writing, for example, taking account of audience when one has not previously done so is not simply a matter of adding an element to the composition task. As we argued in Chapter 1, a substantial overhaul of strategy may be required, such that writing becomes a differently structured process altogether. Furthermore, the *audience* may constitute not just one chunk of information in the mind of the writer but rather a set of procedures—a subtask, as it were—having its own possibly high or possibly low information-processing demand. Whether *taking account of the audience* is a task element that accounts for one unit of information-processing demand, or no units, or several units is an issue for analysis and research, not something that can be assumed by rule.

Difficulties of the sort just noted have made some psychologists skeptical about the value of quantitative theories of information-processing capacity and demand (Flavell, 1978; Shatz, 1977). In science, however, one never expects to be able to measure a variable in every situation where it is theoretically invoked. Other kinds of evidence are normally relied on to provide assurance that principles established in situations where measurement is possible apply in other situations where measurement is not possible. (Consider, for instance, the generalizations made from genes that happen for largely fortuitous reasons to be identifiable to the much larger number of genes that are not yet identifiable.)

The fact is that quite a bit of progress has been made, largely by Case and his coworkers, in analyzing and verifying the processing demand of tasks composed of nonequivalent elements—tasks, in other words, where adding a new element changes the structure of the task (Case, 1985b; Case & Khanna, 1981; Gold, 1978; Liu, 1981). It appears that adding a new loop to a processing strategy does typically amount to adding one unit to information-processing demand, just as adding another stimulus feature does to a combinatorial- or matrix-reasoning task.

As for the problem of determining what constitutes a *chunk,* this appears to be a fatal difficulty only for those who expect that there should be an objective way of doing it. For the special cases mentioned earlier—backward digit span, for instance—it happens that the chunks normally correspond to objective elements or dimensions. But this should not deter us from recognizing that in these cases as in all others, the chunk is a *subjective* unit—it is what the student treats as a unit, not what the experimenter decides to treat as a unit. Identifying such units, given that they may be neither observable nor reportable, is a difficult task but not an unfamiliar task. Indeed, identifying subjective elements of cognition—representations, rules, etc.—may be properly regarded as a constitutive task of modern cognitive psychology, so that if one is not wrestling with problems of identifying subjective elements one is probably not doing cognitive psychology.

A current best guess at the information-processing capacity of normal adults is five chunks (Case et al., 1982; Simon, 1974). This may be thought of as the number of chunks a person can hold in working memory while executing some attention-demanding operation. Higher estimates of capacity, such as that of Pascual-Leone (1970), include capacity required by the operations themselves. We will stick with the lower estimate here, because in the ensuing discussion of processing load in language, we shall consider only items, such as task constraints, that must be held in memory and operated on rather than taking account also of the kinds of operations that must be performed on them.

An important additional consideration has to do with the lower performance of children on processing-capacity tasks. Although there is considerable uncertainty about the cause of this lower performance, it has been observed on a large range of working-memory tasks. On tasks where the adult capacity is four or five units that of 7-year-olds is two units, and of 9-year-olds, three units. (Reviews in Case 1974, 1978c, 1985b.) Indeed the empirical basis for across-task generality of processing capacity is a good deal more solid for children than it is for adults. That is, there is more evidence that a 7-year-old will be able to handle two chunks of information across a variety of tasks than there is evidence that adolescents and adults will handle five.

If, therefore, we are to infer from well-analyzed tasks to language-processing tasks, it would appear that any language task that required the speaker to hold more than five chunks of information in working memory would create an overload and that language tasks that an adult might handle may nevertheless be substantially beyond the capacity of school children. These statements, of course, tell us nothing until we are able to describe language tasks in terms of information-processing load. How complex is a language task that requires holding five chunks of information in working memory? Is it something on the order of composing a sonnet or is it something on the order of carrying on small talk? In order to answer such questions, we must look for evidence, equivocal as it might be, that bears more directly on the subjective units and task demands of language processing.

Information-Processing Load in Language Tasks.

The preceding section has already suggested some of the obstacles to determining the information-processing demand of language tasks. Tasks that lend themselves to such determination are ones in which the strategy for task execution can be clearly specified or experimentally controlled and in which the subjective elements to be processed correspond to denumerable objective features of the task. These ideal conditions are perhaps never met by real tasks, but language tasks do not even come close. The difficulty of specifying executive strategies is exacerbated by the ill-structured nature of language tasks. Thus, on a typical composition task, each writer is pursuing a significantly different goal. The processing load for one writer may be greater than it is for another simply because the first writer has undertaken a more demanding task. The difficulty of specifying subjective units or "chunks" is complicated by the multilevel nature of text processing. As the Hayes and Flower (1980) protocols show, writers continually switch between levels of planning and language generation, and it seems obvious that each switch involves switching to chunks of a different grain. Similarly in text comprehension, readers must switch attention between micro- and macro-propositions (Kintsch & van Dijk, 1978) as well as the surface language units out of which micro-propositions are extracted. Finally, in natural-language processing, what constitutes a chunk is likely to vary enormously depending on the person's knowledge. Whether a phrase like *barometric pressure,* for instance, will be stored as one chunk or two will depend, among other things, on whether the reader understands barometric pressure as a unitary concept or understands it as some kind of pressure (one chunk) associated with a barometer (another chunk).

These kinds of difficulties beset any effort to achieve a detailed understanding of language processes. They are not unique to the investigation of information-processing load. In order to get some leverage on these difficulties, we shall examine a variety of studies in which language tasks have been engineered or controlled so as to reduce some of the uncertainties about strategies and chunking.

There has been quite a bit of research devoted to finding the basic unit of language planning (Reviews in Fodor et al., 1974; McNeill, 1979). One safe conclusion from such research is that people do process language in packets. As Smith (1979) has argued, however, attempts to discover subjective units that correspond precisely to units defined in grammatical theories have failed and are probably destined to keep failing. This is because the considerations that determine what grammarians will treat as a unit have no reference to the performance limitations that constrain what real speakers and listeners will be able to process as single units.

Introspection suggests that anything from a single letter or phoneme up to the topic of a whole composition may at times engage the attention of a language user and thus function as a subjective unit. However, there is evidence that a few basic kinds of units may constitute the main ones that most people use for most of their language processing.

One of these is a phrasal unit influenced by both syntactical and length constraints. The unit tends to run about six words in length but has some syntactic integrity, being either a whole clause or the beginning or end of one. Such a unit has been identified by actual pauses in speech (Chafe, 1985), by having people mark spots in written text where they would expect to pause (Johnson, 1965), by a probe-latency technique (Case & Kurland, 1980), by click-location studies (Fodor et al., 1974), and by writers' reports of language already mentally formed in advance of transcribing it (Bereiter et al., 1979, the "forecasting study" summarized on pp. 102–105). Case and Kurland (1980) tested short-term recall of sentences consisting of varying numbers of these phrasal units. Children tended to be able to recall the same number of phrasal units as they could recall of isolated words. This suggests, accordingly, that the unit in question may commonly constitute a "chunk" in determining the working-memory load of some aspects of language processing.

In studying the generation of text content, we see a unit of larger size, which was referred to in the preceding chapter as a *content unit.* Frequently it corresponds to a sentence but sometimes more and sometimes less. What is more important, however, is that it is a unit of ideational content and not a unit of language; accordingly, the same content unit might appear in text in any of a variety of linguistic embodiments, differing in form and magnitude. Evidence for these units appears most clearly when students talk about problems of text arrangement or when they are recalling their own texts. In an informal study we questioned grade 6 students a month after all of them had written essays on the same topic. Among other things they were asked to identify sentences as their own or not and to state whether or not some additional sentences had occurred between two presented sentences from their old texts. Finally they had to arrange in order sentences from their own text and sentences from another child's. Their discourse on these tasks consisted mainly of sentences like these:

> I might have said x, but I would never say y.
> *I think I remember I said x,* then I said y.
> Something goes between x and y but I can't remember what it is.

In all these sentences, x and y were briefly-labeled items of content such as "we have a right to" or "you have to eat right to be healthy." These had no fixed linguistic rendering, but might be referred to differently at different times. Finally, after the students had done 20 or 30 minutes of work reexamining and making judgments about their original texts, they were asked to recall the texts verbatim. What generally came back was recall of content units rather than verbatim recall.

Several studies using content units indicate that these units also function as "chunks" in the processing load sense. This occurs when the task involves manipulating meanings rather than surface language. McDonald (1980), testing children of ages 5 and 7, used tasks in which the processing load inhered in the inferences drawn from statements. Children heard and repeated back series of sentences like the following:

The desk is in front of the window.
The paper is under the doll.
The doll is little.
The doll is on top of the desk.

Treating each of these statements as a chunk, McDonald classified possible inferences according to the number of chunks that had to be integrated to generate them. In the example, a two-chunk inference is *The doll is in front of the window.* A three-chunk inference is *The paper is in front of the window.* McDonald found that the level of inference children could correctly evaluate corresponded to their estimated working-memory capacity.

Two supplementary findings of McDonald's study are of most direct application to language processing. One is that if the filler item, *The doll is little,* was replaced by a topically irrelevant filler item like *The book is beside the chair,* the apparent processing demand of the inferential tasks was increased by one unit. It would appear that with the first kind of filler item, which gives descriptive information about some previously mentioned topic, the new information is immediately chunked with the topic and so does not survive as a separate chunk. An unconnected item of information, on the other hand, is retained in working memory, waiting for other information to be attached and thus usurps memory resources needed for the making of inferences.

This result is not surprising and was in fact predicted. The difficulty of the irrelevant filler items is not unlike that of multiple-clause embeddings, which are widely recognized as placing a high processing demand on the other comprehender. But the parametric implications are interesting. Suppose each embedding or other bit of dangling information adds one unit to processing load during the time that the information remains unattached. Given a processing capacity of only about four units, an incidental variation in processing load of one or two chunks is a large variation. People can obviously handle a considerable amount of such additional processing load without a breakdown in comprehension. This suggests that either (a) the processing load of language comprehension is normally well within processing capacity or (b) people's processing capacities are frequently exceeded but that what happens in overload is not a dramatic breakdown in comprehension but rather a loss of deeper-level inferences—in other words, a shift to a more simple-minded interpretation of what is said. McDonald's findings are only suggestive on this latter point, but the suggestion makes sense both for language comprehension and production.

The suggestion that deeper inferences are what gets lost under overload may seem to conflict with the well-accepted notion that high-level ideas are the most securely retained in text comprehension (cf. Meyer, 1984). The two notions are not in competition, however. The inference *the paper is in front of the window* is not high-level in a text-structure sense; it is a deeper inference than *the doll is in front of the window* because it requires the integration of more chunks of information. Deep inferences will often not be main ideas. On the contrary, they may be hidden assumptions, subtle inconsistencies, or remote implications not even known to the author.

McDonald's other germane finding was that when children were asked to compose inferences instead of evaluating them, the highest level inference they produced was one level lower than the highest level they could evaluate correctly. The implication is that composition adds one unit of processing load at some point where it interferes with inferencing. Possibly this finding is only applicable to the young ages studied. As was reported in Chapter 4, around the ages of 8 to 10 children begin formulating language during pauses in writing. This might enable them to handle inferencing and writing problems serially rather than simultaneously, thus reducing the processing load.

Some striking findings on the relation between information-processing capacity and ability to handle content constraints have been obtained by Tetroe (1984). Tetroe had students compose stories that would culminate in designated sentences. The ending sentences were designed to vary in the number of constraints they imposed on the plot of the story. An example of a three-constraint ending is:

> That's how Melissa came to be at the laundromat with a million dollars in her laundry bag.

A five-constraint version of the same theme is:

> That's how Melissa came to be at the wrong laundromat with a million dollars in her laundry bag and a trail of angry people behind her.

(Tasks were counterbalanced so that students did not write twice on the same theme.) The information-processing capacity of students was independently estimated by memory-span tests. Each student wrote four stories, with the number of constraints ranging from one less than the student's estimated capacity to two more than the student's estimated capacity. Figure 5.1 shows the average percentage of constraints met by students of different capacity levels on tasks with different numbers of constraints. Graphs for the three capacity levels all show a decline in performance as the number of constraints exceeds measured capacity. The point at which the decline occurs is one constraint higher for each additional unit of capacity. In Fig. 5.1(b), where the graphs are displaced horizontally to conform with hypothetical capacity, it is seen that the graphs for the three capacity levels are rendered virtually identical. This shows that the differences between groups are essentially entirely accounted for by the differences in estimated processing capacity. (Artifacts due to item idiosyncrasies are effectively ruled out as an explanation for these profile similarities: The items on which level-three students scored lowest are the same items on which level-five students scored highest.)

As described so far, these results provide strong support for the conformity of text composition to previously established parameters of information-processing demand and capacity. They show the same extraordinary symmetry found by Scardamalia (1973, 1975, 1977) on highly engineered combinatorial and control-of-variables tasks. But on these logic tasks, performance is generally near perfect when students are working on tasks that are below their measured capacity. By comparison, on Tetroe's composition tasks, *top* performance averaged only about 40%.

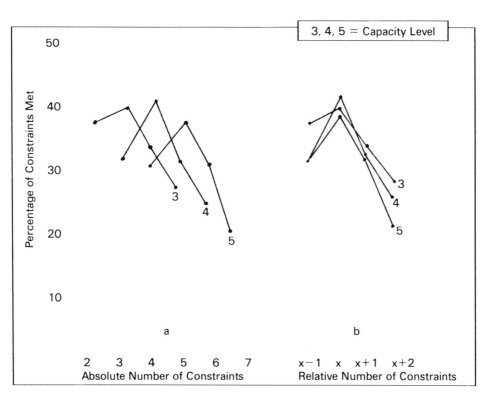

Figure 5.1. Percentage of ending sentence constraints met by subjects at three information capacity levels as a function of (a) absolute number of plot constraints imposed by ending sentence and (b) number of constraints relative to capacity level (x).

Postponing the question of what psychological factors could account for this attenuated performance, we may first ask how the performance displayed in Figure 5.1 could be accounted for formally. It will not do to hypothesize additional factors that add a constant amount to processing load. This would be inconsistent with the fact that performance drops off precisely where it was predicted to. It seems more promising to look for some independent factor that adds a large random element to performance. A physical model of such a situation would be the following: Imagine the task of throwing a ball through a very large frame. The frame is so large that it is almost impossible to miss. However, as the frame is moved increasingly far away, a distance is reached that begins to exceed the distance a person can throw. At that point, balls will start failing to go through the frame because they fall short. This phenomenon corresponds to exceeding a person's information capacity. The drop-off in performance will occur at different distances for different people, reflecting individual differences in the distance people can throw a ball. This would produce differential drop-off curves like those shown in Fig. 5.1(a). But suppose that the frame is covered with a grating such that a ball thrown at the grating has a 40% probability of passing through. This added factor should yield performance graphs that have both the same shape and the same level as those in Figure 5.1(b).

Speculation on what this *grating* factor might be must await further analysis.[16] For purposes of the present discussion, however, the main point is that it does not appear, on formal grounds, that such a "grating" factor would call for an alteration of ideas about processing load in composition. Tetroe's findings support the view that, even in a fairly high level of the composing process, processing load can be counted in subjective units, the same as in other mental tasks, and that people's capacities to handle processing load in composition are equivalent to their capacities as demonstrated on other tasks.

We have so far considered two kinds of units that figure in text processing—a phrasal unit that appears to be a common subjective unit in processing surface language and a content unit that serves as a chunk in processing text content. With respect to both kinds of units, the available evidence indicates that information-processing load and capacity for language tasks is in the same scale as that for other kinds of intellectual performance and reveals the same age norms for functional capacity.

Several cautions must be entertained, however, before we may rest easy with the conclusion that language performance may be treated the same as other kinds of intellectual performance. These cautions are as follows:

---

[16]Although the "grating" metaphor suggests a random factor, it should be noted that this does not suggest a random strategy on the part of the student.

1. What about other subjective elements involved in language, besides the two that have been considered?
2. What about the multi-level nature of language processing, which may require that the several types of units be processed in parallel?
3. What about the modularity hypothesis (Chomsky, 1980), which raises the possibility that the language-processing system may have a different set of parameters and possibly a different structure from the general cognitive system?

That there are other subjective units and that the ones discussed are only a kind of *average* (in the sense of qualitative descriptions of the "average" person), we have already acknowledged. Beaugrande's model (1984a) posits a unit larger than a content unit, a unit he calls the "idea." This is a complex unit in which both content and rhetorical strategy are condensed. Such a unit may figure in the composing process of expert writers, but not in that of novice writers. There may, on the other hand, be units that novice writers use but experts don't. Any attempt at an exhaustive categorization of the elements involved in text processing is bound to describe only an idealized average. Consequently, the only way we have of testing quantitative theoretical notions in language processing is to see whether, in cases where a meaningful average value can be calculated, the value corresponds to theoretical expectations. This seems to have been accomplished in the research reviewed here. This leaves untouched vast areas of performance in which it is not meaningful to predict or compute average values, but there is not much to gain by agonizing over this fact.

The question of parallel processing is an important one that present knowledge doesn't allow us to deal with. May not the person who is manipulating four content units in working memory be at the same time retaining four phrasal units and some other kinds of units as well that must either enter into the same linguistic decision or be held in readiness for the next step? This is certainly a possibility, although Kintsch and van Dijk (1978) offer a theory that allows multilevel text processing to go on with only a single working memory of fixed capacity. At present the best we can say is that whether or not a language task will exceed processing capacity appears to be a question that can be answered satisfactorily by considering separately the different levels of processing that might be involved. Whether this implies separate working memories, time-sharing, or something architecturally more esoteric can be passed over in the present discussion.

Much of the evidence we have brought forward showing that language performance is like other performance in respect to processing demand could be disputed by an upholder of the modularity hypothesis. The argument could be that if you give people memory tasks or problem-solving tasks that only incidentally involve linguistic material, then it is to be expected that they will handle these tasks not with the language faculty but by use of the general-purpose cognitive mechanisms normally employed for memory and problem-solving tasks. Thus it is not surprising that the same performance parameters emerge as with other mental tasks, but this tells us nothing about the architecture or capabilities of the language faculty.

Some observations do involve normal language behavior, however. Kintsch & van Dijk (1978) obtained results compatible with a working memory capacity of one to four chunks using a normal summarization task. In the next chapter we will present findings showing processing loads in the same range, based both on a laboratory-type sentence construction task and on normal school-writing assignments. It may be objected, of course, that in both cases the investigators knew they were looking for something in this range and would no doubt have found some way to reinterpret results that suggested, say, a working-memory capacity in the range of 10 to 40 chunks!

Available evidence on processing load, we are forced to conclude, has nothing to say one way or the other about the hypothesis of a separate language faculty—but the reverse is also true. In other words, there does not appear to be either any empirical or theoretical reason to suspect that the constraints working-memory capacity puts on language performance are of any different kind or degree from the constraints they put on other kinds of intellectual performance.

The reader may well have been prepared to believe this without much argument. We hope, however, to have made it clear that the issue is far from settled.

Minimum Requirements of Text Composition

In text composition, the mental activity that goes into developing the content of the composition is typically regarded as part of the composition process. This being the case, there is obviously no limit to how high the information-processing load of composition can be—except of course, for limits inherent in the capacity of the writer. The information-processing load of composition is at least as high as the load imposed by the most complex content problem the writer wrestles with in the course of composing.

If, therefore, we are to talk about the information-processing burden of writing in any sense that is not dependent on options of the writer, we must talk about some minimal processing load, sufficient for composition that just gets by—whatever that might mean. In this section we shall offer some provisional suggestions about what "just getting by" might mean in terms of composition and its information-processing demands.

The speculations that follow rest on the assumption that there are certain priorities in discourse processing and that when people are faced with overload dangers they will sacrifice performance on low-priority criteria in order to maintain performance at an acceptable level on high-priority criteria. (The human body is full of such back-up mechanisms to preserve vital functions when there is a threatened shortage of some essential resource, such as oxygen. We do not suggest, however, that there is anything innate about the back-up strategies we are talking about.)

In discourse production there seem to be two high and sometimes competing priorities: to produce sufficient language to fill the perceived social void and to maintain local coherence. The void-filling requirement includes such things as the need to forestall extended silences in conversation, the need to write a letter of sufficient length to substantiate one's regard for the receiver, and the need in a school composition to meet the teacher's expectation of effort as it is reflected in quantity. The local coherence requirement is the minimum requirement for upholding the presumption of competence. People whose utterances do not follow in any discernible way from their predecessors are judged to be distracted, drunk, senile, schizophrenic, or otherwise incapacitated.

We do not, of course, mean to imply that void-filling and local coherence are the central purposes of discourse production. It is simply that they are critical functions that, if they fail, result in the failure of most other functions as well. Consequently, the processing demand involved in meeting these top-priority requirements may be thought of as the basic processing demand of composition.

On the basis of efforts to infer information-processing complexity from children's compositions (details of which will be presented in the next chapter), we hypothesize that the minimal processing demand of sustained, locally coherent text composition is, for most genres, two chunks. This demand is critical at the point where a content unit has been expressed, and a next item of content must be selected. At that point it seems necessary to have available in working memory at least one chunked representation of the intention for the whole text (which may amount to nothing more than memory for the topic) and another chunk representing the preceding content item. If the first is absent, discourse will tend to wander away from the topic in an associative chain. If the second is missing, any of several things may happen:

1. A loss of local coherence, resulting in a series of content items each related to the topic but not to each other.
2. Perseveration, repeating past items or starting the discourse over from the beginning (common in inebriates).
3. Termination of the discourse (common in children who experience having exhausted their ideas on the topic).

An apparent exception to the two-chunk requirement is narrative composition. This is an inference based on reports that children as young as 5 or 6 can produce sustained and coherent narratives (Stein & Trabasso, 1982; Mennig-Petersen & McCabe, 1977). Because children of this age are found in other kinds of mental activities to have working-memory capacity to store only one chunk while carrying out another operation (Case, 1974), it should follow that it must somehow be possible to meet the minimal demands of narrative discourse with only this much processing capacity.

Exactly how it is possible to generate a well-formed narrative while holding only one chunk of information at a time in working memory is not clear. No doubt it depends on having a highly efficient discourse schema for narrative (Stein & Trabasso, 1982). In the case of personal-experience narratives, the structure of information in memory may ensure a schematic structuring of items recalled. It may then be necessary only to retain in short-term storage a trace of the previous item expressed in order to activate an appropriate next item. In fictional narrative the dynamics must be somewhat different but perhaps not fundamentally so. It may be that the memory schema for a story episode is so strong that as the child thinks of story ideas they are promptly encoded into long-term memory in a story framework. Accordingly, telling an impromptu invented narrative would be similar to recalling a narrative and would demand only enough working-memory capacity to ensure orderly recall. In trying to explain the coherence of narrative in young children, we should also not ignore the power of the schema in the mind of the listener. People may be so efficient at story comprehension that they are able to form a coherent macro-structure out of much more disconnected material than they are able to comprehend in other genres.

Texts that meet the requirements of sustained local coherence may be thought of as the textual equivalent of small talk, which has similar requirements (Schank, 1977). Small talk, too, probably takes up one or two chunks of working-memory capacity, depending on whether the speaker is relating an anecdote or dispensing facts and opinions. This would explain why small talk is often boring to generate as well as to listen to; it takes up only a portion of available mental capacity yet interferes with using the spare capacity for anything else. We have the impression that school writing assignments are often boring to students for the same reason. Far from straining the limits of information-processing capacity, perfunctory execution of school assignments may be too far below limits to sustain motivation.

As soon as the writer aspires to something beyond minimally adequate text, however, the processing demands of composition can mount rapidly. These additional processing demands may arise from the addition of rhetorical constraints (the composition must be interesting, convincing, original, etc.) or from demands for deeper processing of content, as in critical analysis, synthesis of ideas, or solution of problems discovered in the content.

The knowledge-telling strategy may be regarded as a model of minimal two-chunk composition. Models of minimal performance have an important part to play in the development of text-processing theory, we believe. They allow us to see whether we can account for performance at all within recognized limitations of the cognitive system. If we cannot, then it is likely that our more elaborate models, describing expert performance, are mere metaphors—aids to discourse about discourse but not theories in any serious sense.

CONCLUSION

Although our examination of processing demands in text composition leaves many loopholes and loose ends, we believe that it has arrived at some conclusions. We find that, in spite of formidable obstacles, empirical observations can be made on the information-processing load of language tasks. Language tasks, according to these observations, appear to conform to the same principles as other mental tasks with respect to the size and nature of information-processing capacity and demand. Whereas the processing demand of text processing can run very high, its minimum demand takes up half or less of adult information-processing capacity. It thus appears that under normal circumstances people should have a substantial amount of spare information-processing capacity to allocate to higher-level goals of text processing.

This conclusion has an important bearing on instruction. The prevailing belief in the high processing load of composition has led to the assumption that novice writers will profit from being guided toward load-reducing strategies (cf. Flower & Hayes, 1980b). Although such strategies are undoubtedly an asset to all writers, it may be that where novices most need help is in learning profitable ways to put unused processing capacity to work. Research by Bereiter & Bird (1985) and by Palincsar & Brown (1984) in teaching reading comprehension strategies points to a similar conclusion.

Chapter 6
How Children Cope
with the Processing Demands
of Coordinating Ideas in Writing

*"I have all my thoughts in my mind
but when I come to a word I can't
spell it throws me off my writting."*
— *Tenth-grade student*

PREFACE

In the preceding chapter it was suggested that a minimum requirement for coherent expository writing was holding two mental elements in mind while generating a third. In terms of the knowledge-telling model presented in Chapter 1 this would mean holding two cues in mind while searching for a next item of text content—for instance, holding in mind two topical cues, one topical cue and one structural cue, one structural cue and another drawn from text just produced, or some other combination of two cues. Obviously this is a far cry from holding in mind all the information relevant to choice of a next item of content. What kind of text would result from such a limited sampling of relevant information? What difference would it make if the writer held three items in mind instead of two? Or what if the writer held only one cue in mind while searching for the next thing to say? The present chapter reports text analyses aimed at answering these questions.

This chapter focuses on the ideas expressed in children's texts, but not on what those ideas are nor on how they are expressed. Neither is it simply on how many ideas are expressed—for that may be mainly a matter of persistence. Instead, the focus is on how many ideas the child has been able to coordinate into a single point or argument. Coordinating a greater number of ideas does not lead straightaway to a superior composition. As we shall see, some of the rhetorically most successful compositions drum home a single idea but do it eloquently. On the other hand, some of the more complex coordinations of ideas are delivered in a stumbling fashion—partly, we imagine, because the writer's ideas are evolving during the course of writing.

A major reason for being interested in processing-load constraints on idea coordination is the bearing that this may have on people's ability to adopt a knowledge-transforming as opposed to a knowledge-telling approach to writing. The conclusion reached in the present chapter is that, although fluent and reasonably coherent writing can be achieved by coordinating only two ideas at a time, the knowledge-transforming potential of writing is not fully realized until four ideas at a time can be coordinated.

6

This chapter examines how children at different levels of writing development cope with problems associated with coordinating content ideas. For mature writers idea coordination is probably the overriding challenge of expository writing, yet its development has received little attention in the research literature.

The ability to coordinate ideas has great developmental significance. The ability to coordinate one's own perspective with that of another marks, in Piagetian theory, the transcendence of childish egocentrism (Piaget, 1926); the ability to consider two criteria simultaneously opens the door to cross-classification (Inhelder & Piaget, 1969); and the ability to coordinate weight and distance underlies the logic of proportionality requisite for formal solutions to balance problems. This growing ability to coordinate concepts is illustrated by judgments in balance problems. The child's judgments are initially based on weight (or distance from the fulcrum) alone. Next, the child considers distance and weight factors simultaneously. If weight leads to the judgment that one side of the balance will go down while distance leads to the opposite conclusion, the child cannot resolve the dilemma. Finally the child resolves such dilemmas by coordinating both weight and distance on both sides of the fulcrum (Siegler, 1976). Much of the story of cognitive development may be construed as taking progressively more variables into account during single acts of judgment (Bachelder & Denny, 1977a, 1977b; Case, 1978b; Pascual-Leone, 1969, 1970).

Thus it seems reasonable to expect children's developing expository abilities to show developmental patterns similarly based on increments in information coordinated simultaneously. The ability to coordinate ideas at increasingly complex levels may well underlie advances such as: (a) movement from loosely connected to tightly connected discourse (ability to coordinate increasing numbers of related ideas); (b) movement from unelaborated to elaborated discourse (ability to coordinate increasing numbers of successively reported ideas without straying from the intent of the communication); (c) movement from a single-argument thesis defense to defense that anticipates counter arguments (ability to coordinate an increasing number of reasons bearing on a position); (d) movement from single-episode narration following a chronological sequence to narration with several sub-plots (ability to coordinate increasing numbers of related events within a common thematic structure); and (e) movement from egocentric, non-communicative to decentered, audience-oriented prose (ability to coordinate different points of view).

The emphasis in this chapter is on the cognitive demands associated with the coordination of increasing numbers of ideas in writing. We are not here concerned with the cognitive demands of syntax or vocabulary—the linguistic devices by which such coordinations are expressed. High-level coordinations of ideas can be achieved through several simple sentences or through a single complex sentence. Likewise, complex thoughts can be conveyed with a relatively sophisticated or unsophisticated vocabulary. Examples of children's writing show that they often fail to coordinate ideas when it is safe to assume they have the linguistic competence to express the coordination, and they sometimes produce coordinations without using adult-like linguistic devices. Research in the development of writing abilities has typically focussed on children's acquisition of the linguistic devices for expressing ideas (Hunt, 1965; Loban, 1976; Mellon, 1969; O'Hare, 1973). While use of these devices is inevitably correlated with the final writing achievement (O'Hare, 1973), the use of various linguistic devices is never the end of writing development. This study is an attempt to get closer to the end of writing development—to the attainment of complex coordinations of ideas.

To determine children's level of ideational coordinations in writing, two tasks were presented singly to children at different ages. These tasks exemplify ways in which writing can require the coordination of ideas at increasing levels of complexity. The first task was a simple matrix task for which children were instructed to convey in writing the information contained in the four cells of the matrix. Information in each cell could be conveyed without reference to information in any other cell, or it could be conveyed by interrelating that content with any or all of the other three cells. The second task was one in which children were asked to defend a thesis. Here children could discuss a single point of view or could incorporate opposing viewpoints at varying levels of complexity. The method adopted in this research involved characterizing children's performance as *Level 1, Level 2,* and so on, according to the number of content schemes they appeared to be able to coordinate in these writing tasks. A characterization of a child as Level 1 does not mean that the child is judged incapable of attending to more than one content scheme at a time. The child may well have additional attentional capacity deployed elsewhere. What a Level 1-classification means is that, however much attentional capacity the child might deploy altogether, his writing exhibits attention to only one idea at a time. Thus, we examine writing to determine how many idea units the child has explicitly related and, hence, coordinated.

Our classification system follows Pascual-Leone's lead in defining different levels of task difficulty according to the number of mental units coordinated simultaneously (Pascual-Leone, 1969, 1970). As in Pascual-Leone's studies, the number of figurative schemes (or units of task content) that students coordinate in a single mental operation is the basis for classification. However, we have not attempted a step-by-step reconstruction of the child's thinking process. Rather, we have chosen to analyze those expressed ideas that had to be taken into account simultaneously to produce the most complex idea-coordination displayed in a child's writing. Different levels of idea-coordination are then analyzed to determine what these different levels might tell us about developing writing abilities.

CONVERTING MATRICES TO SENTENCES

The first task was one in which the information to be communicated in writing was provided to children in the form of a matrix. An example is presented below.

The children were taught how to read matrices and then were instructed to write a paragraph or sentence containing all of the information in the matrix. The matrix was in front of the child throughout the writing task.

	STATE	
	Michigan	California
Climate	cool	warm
Fruit Crop	apples	oranges

(left margin label: AT HARVEST)

The matrix task was designed to fulfill two purposes: (a) to provide discrete units of task information that could be combined at any chosen level of complexity, and (b) to provide information in as language-free a manner as possible, thereby minimizing external influences on the child's attempted integrations. Differences in levels of complexity were determined by analyzing the relationships the child made among the independent cells.

In the description of matrix tasks, and of other tasks to follow, the terms *figurative scheme* and *unit of task information* are used interchangeably to denote chunked bits of information. In the matrix task information from a single cell (including row and column labels) constitutes a chunk (e.g., "In the State of Michigan the climate is cool").

At the lowest level of integration (Level 1) the writing lacks integration. For example:

> In the state of Michigan the climate is cool. In the State of Michigan the fruit crop is apples. In the state of California the climate is warm. In the State of California the fruit crop is oranges.

This writing sample is considered to be a Level-1 production because only a single unit of task information at a time is presented. There is no coordination of even highly related units of information.

At the next level (Level 2) two units of task information are integrated. For example:

> In Michigan the climate is cool *and* the fruit crop is apples. In California the climate is warm *and* the fruit crop is oranges.

Consider the first sentence. In order to avoid the redundant use of the phrase *In Michigan,* it was necessary to consider the information from two cells simultaneously. Similarly, in the second sentence the same type of operation was performed in order to avoid the redundant use of the phrase *In California.*

At the next level (Level 3), three units of task information are integrated. The products of the integration take at least two forms. First consider the following example:

> In Michigan the climate is cool *so* their fruit crop is apples. In California the climate is warm *so* their fruit crop is oranges.

The form of the first sentence suggests more than an appreciation of redundant information. It suggests an appreciation of the cause-effect relationship between climates and crops. This cause-effect relationship itself is assumed to be a scheme that is used in the integration process. By integrating the *cause-effect* scheme with the two schemes from the Level-2 operation the child achieves this more advanced Level 3 operation. It could be argued that this seemingly higher-order integration is more an indication of what the child knows about the relation between climate and crops than it is an indication of processing capacity. To be sure, the relevant information must be available in order for the child to integrate it, but that does not alter the fact that the successful use of such information depends on a Level-3 integration. We find the same pattern in matrices from a variety of content areas, and we find children successful on Level-2 integrations but not on Level-3 integrations (e.g., they say "In Toronto in winter it is cold *but* they drink hot chocolate" rather than "*so* they drink hot chocolate"). Still, experimentation with artificial information allowing for the control of knowledge factors would obviously be an asset to research with matrix tasks.

A second form of Level-3 integration was generated from the following matrix:

		HARVEST	
		March	September
COUNTRY	Canada	Wool	Wheat
	Australia	Wheat	Wool

The protocol representing the Level-3 integration is:

> In September Canada harvests wheat and in March we harvest wool. But in Australia they harvest wool in September and harvest wheat in March.

With the exception of the word *but* we have two Level-2 constructions. The redundancy in each sentence suggests that the child has considered the season-crop relationships for each country independently. Yet the conjunctive word *but* implies that he has discovered that similar things happen at different seasons in the two countries. Thus he has discovered an additional unit of information which he proceeds simultaneously to integrate with the specific details of conditions in the two countries.

Finally, at the Level-4 integration, the information from each of the four cells has been considered simultaneously by the child. For example:

> In Michigan's cool climate they harvest apples but with California's warm climate oranges may be grown.

The child here appears to have integrated all four units of information from the table into a single relational structure. Such an operation is of the same order as the proportionality operation already studied by Piaget (Inhelder & Piaget, 1958): cool is to apples as warm is to oranges. At this level, relationships between relationships are formed. In keeping with expectations from both Piagetian and neo-Piagetian research (Pascual-Leone, 1969), this type of construction was found in seventh-grade protocols but not in fifth-grade protocols.

It is important to appreciate that task difficulty is not inherent in any particular logical operation (such as subordination); rather, the difficulty inheres in the number of schemes that must be integrated in order to apply a particular operation in a particular task context. Evidence for this claim has been found with two different logical operations, those of implicative and combinatorial reasoning (Scardamalia, 1975, 1977). Loban's (1976) findings concerning subordination provide further support for this claim. Loban found the use of subordination in sentences such as "I have a cat *which* I feed every day" several years before he found it being used in sentences demanding the integration of particular concepts and a general idea, such as in the sentence "In Michigan it is cool *so* their fruit crop is apples." Our interpretation of this finding is that the use of subordination in the *cat-feeding* example implies a Level-2 integration at most. Cat and feeding co-occur with great regularity. Inferential reasoning is not needed to relate the two. One could even question whether two separate schemes are being coordinated; the child may simply be saying, "I feed the cat every day." At any rate the sentence indicates a less demanding operation than that involved in relating particular concepts (climate and fruit crops) with a general concept (cause-effect).

Furthermore, task difficulty is not inherent in the use of particular words. Although the use of a conjunction such as *notwithstanding* implies a cognitively more demanding integration than the use of *and*, single words can vary considerably in the processing complexity implied by their use. For example, the word *opposite* can be used to contrast simple states of events—fast-slow—or to contrast more complex events as in the following example:

In the country, Canada harvests wheat in September and wool in March while Australia's harvesting is the opposite.

Note another protocol on the same topic.

In Canada we gather wool in March while in Australia they are harvesting wheat. When we harvest wheat in September they are gathering wool!!

Both examples represent Level-4 productions since the information from all four cells of the matrix must be coordinated to appreciate the direct time reversal of harvesting in the two countries. The first example shows greater embedding and greater vocabulary sophistication than the second, yet the latter succeeds in conveying the same level of cognitive complexity through what is essentially an oral-language device. The double exclamation point at the end of an otherwise neutral sentence indicates the contrast with the preceding sentence, as does the child's use of pronouns *we* and *they*.

Level-2 integrations can look quite different for different matrices. For example, if the above Michigan-California matrix is altered to increase redundant information, then a four-cell matrix might be treated like a two-cell matrix. Consider the following matrix and sentence:

	Michigan	Ontario
Climate	cool	cool
Fruit Crop	apples	apples

"In Michigan and Ontario the climate is cool and the fruit crop is apples." This sentence, although it combines all the information in four cells, can be produced by a series of two-scheme coordinations: (a) combine "In Michigan it is cool" with "In Michigan they grow apples" to obtain "In Michigan it is cool and they grow apples" (This is the same two-scheme coordination discussed above); (b) by a similar two-scheme coordination, obtain "In Ontario it is cool and they grow apples;" (c) combine the two (identical) main clauses into one clause; (d) combine the two prepositional phrases into one compound phrase; "In Michigan and Ontario."

What about the phrase, "In *both* Michigan and Ontario..."? It seems likely that this slight refinement involves a three-scheme integration.

PROBLEMS IN DEFENDING A THESIS

Above, we considered levels of achievement on a writing task with a controlled format and short responses. Below we attempt a comparable delineation of successive achievements within the less controlled format of children's essays. In this essay task children were asked to write for 15 minutes on the topic "Should students be able to choose what things they study in school?" In reviewing the protocols of these children it became obvious that staying on a topic was an achievement in itself. Accordingly, we have assumed that the topic is a figurative scheme that must be coordinated with others.

Level 1. The effort to isolate Level-1 behavior began with an attempt to imagine the consequences for writing if one were unable to coordinate two units of task content purposefully. It seemed reasonable to assume that under such conditions a child would fail to elaborate on the topic, or would engage in disconnected discourse, or would engage in connected discourse (rather like story-telling) that strayed from the topic. While there may be other consequences, these were the ones initially considered. A great number of the above consequences appeared in the protocols. An example of disconnected discourse, or possibly a failure to elaborate, is the following (in this as in all subsequent examples in this chapter, children's spelling and punctuation are preserved):

> In School We Should Be Able To Do Any Kind Of We Want To Do We Are Free We Could Do Anything We Want God Us Free We Could Do Anything We Want To Do I'd Like Spelling And Math In School We Should Do It Any Time We Want.

The following two examples represent connected discourse that strays from the topic.

Should Students Be Able Choose What Things They Study In School.
Yes I think we should. Because some subjects are hard like math. And because the teachers give us a page a day. I think the subjects that we should have is Reading. Because that is easyest one. I think we should't have math, science and social studies. Because in social studies and science we have to write up notes and do experments. I think *math* is the *worst* subject. And I *hate spelling* to. Because in spelling there are so many words to write and they are all *hard.* And they waste my time. I think school shouldn't be to 3:45. I think it should be to 2:00. I think school is *too long.*

Spelling
Spelling is my subject because I like it because it is fun to do it, and right after one lesson I can go on to another lesson. Spelling sounds exciting, to me because I can get high marks, and when I have Spelling tests, I get high marks like: 25 out of 25, and 24 out of 25, and those look like good marks to me.

In writing the second protocol above it appears as if the child carried out a chain of operations, but that these operations did not require the simultaneous coordination of two schemes. The child begins with a figurative scheme representing his interpretation of the topic, generates a related idea, and writes it down. The first idea serves as inspiration for the second, but the two are not integrated; the first merely triggers the second. Since the child does not hold both the topic and subsequent idea in mind, the next thought likely will be inspired by whichever of these two schemes is more salient, although it is also possible that a salient but completely unrelated thought will enter.

In the first protocol above the child's thinking seems to be dominated by the idea *we should be free* (which presumably was inspired by the topic). He continually returns to this idea and in so doing fails to effect sequential coordination of ideas. The result is discourse that appears disconnected. It could also be argued that the child never returns to the topic because he never strays from it, in which case what he has written would better be classified as failure to elaborate (i.e., fixation on one idea). In either interpretation, it seems clear that the child is not coordinating information.

The two examples just given of connected discourse that strays from the topic represent the most typical kinds of Level-1 production. If the child does not apply the requisite integrative capacity, then it seems inevitable that attempts at elaboration will result in losing hold of the topic. We suspect that the child's productions at this level are controlled by some affective scheme. That is, the child hits on an emotionally charged content scheme that triggers a host of associated memories. Mennig-Peterson & McCabe (1977) have shown that with 3- and 4-year-olds an affectively laden scheme such as a bee sting can produce detailed memories of past events that children elaborate rather coherently. Within Pascual-Leone's theory of constructive operators (1970), such results would be classified as "A-boosted". That is, only one affective scheme, the one serving to cue relevant memories, is involved, and no attentional effort is required to keep it activated. Such a scheme would explain how young children can produce such elaborated constructions around some topics while not being able to do the same with others (i.e., with ones that fail to spark personal associations).

In both examples above the child failed to hold onto the topic presented. But that topic seemingly has cued more relevant associations for each child, and these cued associations carry the child through to the end of the paragraph. In the first example there is some sense of topic maintenance, but only at the beginning. In the second example there is no sign of a return to the question that inspired the discourse. Bereiter (1980) has labelled this kind of production *associative writing*.

In terms of the knowledge-telling model, Level-1 coordination in writing means that retrieval of content items is cued by the main topic or by some previous item but not both. In narrative writing, such a process could generate a coherent event sequence (in that one thing leads to another) but the story would have a point only in those cases where there was an affectively boosted high-point that continued to cue retrieval without demand-

ing sustained attention. In expository writing, however, the result would almost always be incoherent in one or another of the ways we have illustrated.
Level 2. Coordination of two figurative schemes permits purposeful subordination and coordination of ideas. However, Level-2 coordinations do not permit two consecutive ideas to be interrelated and simultaneously placed in proper relation to the topic. Consider the following example:

> Should children choose what they want to study on? Do you think children should choose what they want for social studies? I do. Because, would you like to study on something you don't like? Would you like to study on Brazil or Peru? Would you like to study on these countries?! Or other countries that are almost unknown to mankind? No. Not I. Who would suffer? We would if we had to study on countries like Brazil and Peru? No! We would only find half as much as is know to man! No! We shall not suffer on this case!! No we won't. Who, tell me who, would like to study on a country almost unknown to mankind?! Almost no one! Only a few! I wouldn't do it! Not at all! We won't suffer doing this. In fact we won't do it at all! Will we?! No! We won't do it!!
>
> Thank you

Notice the continual return to the topic (as somewhat redefined by this child) of freedom from the oppression of set curricula. According to the theory put forward here, a child working at this level cannot both interconnect consecutive sentences and simultaneously place them in proper relation to the topic; the child must either develop the current idea *or* connect the current idea and the topic. The child in the present case seems to have alternated between these choices, first developing his Brazil-Peru idea to include the whole host of "countries almost unknown to mankind," then dropping that line and returning to the theme of combating oppression. He runs through this two-unit cycle twice and then ends.

An interesting additional phenomenon is suggested in the above protocol. The child seems to display a sense of audience, in that he addresses the reader. Sense of audience minimally demands the coordination of two points of view, one's own and another's. Thus the appearance of such behavior is consistent with a Level-2 analysis. Note, however, that it is the child's tone, not his content, that conveys a sense of audience. His content actually ignores the great mass of people who are enchanted by unknown places. It seems likely, therefore, that the child's audience-related stance is another affect-laden scheme—a sort of oratorical wrath—that sustains itself without attentional effort, lending a unified tone to the essay but contributing nothing to the coordination of ideas. Since, at Level-2, processing capacity is taken up with coordinating pairs of ideas and staying on topic, we would not expect additional sentence adjustments aimed at meeting specific audience needs.

Since connected or consistent discourse itself implies awareness of another point of view (the point of view that contradicts the one to be presented) and since a sense of audience likewise implies awareness of another's perspective, it is reasonable that both behaviors should appear, in rudimentary form, at Level 2. It may be the case, however, that extended *and* consistent elaboration actually demand the active rejection of ideas from the opposing perspective—in which case we would not expect extended elaboration to appear until Level 3. Obviously, a good deal of research is needed to determine the relationship between processing demands and adjustments to other points of view.

The next protocol illustrates another Level-2 performance with a different structure from that of the previous example:

> ### Should Students Be Able to Choose What Things They Study in School.
> Students are very sneaky and lazy. Most children would probably choose recess all the time but I still think that it is good. Only is it good though, if the subjects are limited to 4 or 6 things such as Reading, Math, Social Studies Science, art or French. The students though, would probably all ways pick art and not get work done . . .

Here the dominant idea seems to be that students are lazy and that given choice they would not act responsibly. Yet the author wishes to defend the idea that students should be allowed to choose their school subjects. While the author appreciates that the two ideas he has presented are contradictory (a Level-2 ability), he cannot resolve the conflict, so he is left with a pair-wise comparison of ideas that does not further his position. He seems to need some third scheme to break this set, or alternatively to give up one of the two ideas and concentrate on the other.

Level 3.   By virtue of coordinating three figurative schemes simultaneously, preplanning—holding onto the topic while also holding two unwritten thoughts in mind—is made possible. An example of a Level-3 production indicating such qualities follows.

> I think you should not be able to choose you own things to study because of a lot of reasons. The first reason is that some kids might pick easy subjects to learn. Also because I wouldn't know what to learn about it, or write about. I think it alright

for projects to do at home to pick a subject but not at school. If you they were to pick there own book for reading theyed propely pick the easiest one there. For math they would propely just do grade one and two work, and not learn any new things. School won't be like school if you picked your own subject.

The phrase, *because of a lot of reasons,* reflects a kind of thinking ahead that seems to require integration of at least three schemes—the topic and at least two supporting ideas. (Even the rhetorical use of the phrase *because of alot of reasons,* while perhaps not tied closely to the child's thinking, suggests pre-planning exemplary of Level-3 productions). After the phrase *for alot of reasons* the writer proceeds to present two ideas in coordinate form: *The first reason . . .* and *Also. . . .* Accomplishing this should likewise require integration of three schemes. To preserve the parallel structure signalled by the word *also* in the second supporting point, the writer would have to hold in mind the second point and the thesis, as well as the first point with which the second point must be placed in coordinate relation.

After the second supporting point the coordinate structure breaks down. The writer holds on to the topic and does not repeat herself, but she begins stating points that are subordinate to other points already made (such as *If they were to pick there own book . . .* which appears to elaborate upon the first point, *that some kids might pick easy subjects to learn*). The coordinate structure, however, probably could have been maintained if the writer had possessed an executive strategy for testing coordinate structure. Then it would have been sufficient to hold in mind the topic and the new sentence under consideration, while comparing the new sentence with sentences already written. But lacking such a sophisticated bit of rhetorical knowledge, as we presume to have been the case, the writer could have maintained a coordinate structure only by simultaneously considering all the points previously made. Given a Level-3 solution, we should expect this effort to break down just where it did.

The concluding sentence in this example shows another kind of integration not found in the productions of lower-level students. This summary sentence appears to show a three-scheme integration, uniting the conclusion with the thesis and also with what may be called the tenor of the intervening content.

MATCH AND MISMATCH
BETWEEN TASK AND CAPACITY

The complexity of writing tasks is to a large extent determined by the writer. This was evident in the protocols examined in the preceding section, where expressing a position on an issue was implicitly defined by different children as anything from a free-association task to one of considering alternative positions.

The possibility exists that a child may attempt to construct text at a level of complexity that is beyond her capacity, and consequently will produce an objectively unsatisfactory piece of writing. For instance, a child functioning at Level 1, and thus capable, under the right conditions, of producing a reasonably comprehensible series of expressive statements, may set out to produce a thesis supported by a reason, fail to produce a reason that relates to the thesis, and thus produce an anomaly like, "Yes, Richard was cruel because they were all Danes" (quoted from Collis & Biggs, 1976). At a higher level, a child may attempt to produce a thesis, a supporting fact, and a qualification to the supporting fact (calling for Level-3 integrative abilities), but fail to see that the qualification undermines the thesis. Thus, again, the child produces an argument that seems inferior to what she would have produced if she had stuck to a lower level of task complexity—to giving only a thesis plus supporting facts, for instance. Note that these failures, if one is to call them that, are not linguistic failures. On the contrary, the child will often have used a mature syntactical form but filled it with unsuitable content.

If the limitation is primarily a cognitive one, it is reasonable to ask how children can set themselves cognitive tasks that are too complex for them. Isn't the setting of the task itself evidence of a higher level of processing? The answer to these questions probably depends on the conditions under which the child is writing. A likely possibility is that a child who sets himself a Level-3 writing task and then deals with it by Level-2 processing is usually a child who under more facilitative conditions could process information at Level 3. For most children writing is not a situation that facilitates cognitive processing, and so we frequently find children tackling writing tasks that they are unable to handle.

In the following discussion, protocols are characterized as, for instance, *Level-2 task, Level-1 performance.* The level of the task is defined by the level of processing that would be required to coordinate the ideas set forth or implied in the protocol. The level of performance is judged, as in the preceding section, by the complexity of the coordination actually achieved. **Level-1 Tasks.** Since children at Level 1 do not successfully coordinate figurative schemes, an obvious way in which they can avoid inconsistencies is by simply not elaborating on their statements. Thus a successful Level-1 attempt would be one in which the student simply presented a position with no support. The following example illustrates a Level-1 task with Level-1 performance:

Yes I think we should be able to pick our own subjects.

This was one child's complete composition, and its brevity no doubt reflects lack of motivation as much as rhetorical strategy. Be that as it may, it does show that by sticking to a level 1 task the child has successfully avoided inconsistencies. A Level-1 inconsistency is impossible because an inconsistency minimally implies an attempt to integrate two units of content—a Level-2 task.

Level-2 Tasks. In this example the child tries to provide support for his position, but the support statement is not successfully integrated with the position statement. The following is a Level-2 task: Level-1 performance:

No they should not be able choose what to study because sometime if there are subjects that are not very interesting and don't teach you a thing

Notice the attempt to use an *if-then* construction (*if there are subjects...*) in support of his position that students should not choose. Considering just the *if-then* construction (a two-unit coordination) it can be seen that the child failed to execute it successfully. Yet the simple deletion of the word *if* would yield the statement "sometime there are subjects that are not very interesting and don't teach you a thing," a perfectly reasonable support for the argument that students should be free to choose their own subjects. However, the child is trying to support the opposite position. So he has additionally failed in this two-unit position-support integration. Had the child simply stated his point of view with no attempt to elaborate it he would have been classified as successful at Level 1.

A successful Level-2 attempt to integrate position and support ideas is presented below as a Level-2 task, Level-2 performance:

I don't think students should be able to choose their own subjects because then they would pick some dumb topics like *shoes.*

The supporting information presented after the word *because* is perfectly comprehensible and consistent with the argument.

Level-3 Tasks. Children attempting Level 3 generally tried to integrate some qualification into their otherwise Level-2 position-support structure. Below is a Level-3 task, Level-2 performance in which the child succeeded with the position-support structure, but did not successfully integrate a qualification.

> Students should because some people are good in some sub-
> jects and others aren't. The others who aren't good might be
> good in different subjects, while still some are bad.

In her first sentence this child presents her position and a clearly relevant
supporting statement—a Level-2 performance. It is not clear what she was
trying to do in her second sentence—perhaps explain the connection between
her position and her supporting reason, perhaps elaborate on the reason, perhaps qualify it. In any event, the sentence is clearly not integrated with the
preceding two ideas; it is merely juxtaposed. The result is a statement that
is partly redundant, partly irrelevant, and that adds nothing to the argument.
Compare this performance with that of a child who succeeds in integrating a
qualification to his support statement in a Level-3 task, Level-3 performance:

> I think they should because it would be funner than dooing
> borring things. The students could probably get higher marks
> dooing something he wanted to than something borring but
> they could skipe an important lesson and go into life not
> knowing what it was. In a way it is good and in a way its bad. I
> think they should be able to choose some things, but there
> should be somethings they should study.

In this protocol we see a good example of thinking being carried out
through writing, something that becomes possible to a limited extent with
Level-3 processing. The child has stated a position and a supporting reason,
then seen a difficulty with the position and ended up by modifying his
position. Notice that the child has provided two supporting ideas for his
initial position in favor of free choice: it would be *funner* and students would
get higher marks. His integration of these ideas into one supporting argument itself suggests a three-scheme integration—the two ideas and the thesis,
combining to form the assertion that free choice would lead to higher marks
because of students' studying things that interested them.

Then comes a thought opposed to the thesis: *students might miss learning
important things.* It requires only a Level-2 process to recognize the conflict
between a thesis and an argument and thence, perhaps, to reverse one's
thesis. But in the present case the child does not reverse his thesis; he
modifies it to accommodate the opposing argument, and this kind of
constructive thought, we propose, minimally requires Level-3 processing.

When a child can consider simultaneously his thesis, his support for it,
and the opposing argument, he can appreciate the situation as a problem to
be solved; whereas, if he can consider only two of the three schemes at a
time, the best he can do is weigh the opposing arguments and come out for
or against his thesis. What *appreciating the situation as a problem* means is that
the output from evaluating thesis, support, and opposing argument simul-

taneously is a new scheme which constitutes a problem definition. The problem in this case seems to be: how to reconcile the thesis and the opposing argument. In applying a problem-solving strategy to this problem, at least three schemes must be handled simultaneously: the thesis, the opposing argument, and the tentative solution that is being tested for adequacy. Thus, with Level-3 coordinations we can see the beginnings of a knowledge-transforming as opposed to a knowledge-telling process. The effort to deal with opposing arguments rhetorically creates a problem that must be worked out in the content problem space, resulting in a modification of one's original opinion.

Level 3 coordinations are not quite sufficient to handle the complexities of knowledge transforming, however. In the example cited, the supporting argument is left out of consideration. The child, indeed, shows no evidence of recognizing that his modified thesis (allow free choice of some things, make others required) is at some variance with his original supporting argument, in that he would now have students required to study some boring things. To have searched for a new scheme that reconciled thesis, opposing argument, and supporting argument as well would, however, have required a Level-4 process.

Level-4 Tasks.   In the orienting sentence of the following protocol we see what appears to be a solution to problems surrounding freedom to choose subjects, a solution generated after having considered conflicting ideas. Thus the child seems to have anticipated opposing positions to an argument, unlike the above child who recognized a difficulty with his position after he had presented it. Yet on closer analysis we see that while the child anticipated opposing positions, she did not deal with them.

Level 4 Task, Level 3 Performance:

SHOULD YOU BE ABLE TO CHOOSE
WHAT THINGS YOU STUDY IN SCHOOL

This question really depends on the grade you are in (or you are taking.) If you are in elementary school, the subjects should not be *your* own choice, but (the teacher's and) the people who are working for the board of education. In this way, the subjects will give you an idea on, what you have to prepare, for your future and how well you are doing and also understanding them (the subjects). Junior High School's have the same idea as elementary schools, except for the more homework we receive and the work becomes much harder. The way the Junior High School's are organized is fine, in my opinion. We have a few subjects to choose from and that will be enough for us; (to choose from) since our option subjects are just for our entertainment and extra knowledge. I am very

pleased with my educational subjects and I think we should
leave our schooling programs the way it is.

The child's first sentence implies that she is going to coordinate two *if-then* clauses: *If you are in a lower grade then*... and *If you are in a higher grade then*... Coordination of two positions demands the simultaneous coordination of four units of task content. The demand is somewhat comparable to that for the highest level of achievement on the Michigan-California matrix problem discussed earlier in which the child has to work out a proportionality problem (i.e., a is to b as c is to d). But consider what the child does instead of working at this level. She takes one side of the question, the side dealing with children in lower grades. She claims, to paraphrase her, that if you are in elementary school then the board should have control. Having presented this two-unit *if-then* position, she integrates a third elaboration scheme (that this course of action will provide good training for the future). Now we expect her to follow through with the alternate *if-then* construction, implied in the introductory sentence, about conditions in higher grades that make the situation there different. But the child never deals with such ideas. She simply discusses how junior high school is rather like elementary school and that she likes it that way. Here we have an instance in which the language used leads to expectations of higher levels of integration than are actually employed.

Out of the 80 grade-eight protocols (grade eight was the highest grade tested) there was one example of a child successful at coordinating conjectures from both sides of an argument. Here is a Level-4 task, Level-4 performance:

SHOULD YOU BE ABLE
TO CHOOSE YOUR SUBJECTS
Chose is an important thing but a very tricky thing to fool with. I feel that chose of school subjects should be something that is done carefully. A young child given a chose would pick the easy subjects with no foresight into his future. But choose in his later years could be very important. To develop his leadership qualities. To follow and develop his interests and charictor to his fullest. So with these facts I come to the conclution that chose of subjects should not be given until about the age of fifteen. You can not condem or praise what you know little about. Until the age of choise a full and general cericulum should be given. It is not up to the school board to decide your life and until you are old enough to decide it is not your dission ether.

Seemingly, this child is able to take a single factor, *choice,* and work out complex relationships surrounding it. He, like other children, considered the fact that when you are young, you may not make very wise choices. But his method of coping with this factor is quite different from theirs. Other children figure out a way to eliminate factors problematic to their point of view. For example, one girl decides that parents should come into the picture in cases with young children, that parents of *those students* should talk it over with their child. She has simultaneously considered her thesis, an objection to it, and a solution to the objection (a three-unit integration). She therefore seems to feel justified in dismissing the age factor, and proceeds to deal with an unrelated problem. Other children simultaneously consider their thesis, an objection to it, and support for the objection. They thus lose hold of their original support of their position and switch to the other side of the argument. Whatever their course of action, the common feature of these three-unit integrations is that factors are considered one-by-one and a relevant scheme is dismissed rather than integrated.

In the above protocol we see the synthesis of opposing arguments. What clearly distinguishes this child from others is that he appreciates a dilemma surrounding the question of choosing subjects, an operation which demands a four-scheme integration. His introductory statement provides warning that there is no simple solution to the dilemma he sees: choosing is good (position) because choosing is educational (support); but choosing is bad (position) because young children cannot evaluate future consequences of choices (support). By coordinating these schemes simultaneously the child can regroup the four units and recognize that the position *chosing is good* is contradicted by the fact that young children cannot appreciate future consequences; alternatively, the position *choosing is bad* is contradicted by the fact that choosing is educational. The child therefore recognizes that neither position is acceptable and that a different position must be found. If the child has an alternative solution available in his repertoire (perhaps some stock solution such as *let's compromise* or *different people need different things*) this may be triggered by the child's appreciation of the dilemma. Otherwise the child will have to apply a problem-solving strategy.

Let us stop and consider how the present situation differs from that found in the Level-3 protocol in which the child came to grips with a problem. In that case the child gave attention to one thesis (that students should choose what they study), support for it, and an argument against it (that students might miss something important). He did not give attention to the contrary thesis that students should not choose their own subjects. Thus the problem he faced was that of reconciling his chosen thesis with the argument against it. In the present case the child gives attention to both theses and to the objections to each. Thus his problem is a more complex one. He does not have a chosen position but rather sees the question of curricular decision-making as an open one. He must, therefore, hold three things in mind while searching for a solution: the issue of curricular decision-making, the idea that young children are incompetent to choose, and the idea that choosing is itself an important educational activity. Holding these three ideas in mind while testing possible solutions against them constitutes a Level-4 task. From the protocol, it is impossible to tell whether the solution arrived at by the child (no choice up to age 15, free choice thereafter) came from such a Level-4 problem-solving process or whether it merely reflects a ready-made compromise or *split the difference* strategy that is elicited whenever a dilemma is perceived. In any event, the perception of the dilemma itself entails a Level-4 coordination of schemes.

This protocol is unique in another way. It does not stop with the proposing of a solution. The writer then goes on to consider the difficulty of who should decide what young children should study. He does not get very far with this problem (very likely because of time limitations). What he does do, however, is enough to illustrate the ability that is inherent in Level-4 performance to generate a coherent *line of thought*. If the preceding analysis is correct, it is only when one can consider four ideas simultaneously that one is in a position to sustain the dialectical process of thesis, antithesis, synthesis, new antithesis, and so on. It takes simultaneous attention to thesis, antithesis, and the supporting case for each to perceive the need for a synthesis, and it also takes a Level-4 process at the least to generate a novel synthesis.

POSTSCRIPT TO CHAPTER 6

Coordination of four ideas at a time was the highest level of performance observed in this study and in a follow-up study using the same kind of analysis (Bereiter & Scardamalia, 1978). We have not analyzed expert writing to see what the limits of performance might be. Using an analysis similar but not identical to the one used here, Yau and Bereiter (in preparation) found evidence of coordinations of five content units among high-achieving 19-year-olds. If current estimates of working-memory capacity are correct (Simon, 1972; Case, 1985b) we should not expect to see performance much above this level. Also, even if a writer produces more complex coordinations while thinking through an idea, the results are likely to be simplified down to a lower level so as not to overtax the information-processing capacity of the reader (cf. Hirsch, 1977).

Level-4 coordinations appear to be sufficient to sustain a knowledge-transforming process in writing. As we have seen, even Level-3 coordinations have some potential for transforming the writer's knowledge. But below that level of coordination, it would appear that knowledge telling would have to be the principal means of text production. Accordingly, we may take it that fostering a knowledge-transforming strategy entails boosting the level of idea coordination above level 2.

Table 6.1 shows the distribution of levels of coordination found in samples of elementary school writing by Bereiter & Scardamalia (1978). In both narrative and persuasive writing, Level-2 coordinations were the highest levels obtained by most students. Such descriptive data do not, of course, tell anything about causation. Do younger writers follow a knowledge-telling model of composing because they can only coordinate two ideas at a time in writing, or do they coordinate only two ideas at a time because they are following a knowledge-telling model that does not require any higher level of coordination?

Recently Margaret Yau has assessed idea coordination in a study comparing English lánguage compositions written by 15-year-old Canadian students who were native speakers of English and 15-year-old and 19-year-old Hong Kong students who were learning English as a foreign language. The 15-year-old Chinese students typically produced Level-2 coordinations, the 19-year-old Chinese students Level-3 coordinations. The 15-year-old Canadian students were

Table 6.1 Level of Idea-Coordination in Student Essays, by Grade and Text Type.

| Grade | Text Type | Level of Idea-Coordination | | | |
		1	2	3	4
3	Persuasive	11	19	0	0
	Narrative	13	17	0	0
	Descriptive	27	3	0	0
4	Persuasive	3	23	4	0
	Narrative	5	21	4	0
	Descriptive	20	10	0	0
5	Persuasive	0	24	6	0
	Narrative	1	14	11	4
	Descriptive	12	15	3	0

divided between these levels. Analysis of variance showed each group to differ significantly from the others. These results suggest that language was interfering with idea coordination, at least among the younger Chinese-speaking students. Although results reported in Chapters 4 and 5 have made it seem likely that language production does not add greatly to the information processing burden of composition, the present results indicate that it may have such an effect when the language is unfamiliar enough that it requires sustained attention. Similar results might accordingly be observed with native speakers whose dialects were so nonstandard that the production of standard written language required continual attention.

In current doctoral research Yau is experimenting with instructional treatments designed to lessen the effect of language interference in idea coordination. One treatment makes use of sentence-combining exercises aimed at providing syntactic means for handling complex idea integrations in English. The other uses procedural facilitations of planning (similar to ones described in Chapter 12). This study provides the first direct test of the modifiability of level of idea-coordination in writing. Both treatments produced significant gains in complexity of content integration, with the facilitation of planning producing the greater gain.

Part III
Perspectives on the Composing Strategies of Immature Writers

Much has already been said in earlier chapters about the composing strategies of young writers. Part III, however, comprises three chapters that deal specifically with these strategies, each from a different perspective.

In Chapter 7, the knowledge-telling strategy is dealt with from a broad educational perspective concerned with functional and dysfunctional ways in which students deal with knowledge. From this perspective knowledge telling is seen as a strategy for coping with school tasks, but one that undermines broader education purposes. Worse, by adapting to students' knowledge-telling tendencies, schools encourage persistence of these tendencies and create a learning situation that fosters "inert" knowledge.

In Chapter 8, composing strategies are viewed from the perspective of the development of planning abilities in writing. It is sometimes tempting to think of young writers as not planning at all. By eschewing "can they/can't they?" types of questions, however, and looking closely at what does go on when young writers are asked to plan, we can see that there is quite a complex development of planning abilities, even within the limits of a knowledge-telling approach to writing.

In Chapter 10, writing strategies are viewed within the larger context of text-processing strategies, which include strategies of reading comprehension and summarization as well as composition. Striking parallels to knowledge telling are found in other text-processing activities, thus strengthening confidence in the knowledge-telling model on one hand and on the other hand suggesting that it is but one reflection of a more pervasive way of dealing superficially with text.

Chapter 7
Knowledge Telling
and the Problem
of "Inert Knowledge"

PREFACE

This chapter sets forth an early version of the knowledge-telling model. The findings on which it was based have almost all been presented already in previous chapters. Thus, the model came about not from any particular new finding but from a sustained effort to make sense out of what had already been found. This effort, however, included not only studying the results of experimental studies but also studying several hundred thinking-aloud protocols from writers of different levels of skill. The guiding question was *what tasks are these writers actually trying to accomplish and what uses are they making of their knowledge in order to accomplish those tasks?* The realization that immature writers were using their knowledge in ways that left it little better integrated than it was before they committed it to text pointed to the larger problem that Chapter 7 addresses. This is the problem of the tendency of schooling to propagate "inert" knowledge—knowledge that is relatively inaccessible for any purpose other than stating it.

This chapter expresses a more severe view of the knowledge-telling strategy than we currently hold, denying it any value except as an academic survival strategy. As Chapters 1 and 14 indicate, we now see it as a serviceable strategy for much routine writing and as having some epistemic benefit as well. But subsequent research, such as that reported in Chapter 9, has also borne out our original sense that knowledge telling is more than a writing problem, that it has wide and serious implications for the way people acquire and use their knowledge.

7

Alfred North Whitehead (1929) decried what he called "inert ideas"—propositional knowledge that the student could express but not use. Whitehead declared that the central problem of all education was "the problem of keeping knowledge alive, of preventing it from becoming inert." His view of this problem was essentially a cognitive one; that is, he saw the problem as residing, not in the knowledge itself, considered epistemologically, but in the way this knowledge was represented in the student's mind. The "parroting" problem has long been recognized, the problem of students learning propositions by rote that were intended to be meaningful. But Whitehead saw beyond that to recognize that propositions could be comprehended and still constitute inert knowledge.

Whitehead took a large view of the sources of this problem, but mainly he found them in the fragmented character of the curriculum and the lack of active application, which together resulted in "the passive reception of disconnected ideas." In other words, Whitehead saw the problem of inert knowledge to arise from the way knowledge is presented to students and from the kinds of operations they are asked to perform on it. In this, also, Whitehead was in tune with contemporary cognitive notions. We think, in fact, that among educational philosophers Whitehead is particularly good reading for "cognitivists," because he shares their basic view, while considerably enriching and humanizing it.

Much of current cognitive research in education is serving to provide a theoretical basis for Whitehead's intuitions. Thus we are coming to understand more explicitly what connectedness and unconnectedness of knowledge mean psychologically and to know more about the effect that different kinds of processing have on the way knowledge is encoded and on its subsequent availability for use.

In this chapter, however, we want to go back to the "inert knowledge" problem and add a different dimension to it, one that Whitehead does not seem to have treated and that may have some novelty within the current scientific context as well. The dimension is a cognitive-developmental one. We want to suggest that children may early in their school careers develop certain cognitive coping strategies that prove to be powerful enough that they continue in force and override educational efforts to get students to encode knowledge in certain ways and to perform certain operations on it. Accordingly, efforts to solve the "inert knowledge" problem may fail if they deal only with how knowledge is presented to students and what they are asked to do with respect to that knowledge. Unless direct attention is given to the coping strategies children bring to knowledge-use tasks, those strategies may defeat instructional intentions.

EXPOSITORY WRITING AS A PARADIGM TASK FOR KNOWLEDGE USE

To say that knowledge is inert is to say that it is seldom put to use in those situations where it is potentially applicable. Research on "insight" problems (e.g., Duncker, 1945; Maier, 1930) revealed many instances of people failing to solve problems because some critical item of knowledge available to them was not brought into play. Although these special instances are relevant to the general topic, logic problems and concrete puzzle problems are not very good paradigms for everyday problems of knowledge use. They typically involve very small amounts of relevant information. Typically, moreover, the solver is forbidden to make unrestricted use of knowledge resources. In the familiar problem of getting cannibals and missionaries across a river in a small boat, for instance, it is quite out of the question to draw on one's knowledge of alternative means of crossing a river. We may describe problems of these contrived kinds as occupying knowledge-restricted problem environments. By contrast, real-life problems, of the kind to which we must attend if we are concerned about inert knowledge, are problems that occupy knowledge-unrestricted problem environments. The problem, that is, imposes no limits on the knowledge that may be brought to bear on it. Furthermore, the problem as encountered often gives little suggestion as to what knowledge may be relevant to solving it, and so the likelihood of solving it will depend much more on the characteristics of one's knowledge and of one's means for accessing it.

Ordinary real-life problems, such as deciding which candidate to vote for in a local election, open up vast areas of knowledge as potentially relevant. Identifying what knowledge is relevant and gaining access to it become an important part of real-life productive thinking. It is also characteristic of real-life productive thinking that the relevant knowledge is sufficiently diverse that it cannot be accessed efficiently by a top-down search. Thus, the knowledge relevant to deciding on a city council candidate is not all accessible by starting with one's highest-level knowledge about city government and working down until appropriate specific items of knowledge have been found. Some knowledge may be "filed" under politics, some under ecology, some under current events, and some may be episodic. Successful thinking will therefore require flexible access (Brown & Campione, 1981) to long-term memory stores. To the extent that people have fixed access, dependent on very specific cues, it will be difficult for them to make use of stored knowledge in coping in a flexible forward-and-backward manner with the kinds of mental tasks normally encountered in real life.

Most school tasks, however, do not pose the kinds of knowledge access demands that the tasks of everyday life do. Even when a test or homework assignment is high in Bloom's hierarchy of cognitive demands, its knowledge demands are generally confined to retrieving information dealt with in the particular course (fairness in grading more or less requires this). This knowledge, moreover, is likely to be organized in a way that facilitates search—if not organized hierarchically, at least organized into learning episodes that will have some logical sequence to them. One might go farther and say that the conscientious teacher *conspires* to see to it that there is a congruity between the way students encode knowledge on acquisition and the retrieval requirements of course assignments and tests. "Teaching for the test" is an epithet applied to going to the extreme in this effort, but testing for what was intended to be taught is considered a virtue.

At the end of this chapter, we speculate on the consequences of this affinity between encoding and retrieval in school instruction. There is, however, one kind of school task where this affinity is not so close, and where, accordingly, the knowledge-retrieval demands are somewhat closer to those found in out-of-school life. This is the task of expository writing, as represented in term papers, "projects," opinion essays, and other writing assignments that are not precisely bounded as to the range of knowledge that it is appropriate to draw upon.

Expository writing, if it is not simply a disguised recall task, is a good example of problem solving in a knowledge-rich domain. Consider the primary-grade Canadian child setting out to do a paper on Canada. The task space is knowledge rich in that the child has a wealth of potentially usable knowledge of many different kinds and may rapidly acquire more by "research." Given that, for a person growing up in Canada, *Canada* is such an inclusive concept that it would subsume a large part of the child's stored experience, a top-down search, with *Canada* as its starting point, is not likely to be adequate. Expert writers put much of their planning effort into elaborating constraints, setting subgoals, and, as composition proceeds, reevaluating and adding to these (Flower & Hayes, 1980a). However, because writing is also an "ill-structured" task, in which the end state is largely defined by the writer, one cannot say that the task *demands* forward and backward processing in the sense that missionary and cannibal problems do—in the sense that an inadequate executive strategy will with high probability lead to an impasse, halting progress short of the goal. Expository writing, like many other real-life tasks, may involve accessing varied stores of knowledge in the course of working forward and backward in relation to goals. But it is also possible to go at the task with simpler, forward-acting strategies, drawing only on spontaneously recalled (i.e., associatively cued) knowledge. The result will not be failure to reach a decision, but only a suboptimal decision that may nevertheless be sufficient.

Expository writing, therefore, is a normal school task that has about it many of the properties of everyday-life uses of stored knowledge. Study of children's composing processes provides insights into how accessible their knowledge is for use on such tasks and what kinds of strategies they employ for bringing it into use.

When knowledge access is studied in any practical context, the inquiry inevitably spreads across the boundary between memory and problem solving. This is inevitable because whenever the task environment does not provide sufficient cues for directing memory search, a person must carry out some intermediate analysis to determine what information is required, and this is by definition problem solving. Accordingly, in the discussion that follows, we do not presume to separate the problem-solving aspects of composition from the knowledge-access aspects, but instead will try to draw from the area of their overlap such insights as are particularly applicable to questions of promoting knowledge acquisition in school.

THE KNOWLEDGE-TELLING STRATEGY

The reader may have had an experience that both of us recall having had as students. In an essay examination, you discover that you don't have the knowledge necessary to answer one of the questions. Instead of leaving the question blank, you write down whatever you know about the topic of the question, even though it in no way constitutes an answer. When the examination paper is returned, you are surprised to find that your response received a middling mark, whereas you had expected at best a charity point or two.

From later experience as markers of examination papers, we can understand why such bluffing passes without condemnation. It is only doing deliberately what many students do unwittingly as a standard mode of response. They produce information that is on the topic and that is influenced by the form of the question, so that the response has a kind of genre appropriateness as well as topical appropriateness. But it doesn't answer the question; that is, it doesn't achieve the intended goal of explaining such and such, specifying the difference between this and that, or whatever the question might demand. Instead, it *tells what the writer knows* within a domain demarcated by key words in the question and by the question's general form. Accordingly, we call the strategy that gives rise to this type of response the *knowledge-telling strategy.*

We explicate a first-approximation model of this strategy and indicate how the strategy circumvents the difficulties of knowledge search described previously. The general phenomenon illustrated in examination writing has been recognized from other viewpoints. Flower's (1979) characterization of "writer-based" prose is compatible with the model we sketch. "Writer-based" prose, according to Flower, is dominated by the way knowledge is represented in the writer's own memory instead of being shaped to the needs of the reader who will be trying to take this knowledge up. Britton et al. (1975) have identified "expressive" writing as a kind of writing directed by internal needs and developmentally prior to "transactional" writing, which is writing directed toward external objectives. Similarly, Graves has noted what he calls "all about" writing, in which children record whatever information comes to mind about a composition topic (Graves & Giacobbe, 1982).

Analyses of thinking-aloud protocols reveal what poor writers don't do that expert writers do. Mainly, they do not, to nearly so great an extent as experts, elaborate goals or consider actions in relation to goals (Chapter 8; Flower and Hayes, 1980a). That much is certainly consistent with the brief characterization we have already given of a knowledge-telling strategy, but it leaves unanswered how such a strategy actually works.

In Figure 7.1 we present a rough model of knowledge telling. It leaves much unaccounted for, but it is a model in the sense that it describes a process that could generate products having the main attributes we see in examination papers and student essays. (See Chapter 1 for a more elaborate version of the model.)

The knowledge-telling strategy requires that two things be extracted from an essay examination question or writing assignment. One is a set of descriptors drawn from key lexical items in the assignment, and the other is information to guide the choice of a schema for the text to be produced. These schemata would be comparable to story grammar schemata, representing such discourse forms as explanation, thesis and defense, comparison and contrast, etc. Their precise nature need not concern us here, nor need we assume invariance across persons or genres. We do assume, however, that they provide general types of elements to be used in discourse, that some of these elements may be necessary and some optional, and that some may be reusable in the same discourse and some (such as concluding statement) may not be.

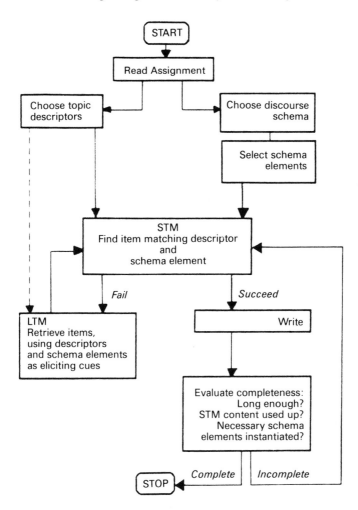

Figure 7.1. A model of the knowledge-telling strategy as applied in expository writing.

Discourse generation is set in motion when short-term memory (STM) is examined for an element that matches the selected schema requirement and the descriptor (or chunked descriptor set). One might suppose that at the start nothing would be in STM waiting to be tested. That may often be the case, but we assume (as suggested by the broken line in Fig. 7.1) a more direct route from descriptors to long-term memory (via the limbic system, perhaps) that may already have produced spontaneous recall of relevant material to STM. This would be especially likely if the descriptor happened to have emotion-laden associations. If, however, no match to requirements is found in STM, new items are retrieved from long-term memory (LTM). Both the descriptors and the schema elements will serve as cues for retrieval. (For evidence that schema elements can serve as cues for content retrieval, see Bereiter, Scardamalia, Anderson, & Smart, 1980; Paris et al., 1980). When an item has been found that matches both descriptors and schema element, it is translated into text, and the process repeats until the text is judged finished.

Figure 7.1 does not show what happens if search of LTM keeps failing to bring forth a matching item. Different recourses are available, and we have seen evidences of each one being used. One is to choose a new schema element. Another is to go back to the assignment and search for additional descriptors (Flower & Hayes, 1980a, note this as a common practice of novice writers when stuck). Yet another common practice is to mine what one has already written for eliciting cues.

On first inspection, it may not be obvious why this would be called a model of an immature or inadequate strategy. In fact, the strategy is adequate for many school tasks. It is well suited to writing assignments of the "What I Did on My Summer Vacation" or "An Interesting Character" type, and also to essay examination questions like the old college literature standby, "Discuss the use of such-and-such in the work of so-and-so." These are assignments in which key words, together with contextual clues as to the desired genre, are sufficient to make the model work. The model will work even better if the topic is one that evokes strong associations, or if the teacher has taken the trouble through prewriting activities to prime relevant stores in long-term memory. Then the ready flow of material to STM will ensure fluent and sometimes quite coherent and expressive writing.

As we indicated in Chapter 1 and will elaborate further in Chapter 14, the model fits a variety of observables parsimoniously and is not incompatible with any observations we are aware of. For purposes of advancing the present argument, we need not press the issue of the model's validity any farther than that. Accordingly, we proceed to the final section, where we treat this model as describing a disquieting type of school outcome.

THE ROLE OF KNOWLEDGE TELLING IN KNOWLEDGE ACQUISITION

Viewed pragmatically, the most interesting thing about the cognitive strategy depicted in Figure 7.1 is that it is virtually worthless for any purpose other than getting through certain kinds of school assignments. There are few instances in real life where telling what you know, within a few topical and discourse constraints, is called for. Sustaining small talk with a taciturn partner is one. Serving as a witness is another. Both instances are revealing, in that they involve suspending the usual purposefulness of discourse. In both cases the construction of personal meaning is superceded by subsidiary goals—in the first case the goal of fluency, and in the other case the questioner's goals. In all normal forms of discourse—and this applies to private mono-logue as much as to communicative expression—there is problem solving or goal directedness of some sort that requires that knowledge be sought and manipulated in ways that the knowledge-telling strategy does not provide for.

Whereas the knowledge-telling strategy is surely something for teachers of writing to be concerned about, it is not as a writing strategy *per se* that it seems most worrisome. It is more worrisome as a strategy that, if students use it "across the curriculum," may come to influence very broadly the way in which they manipulate and perhaps even the way they encode propositional knowledge.

The possibilities for a knowledge-telling strategy to have an effect on the actual encoding of knowledge are twofold. The first has to do with what is sometimes glamorously referred to as "language as a way of knowing" (Nystrand, 1977). When we think of knowledge stored in memory we tend to think of it as situated in three-dimensional space, with vertical and horizontal connections between sites (Wickelgren, 1979). Learning is thought to add not only new elements to memory but also new connections, and it is the richness and structure of these connections that would seem, as Whitehead said in his own way, to spell the difference between inert and usable knowledge. On this account, the knowledge-telling strategy is educationally faulty because it specifically avoids the forming of connections between previously separated knowledge sites. An intriguing extension of this idea comes from Gazzaniga and LeDoux (1978), who hypothesize that not all memory contents are internally connectable, so that the mind may have to form relationships among memory contents by observing their manifesta-tions in the integrated external behavior of the organism (see also Luria, 1973, p. 31). In other words, the way the mind gets to know itself is not altogether different from the way it gets to know other minds. To the extent this is true, expository writing and similar forms of expression potentially have an even more vital role to play in knowledge acquisition than even the most ardent advocates of the rhetoric of invention (e.g., Young, Becker, & Pike, 1970) have supposed. Knowledge telling, on this account, would be severely limiting to the growth of knowledge because it only externalizes mental content that already is easily amenable to internal connection.

The other way in which the knowledge-telling strategy may influence knowledge acquisition is through a social route. This is the route whereby the instructional system adapts to the cognitive strategies of the student rather than the reverse. (Presumably both kinds of adaptation must go on in any self-maintaining social system.) What we are suggesting, in brief, is that over the years school practices for presenting, reviewing, and assessing knowledge may have accommodated to students' cognitive coping strategies so that finally what is taught is what the knowledge-telling strategy is equipped to handle—and that is, precisely, inert knowledge.

Consider the following list of school practices, each quite justifiable in its own right, yet each of which in some way plays into the knowledge-telling strategy and quite inadvertently encourages its persistence:

1.   Testing only on content taught in the course.
2.   Reviewing by identifying superordinate categories of the specific items called for on the examination, thus priming those knowledge stores that will serve for knowledge telling.
3.   Presenting test items in an order corresponding to the temporal sequence of topics in the course, which is a boon to those who store course content episodically.
4.   Teaching concepts in hierarchically ordered fashion. (Who could object to this? But it does mean that recall cued by descriptors will suffice, without the need for goal-directed search.)
5.   Phrasing test items to specify the discourse schema, as in compare-and-contrast questions.
6.   Referring to course content by its temporal connections (what we studied last week, etc.).
7.   Assigning long course papers calling for assembling knowledge on a single topic such as women's rights, the Industrial Revolution, Captain Cook, etc. (Clearly an opportunity for integrating knowledge, but also an assignment tailor-made for knowledge telling.)
8.   Teaching topic outlining and procedures for putting content items on separate note cards and arranging them, which is valuable for some writers, but permits purely formal arrangements of items without need to have a goal.
9.   Assigning topics that "turn students on" and therefore provoke a ready flow of spontaneously recalled content.
10.   Using "prewriting" activities—films, discussions, interviews, and the like—to activate knowledge stores or provide fresh new knowledge for students to draw on in writing.
11.   Giving passing marks to students who don't actually address presented problems but who "show that they learned something in the course."

Let us repeat, these are all justifiable practices and some are virtually indispensable. Our only point is that they are all compatible with a knowledge-telling strategy. One would be hard put to come up with a comparable list of instructional practices that make it rough on students who use this strategy. Thus, it is not unreasonable to conjecture that these school practices have survived at least in part because they accommodate the cognitive coping strategies of students. But to the extent that school practices simply accommodate, they defeat their intended educational purposes and become practices for instilling inert knowledge.

One danger of attributing to children general coping strategies that defeat educational efforts is that it can easily slip over into blaming the child for educational shortcomings. When someone attributes to children a naive strategy for doing balance beam problems, there is no implication that the child really ought to know better. But when one attributes to them a general strategy that subverts teachers' efforts to confront them with intellectual challenges, then one is dangerously close to implying that children are mentally lazy and refuse to be educated.

We want to make it clear that no such implication is meant or endorsed. We see the knowledge-telling strategy being carried out by children who, as far as we know, have the best of intentions and think they are giving their best to the educational enterprise. They did not develop the knowledge-telling strategy as a way to avoid work but as a way to do work that, without such a strategy, would have been beyond them. Knowledge telling is not a conscious strategy and they have no reason or means to evaluate it. Because it goes on working, they go on using it; that's what one expects of adaptive organisms. But its effectiveness is all in the short run, whereas in the long run, it is bound to be a losing strategy. Children cannot be expected to know this, and so it is the responsibility of educators to know this and try to do something about it.

Chapter 8
The Development of
Planning in Writing

PREFACE

This chapter represents our most systematic look at what young writers do when they plan. It shows that there is a definite development over the elementary school years of planning as an activity distinct from text generation. Although changes between the ages of 10 and 14 are dramatic, they appear to take place within the general procedure described by the knowledge-telling model, rather than representing an outgrowing of it. This conclusion is brought home when, as is done toward the end of the chapter, planning protocols of children are compared with those of adults.

8 Writing permits and sometimes requires deliberate planning. Unlike the speaker, who must maintain a certain pace of discourse in order to hold the attention of an audience, the writer is usually free to give extended periods of time to reflection, both before and during writing. Also, because of the freedom that writing allows for revision, plans may alter or grow over successive drafts of a composition. On the other hand, speakers can use the rapid give-and-take of conversation to compensate for a lack of planning. A speaker can produce a hastily constructed utterance and rely on the ensuing interchange to clarify, alter, or enlarge upon the message. In written composition more is at stake in the document as it first reaches the reader. Consequently there is a greater need for the writer to plan a message so that it is understood and achieves its desired ends without further cycles of communication. Planning is also called for in order to handle the complexity and the quantity of ideas that go into a long composition. Flower and Hayes (1980a) recommend planning as a way of reducing the cognitive strain of writing without sacrificing attention to requirements of the task.

We do not wish to overstate the distinction between speaking and writing as far as planning is concerned. Certainly there are times in conversation when one must think out a statement carefully before uttering it. But such circumstances occur much more often with written communication. Similarly, there are times in writing when spontaneity has preference over deliberation—as in "expressive" writing, for instance (Britton et al., 1975), or in chatty correspondence with a friend—but these are more common in conversation.

It would be foolish to maintain that all writing must be planned. But it does not seem unreasonable to assert that good writers must be able to plan. Flower and Hayes (1980a) find, in fact, that expert writers can be distinguished from inexpert ones not only by the compositions they produce but by the amount and kind of planning they carry out.

In this chapter we address the question of how the planning process evolves. The available data might be examined for answers to questions such as Do young children plan?, How well?, How much?, and so forth. Questions of this type, though, are apt to turn on one's definition of planning, and hence to be ultimately unresolvable and not worthwhile. The approach we will take instead is to construct a developmental scenario, based on trying to understand what is actually going on in the minds of writers. The developmental scenario may be summarized as follows:

In the course of writing development, planning becomes gradually differentiated from text production. This differentiation involves at least the following two steps that we can identify. In the beginning years of composition, children's mental activity is so closely tied to producing the written composition that it is difficult to identify much in the way of separate thinking that can be called planning. Gradually, as writing ability develops, there is a separation of the problem of finding content for a composition from the problem of actually writing the composition. At this point, clearly identifiable planning can be seen, but the planning remains at the same time tied to the content needs of text production, so that the plan that is generated consists of a listing of content possibilities. In adolescence, planning starts to become sufficiently differentiated from production that we begin to see the plan as having properties and containing elements that have only an indirect bearing on the content of the text. This emergence of the plan as an object of contemplation in its own right marks, we believe, a major advance in the student's development. It is probably an essential step in movement toward knowledge-transforming in composition. For able writers, the plan comes to include the consideration of organizational possibilities for the content and becomes a medium in which goals and strategies may be formulated that shape the emerging composition but are not themselves part of it.

PRELIMINARY OBSERVATIONS

The term *planning* has a variety of meanings in current usage, and one can find it applied to almost any kind of constructive mental activity. We use planning here in the sense defined by Hayes-Roth and Hayes-Roth (1979) as "the predetermination of a course of action aimed at achieving a goal." That defines the ultimate or ideal form of planning activity, however. Most of our attention will be directed toward the rudimentary forms of goal-directed planning. At what point in development activities begin to merit the label "planning" is a matter of judgment not in itself crucial to understanding the course of development.

One early glimmering of "predetermination of a course of action" is revealed in children's vocalizations or lip movements when they write (Chapter 4; Simon, 1973). In the first two years of writing, children almost all show some indications of vocalizing or subvocalizing as they write, and these vocal movements appear to be synchronized with their writing. Children are spelling or sounding words as they write them. By the fourth year (around age 10), however, this type of mouthing of words had largely disappeared among the children we studied and was replaced by a process of constructing a segment of language subvocally, then writing it, constructing another segment, writing it, and so on. This type of activity was found to be more pronounced in the students judged to be better writers. Hence there is reason to suppose that it represents a cognitively more advanced way of composing. When we call this preformation of language "planning," however, we must be aware that it is still very closely tied to immediate text production needs.

Elementary school children tend to start writing almost immediately when given a writing assignment. The delay in starting, although usually less than a minute, nevertheless varies with the task, which suggests that some kind of task-relevant thinking is going on during this brief period. The delay in starting to write an argument to parents on a familiar household issue is less than the delay in starting to write an opinion essay on a similar issue

(Scardamalia and Bereiter, 1981). The delay in starting to write an opinion essay that starts with a statement of belief is shorter than the delay in starting with a less conventional opening (Paris, 1980).

These delays are far too short, however, to allow much in the way of goal-setting or explicit planning with respect to the text as a whole. More likely is the condition that would be predicted from the knowledge-telling model—that the time spent is that required to find an appropriate first thing to say. Still, the criterion of appropriateness implies that the first item must be judged against some more global intention, and this is certainly a kind of implicit planning. In the knowledge-telling model, "appropriateness" consists of topical relevance and conformity to text grammar requirements. The amount of planning required to discover a content item appropriate in this way could plausibly be carried out in half a minute or less in most cases.

A fourth-grade student once related to us an incident that was remarkable to her because it involved the whole class being stumped for several minutes before starting a writing assignment. The assignment given by the teacher was to write a story on the theme, "The Christmas That Almost Wasn't." The class, according to our informant, sat in puzzlement until one child whispered to the others, "Santa was sick!" Immediately all the children started writing.

The story is believable, even if not well authenticated. Children evidently have readily available schemata to handle the form of narratives, but in this case the assignment did not give sufficient clue to a topic to guide a search for relevant content. The phrase "Santa was sick," however, did provide necessary topical information, and accordingly the knowledge-telling strategy could be set in motion.

The fact that children do little planning in advance of starting to write does not mean that they do not plan during other phases of composition, of course. It is by now well known that expert writers often do much of their planning while they write rather than before they start writing. Nevertheless, planning in expert writers stands out as a distinct mental activity, concentrated largely though not exclusively in the early phases of producing a composition (Hayes and Flower, 1980).

In their studies of adult writers thinking aloud while they compose, Hayes and Flower (1980) identified three kinds of planning episodes: generating (which means retrieving information relevant to the writing task), organizing, and goal setting. Together these comprise about 80% of the thinking-aloud content statements produced early in the process of composing. In the latter portions of work on a composition, translating (the actual production of written language) and editing come to predominate.

Thinking-aloud protocols were gathered from 20 students writing one-page essays on the topic, "Do you think that women should have jobs that take them away from their homes?" There were five students at each of grades 4, 6, 10, and 12 (approximate ages 10, 12, 16, and 18). Table 8.1 presents frequencies of different kinds of protocol statements. Dictating and rereading include the verbatim recitation of text as it was being written or read over; Content includes statements that provide content for the text; Language includes statements concerned with spelling, grammar, punctuation and the like; and Organization, Goals, Reader, and Difficulties include statements that indicate planning of four specific kinds: organization of the text, setting goals, considering the reader, and dealing with expository problems. Among ten-year-olds the majority of protocol segments consist of dictating or rereading text, and almost all the rest is taken up with content generation. Content generation remains the predominant kind of planning at all ages, but by age 18 other types of planning have begun to appear with sufficient frequency to account for 13% of protocol segments.

Eighteen-year-old performance does not appear to be out of line with that observed in expert writers. Hayes and Flower's experts devoted much more thought to organizing, but they were writing longer compositions. The youngest students, however, do not look much like the experts at all. They are primarily engaged in thinking of content and writing it down.

Several problems with studying the development of planning are suggested with this investigation. First there is a problem of the method possibly interacting with age. Perhaps children think of all the same kinds of things that adults do, but they don't report certain kinds of thought—possibly because they don't think they are appropriate, possibly because things like goal setting are carried out at not quite so conscious a level in children. Both possibilities are plausible.

A further difficulty is that, even if thinking-aloud protocols give us a realistic picture of what goes on in children's minds when they write, they may not tell us anything about children's competence. Given a short essay-writing assignment, young writers tend to start writing almost immediately and to write down additional items of content as they think of them. This "what next" or "knowledge-telling" strategy has little place in it for con-

Table 8.1 Analysis of thinking aloud protocols collected during the writing of an argument essay. Percentage of total protocol devoted to each type of statement

Age	Dictate and reread	Language	Content	Organization	Goals	Reader	Difficulties
10	54	9	37	0	0	0	0
12	53	9	35	1	0	0	2
16	31	17	49	0	3	0	0
18	23	20	45	2	3	1	7

scious goal setting or organizational planning. But perhaps this is just the way students are in the habit of going about school writing tasks. What would happen if students were induced to plan for a while before starting to write and to think about such things as what they were trying to accomplish, how they might present their ideas, and what a reader might think of them? Perhaps students would then exhibit the same kinds of planning that adults show, and thereby demonstrate that they have the competence to plan even if they don't routinely use it. Or perhaps they would be at a loss and have no idea how to fill the time designated for planning.

The study to be reported in the next section was an attempt to find out. The study, accordingly, involved students in planning and note-taking activities taking place in advance of their actually producing a text. In this study we also looked at notes taken during planning and at the texts produced afterwards, in order to avoid complete dependence on thinking-aloud protocols as a source of data on planning.

AN EXPERIMENT
IN ADVANCE PLANNING

The research considered in the preceding section of this chapter leaves the impression that planning by young students is dominated by concerns of producing content in sequential order—of what to write next in a composition. We have suggested, however, that this research may only be telling us about the habitual behavior of younger students in assigned writing tasks and may not be telling us about their abilities to plan.

In the experiment to be reported here we took a direct approach to inducing students to put their planning abilities to work. We made it clear to students that we wanted them to plan, and we introduced a variety of increasingly explicit guides as to what was expected—guides designed to encourage a range of planning activities, including goal setting and problem identification as well as figuring out how to attain goals and solve problems.

Students were asked to carry on planning, making notes as they proceeded, but not to begin actually writing their text until they had done as much planning as they could. This approach was taken because of our finding that under ordinary circumstances children tended to plan only one point at a time. Although mature writers do not typically plan very extensively in advance of starting to write (Emig, 1971; Gould, 1980), we have found that they have no difficulty doing so on request. Some data from adult advance-planning protocols will be discussed later in this chapter. Advance planning seems to involve a relatively minor adjustment of adult composing strategies. In asking children to do advance planning, our thought was that by removing them from the think-write-think-write pattern we might give them an opportunity to reveal a greater range and depth of planning capabilities.

When, in exploratory interviews, we told children that adults sometimes think for 15 minutes or more before starting to write, many children were incredulous. They could not imagine what there was to think about for that length of time. They were inclined, in fact, to think that such a slow start was a sign of incompetence and that expert writers, being smarter, should be quicker off the mark. In order to overcome misconceptions of this kind, we built into the experiment different ways of indicating the kinds of mental activities that might go on in advance planning. The result, of course, is that if the planning behaviors fail to appear even though they were directly suggested, this may be taken as an indication that such behaviors were not readily available to the students.

The study was conducted with 72 students, 24 from each of grades 4, 6, and 8. The approximate ages of the three groups were 10, 12, and 14 years. At each grade the students were divided equally into four groups which differed in the kinds of guidance given. Each student was interviewed individually, in a session lasting from about 45 minutes to an hour.

All students were assigned to write a brief essay on the topic, "Should children be able to choose the subjects they study in school?" This topic had been used in a number of other studies and was known to produce a range of opinions varying in the amount of thought that appeared to have gone into them (see Chapter 6). It was therefore of interest to see what kinds of planning this topic would provoke. Students were asked to plan aloud for as long as they could before actually beginning to write. Paper and pencil were provided, and they were encouraged to take notes as they planned. All students received the following general instructions, suggesting five things they might think about in their planning. Italicized phrases indicate the five points that were suggested as planning focuses.

> . . . Just plan out loud the kinds of things you usually plan when you're going to write something. You may think of things like what *difficulties* might come up while you're writing, you know, what problems you might have and how you'll handle those problems. And you might want to think about the topic, trying to *remember what you know* about it and what kinds of things you want to put in your paragraph. Also, you might want to think about *what your goal is* in writing this— what you're trying for in what you write. There are also things to think about like *how the people who read this will react* to it, what they'll think and what that means for how you should do

things in the paragraph. Then, of course, you need to figure out *how to put everything you've thought about together* to come up with a really good paragraph. So really, I just want you to think about the kinds of things you and other writers usually think about when they're planning to write something . . .

Students in the Control condition received only these general instructions. Students in the Card condition were, in addition, provided with five cards to serve as reminders of the five kinds of planning. Each card contained a short phrase: Thinking about difficulties and how you will handle them; Remembering what you know about the topic; Thinking about your goal—thinking about what you're trying for; Thinking about the reader; and Putting your plan together. No particular way of using the cards was prescribed; they were simply made available to students with the suggestion that they might be helpful if they got stuck in planning.

Students in the remaining two conditions viewed a specially made videotape in which an adult writer planned an essay (not on the assigned topic) and modeled thinking aloud about each of the five areas of planning referred to in the general instructions. Each area was represented in a short segment of three or four minutes. The tape was stopped after each segment and the student was asked to indicate, by referring to the five cards described above, which kind of thing the planner was mainly thinking about during that segment. The reason for adding this discrimination task was to direct attention to relevant aspects of the videotape demonstration. However, it also provided supplementary data on students' metacognitive knowledge of planning—that is, conceptual knowledge of the cognitive process, as compared to tacit "know-how" (see Flavell, 1979). Students in the Modeling Only condition then planned their own compositions without having cards available as reminders, whereas students in the Modeling Plus Card condition retained the cards and were invited to use them, as in the Card condition.

Finally, all students were told to keep planning for as long as possible before starting to write. It was mentioned that writers often plan for 20 minutes or even longer. During the actual planning aloud, each student was prompted once to continue planning after he or she indicated being finished planning.

RESULTS

Among the kinds of data to be considered here are accuracy in identifying planning behaviors on the part of those students who viewed the model videotape, the relation between notes taken during planning and texts written afterward, and the appearance of different kinds of planning in the thinking-aloud protocols. There were pronounced age differences in each kind of data, but each highlights a somewhat different aspect of the overall developmental process. We had expected that there would also be pronounced differences between experimental conditions, but this proved not to be the case. There were some differences, which will be noted, but they are overshadowed by and also linked to the age differences, which will be the main object of our attention.

Identification of Videotape Planning Segments

In the videotape produced to model advance planning, the focus of the different segments on audience, organization, content, etc., was intentionally made very obvious and consistent. Adults on whom we pretested the videotape had no difficulty identifying the five segments according to their intended focuses. The mean number of segments correctly identified by students in the experiment was 2.17 at grade 4, 4.00 at grade 6, and 3.83 at grade 8. The large jump in accuracy between grades 4 and 6 suggests that during this period students are making a major advance in their *conceptual* grasp of text planning. This could come about either through gaining an understanding of the abstract notions involved or through becoming able to view cognitive behavior more analytically. It is interesting that no further gain occurred between grades 6 and 8 (if anything, a slight loss), even though these grades span an age range during which major gains in abstract conceptualization are often observed (Inhelder & Piaget, 1958). Of more immediate concern, however, is whether changes in actual planning behavior are linked with these conceptual advances.

Notes and Text

The way in which the notes are used to generate text was found to change considerably in the age-range studied.

Let us begin at the most advanced level, with an example of notes written during the planning phase and the subsequent text produced by one of the better planners in the group (on the subject "Should students be able to choose the subjects they study in school?"):

NOTES
—opinion (mine)
—responsibility of the children—their goal in life
—parents—their understanding of their children
—what will happen with what they take
—examples
—what rights do they have
—what I think about it
—the grade (if they chose) should be 7 and up
—school subjects should be made more interesting
—how future will be

TEXT
I personally think that students should be able to choose which subjects they want to study in school. In grade 9 students are allowed to choose certain subjects which they want to but even then the students aren't sure. Many don't know because they don't know what they want to be when they get older. If they choose the subjects they wanted most students would of course pick easier subjects such as art, gym, music, etc. I think that this doing is partly the schools fault. If the school made math classes more interesting students would more likely pick that. Their parents should be able to discuss with the children what they should take. The parents of course have more responsibility and of course want the best for their children. Many children (if they could pick their own subjects) would pick something their parents didn't approve of if their parents were mean to them. Then the children would be ruining their own life. This would probably go around in circles. The world is a very mixed up place but it would be even worse if there wasn't any control. Control must begin with children of today because they will become the adults of tomorrow.

Although the composition itself may not be particularly distinguished, this 14-year-old student has gone about producing it in a relatively mature fashion. Her notes represent gists of ideas that are expanded into complete thoughts when the text is written. Some of them (e.g. "my opinion") indicate her intention without giving the contents of it. When the notes are used in the text, they are used in a rearranged order, and a single note may be expanded into two sentences or two notes collapsed into one. Some notes are not used, and some new material is added. Thus a large variety of transformations are made in passing from the notes to the text.

For contrast, here are the notes and text of a 10-year-old:

NOTES
I don't like language and art is a bore
I don't like novel study
And I think 4s and 3s should be split up.
I think we should do math.
I don't think we should do diary
I think we should do French

TEXT
I think children should be able to choose what subjects they want in school.

I don't think we should have to do language, and art is a bore a lot. I don't think we should do novel study every week. I really think 4s and 3s should be split up for gym. I think we should do a lot of math. I don't think we should do diary. I think we should do French.

In contrast to the age-14 protocol, the age-10 example shows very little transformation taking place between the notes and the text. The notes are already complete sentences, and they are used in the text with minor modifications, and in the same order as they were listed. Only the first sentence of the text is new, and forms a sort of title for the essay. (The space between the first sentence and the rest of the text appears in the original.) For the rest, the notes themselves are copied as if they already constituted a complete first draft of the essay.

These examples highlight the main developmental trend that we find in the notes-to-text data. For the older students the notes represent ideas that are later worked into a composition. For the younger students the notes represent a first draft of a composition, which is then edited into a final draft. In order to quantify this age trend, we counted the number of transformations of different kinds between notes and text for the three age groups. Table 8.2 shows the resulting frequencies. There is a clear increase from age to age in the amount of transformation done on notes to convert them into text.

These findings do not tell us anything directly about the process of planning but they tell us something quite remarkable about the product of planning. In younger children the product of planning is text. There does not seem to be any intermediate product. For the more mature students, however, the product of planning is a plan. It is not just a stripped-down text, for it contains elements texts do not contain—notes to oneself, as it were—and it bears little structural or stylistic resemblance to the subsequent text. The construction of such plans, and the underlying ability to represent text contents in a variety of abstract ways, is critical, as we elaborate in Chapter 14, to writing as a knowledge-transforming activity.

In effect, the younger students subverted our effort experimentally to separate planning from production. Asked to plan before writing, they simply used note-taking as a way of producing text and so were able to go about composing in their accustomed way. This binding of planning to production is not a phenomenon that can be easily attributed to motivational factors or to some residual confusion about what was expected. In clinical work with a small group of children, sustained over a period of weeks, Robert Sandieson tried to initiate the children into the planning strategy that we find older students using spontaneously—the strategy of jotting down ideas in telegraphic form that are later used as raw material in a composition. In spite of modeling and face-to-face coaching and monitoring, the children showed a persisting inclination to produce continuous text (even though it was superficially in list form), thus losing the advantages of brainstorming because of having to deal with all the travail of text production from the beginning. Only by introducing formal procedures such as a list of questions to be answered—procedures that effectively disrupted the continuity of production—was it possible to get idea generation to take place apart from text production. It is interesting in this regard that a variety of current methods for enhancing the thought content of students' writing have this property (e.g., Jones and Amiran, 1980; Robinson, Tickle, & Brison, 1972; Young et al., 1970). A prevalent form in all these approaches is the matrix, which introduces a geometric framework not easily assimilated to the continuous production of linear text.

Table 8.2   Changes made in passing from notes to text. Percentage of notes undergoing each type of transformation. (Transformations are not mutually exclusive.)

Age	Minor changes only	Elaboration	Reordering	Division	Combination	Omission	Addition
10	31	42	5	5	5	29	15
12	4	65	9	3	11	32	7
14	0	73	18	11	11	25	15

Use of Conceptual Planning Cues

Inasmuch as all the forward-looking thought involved in composition can be called planning, we need a special term to distinguish those kinds of forethought that deal with goals, strategies, organization, and the like, from those that amount to the actual mental generation of text. We will refer to the first kind as *conceptual planning*. The outcome of conceptual planning is not text content or language, rather it is knowledge that guides or interprets the choice of content and language. We will use the term *content generation* in referring to the generation of material intended for actual use in the text. The distinction cannot always be made confidently on the basis of thinking-aloud protocol statements. A statement of the type, "The main point I want to make is . . . ," may be a conceptual planning statement about the composition but it may also be a statement intended for actual inclusion in the text. In this section we examine a class of planning statements that are especially revealing as to the distinction between conceptual planning and content generation.

The general instructions, the videotaped modeling, and the cue cards were all designed with a view to encouraging conceptual planning. It was to be expected, of course, that some students would try to follow the model and the instructions even though they did not understand them. This could be observed in planning protocols when students used the vocabulary of planning that we had given them but used it in a way sharply at variance with its original intention. Examples of this occurred with each of the five types of planning highlighted by the experimental procedures.

With respect to thinking about goals, for instance, we get the following examples of students using the Goals card but with quite a different function from that of conceptual planning:

> The goal is that you have to be very good in school, and the thing that you're trying for is to get a good mark.

> Think about which subject would be helpful to you in the future, things like math or languages.

> I don't know if they mean it like that, but if they're picking their subject they should think about what they're going to be doing later in life.

Here we see that the idea of goal is used as a theme or cue for generating content to be used in the text, rather than as a cue for thinking about a goal of the text.

A similar phenomenon occurred with the Difficulties card, intended to elicit thinking about rhetorical difficulties or difficulties with the argument the writer was advancing. Instead some students used difficulties as a content theme:

> Like if you have a problem in math or something you should try to get a tutor.

> If you run into difficulties in a subject that you took as an option. . . .

> You should pick like a subject that would help you deal with your difficulties.

One student was ingenious enough to turn Organization into a content theme relevant to the essay topic:

> You should organize yourself so that you don't wind up in a trap like you take a course that you thought would be useful but it doesn't turn out that you really need it.

One of the cue cards, "Remembering what you know about the topic," was a directive to generate content. Some students, however, took even this cue as a content theme rather than as a suggestion of a type of planning:

> If you forget about the topic later on when they come to mark it and you don't have that much information on it you won't get very good marks.

> Maybe you'd think back about what your teacher explained, and you'd remember it.

The extent to which students used planning cards for conceptual planning is shown in Table 8.3. Notice that 14-year-olds who saw the model videotape show a greater percentage of conceptual planning uses than others, which suggests that they, but not the younger students, were able to gain from the videotape some grasp of the implicit distinction between conceptual planning and content generation.

Table 8.3   Use of cards. Percentage of occasions on which cards were used for conceptual planning. (See text.)

| | Group | |
Age	Card	Card and Film
10	8	0
12	12	27
14	14	60

The point we want to make from these data is not that many students misunderstood the directions. This may be true, but it is not enlightening. What is enlightening is that students who distorted the planning task did so in a highly systematic manner. It appears that for these students planning is content generation. When, as cooperative experimental students, they try to make use of the material and guidance given to them, they try to incorporate these into the process of content generation. As the examples show, they sometimes did this with considerable ingenuity.

The power of content generation as a planning mode is dramatized in the following instance of a 10-year-old student who seems to have come close to catching hold of conceptual planning but then let it slip out of his grasp. These are the student's notes:

NOTES
Getting basic subjects
Think about what you want to major in
Keep information remembered so you get smarter
Think of all the subjects to go together so you get a good education
Think how a reader would react to the story (kind of a story)
Remember how to figure out your problems

Notice that the last two notes reflect two types of planning encouraged by the experimental procedures—thinking about the reader, and thinking about problems or difficulties. The student did not actually get into planning in either of these areas but did record notes that might serve as reminders to himself to keep these matters in mind when composing the text. Here, however, is the text the student produced:

TEXT
I think students should be able to pick their own subjects if they had some guidance. One thing to start off with is for you to take your basic sujects like math, language, gym, music, and maybe history. In school start thinking what you want to be so you can take those subjects for a start. If you did want to be say a teacher (just math) keep remembering the things you've learned so you will be a better teacher (you will be smarter). So you do become a good teacher even if you just want to teach math you would still need other subjects so you would have to take ones that go together. To this story a reader's view may think it is kind of silly but maybe not. If you do run into problems you must learn how to cope with them and work them out.

It appears that when the student came to write his text, he used the conceptual notes as if they were content and worked them directly into the text.

Classification of Thinking-aloud Protocol Statements

In order to test further the conclusions suggested thus far, we classified statements in the thinking-aloud protocols so as to distinguish between episodes of content generation and episodes of conceptual planning. We tried to follow the same general approach to classifying protocol segments as used by Hayes and Flower (1980), with differences due to our interest in a finer-grained analysis of types of planning and to the fact that our protocols extend only up to the point where writing begins and thus do not contain episodes of transcribing and editing. Each transcript was first segmented into idea units and each unit was then coded as belonging to one of six categories: language considerations (spelling, grammar, vocabulary), content generation, organization, reader awareness, overcoming difficulties, and considering goals. The last four categories, when combined, make up the category of conceptual planning. The frequencies reported in Table 8.4 are the average of data from two independent coders.

As we have noted previously, it is often uncertain in judging individual protocol statements whether the statement is a statement *about* the composition, in which case it belongs in one or another category of conceptual planning, or whether it is a statement intended to be *part of* the composition, in which case it is an instance of content generation. In fact, one of the coders placed many fewer statements into the conceptual planning categories than did the other. The actual percentages indicated in Table 8.4 must accordingly be taken with discretion. They could move up or down depending on subjective criteria. We doubt, however, that by any reasonable criterion conceptual planning would be found to account for more than a small part of the planning done by students of the ages studied. Because the coders were blind to the ages and experimental conditions involved, greater confi-

Table 8.4 Analysis of thinking aloud protocols collected during planning in advance of writing. Length of protocol (in idea units) and percentage of total protocol devoted to each type of planning

Age	Length	Language	Content	Organization	Goals	Reader	Difficulties
10	18	1	91	1	5	1	1
12	42	0	89	4	3	1	3
14	37	2	90	3	3	1	1

dence may be placed in the relative percentages associated with the different ages.

The number of idea units per protocol gives a rough index of the total amount of planning of any sort done at the different ages. There is a sharp increase from a mean of 18 units at age 10, to 42 and 37 units at ages 12 and 14, respectively. Thus the gross amount of planning activity revealed in the protocols more than doubles between the youngest and the older ages. This large age difference in the amount of planning is not accompanied by much of a change in the type of planning, however. Content generation remains at about 90% of the total at all ages, while conceptual planning remains at about 10%. The amount of planning of all sorts increases, but the amount of conceptual planning remains a constant, small percentage of the total.

Thoughts During Pauses

Because students may differ in the extent to which they report their thoughts while thinking aloud, we took the precaution of questioning students about what they were thinking whenever they lapsed into extended silence during a planning session. Replies were sorted into four categories:

Negative replies: "I'm stuck," "I can't think of anything," etc.

Direct content replies: These were replies comparable to those scored as content generation in the protocol analysis. That is, the student responded with some item of content that seemed intended for inclusion in the text.

Indirect content replies: These replies took a form such as "I was thinking that. . . . " or "It seems to me that. . . . " Even though the idea that followed might be similar to the kinds scored as direct content, the presence of self-referencing phrases like those noted above suggested that the speaker was thinking *about* the idea or *about* its appropriateness for the essay rather than directly generating content for the essay.

Conceptual planning replies: These were replies such as "I'm thinking about the reader" or "I'm thinking how to write this," where the speaker indicated a concern about the structure, form, or style of the essay, or about some general issue of content, but was not proposing a specific item of content.

Briefly, negative replies and direct content replies were found at all ages. Indirect content replies and conceptual planning replies appeared rarely at age 10 but were common at ages 12 and 14, increasing from about 10% to over 50% of all replies. The age effect in conceptual planning is thus very clear here, in contrast to the regular thinking-aloud data discussed previously. Although these replies to "What are you thinking?" are retrospective reports and thus have validity problems of their own (Ericsson and Simon, 1980), they suggest that the silent part of young students' thinking is not much different from the part verbalized in their thinking-aloud protocols, but that the older children are engaged in at least some conceptual planning that does not appear in the regular thinking-aloud data. At the same time, if the conceptual planning of the older children is still largely restricted to those brief periods when they are silent, it cannot constitute more than a small percentage of their total planning.

It is interesting that the older students do fall silent when they are engaged in conceptual planning, because it suggests that conceptual planning is competing with talking for their attentional resources. We have often noticed that students of all ages who are thinking aloud fall silent at exactly the point where the most demanding—and most interesting—thinking seems to be occurring. Their silence indicates that the 14-year-olds, in conceptual planning, are attempting something that is difficult for them to achieve.

Adult Replication

Six university undergraduates were tested in a replication of the Control condition of the main planning study (no cards, no videotape). There were two main reasons for this replication. The first was to get a more extended developmental picture. Although some striking changes were observed during the age range of 10 to 14 years, the incidence of conceptual planning in the thinking-aloud protocols appeared low at all ages—a possible indication that knowledge telling was still the prevailing model, even among 14-year-olds. To have confidence in such a conclusion, however, it appeared important to verify that there was in fact an age gradient in this planning behavior and to ensure that there was not some experimental artifact serving to diminish planning even in proficient writers. We will not give a detailed account of the adult-level findings, but will give an overview that serves as well to pull together the findings on school-age writers.

With respect to the phenomena that we have noted thus far, the adult writers were very similar to one another and markedly different from the children and adolescents observed in the main study. The outstanding difference in planning between the adults and the children was that the adults explicitly planned out the organization of the entire essay during the planning period. Let us consider briefly the adult data in each of the areas of development that we examined in the main study, to see how this difference manifests itself.

The relation of the notes to the text in the adults is no longer traceable in the same terms that it was with the children. The notes have become much too complex and much too condensed. For most of the adults, the notes consist of multiple small lists of ideas here and there over the page, with arrows and lines connecting them. They have a diagrammatic, structural quality. They often are so abbreviated that they cannot be easily interpreted by a reader. Conceptual planning notes are everywhere. Marks that indicate the value of notes are frequent—asterisks, boxes, question marks, and exclamation points. Ideas are grouped and labeled according to content—"pros" and "cons", "early grades" and "high school"—or structural position in the essay—"introduction" and "conclusion." There are sometimes notes that refer to the planner's current concerns—"this is no good," "am I answering the question?," "stay on topic," or "relate paragraphs." None of these features occurred in the notes of the children. They all came about because the adult is concerned with the structure of the essay during the planning phase, and most of the notes obviously play a supporting role for this type of conceptual planning.

The thinking-aloud protocols, too, show much more conceptual planning. We did not give cue cards to the adults, who no doubt would have used them correctly, but in any case they were not needed, as most of the areas of conceptual planning are represented (with the notable exception of audience considerations). The adults only infrequently had to be asked what they were thinking, so that there are few replies to compare to the children's, but the replies that did occur were of all types, with perhaps more indirect content replies.

About 33% of the protocol idea-units were explicitly concerned with the areas of conceptual planning that we defined. In fact, the adults' whole approach to content, which covered the other 67%, was also typically more goal-oriented, more oriented toward overcoming difficulties, and more oriented toward establishing structure ("putting your plan together" as the card said) than that of the children. There is a great deal of repetition of content in the adults' protocols, too, where they are reviewing and reconsidering aspects of the planned essay.

Finally, there are many cases of clear, explicit planning of the structure of the essay during the advance planning phase. The adults say things like "I'll start with the idea that . . . then I'll talk about . . . and I'll finish with . . . ", showing that they do consider the essay as a whole during the planning period. None of our school-age writers planned the organization of the essay in advance to this extent.

CONCLUSION

Let us briefly recapitulate our experimental findings on the development of planning abilities. At the level of metacognition—that is, the level of knowledge about the cognitive process of planning—10-year-olds showed little accuracy in identifying the kinds of planning carried out by an adult model. By age 12 accuracy had risen to close to an adult level. In attempting to carry out suggested kinds of planning, however, students across the 10- to 14-year range showed a tendency to distort all kinds of planning into content generation, although this tendency diminished significantly across the age range.

Between the ages of 10 and 12 there was also a major jump—a doubling—in the gross quantity of planning indicated in thinking-aloud protocols. Conceptual planning increased slightly across the 10- to 14-year range, but was infrequent at all ages. Only 14-year olds, however, showed evidence of a response to videotaped modeling of conceptual planning. Adults showed a higher incidence of conceptual planning, even without modeling or instruction.

At age 10 there was a close resemblance between notes taken during planning and the text written afterwards. This resemblance declined in the following years. With adults, planning notes were obviously a different kind of thing altogether from the text later produced from them, differing from it both in form and in types of content.

These findings are all congruent with the thesis that what happens in writing development is the increasing differentiation of planning from text production. Different aspects of the differentiation are observed at different levels. At the metacognitive level it is shown in an increasing ability to recognize a variety of planning activities involved in composition that are distinct from a direct "thinking of what to write." At the level of thought tapped by thinking-aloud protocols it is shown in the apparently slow emergence of what we call conceptual planning—planning that consists of thinking *about* the composition rather than planning that consists of mentally rehearsing or creating the composition. At the level of product it is shown in the emergence of the *plan* as a formally and substantively distinct entity that can be operated on apart from the composition itself.

Our experimental procedures, by forcing planning to precede text production, undoubtedly favored the creation of tangible plans. It is therefore noteworthy that, in spite of this bias, 10-year old writers tended not to produce plans that were distinct from text. This strengthens, therefore, the conclusion that for children of this age planning is not differentiated from production. What the youngest writers seemed to do was discover a way to smuggle text production into the planning period by using note-taking as a way of producing a first draft of text.

We know that mature writers, left to their own devices, will often intermix planning with production (Hayes and Flower, 1980). In these cases the plan may exist only in the mind of the writer, having no physical embodiment and taking shape along with the composition instead of antedating it. It remains in these cases that the plan for a text is conceptually different from a mental representation of the text itself. The plan exists on a different conceptual plane and has different content. It contains intentions, strategies, priorities, alternatives, evaluations, justifications. Much or all of this may be reflected in the text, but there it is implicit and deeply enmeshed, whereas in the plan it is more explicit and susceptible to direct operation. The plan may have strengths and weaknesses distinct from those of the text. Large changes in the plan may show up as small changes in the text or small changes in the plan may show up as large changes in the text. The plan, in short, represents a different sort of thing to work with, in which the writer can accomplish things that are not readily accomplished in working directly with the text. Conversely, as many a writer testifies, things happen in working directly with the text that could not have been prefigured in the plan. Expert writers keep switching back and forth between planning and production, we suspect, because each complements the other; it is not a one-way affair in which planning feeds production. This complementary function, however, is one that depends upon planning and production becoming sufficiently differentiated.

In our analysis the developmental scenario goes approximately like this: At first all the child's conscious attention is involved in the immediate written expression. Global intentions, world knowledge, discourse knowledge— these all have their influence on the child, as can easily be demonstrated, but it appears that their influence is tacit and unconscious, like the influence of our syntactic knowledge on our everyday speech. Over the course of childhood and early adolescence, thought becomes sufficiently detached from immediate expression that the young writer can generate text content in abbreviated forms and mentally manipulate it—delete, arrange, seek new content, etc. At this stage we may accordingly speak of the plan as distinct from the text and existing more or less as a mental table of contents for the text. Not until later adolescence do we typically see the plan taking on conceptual properties of its own, so that text organization, intentions, problems, strategies, and the like are clearly represented and capable of being operated upon, rather than remaining implicit and in the background.

In concluding, we need to say something about how firm and generalizable we take these findings to be. Let us first make it clear that we have no stake in assigning age norms to the developmental scenario we have sketched. Other student populations with different educational histories might be considerably advanced or retarded compared to the students we studied. Although age-norm questions are potentially interesting, our research cannot answer them, nor do such questions have a significant bearing on the conclusions we have drawn. We are interested, here, in understanding the nature of planning in writing and how it develops. The developmental scenario that we have arrived at is supported by a sufficient variety of converging types of evidence that we have considerable confidence in it as a description of the student population we studied. The basic developmental process also seems to have such a strong internal consistency to it that we find it hard to imagine that it would not be found in other populations, even though the age norms might be considerably different.

One type of apparently contrary evidence may be anticipated, however. That is evidence from school situations that feature a great deal of social support for the composing process—peer discussions, cooperative writing, conferencing, etc. Anecdotal reports already suggest that instances can be found where rather sophisticated planning seems to be carried out by children of ages younger than the youngest in our population.

This raises an important issue. Even without such evidence it is clear that young children have a good deal of competence in planning. They set goals in their daily lives, select strategies for reaching those goals, anticipate obstacles and think of ways to get around them, and so on. It is not surprising therefore, that under the right sort of circumstances they can demonstrate these same kinds of planning abilities in writing. How do such occurrences fit with the picture of a slow, difficult course of development in planning abilities?

It will be instructive to consider several different circumstances in which precocious composition planning may appear. First, it is no doubt possible to produce a demonstration such as Socrates did in the *Meno,* leading a child solely through questioning to carry out rather sophisticated planning. We have done something like this with individual students ourselves, and it is a key element in teacher-pupil conferencing. In Chapter 3, we presented a group planning protocol that shows planning far beyond the normal 12-year-old level, in this case stimulated by the group process. Because different children had different ideas about what to include in a story, the planning was forced to a more conceptual level where alternatives were explicitly weighed and analyzed. Another circumstance that might provoke higher-level planning would be one in which the child faced a significant communication problem—a strong need to convince a hard-to-convince reader, for instance. In such a case, problematic aspects of the communication task might be sufficiently salient that the child would be found giving conscious attention to questions of strategy, subgoal specification, anticipation of obstacles, and the like.

Educators, considering such instances, are sometimes inclined to declare that there is no developmental barrier to reckon with and that the problems of writing instruction are solved: simply engage students in the conferences, group efforts, and real-life problems that have been found to enhance planning and other aspects of composition. These may well be good instructional approaches, but one should be clear about what they are doing and how they relate to development.

Cognitive development, as Donaldson (1978) among others has argued, does not consist of the acquisition of new elementary logical operations. It consists, from one perspective at least, in the acquisition of knowledge structures and control structures that enable the child to bring these elementary logical operations to bear on increasingly complex tasks, in increasingly flexible and deliberate ways. That is, generally, how we see the development of planning in writing. Young writers may have the elementary logical operations of planning available to them, but it takes the guiding questions of an adult or a favorably structured situation for these operations to be brought effectively into use. With maturity, writers become less dependent on external conditions and events to organize and stimulate their thought. Instead of having to be led by questions, they ask their own questions. Instead of needing to argue alternatives with their peers they produce and analyze alternatives themselves. Instead of needing a real-life problem context to stimulate goal-directed planning, they can start cold with an unchallenging topic and begin to formulate goals and problems of their own. That is what the development of planning ability seems to be about. Our effort in this chapter has been to look beneath the surface of this ability to learn something about the conceptual and procedural knowledge of which it is constituted.

POSTSCRIPT

The preceding results pertain to planning in expository writing. It seems to be widely believed that young writers are more advanced in their ability to produce narrative than exposition, although it is not clear how such a belief could be tested (cf. Hidi & Hildyard, 1983). Even if the premise is accepted that children's narratives are better developed than their arguments or explanations, however, it does not follow that their planning abilities are more sophisticated in narrative. It could simply be that a good narrative can be produced with less planning than is required to produce a good exposition (however "goodness" is to be equated across these genres).

In order to compare students' planning in narrative and argument writing, Burtis (1983) carried out a replication of the study reported in this chapter, simply altering the task to that of planning and then writing a story on the topic, "The Kid Who Lost Things." Eight children at each of grades 4, 6, and 8, plus eight adults were examined. The results were essentially identical to those for expository writing. In the planning portion, grade 4 students essentially generated drafts of their stories. Grade 6 and 8 students made notes that were carried fairly directly over into their stories, but with a greater amount of revision.

Summarizing adult-child differences, Burtis reported:

> Some of the adults, but none of the children, searched for a main point for their story and built the rest of the story around that point. Some of the adults, but none of the children reviewed their entire story several times before beginning to write. . . . Also, the notes of some of the adults, but not the children, in narrative planning had the same structural quality found in the adult notes of argument planning (p. 2).

Burtis concluded that, rather than being more advanced, "if anything, planning in narratives lagged behind planning in arguments" (p. 2). Such a conclusion might seem paradoxical, but it is understandable on the basis of the knowledge-telling model (Chapter 1). According to this model, the two main determinants of coherence in immature writers' texts should be the organization of content in memory and the degree of organization imposed by the discourse schema. Personal experiences would tend to be coherently organized in memory, compared to knowledge about topics, which would probably have been acquired here and there, possibly with little interconnection. And, as we argued in Chapter 3, the closed character of the narrative schema should make for more coherent text production, compared to the open character of other discourse schemata, which are designed for accommodation to conversational inputs. Thus, an amount of planning that might produce an incoherent argument or exposition might produce a highly coherent narrative—especially if the narrative was one that drew on well-remembered personal experience.

Chapter 9
Links Between Composing
and Comprehending Strategies

PREFACE

This final chapter in Part III reports investigations of strategies in reading comprehension. This research was originally undertaken as a way of testing whether the knowledge-telling model was on the right track. It was reasoned that if young writers actually do what the model proposes, then they ought to do something similar in reading. One of the experimental tasks, in fact, stands right at the intersection of reading and writing. It is the task of arranging sentences to reconstruct a text. Like reading, it involves making sense of already-formed written language; but, like writing, it involves the creation of a linear text out of nonlinearly arranged material (cf. Beaugrande, 1984b).

This research turned out to do more, however, than confirm that a strategy similar to knowledge telling could be identified in reading. A key issue in reading is what kind of mental representation is constructed of the text (Kintsch & van Dijk, 1978). By analyzing kinds of mental representations students were constructing as they thought aloud while reading or arranging sentences, we could begin to see how intimately related text-processing strategies are to the kinds of mental representations they operate on.

Knowledge telling locks the immature writer into working with only a limited range of mental representations of
text, and a limited range of representations keeps the immature writer locked into knowledge telling. The work to be
reported in this chapter suggests that similarly narrow ranges
of text representations lock students into immature reading
strategies. This theme will be taken up in more detail in the
concluding chapter of this book where we deal with the
broad range of text representations that underlie knowledge-
transforming operations with text.

9

The two studies to be reported in this chapter sought to
obtain information, primarily through the use of thinking-
aloud protocols, on how young readers deal with text
comprehension difficulties. There were two reasons for
focusing on situations in which comprehension is prob-
lematic. The first is methodological. Fluent, easy reading is a fairly automatic process in which little of the mental activity is available for self-report
(cf. Just & Carpenter, 1980; Perfetti & Lesgold, 1977; Woods, 1980).
Consequently, text-processing tasks are used that contain problems or impediments intended to bring normally covert processes into sufficiently deliberate use so that relevant kinds of self-report data may be obtained. The
second reason—and the more significant reason—is an interest in educational
applications.

When students try to comprehend and learn from written texts, they often
work under the combined handicaps of having limited knowledge of the
subject matter and limited familiarity with the genre they are reading. Thus
they lack the benefits that Voss (1984) attributes to "high knowledge" in a
content domain and the benefits that Stein and Trabasso (1982) attribute to
having a well-developed discourse schema that organizes information for
memory storage and serves to guide inferencing into relevant channels. If
students are to be successful at learning in such situations—situations that
are normal rather than exceptional in formal education—then they need
powerful problem-solving strategies. Studying what strategies they do have
available and how these compare to expert strategies would seem to be a
vital first step in building a developmentally sound program of instruction
(Case, 1978a).

There is evidence that skilled readers have special strategies that they can
bring to bear in cases where comprehension is difficult. Flower, Hayes, and
Swarts (1980) found that in trying to make sense of complex regulations,
skilled readers constructed scenarios or narratives that permitted them to
restructure the text content in a way they could better comprehend. Bird

(1980) collected thinking-aloud protocols from adults reading a variety of texts. Among the strategies she found skillful readers using when they encountered comprehension difficulties were the following:

1. Ongoing summarization. It appeared that readers were consciously creating the macro-structure that normally, according to Kintsch and van Dijk's model (1978), is created automatically.
2. Strategic backtracking. Bird found that both more skilled and less skilled readers backed up and reread when they encountered difficulties, but skilled readers appeared to back up to where the information they needed was located, whereas less skilled readers tended to backtrack only to the beginning of the sentence in which they experienced difficulty.
3. Problem formulation. Skilled readers tended explicitly to formulate their difficulty as a problem, which they then tried to solve. Although this does not sound like a strategy in itself, it apparently has strategic value, in that it helps the reader bring general-purpose problem-solving procedures to bear on the comprehension difficulty.
4. Setting up "watchers." Rieger (1977) proposed that in story comprehension certain story elements activate "watchers" in the reader's mind, which remain active until a particular kind of required information is received. Olson, Mack, and Duffy (1981), as well as Bird (1980), found direct evidence of readers setting up such watchers, thus anticipating categories of information to appear in the text—reasons to support opinions, definitions to explain unfamiliar words, examples to illustrate general statements, etc.

In subsequent analysis of protocols from seventh- and eighth-grade students, Bird (1980) found some incidence of all these strategies. However, only 17 out of 46 students showed a single instance of problem formulation in the course of reading about 1500 words of expository material, even though comprehension was only about 60%, as measured by factual and inferential test items following brief passages. Direct instruction with modeling boosted this incidence to approximately 2.5 problem formulations per student on a post-test with large increases also in the use of ongoing summarization and strategic backtracking. Comprehension test scores likewise showed significant increases.

These findings indicate that young readers do not make optimum use of strategies experts use for dealing with comprehension difficulties, but they do not show us: (1) to what extent the strategies are available but simply not called up; and (2) what strategies students do employ that may be different from those observed in experts. Answering the first question requires experiments that try to maximize the likelihood that students will use the most powerful strategies they have available. The second study reported in this chapter attempts to maximize use of problem-solving strategies by means of sentence arrangement tasks that pose clear-cut problems for putting together meaning in text. The first study to be reported involves a more ordinary reading activity designed to bring out the strategies students normally employ. Students think aloud as they read texts that pose difficulties for comprehension.

STUDY 1

The purpose of this study was to obtain descriptive information on comprehension strategies used by students in the middle years of school in reading expository texts. Protocol data were obtained by having students think aloud while reading (Bird, 1980; Olson et al., 1981; Swaney, Janik, Bond & Hayes, 1981), expressing any thoughts as soon as they occur. Examples of the protocols thus obtained are shown in Table 9.1.

As the examples show—and as was also true of the protocols collected by Bird (1980), who studied readers in the same age range—reading protocols are not nearly so rich in detail as those obtained from slower-moving problem-solving activities. Consequently, one cannot expect to construct a complete strategy on the basis of a single student's protocol, as is frequently done in other domains (Newell & Simon, 1972). Strategy descriptions must instead be constructed from fragmentary data obtained from a number of students.

The texts that students read were two paragraphs taken from a study by Markman (1979). These constitute the unitalicized portions of the protocols shown in Table 9.1. Each paragraph contains an item of information intended to be incongruous or logically inconsistent. In the Fish passage, the statement that fish at the bottom of the sea know their food by its color is incongruous with the preceding statement that there is absolutely no light there. In the Ice Cream passage, the statement that Baked Alaska is made by putting ice cream in a hot oven clashes with everyday knowledge about the propensity of ice cream to melt.

Markman (1979) used these passages in a study that indicated striking deficiencies in comprehension monitoring among children and early adolescents. Markman's research has stirred up considerable controversy and follow-up research (summarized in Brown, Bransford, Ferrara, & Campione,

Table 9.1   Sample Reading Protocols

"Fish" Passage

Many different kinds of fish live in the ocean. Some fi . . . some fish have heads that make them look like alligators and some fish have heads that make them look like cats. Fish live in different parts of the ocean *um . . . What's happening there! Like where . . . where.* Some Fish live near the surface of the water. *um There's the answer.* Some fish live at the bottom of the oceans. *So I think those kind of fish are probably shrimp and lobster.* There's absolutely no light at the bottom of the ocean. *So the problem's cold.* Some fish that live at the bottom of the ocean know their food by its color. *What's its color got to do with it? Color, color doesn't mean anything . . . Yah, that's all. Some of that stuff wasn't relevant. Like it doesn't . . . the color . . . what does color of the food . . . Doesn't matter to them. I don't think they can see very good. We did that last year. And a and a that's about it. And living at the bottom. That's . . . That was OK . . .*

"Ice Cream" Passage

Lots of different kinds of desserts can be made with ice cream. Some fancy restaurants serve a special dessert made out of ice cream called Baked Alaska . . . *I don't know what "Baked Alaska" . . . Never seen the word "Baked Alaska" . . . Looks like . . . To make it . . . To* make it they bake the ice cream . . . *If they bake ice cream it would melt . . .* As soon as it is finished baking they cut it into pieces with a knife and serve it right away . . . *How could, how could they . . . cut ice cream? Oh, and when it's been in the oven heated, it would be just milk . . . Like water . . .* One of the things children like to eat everywhere is . . . in the world is ice cream. Some, some ice cream stores sell many different flavors of ice cream, but the most popular flavors are chocolate and vanilla . . . *Not to me . . . orange is.*

Note: Portions not italicized indicate reading aloud from text. Italicized portions indicate thinking-aloud statements. Texts are taken from Markman (1979). The ice cream passage was rearranged to avoid having the anomalous information come at the end in both passages.

1983). It must be made clear that the present study was not concerned with confirming, disconfirming, or explaining Markman's findings. The objective was to have participants in the study read texts that presented obstacles to comprehension but not obstacles of an obvious kind (such as unfamiliar vocabulary) that would immediately alert them to the problematic nature of the task. Any of a variety of texts might have served the purpose, but Markman's paragraphs had a special advantage. Markman had found that students in the age range used in the present study detected the anomalous information when alerted to be on the watch for something wrong, but tended to miss it if not alerted. Thus, the critical items of information in these paragraphs seemed to meet the twin requirements of (1) not being obvious and (2) not being so esoteric or subtle as to lie entirely outside the grasp of the students. These requirements were intended to ensure that the texts provided some scope for the operation of text-processing strategies rather then depending entirely, for instance, on the availability of subject-matter knowledge.

Method

The study used 12 students from sixth grade and 12 students from tenth grade (approximate ages, 12 and 16 years) in Metropolitan Toronto schools serving middle-class populations. Each group received 45 minutes of preliminary training in thinking aloud while reading, using methods devised by Bird (1980). The training conducted by Bird included demonstrations of the major types of reading behaviors and protocol statements she had identified in previous research, followed by supervised practice. On the following day, in individual sessions, students were tape-recorded as they read the two passages discussed previously. Students were told that the purpose of the study was to find out what goes on in people's minds when they read, and they were encouraged to read normally. They were not alerted to the possibility of there being anything unusual in the texts, and the Fish passage was always presented first, because prior testing had indicated its anomaly to be less frequently recognized than that in the Ice Cream passage. After reading a passage, students were encouraged to continue thinking aloud. It was thought that efforts to resolve a detected anomaly might surface at this time. Then students were asked to recall the passage orally, as completely as possible, and then to write a summary of it from memory.

Findings

Analysis of Protocol Statements.   Each protocol statement made during or immediately after reading was typed on a separate slip of paper and independently classified by two raters. Three-fourths of the statements were judged to be concerned with interpretation of the text and to be clear enough in reference to be classifiable. (Statements such as "That's weird," for instance, were eliminated because it could not be determined whether such a statement referred only to the immediately preceding item of text or to a larger unit.) The interpretive statements that remained were sorted into the following two categories:

> 1. *Detail interpretations.* These were protocol statements that interpret, paraphrase, or question particular items of text content without reference to other items or to more inclusive propositions. Typical items scored as detail interpretations are "Cats?" (referring to the statement that some fish look like cats) and "Why would they live at the bottom of the ocean?" Inferential statements were included in

this category if they were judged to involve only a single item of text content related inferentially to the student's world knowledge. A frequent inference of this type was that the fish said to look like cats must be catfish.

2. *Macro-interpretations.* These are statements concerned with relating particular text elements to other elements or to the overall gist of the paragraph. For example, one student, on reading the statement about no light at the bottom of the ocean, remarked, "which means that these fish that live at the bottom of the ocean live in the dark." This statement adds little content to what has already been explicitly stated in the text, but it performs the important function of connecting the fact about no light to the fact that there are some species of fish that live at the bottom of the ocean and, consequently, live in darkness. Also included in this category were statements referring to the topic or intent of the discourse, such as, "So it's just sort of a summary of the fish and their existence."

These two categories have obvious similarities to the categories of micropropositions and macro-propositions defined by van Dijk (1980). The difference is that the categories used here include not only statements of text content but also comments and questions related to it.

Table 9.2 presents data of the frequency of the two types of protocol statements in sixth and tenth grades based on averages of the two raters. The correlation between raters was .90 for detail interpretations and .81 for macro-interpretations. Detail interpretations are the more numerous at both grade levels with a nonsignificant tendency for the younger students to produce more of them. The older students, however, produced on the average almost four times as many macro-interpretations as the younger students.

Recognition of Anomalies. All but two of the students explicitly recognized the anomaly in the Ice Cream passage (concerning baking ice cream in the oven), making a comment such as "It would melt." Of the two who did not make such a remark, one indicated a familiarity with Baked Alaska. We will later consider what may have made this item so easy to detect, but for the present we will examine results for the Fish passage on which performance was considerably more variable. Eight of the 24 students made no comments at all related to the sentences about there being no light at the bottom of the ocean and about fish finding their food by its color. For the other 16 students, all comments related to these statements were extracted from the recall protocols, along with any statements that contained other than literal repetition of the two points. Each student was then rated on a 0-to 3-point scale, with scale points indexed as follows: 0 = no sign

Table 9.2 Reading Protocol Data

	6 (n = 12)		10 (n = 12)			Some (n = 9)		None (n = 15)		
Variable	M	S.D.	M	S.D.	t	M	S.D.	M	S.D.	t
Detail inter-pretations	4.42	2.18	3.75	3.23	<1	5.28	3.37	3.37	2.04	1.74
Macro-inter-pretations	.54	.78	1.96	1.78	2.52[b]	2.44	1.49	.53	1.04	2.73[a,b]
Anomaly Recogni-tion Score	.54	2.08	1.00	1.30	<1	2.06	.68	0	0	—

The table has two spanning column headers: "Grade" over the "6 (n = 12)" and "10 (n = 12)" columns, and "Group Recognition of Anomaly" over the "Some (n = 9)" and "None (n = 15)" columns.

[a]Tested against $H_o: \mu_1 - \mu_2 = 1$.
[b]$p < .05$

of recognition of the anomaly, 1 = vague indication of concern, 2 = raising the issue of vision in a relevant way but without clear recognition of the conflict between *no light* and *find food by its color,* and 3 = clear recognition of a conflict between the two statements. (The conflict did not have to be accurately formulated; most students who recognized the anomaly declared it would be difficult, rather than impossible, to see with no light.)

Mean scores on the scale of anomaly recognition are presented in Table 9.2. The mean score is higher for tenth-grade students, although this effect is not statistically significant, mean scores being small in relation to variance. Only nine students in all obtained nonzero scores on the scale of anomaly recognition, and of these only five (two sixth-graders and three tenth graders) were credited with explicit recognition of the inconsistency. Table 9.2 presents a comparison of reading protocol data for the group of nine students with that for the remaining 15. The some-recognition group averaged 2.44 macro-interpretations each, compared to .53 for the no-recognition group. (Because a statement recognizing the Fish anomaly would itself be scored as a macro-interpretation, the difference between groups was tested against a null hypothesis of one point, rather than the customary null hypothesis of zero difference.) The some-recognition group also exceeded the no-recognition group in detail interpretations, although not to a statistically significant extent. When the number of detail interpretations is partialed out, there remains a significant correlation of .51 between macro-interpretations and anomaly score. Accordingly, it is concluded that although recognition of the Fish passage anomaly is not significantly associated with school grade, it is significantly associated with reading strategy. The favorable strategy is one that includes explicit attempts to formulate macro-propositions.

Clues to the Nature of Immature Strategies

The quantitative data reported in the preceding section characterize skilled readers in a way that is congruent with the Kintsch and van Dijk (1978) model of text comprehension. Because the validation of that model has rested on indirect evidence, it is gratifying to find in reading protocols direct indications of readers constructing macro-propositions. Unfortunately, however, the quantitative data leave us in the position of defining novice competence solely in terms of lacks. Younger students were found to engage in element-by-element interpretations of text details but so were older students. The difference was that in addition the older students engaged in higher-level interpretations relating details to one another or to the gist of the text. In this section a more holistic look at reading protocols is taken in an effort to see if it is possible to characterize younger readers in terms of what they do do rather than solely in terms of what they do not do.

First, to provide a basis for comparison, we will look at a reading protocol excerpt from one of the more sophisticated tenth-grade students. This excerpt shows the student coming to grips with the Fish passage anomaly:

> There's absolutely no light at the bottom of the ocean, *which means that these fish that live at the bottom of the ocean live in the dark. They probably can't see much of anything—either that or they have very good vision.* And some fish live at the bottom of the ocean know their food by its color *and how could they see the color of the food if it's dark unless they had really good vision?*

In this protocol the reader actively formulates propositions that synthesize information contained in several text propositions, and formulates tentative macro-propositions that are subsequently tested against text content.

The Ice Cream passage protocol shown in Table 9.1 is representative of the younger subjects, who show active interpretation of details but little or no interpretation at the macro-level. These students appear to do the same kind of questioning and inferencing as the older students. The difference is in their exclusive focus on single details: What kind of fish look like alligators? What is Baked Alaska? Are chocolate and vanilla really the most popular ice cream flavors?

Worth examining more closely is the response shown to the baked ice cream anomaly by the protocol in Table 9.1. Almost all students, as noted previously, registered some objection to the effect that ice cream would melt. In the protocol in question, the student is seen going on to question how the ice cream could later be sliced, because it would have been reduced to liquid. Seven of the 24 students raised such an objection, all but one of them being from the lower grade. Recognition of the slicing ice cream anomaly is unrelated to recognition scores for the Fish anomaly ($r = .07$).

One could well argue that the chain of inference involved here is as sophisticated as that involved in recognizing the Fish passage anomaly. In the one case, *no light* implies *darkness* which contradicts *know food by its color*. In the other case, *bake ice cream* implies *melt* which contradicts *slice*. The difference, then, is not in the logical operations involved. The difference, we would argue, is in the kind of text processing that is required in order to set inferencing in motion. In the case of the Fish anomaly, inferencing must be applied to items of content that have no obvious relation to one another except for the fact that they follow one another in the text. In other words it is not a perceived conflict between factual statements that sets inferencing in motion in the case of the Fish anomaly. It is the effort to construct a coherent connection between the *no light* sentence and the *find food by its color* sentence that brings the factual discrepancy to light. In the case of the Ice Cream anomaly, on the other hand, the statement that ice cream is baked in an oven is immediately recognized as discordant with known facts. Once this discrepancy is noted, the further statement about slicing the ice cream is also recognizable as discordant with world knowledge. Thus, the important difference between the two anomalies from a text-processing point of view is that the Ice Cream anomaly will be recognized by someone who actively questions the plausibility of individual statements as they are encountered, but the Fish anomaly will be recognized only by someone who is in addition trying to construct macro-propositions linking apparently disjointed statements.

As a first step toward characterizing immature comprehension strategies, then, it may be proposed that young readers appear to proceed through text by testing individual items of information against their world knowledge. If the item is seen as inconsistent or uninterpretable (if, for instance, it involves an unfamiliar key word), then inferential processes are set in motion, otherwise they are not. This conjecture is consistent with observations by Markman (1981) on younger children who were directed to search for anomalous information in texts. She found that they questioned the truth of individual claims but did not consider the relation of one claim to another.

Children who do nothing but interpret details one-at-a-time could never grasp the gist of a text, however. Summaries produced by the students in the present experiment all show at least some evidence of gist construction. The following examples give an idea of variations in the amount of synthesis of details into statements of gist:

1. There are many fish living in all parts of the ocean. Some have heads that look like other animals. It seems most fish have extremely good vision.
2. There are many kinds of fish. Some fish have heads like cats or alligator. Some fish live near surface of the water. There are many fish in parts of the ocean.

Example 1 consists of constructed statements that interpret sets of propositions included in the text, whereas example 2 consists of paraphrases of selected statements from the text. But the selection of statements in example 2 is clearly not random, two of the four statements being high-order ones. The performance of students in this study was consistent with that found by Brown and Day (1983), with the less mature students relying on deletion and selection and only the most mature using invented statements of gist.

Brown, Day, and Jones (1983) propose a strategy that they call "copy-delete" to account for the way fifth-grade students were found to summarize texts. The strategy consists of reading text elements sequentially, deciding for each element whether to include or delete it, and copying out any items selected for inclusion. The copy-delete strategy has an obvious parallel in the element-by-element interpretation of details that was suggested previously.

In the Kintsch and van Dijk (1978; van Dijk & Kintsch, 1983) model, text comprehension is conceived as cyclical, with deletion, selection, and construction of new propositions going on during each cycle, with previously selected details sometimes being deleted in later cycles and previously deleted details being called back for use in constructing revised macro-propositions, and so on. The reading protocols of the more mature readers that were examined in this study are congruent with such a cyclical model of text comprehension. Protocol data from the less mature readers, however, along with the observations of Markman (1981) and of Brown and her co-workers, all point to the possibility of a different control structure for novice readers. Comprehension in immature readers shows signs of being more of a single-pass process, with details being definitively matched to existing knowledge and assessed as important or unimportant, true or false, at the moment of first encounter. The interpretive rules that immature readers apply are perhaps no different from those applied by experts, but they tend to be applied in a once-and-for-all manner and the order of their application is keyed to the order of elements in the text rather than to processing cycles.

Labeling a mature comprehension strategy as "cyclical" and the immature strategy as "single-pass" is, of course, an oversimplification. At a sufficiently detailed level of analysis, all comprehension probably involves cyclical retrieval of elements into short-term memory (Kintsch & van Dijk 1978). At a more molar level of analysis even mature readers are found to proceed in a largely single-pass manner (Just & Carpenter, 1980). A comparison of mature and immature comprehension strategies must accordingly be made relative to a specified level of analysis. In the studies reported in this chapter, the level of analysis is the relatively molar level that is tapped by thinking-aloud protocols (Ericsson & Simon, 1980). At this level, marked differences do appear in the extent to which readers recall and reconsider previously processed units of text content.

In considering the possibility of qualitative changes in reading comprehension strategies, it is interesting to look for transitional cases—cases that might illustrate the breaking up of an immature strategy and the beginnings of a new one. Such a case seems to be represented in the Fish passage protocol in Table 9.1. It comes from a tenth-grade student who generated above-average amounts of both detail and macro-interpretations. Twice in the Fish passage protocol she indicates a concern about the relevance of particular items to the gist of the text ("What's happening there? Like where . . . where" and "What's its color got to do with it?"). Thus, she does not simply judge items singly as important or unimportant but raises questions and looks for connections. On the other hand, she shows signs of interpreting details in isolation and in a once-and-for-all fashion. Fish living at the bottom of the sea are interpreted to be shrimp and lobster. The implication of no light at the bottom of the sea is determined to be coldness. Both of these are, of course, reasonable interpretations. It is their finality that stands in the way of successful gist-construction. The student worries at some length about what to make of the subsequent sentence about fish knowing their food by its color but in the process does not consider alternative interpretations of the earlier sentences that might make sense in relation to the item about color. On matters of topical relevance, it appears, the student has learned to apply provisional operations that keep data available for further processing, whereas on matters of factual interpretation, she appears to apply prematurely strong macro-rules that eliminate data from further processing (cf. van Dijk, 1980, pp. 49–50).

STUDY 2

One way of getting more insight into text processes is to employ special tasks that render aspects of the process problematic that are not normally problematic. Such a strategem runs the risk, of course, of so altering the task that it no longer elicits the same cognitive behavior that one sets out to investigate. In fact, it probably goes without saying that in any experimental task some unspecifiable amount of what one observes is task specific.

Consequently, in the end one can only rely on findings that converge under principled interpretations. That is the basis on which we try to advance our understanding of text processing in the present study.

The experimental task is that of arranging a set of sentences to make a coherent text. In Study 1 it remained unclear how, or to what extent, the younger students were forming a coherent mental representation of the texts they read, inasmuch as their thinking-aloud statements were focused overwhelmingly on individual details. It is possible that their silence on matters of overall text meaning simply indicates that they encountered no problems in this respect. In sentence arrangement the task of producing a coherent representation is rendered salient and concrete. It was therefore hoped that this task would bring into the open whatever strategies young readers have available for dealing with problems of coherence and overall meaning.

Sentence arrangement also resembles the reading of difficult texts in the kinds of difficulties it imposes:

1. Interpretation of individual sentences often requires a search through other sentences in order to discover referents or to establish the semantic context.
2. Initial hypotheses about meaning will often prove inadequate in the light of subsequent information. Ways in which students dealt with these problems in sentence arrangement were studied by investigating their behavior in reading the sentences, the extent to which they made provisional orderings and groupings, and the kinds of justifications they gave for sentence placements.

Method

The same 24 students of the previous study (12 in each of the sixth and tenth grades) served in the present study. They received the scrambled-sentence tasks the day after completing work with the anomalous texts.

These students received, in a counter-balanced order, two sets of sentences to unscramble. One set, consisting of 10 sentences, formed the text of a narrative fairy tale (a summary of Saint-Exupéry's *The Little Prince*). The other set, consisting of six sentences, formed an expository text about early travel to the East Indies for spices. The two texts are shown in Table 9.3. The sentences are shown in their original order, with numbering added. Students saw the sentences on separate slips of paper randomly arranged. They were instructed to put sentences into the order they thought best. Students were tested in tape-recorded sessions during which they were free to work on the tasks for as long as they wished. They were instructed to think aloud as they worked. Experimenters intervened freely to clarify statements and were directed to elicit a justification of any sentence placement that a student did not explain spontaneously. Experimenters recorded all sentence placements in a way that permitted subsequent coordination with protocol statements.

Table 9.3   Sentences Used in Sentence Arrangement Task

"Prince" Passage
1. The little prince lived alone on a tiny planet.
2. The planet was so tiny, it was no bigger than a house.
3. There were three volcanoes on such a small planet.
4. The prince had a flower.
5. It was unlike any flower in the galaxy.
6. It was special because it could talk.
7. One day, something the flower said made the prince very unhappy.
8. It was this unhappiness that started the prince on his travels.
9. He met a magic fox on another planet.
10. The fox told him the secret to happiness

"Spices" Passage
1. In ancient times and throughout the middle ages, all the spices known in Europe, such as pepper, cloves, mace, nutmeg and cinnamon, were obtained from India and the East Indies.
2. These were in great demand since Europeans, who were heavy meat eaters, had discovered that these substances would not only flavour, but help preserve meat.
3. At first the overland route was used, and spices were carried across the middle east to Europe by caravans.
4. When the Turks captured Constantinople in 1453, and extended their rule into the eastern lands of the Mediterranean, this route became too dangerous.
5. Fortunately, ships were soon improved enough that navigators could sail into unknown seas in search of a water route to the famous spice islands, the East Indies.
6. In fact, one of the aims of Columbus on his celebrated voyage was to find spices.

Findings

Sentence Manipulation Strategies. Two statistical analyses were carried out on students' manipulations of the slips of paper on which sentences were written. The variable *linear placement* was defined as the number of moves in which a single sentence was added to an existing series minus the number of moves in which a sentence was either inserted or moved from its original placement. The mean linear placement score for the two texts was 2.38 at the sixth grade. For the tenth grade, it was −1.04, indicating a preponderance of moves involving insertions or reorderings. The difference between grades was significant at the .05 level ($t(22) = 2.14$). There was a substantial correlation between scores for the two texts (.80 in sixth grade, .70 in tenth grade) suggesting consistent individual differences in approaches to the task.

In the other analysis, students were classified according to whether or not they put sentences into clusters or subgroups prior to assigning them a place in the reconstructed text. Only 3 of the 12 students in sixth grade ever grouped sentences, whereas 9 of the 12 students in tenth grade did so ($p <$ .025, Fisher's exact test).

These analyses indicate markedly different overt strategies predominating in the two grades, with the younger students tending to add sentences one at a time to an arrangement with little subsequent alteration to the linearly developed text, whereas the older students more often made use of preliminary groupings, insertions, and revisions.

Reading Strategies. Linear placement of sentences could reflect a sophisticated or an unsophisticated approach to sentence arrangement depending on the intellectual processes involved in selecting the sentences to place. With a simple text involving few sentences, one could imagine an expert working the whole arrangement out mentally and then placing the slips one-by-one to display the order. Verbal protocol data were examined from two different perspectives to obtain information on intellectual processes. In this section, global reading strategies that students applied to the text sentences are examined. In the next section, the justifications students gave for the sentence placements they made are analyzed.

The protocol of each student on each of the two sentence-arrangement tasks was rated for the presence or absence of the following three types of reading activity: (1) Surveying content—defined as reading ahead of the sentence being placed; (2) Rereading and checking—defined as rereading more than the sentence just placed or making any statement indicating that a placement was temporary, and (3) Summarizing content—defined as stating the gist of information contained in more than two sentences. Two raters independently scored one-fourth of the protocols. Agreement was obtained on 92% of the 36 judgments involved. Final scores were determined by consensus on the three strategy scores on which there was disagreement. The remaining protocols were scored by only one rater.

Surveying content was shown on at least one task by 9 of 12 sixth-graders and 10 of 12 tenth-graders. Rereading and checking was shown by 7 sixth-graders and by all of the tenth-graders—a difference significant at the .05 level by Fisher's exact test. The most pronounced difference between grades, however, was in the incidence of summarization. None of the sixth graders was rated as showing summarization on either task, whereas 8 of the 12 tenth-graders did so ($p < .01$, Fisher's exact test). Summarization was more often elicited by the expository than the narrative passage. The eight students who showed evidence of summarization all did so on the expository passage, but only four of them also did so on the narrative passage.

The relation between reading strategies and sentence-placement strategies was tested by correlating the linear placement score described in the preceding section with the number of tasks (zero to two) on which each student exhibited the various reading strategies. The resulting correlations are shown in Table 9.4. Use of each of the three strategies is negatively associated with linear placement of sentences, the correlations involving the rereading and checking and the summarization strategies both being significant beyond the .05 level. Table 9.4 also shows the correlations between reading strategy use and use of macro-interpretations, as assessed on these same students in Study 1. Summarizing, the strategy most clearly related to macro-interpretation, correlates .60 with that variable indicating a significant degree of stability of reading strategy across the two quite different kinds of tasks.

Findings considered up to this point indicate a developmental trend toward handling sentence arrangement problems by means of tentative groupings and placements of sentences guided by rereading and checking and by summarizing portions of text already assembled. The approach taken by the more mature students appears, therefore, to parallel the process of gist construction posited by the Kintsch and van Dijk (1978) model. This parallel is reinforced by a significant correlation between use of summarization in sentence arrangement and the use of interpretations oriented toward

Table 9.4 Correlations of Reading Strategy Use with Other Strategy Variables

	Correlated Strategies	
Reading Strategy	Linear Placement	Macro-interpretation
Surveying content	−.29	.16
Rereading and checking	−.58[b]	.09
Summarizing	−.50[a]	.60[b]

[a]$p < .05$.
[b]$p < .01$.

macro-structure in ordinary reading. Younger students, on the other hand, tend to approach sentence arrangement in the same element-by-element fashion that it has been hypothesized they use in normal reading. They seldom reconsider judgments about the placement of sentences, much as they appear to make once-and-for-all judgments about the significance and meaning of statements as they encounter them serially in reading texts. How they make these placement decisions has not yet been made clear and is a question that will be pursued in the next section. Results noted thus far indicate that young students make about as much use as older ones do of surveys of content, reading ahead of the sentence under immediate consideration. What is attended to in such surveys could vary, however. Surveying content might involve looking for unifying themes or topics, or it could involve only the serial consideration of alternative sentences for the next placement. For indications of what students may be attending to in their examination of sentences, the explanations students offered when asked to justify sentence placements are discussed.

Justifications of Sentence Placements.   One student from sixth grade and two from tenth grade were eliminated from the following analyses because of experimenter failure to probe for justifications. Each statement by the remaining 21 students justifying a sentence placement was typed on a separate slip of paper and classified by two raters who were blind as to student identity and grade. The total corpus consisted of 242 justifications, 133 from sixth grade and 109 from tenth grade. Six of these justifications were rejected by one or both raters as unclassifiable. The remaining sentences were sorted into the 13 categories shown in Table 9.5. Table 9.5 also presents mean frequencies for each grade and reliabilities, which were estimated by the Spearman-Brown prophecy formula applied to the correlation between frequencies assigned to each student by the two raters.

The grouping of categories in Table 9.5 into five types is conceptual. Only in the case of the *Meaning Construction* group does the grouping prove to have an empirical basis as well.

Unexplained justifications are ones in which the call for justification produced a relevant response but one that did not actually say what it was about a sentence that justified its placement. One kind was *paraphrase* of the sentence in question (e.g., "It's about the route they were taking and it gets too dangerous," which paraphrases a portion of one sentence of the expository passage). Another was *default*, where the reason given for placing a sentence was that no better placement could be found. By far the largest number of unexplained justifications, however, were of the kind labeled *general effect*, which included statements that sentences "sounded good" and responses such as "Because this one says . . . ," followed by reading of the sentence, sometimes in context with or in contrast to another sentence but with no explanation. Not surprisingly, sixth-grade students exceeded tenth-

Table 9.5   Mean Frequency of Types of Sentence Placement Justifications

Justification	Reliability	Grade 6 (n = 11)	Grade 10 (n = 10)
Unexplained			
Paraphrase	.67	.59	.10[a]
Default	.94	.55	.05
General effect	.98	4.41	1.65[a]
Argument overlap			
Single topic	.98	2.18	.40[b]
Multiple topic	.88	.18	.25
Text function			
Beginning/ending	.95	1.32	1.35
Implicit function	.74	.50	.35
Explicit function	.85	.32	2.70[c]
Meaning construction			
Elaborated topic	.66	.27	.75
Linking inference	.91	1.09	2.70[a]
Extrapolation	.97	.05	.35
Cohesion	.91	.23	.65

[a]$p < .05$, two-tailed, for difference between grades.
[b]$p < .01$.
[c]$p < .001$.

grade students in all these categories, significantly so in the case of *paraphrase* and *general effect*.

Argument overlap is a term taken from Kintsch and van Dijk (1978), who propose that a fundamental process in comprehension is the construction of a text base composed of propositions that are cohesively linked by the overlap of arguments with terms in preceding propositions. Here we use the term to refer to justifications that rest solely on the match or mismatch of arguments without reference to predicates. Examples of *single topic* overlap justifications are "It's still talking about the spices" and "It tells you about Europe again." Any argument overlap justification that mentioned or implied more than one topic was classified as *multiple topic*—for instance, "It's talking about a flower, then all of a sudden it's talking about the planet. . . . It doesn't go well together." Sixth-grade students gave five times as many *single topic* argument overlap justifications as did tenth-grade students. With *multiple topic* justifications there is a slight trend in the other direction.

Text function justifications were statements that referred either to the structural role of a sentence in a text or to the kind of information it provides. *Beginning/ending* justifications were ones that asserted, without further explanation, that a certain sentence looked like an appropriate beginning or ending sentence. Such justifications averaged about one per student at both grade levels. An example of *implicit function* justification is the statement, "Why it's special," referring to the sentence, "It was special because it could talk." It is inferred that this means the sentence explains the preceding sentence, which says the flower "was unlike any flower in the galaxy." A justification that spelled this relationship out would be classified as an *explicit function* justification. The statistically most significant difference of any between the grades is in the incidence of *explicit function* justifications, which are almost an order of magnitude more frequent in the tenth grade than in the sixth grade. *Implicit function* justifications are less frequent and slightly favor the younger group.

Meaning construction includes types of justifications that reflect an effort to construct a gist that is superordinate to the particular sentences under consideration. *Elaborated topic* justifications refer to topics, but they go beyond *argument overlap* justifications by indicating some meaningful relationship between arguments. An example is, "That one is talking about land, and then it says ships were soon improved." *Linking inferences* offer some deductive reason for relating two sentences. For instance, one student related the sentences "It was special because it could talk" and "One day something the flower said. . . . " by inferring, "So we know it's the flower that could talk." *Extrapolation* involves inferences to sentences anticipated but not yet encountered. For instance, one student, after arranging sentences that established the prince as living on a tiny planet, said "Now to find out what he's doing there, or what's there." Tenth-grade students exceeded sixth-grade students in all three types of justifications in this group, although the difference was significant only in the case of *linking inference,* which was the most frequent of the three types. This was the only homogeneous group of justification types in terms of intercorrelation (coefficient alpha = .66), and so combined scores for these justifications are used in some later analyses.

A final type of justification was justification on the basis of *cohesion.* Examples of this type are "It can't be the fox because it says 'it' instead of 'he' " and "This 'in fact' sounds like a followup." The few such justifications found at each grade level did not differ significantly in frequency.

Relation of Justifications to Other Variables.   Each student's final arrangement of sentences for the two texts was rated for coherence by two raters on a 5-point scale. There was no difference between grades in the combined ratings ($t(22) < 1$), but coherence ratings for the final sentence arrangements correlated significantly with the use of *meaning construction* justifications ($r = .54, p < .05$). The only other variable that correlated significantly with coherence ratings was *beginning/ending* justifications, which correlated negatively ($r = .60, p < .01$). Evidently, judgments as to what looked like an appropriate beginning or ending sentence tended to be ill-founded. It is interesting that use of *explicit function* justifications did not correlate with coherence rating (r = .03). Although this type of justification was highly related to grade level, it appears not to have been carried out in such a way as to be effective for solving problems of coherence, whereas *meaning construction* was. Evidence of a direct connection between *linking inference* and coherence of the resulting sentence arrangements comes from separately correlating scores for the two texts. Amount of inference on the expository passage correlates significantly with coherence rating for the expository passage but not with coherence rating for the narrative passage. Conversely, amount of inference on the narrative passage correlates significantly with coherence rating for that passage but not with coherence rating for the expository passage.

The *linear placement* score, based on overt sentence manipulations, correlated .47 (p < .05) with use of *single topic* argument-overlap justifications, which suggests that the kind of superficial analysis involved in argument overlap justifications is compatible with an overt strategy involving few modifications in sentence arrangement. The only other significant correlation involving *linear placement* was a negative one (–.50, p < .05) with use of *cohesion* as a justification. This may indicate a tendency for cohesion to be used as a criterion for altering arrangements originally made on some other basis.

The *macro-interpretation* score from Study 1, which was previously shown to correlate with use of summarizing in the sentence arrangement task, also proved to correlate significantly with use of *meaning construction* verifications (r = .44, p < .05). Thus, again, we find macro-interpretation in ordinary reading to be correlated with its most obvious counterpart in sentence arrangement. Macro-interpretations did not correlate significantly with any other justification variables.

Summary of Quantitative Findings.   The approach of the more mature students to sentence arrangement was found to be characterized by tentative placements of sentences and use of preliminary groupings, rereading and checking, and summarization of text. Placement decisions were justified mainly on grounds of their explicit function in the text or on grounds of the meaning generated by a sentence string. If the word *placement* were replaced by the word *interpretation* one would have an approximate description of the ordinary reading behavior of the more mature students as observed in study 1. Indeed, the use of macro-interpretations in Study 1 was significantly correlated with the use of meaning construction justifications in Study 2. Thus, as far as more mature competence is concerned, Study 2 serves mainly to reinforce Study 1 and to provide some basis for confidence that the strategies revealed in sentence arrangement are the same strategies that are used in reading.

Unlike Study 1, however, Study 2 reveals distinctive characteristics in the approach of the less mature students as well. The less mature students were characterized by a linear placement of sentences with little revision, by little rereading and checking and a complete absence of summarization, and by sentence-placement justifications that were either unexplained or explained in terms of overlap between arguments. The unexplained justifications mainly consisted of appeals to the general effect of a string of sentences.

These characteristics seem to add up to a strategy that makes it possible to deal with a sentence-arrangement task without having to construct the overall meaning of the text. The behavior of the younger students in sentence arrangement is consistent with that attributed to them in Study 1: element-by-element interpretations that are not analyzed further in the light of subsequent information. But does their behavior in sentence arrangement tell us anything about how they manage to comprehend text with such a limited processing strategy? That question will be considered by a more detailed examination of selected protocols.

Ways of Reconstructing Texts

In reading through the protocols of both the most sophisticated and the least sophisticated students, the orderliness and apparent ease with which they go about their dramatically different treatments of the sentence arrangement problem becomes obvious. One of the most sophisticated students, after selecting a likely beginning sentence for the expository (Spices) passage, begins his deliberations by formulating an overview:

> So that, you know, it looks like it's going to be something about spices. So it gives the time period—in ancient times and throughout the middle ages—and it gives the subject, all the spices known in Europe.

Thus oriented to the topic, he proceeds to select sentences on the basis of inferences about the meaning of the text aided by summary statements that consolidate what he has established up to that point. For example:

> So—so now we know that they [spices] are in great demand, so we have to have some way of getting them there. . . . So I guess it's that the overland route was used. That's at first, so we know that's the first one. . . .

Were it not known that this was a sentence-arrangement protocol, one might suppose it was the protocol of someone carrying out a very careful reading of an intact text. What the sentence-arrangement task seems to do in a case such as this is to produce an overt display of the macro-operations that are presumed to go on covertly in normal text comprehension (cf. Kintsch &

van Dijk, 1978). For sophisticated students, then, sentence arrangement appears to consist of constructing a mental representation of text meaning and is accomplished by the processes normally employed in comprehension.

A quite different sort of orderliness is displayed in the protocols of less sophisticated students. The following, for instance, is the complete set of comments of one student assembling the Spices passage, minus references to the physical placement of slips of paper:

> . . . because it sort of starts "in ancient times."
> . . . because it just seems to carry it on.
> . . . It's the only one that sounds right.
> . . . because it's talking about . . .
> . . . It's still talking about the route.
> . . . It's the only one left and it sounds okay.

Here there is no apparent effort to grasp the meaning of the text. Argument overlap and general effect are the main criteria applied. Nevertheless, this student produced a reasonable sentence arrangement, one that received a rating of 4 on a 5-point scale of coherence.

Two questions are raised by protocols of this kind:

> **1.** Is the behavior displayed here unique to the sentence arrangement task or does it, as appears to be the case with the more sophisticated students, reflect more general ways of processing text?
> **2.** How is it possible to construct coherent text by means of the kinds of operations displayed?

Studies of children's writing have identified both argument overlap and general effect as playing central roles in children's composing processes. In a study of coherence in children's texts, McCutchen and Perfetti (1982) found that most of the connections in the texts of second graders were on the basis of reference (argument overlap), whereas by the eighth grade, students were beginning to make use of complex syntactic connections. They observed:

> A simple count of repeated words, or argument overlap (Kintsch
> & van Dijk, 1978), would overestimate the degree to which
> coherent texts are produced by young writers.

The same would be true in sentence arrangement. Use of argument overlap justifications did not correlate significantly with rated coherence of the resulting arrangements (r = .29 for the narrative passage, .19 for the expository passage).

In a study of revision abilities, Bartlett (1982) found that elementary school students could recognize that something was wrong in passages where there were failures of cohesion (as in faulty reference), but they could not locate the source of the trouble. Their appeal, instead, was to the general effect or sound of the language.

Thus there is evidence from other areas of text processing that children make use of argument overlap and general effect in cases where more mature people would make use of meaning-based inferences and connections. In sentence arrangement, children appear quick to recognize overlapping arguments even when they are not based on exact repetition of words. This apparently well-practiced skill suggests that the micro-operations that Kintsch and van Dijk (1978) specify for creating a cohesive set of propositions are part of children's repertoires. In addition to connecting one sentence to another, however, children show signs of identifying those particular repeated arguments that indicate the topic of a text segment. This is clearly a kind of macro-operation, although it is one that can be carried out without reference to text meaning.

Children's appeals to *general effect* are difficult to interpret, because it is not clear to what extent the vagueness resides in the child's comprehension of text and to what extent the vagueness resides in the child's expression. Notions such as *flow* and *sound* are common in expert discussions of text and point to the fact that mature language users often have global impressions of the appropriateness or inappropriateness of a text sequence without a statable explanation. Such global impressions of coherence, together with a recognition of topical connections, could provide a workable basis for comprehension monitoring in children. Such a basis would often permit superficial or incorrect comprehension, as indicated in children's response to anomalous texts, but it would probably serve for most kinds of easy reading. Thus, it is not unreasonable to suppose that the processes that immature students display in sentence arrangement are processes that serve them in normal reading and writing as well, enabling them to achieve a degree of coherence through limited processing of text meaning.

The two approaches to sentence arrangement illustrated above seem worlds apart. In an effort to gain insight into what is involved in changing from one approach to the other, we shall examine, as was done with Study 1, what appears to be a transitional case. It is perhaps worth noting that the two selections of transitional cases were carried out by Bereiter and Scardamalia independently, but the same student turned out to be chosen in both cases. In Study 1 this student was observed to be carrying out sophisticated interpretations of individual statements and to be showing concerns about relevance, but to be hampered in making sense of the text by the persistence of a strategy of element-by-element interpretation. In sentence arrangement she again makes sophisticated inferences, but is unable to integrate these inferences into a coherent interpretation of the text.

In tackling the Spice passage, this student first infers a sequential relationship between the sentence that begins "When the Turks captured

Constantinople in 1453. . . . " and the sentence about Columbus by drawing on (slightly inaccurate) world knowledge that associates Columbus with the year 1497. Later she establishes a meaning-based connection between the sentence referring to caravans and the sentence about ships being improved: "The caravans, see, at first—makes you think, like, that was at first, then ships came along." A number of other connections are established on the basis of logical inference or discourse-structure knowledge.

Where this student runs into trouble is in trying to combine all these separate insights into a basis for ordering the complete set of sentences. In attending to one relationship she loses track of another; for instance, the 1453–1497 connection later disappears without comment. She attempts an overall ordering on the basis of temporal cues, but there are not enough of those. She ends up placing some sentences on the basis of argument overlap (spices), one on the basis of its being "like a beginning statement," and then subjecting the whole to rereading to test how it sounds.

This student appeared to have the elements of a sophisticated text-processing strategy but to lack the higher-level executive procedures that could make these elements work effectively in producing a coherent text representation. Unlike the more successful student whose protocol was examined previously, she attempted no overview of what the text was about. Although she reread sentence sequences to see how they sounded, she did not generate summary statements that might have enabled her to see where the text was heading or to spot out-of-place sentences. Unlike the other two protocols cited, this student's protocol does not convey an impression of orderliness and ease. Confusion and struggle are evident. It seems that she was trying to handle meaning-construction processes like those of the more mature student but with an executive structure more like that of an immature student.

Individual cases can, of course, only illustrate, not prove points. The point this transitional case illustrates is that progress toward mature text processing involves not only acquiring particular macro-rules, but also developing an executive structure within which those rules can be applied effectively and without overloading or disrupting the cognitive system.

GENERAL DISCUSSION

Although the two studies reported in this chapter used unconventional tasks, their intent was to yield information about normal text processing—in particular, about how immature readers deal with difficult texts. Let us be clear about what is and is not being assumed when we try to generalize from experimental tasks like sentence arrangement to everyday activities of reading and studying from texts. We do not assume that the calibre of performance, however measured, is the same. Experimental conditions might degrade performance to a less mature level, or they might, on the other hand, provide motivation and aids to the structuring of cognitive behavior that enable students to perform above their normal levels (cf. Bransford, 1981). It is assumed, however, that the cognitive strategies students use in experimental tasks must have had a life outside the experimental situation. They may be adapted to experimental task demands, but they could not have been created *de novo* for the experiment. This assumption receives empirical support from the cross-task correlations observed in the two studies, which were run on the same students, as well as from the general conformity of the behavior of more mature students to that expected from existing knowledge of the comprehension process. Accordingly, although findings from these studies cannot be taken as normative measures of the competence of 12-year-olds and 16-year-olds, they can be taken as indicative of developmental changes in the strategies students have available for dealing with text processing difficulties.

The characterization of the more sophisticated text-processing strategies that emerges from these studies contains no surprises. The sophisticated student approaches both ordinary reading and sentence arrangement tasks as tasks that call for the construction of a coherent gist or message. In ordinary reading, inferential processes are brought into play not only when there is an inconsistency between text statements and world knowledge but also when there is a difficulty in making a coherent propositional connection between textually linked statements. Sentence arrangement differs from ordinary reading for these students primarily in that establishing coherence is problematic throughout and thus requires more of what they do normally. This characterization, as noted several times previously, is virtually a gloss on the Kintsch and van Dijk (1978) model of text comprehension, its only novelty arising from the fact that it is drawn from quite different kinds of data.

It is easy to characterize younger students by the absence of features of mature competence. Data from the present studies support the notion that the kind of competence represented in the Kintsch and van Dijk model is not inherent in the human information-processing system but is an acquisition. In both studies, younger students showed significantly lesser amounts of the kind of activity associated with construction of macro-propositions—less summarizing, less rereading and checking, less questioning of intersentence connections, less production of linking inferences.

These characterizations have relevance to instructional design, supporting efforts like those reported by Palincsar & Brown (1984) to teach expert-like strategies of text processing. It has been intended, however, in carrying out the reported studies, to go beyond identifying what students lack and to obtain insight into the strategies immature students actually use. This is a much more speculative venture than identifying what students lack, but the studies have provided a basis for at least the beginnings of such a venture.

A starting premise, which has support from other research, is that young students have the capacity to make the same kinds of inferences as older ones (cf. Trabasso, Stein, & Johnson, 1981). In Study 1 such inferencing was sparked by conflicts between text statements and world knowledge but not by problems of text coherence. The protocol statements of younger students in Study 1—heavy on detail interpretations, light on macro-interpretations— and the linear placement strategy they exhibited on sentence arrangement tasks in Study 2 suggest a common underlying strategy of text processing. It is a strategy that proceeds element by element, relying to a large extent on text characteristics that can be extracted without deep analysis—on the sharing of arguments among propositions and on a general impression of flow that may result both from surface cohesiveness and local coherence (McCutchen & Perfetti, 1982).

The mental representation of a fully comprehended text, as described by van Dijk (1980) for instance, consists of hierarchically arranged propositions. At the top of the hierarchy are topics—propositions that indicate what the text is about. At a lower level are propositions that summarize major substantive points in the text. Much of the activity of comprehension, according to Kintsch and van Dijk's model, goes into the construction of these macro-propositions. At a still lower level are propositions capturing the detailed content of the text. An immature processing strategy of the kind described would be capable of generating high-level propositions of the "what it's about" variety, because these could be derived from the analysis of argument overlap that has been evidenced in young readers. But such a processing strategy would not generate macro-propositions of the "what it says" variety. Hence the absence of invented summary statements in the summaries of young readers studied by Brown and Day (1983).

The resulting mental representation of text, then, would consist of high-level nodes representing topics, directly connected to low-level nodes representing details of content. Missing would be the intermediate level of macro-propositions that distill the substance of the text. Such a *topic-plus-detail* mental representation is obviously deficient from the standpoint of meaningful learning from text. Most of the knowledge worth carrying away from an instructional text is captured in macro-propositions of the "what it says" type. "What it's about" propositions encode information mainly about the text itself rather than about the world and consequently are of limited long-term value; also, propositions representing single details have obvious inadequacies as knowledge.

Although the structure of this hypothesized topic-based strategy is but crudely sketched in these remarks, and although much of what has been said is speculative, collateral evidence makes it seem likely that some kind of strategy based on element-by-element interpretation and a shallow structure of mental representations underlies immature text processing. The previously cited *copy-delete* strategy identified by Brown, Day, and Jones (1983), seems to be the same kind of strategy applied to summarization that is applied to ordinary reading and to sentence arrangement. It parallels the knowledge-telling strategy for composition that consists of generating text content serially under constraints of topic and discourse schema—essentially the same process displayed in the more immature approaches to sentence arrangement in Study 2. There is, thus, a certain convergence of results from varied data sources. Progress toward a more general and definitive description of immature text-processing strategies will likely depend on such convergence, rather than on exploiting particular experimental paradigms.

Brown, Bransford, Ferrara, & Campione (1983) have discussed the copy-delete strategy of summarization and the knowledge-telling strategy of composition as examples of immature strategies that tend, because they work moderately well and demand less mental effort than more sophisticated strategies, to persist beyond the age when they might be outgrown. Because strategies for learning from text are mainly acquired and applied in school, it may be important for educational planning to examine the conditions of schooling that sustain or thwart various cognitive strategies. In Chapter 7, 11 common school practices were itemized that would tend to support the knowledge-telling strategy. Is it possible also that there are school conditions that support persistence of immature comprehension strategies?

A likely candidate is the pervasive school practice of question-and-answer as the instructional technique for testing and practicing learning from text (cf. Bellack, Kliebard, Hyman, & Smith, 1966). While a reading strategy that leads to a topic-plus-detail representation of text may not be an effective way for independently acquiring world knowledge, it may be an effective way of preparing for school tests and lessons. Such a way of organizing information is effective for retrieving details, given either a topic or a related detail. It may also be an efficient way of preparing for "thought questions" because it avoids commitment to high-level propositions that might prove inappropriate to the questions. From this standpoint, the immature topic-based as contrasted with the mature proposition-based strategy may be seen as a strategy of incomplete text processing, which depends on class discussions or other school learning activities to complete the processing of text details into macro-propositions that will be incorporated into world knowledge.

Data reported in this chapter show indications of substantial development toward more mature reading strategies occurring between sixth and tenth grades, but they also suggest that development is not universal. One-third of the tenth graders made no overt use of summarization in sentence arrangement.

Only one student showed consistent efforts at gist construction in all the experimental tasks. How prevalent different kinds of reading strategies are, and to what extent immature strategies persist in older students and adults, are important questions that cannot be answered on the basis of present evidence.

POSTSCRIPT
THREE FOLLOW-UP STUDIES

An informal study was conducted by Woodruff and Scardamalia to see whether children would apply the same strategies to computer program arrangement that they apply to arranging text sentences. The participants were elementary-school students of varying ages who had spent the preceding term learning to use the LOGO programing language (Papert, 1980). Each child was given the sentence arrangement tasks described previously and in addition was given the statements of a LOGO program in scrambled order. The program consisted of eight statements which, when run in the proper order, would produce the picture of a flower on the monitor screen. All but one of the children used the same kinds of low-level strategies for program arrangement as for text arrangement. They would group together statements that contained the same terms and then would try to sequence them on the basis of local considerations. Only the one student who was the most talented programer did what adult programers did—try to figure out what the program was supposed to do (the equivalent of gist construction) and then arrange the program statements so that they would do it.

This study adds further evidence of the generality of immature text-processing strategies. Here the strategies were found being applied in a situation quite removed from classroom reading and writing, and applied to a task where students could be assumed to be motivated to bring their most sophisticated strategies into play. Moreover, the program arrangement task, unlike ordinary sentence arrangement, is a task in which it should have been clear to the students that there is a central idea or purpose to be identified.

The second follow-up study was a replication of the sentence-arrangement Study 2 reported in the main body of this chapter, using a different way of presenting the scrambled sentences, and including adults as well as school-age students (Burtis, Bereiter, & Scardamalia, 1984). Although younger and older students in the original study revealed significantly different approaches to the task, they did not differ significantly in their actual success in reconstructing the original texts. Apparently, both the more mature and less mature strategies worked reasonably well for recovering the original text. We reasoned that this might be true because the format of the task, in which sentences were spread out in front of the students, facilitated the immature strategy of scanning the sentences for common topics. If our analysis of immature versus mature strategies was correct, then introducing a procedure that prevented people from scanning the sentences for common topics ought to lower the performance of younger students but should not affect the performance of students using a higher-level, gist-oriented strategy. Such a study, therefore, could serve as a validation of the original analysis of text-processing strategies.

The new procedure that blocked scanning for common topics consisted simply of presenting the scrambled sentences one at a time rather than simultaneously, and requiring participants to make a tentative placement of each sentence before the next was presented. Briefly, the results for sixth- and tenth-grade students were exactly as expected. When judged according to the coherence of the texts they constructed, sixth-grade students did significantly worse than before, whereas grade 10 students were unaffected. The justifications students gave were similar in distribution to those in the previous study, indicating that the same strategies were being used. What changed was how well the strategies worked. A correlation of .78 was found between level of strategy (as indicated by the use of gist-oriented versus surface-oriented justifications) and rated coherence of the reconstructed texts.

A final study, carried out by Earl Woodruff, was concerned with whether students would change toward higher-level strategies over a series of trials if they had continuous access to feedback that would show when their existing strategies were not working. A computer program was constructed that presented text sentences one at a time in scrambled order. Students made tentative placements of the sentences and were free to rearrange them at any time, as in the study just described. In addition, however, there was one condition in which students could call, whenever they had placed a sentence, for feedback on how well their reconstructed text at the moment corresponded to the original text (the correspondence being expressed as a percentage). Justification protocols, like those obtained in the preceding studies, were collected before and after a six-paragraph training series. Unfortunately, these protocols have not yet been analyzed at this writing. What is known, however, is that sixth-grade students in the feedback condition increased significantly the amount of time spent trying to solve the sentence arrangement problems. This suggests that at least the conditions for strategy change existed, so that it will be quite remarkable, and a further testimony to the strength of immature text processing strategies, if there is no change after such concerted effort by students to improve their performance.

In summary, the further research that we have been doing adds reason for confidence that the immature strategy identified first in writing and then in comprehension is not a procedural fluke. It appears in a variety of tasks and behaves in a lawlike way under varying conditions. To what extent it can be changed remains to be seen. Instructional possibilities are explored in Part IV.

Part IV
Promoting the Development of Mature Composing Strategies

Although this part of the book deals with efforts to advance young writers' composing strategies, it can also be read as a continuation of research into the nature of composing strategies. This is because the instructional experiments to be reported were conceived as varieties of "simulation by intervention," as described in Chapter 2. None of the studies are aimed at producing overall improvements in writing performance. Rather, each study typically focuses on the possibility of producing some particular change in students' composing processes. Changes in writing performance are then examined to see whether they are consistent with the intended effects on cognitive processes and whether they are consistent with theoretical notions. In this latter connection, those aspects of writing performance that do not change (or those that may even change for the worse) are often as informative as those aspects of performance that improve as a result of the intervention.

The following chapters do not address the large question of how writing should be taught (much less take sides in the controversies that inevitably attend that question). Instead the chapters address an aspect of learning to write that until recently has received almost no attention—namely, the aspect that has to do with how the composing process is structured in the mind of the learner.

The question we would like ultimately to answer is whether knowledge tellers can become knowledge transformers and, if so, how. But answering such a question is almost certain to take long-term interventions, measured in years. No short-term intervention can be expected to produce the reorganization of cognitive processes that we believe to be required. But long-term experimental interventions are almost nonexistent in educational research and will probably, for practical reasons, continue to be. Some of the interventions we have used lasted less than an hour and were essentially probes to see whether some particular process was amenable to facilitation. The longest intervention, reported in Chapter 12, ran for half a year. Accordingly, conclusions about major changes in the composing process have to be based on inference from short-term indicators.

It is because of this need to infer long-term consequences from short-term effects that theory is vital in instructional research. Without it, one is left with guesswork and unfounded extrapolation. In instructional research on writing, the common assumption is that anything that produces an improvement in the quality of student writing is of long-term benefit, but this is obviously a risky assumption. As we saw in Chapter 4, you can improve the rated quality of students' writing simply by asking them to write more. Changes in the nature of the task, in motivating conditions, or in the kind of help given students may all improve the quality of what they produce without producing any but a transitory change in the students themselves.

The knowledge-telling and the knowledge-transforming models provide theoretical grounds for regarding several kinds of short-term effects as indicators of more fundamental change:

1. *Signs of problem-solving effort.* The main thing that distinguishes knowledge transforming from knowledge telling is the involvement of problem-solving processes in the former. Evidence that students are wrestling with problems in their compositions—either problems of substance or problems of presentation—is therefore a hopeful sign.

2. *Internalizing a new feedback loop.* Knowledge telling is primarily a straightahead process of text generating. It is therefore a hopeful sign whenever students independently

reconsider a decision or make a new decision on the basis of evaluating what they have already done. Such evidence of feedback-controlled activity in writing is favorable even when the rethinking is of such a local nature that it can easily be accommodated within a knowledge-telling model (for instance, thinking of a fact to state, deciding it is uninteresting, and thinking of another one). Such limited backward looping may establish patterns of rethinking that eventually give rise to more extensive reconsideration of decisions.

3. *Self-reports of cognitive change* (to be distinguished from reports of enjoyment or improved performance). Even though there is good reason to be skeptical about self-reports of cognitive processes (Nisbett & Ross, 1980), a case can be made for taking certain kinds of reports of cognitive change seriously. When children, without undue prompting, report changes in how they are thinking or in how they see what they are doing, and when these reports are consistent with theoretical expectations, and when it is unlikely that the children would be sophisticated enough to have figured out what those expectations were, then it seems reasonable to infer that some change worth taking seriously has occurred. This is true even when there is no corresponding change in performance since, as we have seen repeatedly in earlier chapters, there are many reasons why a particular competence might not be reflected in performance.

These evidences of cognitive change have appeared almost universally in the instructional studies to be described in this section. This is not to suggest that a shift toward knowledge-transforming processes is easy to achieve. When we have used interventions that focused on the surface text or on overt behavior (as in some of the studies reported in Chapter 3), evidences of cognitive change did not appear. What is suggested, however, by positive results from even very brief interventions, is that students have cognitive resources ready to be brought into the composing process. They typically show motivation to acquire more sophisticated writing strategies and such necessary components as evaluative and general problem-solving skills. The instructional challenge, then, is to help them develop an executive structure for applying these resources. That is the problem to which the studies reported in this section were addressed.

Chapter 10
Fostering Self-Regulation

PREFACE

There are two quite different senses in which one may talk about strategies in writing. One sense refers to *rhetorical* strategies. These are strategies for achieving effects or purposes of the composition. An example would be the strategy of beginning the narrative in the middle of an event, without any establishment of setting or character—a strategy that might serve, among other things, for arousing curiosity in the reader. The study of such strategies has, of course, been the province of rhetoric. There has, however, been a recent interest in the psychological study of rhetorical strategies (Beaugrande, 1982b; Brewer, 1980) and some beginnings have been made at finding out how rhetorical knowledge is acquired from reading model texts (Bereiter & Scardamalia, 1984; Church & Bereiter, 1983).

The other sense of strategies in writing refers to *self-regulatory* strategies. These are strategies for managing one's own cognitive behavior during writing. Knowledge telling is a strategy in this sense. It is a way of going about the writing task that is, as we have seen, effective for some purposes and not for others. Other self-regulatory strategies in writing might range from simple procedures of checking over pronouns to make sure their reference is clear, to the elaborate rituals some writers construct to guide their work (Wason, 1980). The research described in previous chapters has focused on self-regulatory strategies, not on rhetorical strategies. We retain this focus in the instructional research reported in the following chapters.

This is not to diminish the importance of rhetorical strategies. To be an expert writer you must obviously have a repertoire of powerful rhetorical strategies; by contrast, the best self-regulatory strategies in the world will not make you a good writer. Therefore it is not surprising that college composition courses have tended to concentrate on teaching rhetorical strategies, especially through the study of model texts in which such strategies are represented.

But the learning of rhetorical strategies presupposes an executive structure within which those strategies may function. That implies a structure for setting goals to be achieved through the composition and for monitoring progress toward those goals, for identifying obstacles, solving problems, and so on. As we have seen, the executive structures that guide the composing processes of novice writers tend not to have these capabilities. Acquiring them is a matter of learning self-regulatory strategies. The difficulties of learning more sophisticated self-regulatory strategies in writing, and general approaches to overcoming these difficulties, are the topics of the present chapter.

10

This chapter deals with ways to help children improve their strategies for handling complex knowledge-processing tasks. In chapter 7, "Knowledge Telling and the Problem of 'Inert Knowledge,'" we described a common strategy by which children reduce a number of potentially difficult tasks to a relatively simple task of "knowledge telling." Although this strategy has great coping value, enabling children to handle school tasks that would otherwise exceed their performance limitations, the strategy tends to defeat the educational purpose of much school work. There is a broad range of complex knowledge-processing activities in which the immediate consequences of deficient strategies are not definite enough to induce strategy change. In these activities, instruction therefore has an especially important role to play, but also an especially difficult one.

Expository writing is paradigmatic for a range of intellectual tasks occurring in everyday life. These are tasks in which the goal is at least partly emergent—your knowledge of what you are after grows and changes as part of the knowledge-constructing process—and in which there is a wealth of potentially applicable knowledge and potential routes to the goal. Tasks that have these properties fall within the category of what Greeno (1978) calls composition problems. We refer to the whole category as *compositional* tasks, to distinguish them from written *composition*, which is a subclass. Whether these are humble tasks of planning a birthday party or grand ones of constructing a scientific theory, they all present formidable obstacles when it comes to teaching someone better strategies for doing them.

To get a general sense of these obstacles, one need only reflect on the conditions that favor rapid learning of new strategies. These are a clear-cut goal, against which to judge the efficacy of one's current strategy, and the opportunity to observe or be coached in a more effective strategy (cf. Case, 1985a). In tasks that have emergent goals, however, the goal is in large part a product of actions taken in pursuing it, and so its value as a standard and as a motivator of change is ambiguous. This also means that the advantage of a more sophisticated strategy may not be obvious, because different strategies entail different goals, not merely different ways of pursuing the same goal.

There is a deeper difficulty with teaching new strategies for compositional tasks, however, which has to do with the level of specificity at which strategies may usefully be presented. A strategy for executing a task may be described at a range of levels of specificity, from the detailed level of production systems or computer programs to the level of very broad descriptive statements. Successful efforts at cognitive strategy teaching, such as those by Case (1975, 1978c, 1985a), have tended to use strategies of quite fine grain—strategies more or less at the level of specificity of computational algorithms. Teaching strategies at what we may accordingly call the algorithmic level is evidently powerful, but unfortunately it is practical only within a very restricted range of activities. It is restricted to activities for which algorithms can be written with a small enough number of rules that it is reasonable to expect that the rules can be learned. Such activities are largely confined to the realms of logico-mathematical problem solving. Outside that realm, most intelligent activity depends on context-sensitive rules (Bobrow & Norman, 1975). Grammar is a good example. A complete description of English grammar at the algorithmic level remains yet to be written, because each rule for a particular linguistic feature has many conditions attached to it relating to other feature combinations. Supposing an algorithmic description could be worked out, however, it is clear that it would be far too complex to teach. The same is true for any compositional task. In tasks to which large amounts of propositional knowledge are relevant, choices of action become complexly contingent on the knowledge context. The result is that, even if it were possible to abstract and teach an algorithm for writing a good essay about dogs, there is no assurance that it would work for writing an essay about cats.

The obvious recourse is to move up to a more general level of strategy description. This is the level of heuristics (Polya, 1945) or tricks of the trade. A great deal of advice is given at this level pertaining to writing, ranging from the introspections and commonsense injunctions of innumerable books on the art of writing, to systematic schemes for developing compositions (e.g., Young et al., 1970), and most recently to suggestions drawn from research on the composing processes of expert and novice writers (Flower, 1981). We have no doubt that strategy teaching at these levels can be helpful, having profited from it ourselves. But it is limited by two important presuppositions. First, it presupposes a high level of metacognition so that one is able to assess and consciously manipulate one's cognitive strategies. Second, it presupposes an existing executive strategy that is already highly enough developed to incorporate suggested new procedures as minor altera- tions or additional "loops" (cf. Case, 1985a). We presume, in other words, that it is not possible to build or rebuild a complex executive strategy from the ground up through the use of verbal strategy descriptions. Thus strategy teaching at this level offers little hope for dealing with the kind of problem that motivates the present inquiry—the problem of students who use the knowledge-telling strategy, which bypasses problems that such high-level strategic advice is intended to help people contend with.

The strategy-teaching approaches we have just discussed, ranging from those that work at the algorithmic level to those that work at very general levels of description, may all be thought of as approaching strategy change through the implicit or explicit teaching of *rules*—rules that constitute principles or procedures of task execution.

We are convinced that rules of task performance do not represent the most promising objects of instructional effort when one is trying to upgrade immature strategies for complex knowledge-processing tasks, and that this is true regardless of the level of specificity of the rules and regardless of whether they are taught verbally or instilled through some more ingenious method. Instead, we believe that instructional efforts in this context are better directed at what Brown and Campione (1981) call "self-regulatory mechanisms."

As examples of self-regulatory mechanisms, Brown and Campione list *checking, planning, monitoring, revising,* and *evaluating.* We prefer to work with a somewhat more fine-grained specification than this, as is illustrated in the next section, but these examples nicely indicate the sort of cognitive entity we are talking about. Each one represents an information-processing skill or executive function amenable to improvement in its own right, a function that involves its own goal setting, knowledge retrieval, processing, and storage operations.

These self-regulatory mechanisms may be thought of in two ways. In one way, they may be thought of as building blocks or subroutines that can be assembled along with other subroutines to constitute a program for accomplishing some task. That is how they are treated, for instance, in Hayes and Flower's (1980) model of the composing process, where many of the same mechanisms mentioned by Brown and Campione are explicitly represented. The composing behavior of expert writers may in these terms be distinguished from that of novices by the greater frequency with which regulatory mechanisms are used compared to nonregulatory mechanisms such as generating and transcribing.

But there is another way of looking at self-regulatory mechanisms that has more long-range educational significance. It is to see these mechanisms as contributing not only to immediate performance but also as contributing to the further development of the cognitive system. When executive functions such as planning and evaluating are incorporated into the system of cognitive behavior, they generate information that may lead to strategic changes in behavior (Flavell, 1979). In other words, these self-regulatory mechanisms may constitute change-inducing agents that will have the effect of altering the rules by which the system operates. Thus, whereas introducing new self-regulatory mechanisms into children's cognitive behavior does not in itself constitute teaching new rules or strategies of task performance, it may result in the child's acquiring such new rules. In task domains where the rule systems are too complex to be teachable, it would seem that the best hope for promoting learning would be to promote self-regulatory functions that will help children acquire rules through their own activity (cf. Krashen, 1976).

The instructional methods that we propose in this chapter are, then, methods aimed at promoting more mature cognitive strategies through the action of the children's own self-regulatory mechanisms. The first method is procedural facilitation, some applications of which have already been described in Chapter 3. It consists of routines and external aids designed to reduce the processing burden involved in bringing additional self-regulatory mechanisms into use. The second method, *goal concretization,* uses substitute goals of a more concrete and stable type than those naturally occurring in compositional tasks. These goals serve as the basis for learning activities in which self-regulatory mechanisms can serve goal-directed functions that may later be transferred to natural tasks. Although these two methods can be—and we think should be—combined in practice, they are conceptually quite different, and so for clarity of exposition we treat them separately here.

PROCEDURAL FACILITATION

We start with the assumption that for any compositional task that might be presented to children they already have an executive procedure available for dealing with it—a procedure that will enable them to undertake the task and carry it through to some kind of completion. The situation is different with many logical or practical tasks, in which it is quite possible for a person confronted with the task to declare, simply, "I don't know how to do this." Thus, in the case of compositional tasks, instruction must always be brought to bear on a procedure that already works in some fashion and that the child may well believe to work perfectly.

Our instructional goal is to introduce an additional self-regulatory mechanism into this executive procedure, for instance, one for planning or for evaluation. Adding such a mechanism inevitably increases the information-processing load on the executive system. This occurs in two main ways. First, in order to bring the new mechanism into use, the executive system must switch attention to it at appropriate times and then switch attention back to the interrupted procedure. This requires active attention and recall of quite a demanding kind. One of the problems people have in incorporating new behavior into their habitual routines is that they simply don't remember to do it when they should (Wilkins & Baddeley, 1978). Second, the new mechanism itself requires processing capacity, possibly a large amount because of the newness of the function, and this may wipe out short-term stores of information needed for other parts of the task procedure that have been momentarily suspended. This would be experienced as losing one's place, forgetting what one was doing, etc.

One of the conjectures that led us to explore procedural facilitation was that children might have appropriate self-regulatory mechanisms available, and even know that these procedures would be good to use, and yet fail to use them because they were unable to place them in their existing executive procedures. Accordingly, we set out to design special supportive procedures that would (1) provide cues or routines for switching into and out of new regulatory mechanisms while keeping the executive procedure as a whole intact and (2) minimize the resource demands of the newly added self-regulatory mechanisms.

The main steps in designing a procedural facilitation are as follows:

1.   Identify a self-regulatory function that appears to go on in expert performance but that does not go on or that goes on in an attenuated form in student performance: for instance, revision (Nold, 1981) or composition planning (Chapter 8 of this book; Flower & Hayes, 1981).

2. Describe the self-regulatory function as explicitly as possible in terms of mental operations or functions. For example, *revision* can be described in terms of the mental operations of *comparing, diagnosing, choosing a revision tactic,* and *generating* alternatives to previous phrasing and structuring of text (Chapter 11). *Planning* can be described in terms of mental operations that sustain a dialectic between rhetorical and content concerns (Chapter 12).

3. Design a way of cuing or routinizing the onset and offset of the process that makes minimal demands on mental resources. Thus, we may think of the four revision operations listed previously as a loop that is set in action when some mismatch has been detected between written text and intention. After that the output from each operation triggers the next until the comparison operation no longer detects a mismatch. Figure 11.1 shows a flowchart model of this process, which for brevity we call the CDO process (for COMPARE, DIAGNOSE, OPERATE). Likewise, we may think of the dialectic in *planning* as a loop set in action when a perceived content or rhetorical problem is translated into a problem of the other sort. As a way of facilitating the onset and offset of such processes, and for purposes of getting the function introduced into a child's executive procedure, we may teach the child to initiate it routinely, and to end the process after only one cycle.

4. Design external supports or teachable routines for reducing the information-processing burden of the mental operations. For instance, to facilitate *comparing* and *diagnosing,* we may reduce the task to a choice among a limited set of alternative evaluations ("This is good," "People may not understand this point," etc.). Similarly, we may reduce choosing a revision tactic to a finite choice (leave the text unchanged, delete, change wording, replace whole sentence, etc.). In *planning* we can reduce the rhetorical and content concerns to a finite set (see Chapter 12, Tables 12.1 and 12.2). These choosing operations may be given external support by presenting the sets of alternatives on cards or in lists.

What we end up with, then, is a much simplified version of the self-regulatory function. The purpose of the simplifications is to enable children to start performing the self-regulatory function with as little additional burden on their processing capacities as possible. As they become practiced at it, the function should begin taking even less capacity, so that the simplifications can be withdrawn.

There is obviously a danger that in simplifying a self-regulatory function it will be so altered that practicing it will have no value in preparing children to carry out the normal function independently and might even interfere, by teaching bad habits. The likelihood that this will occur cannot be determined by surface appearances or commonsense assumptions. Indeed, it should be apparent that a procedural facilitation cannot be either constructed or evaluated except on the basis of a reasonably strong theory of the process—so that in the end testing the facilitation becomes a way of testing the theory. (See the discussion of *simulation by intervention* in Chapter 2.)

The intimate connection between procedural facilitation and process models will become evident in Chapters 11 and 12, which report instructional studies using procedural facilitations of revision and of reflective planning. Each chapter begins with a model which is at the same time a hypothetical model of the mature process and a framework for the facilitating procedures. It will also be evident in the postscript to Chapter 11 that the process model provides the basis for assessing what the intervention has and has not accomplished and for designing further procedures to provide more complete or effective facilitation.

In ending this section we want to underline the discriminative force of the adjective *procedural* in procedural facilitation. There is another much more common type of facilitation used in teaching, which we may call *substantive* facilitation. In substantive facilitation the overall executive burden is reduced by having the teacher or some other agent directly assume part of it and thus function as an active collaborator. With respect to the CDO process, for instance, a traditional school practice is for the teacher to do all but the last phase of it. Through comments on the student's composition, the teacher evaluates, diagnoses, and sometimes suggests the general type of remedy (to split up an overlong sentence, recast a paragraph, etc.), leaving GENERATE ALTERNATIVE as the only part of the process for the student to perform. In planning compositions, teachers sometimes collaborate in the selection of topics and content by asking questions and responding with encouragement to promising ideas. Substantive facilitation can no doubt be educationally worthwhile through freeing the student to attend to one function by taking over responsibility for others. It is not our intention to evaluate substantive facilitation here but only to point out that it is different from procedural facilitation. In procedural facilitation the facilitator, be it live teacher or inanimate set of cards, functions somewhat as conductor to soloist, but neither as puppeteer to puppet nor as partner in a duet.

CONCRETIZING OF GOALS

With the half-dozen different kinds of procedural facilitation in writing that we have investigated, we find in every case some children who seem to use the added support as a way of tackling higher level goals. These are children who seem already to have a notion of what they would like to achieve in writing that exceeds their executive capabilities, so that any boost to these capabilities is exploited in the service of goals. Other elementary school children, however, appear to assimilate the new executive function to their established way of writing and exploit it as a way of making their job easier.

As we have tried to show with the knowledge-telling model, children tend to approach expository writing as a task of telling what they know rather than a task of reaching some composition goal. Procedural facilitation cannot directly alter this tendency. But it also seems that a reorientation cannot be achieved by exhortation or other frontal means, because of the subtle and complicated nature of goal pursuit in compositional tasks. Accordingly, we have sought to devise some means whereby children who have not yet reached the point of formulating compositional goals for themselves could gain experience in pursuing such goals and begin to develop executive strategies for pursuing them.

For this purpose we used the technique of goal concretization. This technique is the stock-in-trade of developmental research with logico-mathematical problems. If the child cannot understand a problem formulated in abstract terms—a proportionality problem, for instance—then find a concrete representation of the problem with a goal the child can understand—like the goal of getting a balance beam to balance. In the logico-mathematical realm, concretizing of goals depends on being able to demonstrate the logical equivalence of semantically different problems. In other task realms, however, logical equivalence is either not demonstrable or not germane. What we need instead is psychological equivalence. Thus, what we seek with compositional tasks is a way to create concrete, stable goals that will evoke the same kinds of mental activity as the more abstract, unstable goals of real-life compositional tasks. This is not easy, but we believe it is possible. To illustrate, let us review the characteristics of goals in compositional tasks:

1. At the outset of a compositional task, the goal is global—to find a rewarding job, to have a good time, to write a good story, etc. To say that the goal is global is to say that it does not specify (or even necessarily suggest) the nature of the end state. Typically, there are many different end states that might satisfy the goal—for instance, many different rewarding jobs. This is in contrast to commonly studied logico-mathematical problems where there is only one satisfactory end state and it is fully specified by the goal statement and is

therefore known from the beginning—all the cannibals and missionaries are across the river, the balance beam balances, etc.

2. Success in achieving the global goal is typically not all-or-none, and evaluation of success is hampered by not knowing what the alternatives might have been. Thus it is possible to be satisfied or dissatisfied with a range of outcomes.

3. The desired end state becomes increasingly specified as work proceeds. For instance, in exploring different job possibilities, more definite constraints on what constitutes a "rewarding" job are established.

4. Some of these constraints may have to be abandoned because they are later discovered to be incompatible with other desired conditions or practical limitations. For instance, inability to find a house meeting certain livability requirements might force the house hunter to reconsider an initial constraint that the house be near to work.

Starting with such a global goal, there are basically two ways of proceeding, which for simplicity we may call the "high road" and the "low road" (Bereiter & Scardamalia, 1983a). The high road requires that one keep reassessing partial solutions and goal constraints in the light of each other and of the global goal. Thus there is a great deal of forward and backward analysis, making for an intellectually demanding task. The low road proceeds by avoiding goal constraints. The global goal is retained and influences the choice of actions, but finally whatever end state is achieved will probably suffice because it will in some degree satisfy the global goal and one will be unaware of the alternative end states that might have been achieved. The low-road way is not necessarily thoughtless, but it is entirely forward moving, concerned only with what comes next, rather than with the more difficult problem of closing a gap.

What we want to achieve instructionally, then, is some concrete goal that will get children who are accustomed to the low road to practice the kinds of mental operations required on the high road. Let us consider first a simple everyday task that illustrates how a concretized goal might induce high-road mental activity.

The task, let us say, is to take two small children for an outing. The global goal is simply that adult and children should have a pleasant time. The high-road thinker may begin by considering various alternatives and rejecting them because they are too costly, because they involve too much travel, because they are too commercialized, etc. Out of these trial solutions a clearer goal specification emerges—going someplace not too far away, not expensive, and of some "worthwhile" entertainment value. Search of the newspaper brings to light a free puppet show that will meet these goal requirements, but it promises to draw a big crowd, and so it will be necessary to go early to get a good seat. This, however, raises the prospect of waiting in line a long time, a problem with young children, and so that solution is also set aside, with "no waiting" added as a specification to the goal state. However, no better alternative can be found, so the puppet show is reconsidered along with the subgoal of finding a way to keep the children entertained while waiting to get in. A bag lunch, books to read, and games to play are added to a plan that finally conforms to the now-elaborate definition of the goal state.

The low-road way, of course, is to pack the kids into a car, ask them what they would like to do, and take it from there. We have no wish to argue that in this particular instance the high-road way is best, only that it involves a distinctly different mental process. Now how might one induce this mental process? The way we suggest is by giving someone a problem like the following: Plan an outing with two small children so that when it is over you could say, "It was worthwhile for the kids and I enjoyed it too. It was economical, and, because of my careful planning, the kids were kept happy all the time even though we had a long wait."

In order to solve that problem, it would seem that one would have to go through much the same mental process that our high-road thinker went through in arriving at the same end state. There is an important difference in that the high-road thinker had to construct this end state, whereas now we are specifying it at the beginning. But it still seems reasonable that practice with goal-specified tasks like this would induce the kinds of goal-directed processing that would help people develop toward becoming high-road thinkers themselves. Note, furthermore, that we have not fully specified the goal. The solution need not be the puppet show; it could as well be going fishing off a pier. The point, simply, is that enough specification has been supplied to induce the desired goal-directed processing. As we indicate later, the amount of specification required to do this is a researchable variable.

An essential property of the goal specification is that it set up interdependent constraints. In our example, a single activity must be found that meets the constraints of economy, value for children, interest for an adult, a long period of waiting, and the possibility of keeping children entertained during the wait. The instructional purpose would not be served by specifying a set of constraints that could be met by dealing with them one at a time. As we see, students tend to try to deal with constraints one at a time anyway.

We have already reported, in Chapters 3 and 5, experiments using this way of specifying end states in composition. These were experiments in which children were given ending sentences and asked to produce compositions leading up to the specified ending sentence (see Chapters 3 and 5). Thinking-aloud protocols showed that children do, in fact, engage in more goal-directed processing when given an ending to work toward than they do in the more common task of working forward from a topic or initial statement (Tetroe et al., 1981).

There is another kind of goal concretization that we have investigated casually, and for which we have designed a large number of learning activities called "consequential tasks" (Scardamalia, Bereiter, & Fillion, 1981). In consequential tasks, the goal is made concrete but its specifications are left up to the learner to construct. Here, for instance, is an activity in which the global goal is to achieve realism in a narrative. This goal, however, is concretized in the following activity:

> Students are grouped into teams of three to discuss interesting personal experiences. They choose one person's experience, discuss it in detail, and each student goes off to write about it as if it happened to him or herself. The teacher may remind students that their stories should contain no real names. Each student in a team reads his or her story aloud and the class tries to guess which of the three stories was written by the person the experience actually happened to. The writer succeeds by convincing the class that his or her narrative is the true account.

Thus the abstract and intangible goal of realism is replaced by the concrete goal of producing a fictitious narrative that will pass for a true account. Yet the actual characteristics of the end state, the constraints that must be met in order for the concrete goal to be achieved, are left entirely to the student. Tasks of this sort, we believe, bring the student just one step short of the full act of dealing with emergent goals. The remaining step is to go from global goals to progressive goal specification without need for an intervening concrete goal. We turn to that as yet unsolved problem in the next section.

GOAL CONSTRUCTION

The two instructional approaches described so far—procedural facilitation and goal concretizing—clearly need to be used in combination. One influences the cognitive means children employ but leaves the goals open, the other influences the goals they pursue but leaves the means open. Even in combination, however, they do not deal with the whole of what is involved in mature performance on compositional tasks. The missing element, as we have indicated, is movement from initial global goals—which are more or less in the nature of felt needs—to the specification of an end state that arises out of and further guides purposive behavior. This goal-constructing activity, and self-monitoring of progress in light of goals, provides the foundation for *intentional cognition* (Bereiter & Scardamalia, 1983b; see also Chapter 14). Instead of only responding to problems, ideas, and opportunities that happen to arise, students can then begin to decide where they want to go cognitively and apply their mental resources to getting there. It would seem that only within such a context of self-directed cognitive activity can a knowledge-transforming approach to writing really be expected to materialize and function.

The ability to pursue cognitive goals in knowledge-rich domains is a complex and many-sided achievement that it appears many people in our culture fall short of. This achievement will not be brought about, we fear, by instructional approaches of either a technical or a romantic simplicity. As Whitehead (1929) said, "You are up against too skillful an adversary, who will see to it that the pea is always under the other thimble." It seems essential to enlist children's full support in the educational effort, to communicate to them somehow, through modeling or precept, an image of the psychological state they are to attain. Experience to date encourages us to believe that children become willing allies in the instructional process once they glimpse what it means to construct cognitive goals for themselves and to regulate their cognitive activity in light of such goals.

POSTSCRIPT

Two instructional approaches were discussed in this chapter— procedural facilitation and goal concretization. The next two chapters will report several applications of procedural facilitation, and a number of other applications have been or are being developed among our research group. There was an obvious reason for giving priority to work on procedural facilitation. As was brought out in Chapter 3, procedural facilitation has been a tool for investigating the competence of immature writers, finding out what knowledge and abilities they had that were not being put to full use, and identifying the strategies they were using in composition. Thus it is fundamental to other kinds of instructional work, including work on goal-directed processes. Indeed, without findings brought to light by procedural facilitation it would be difficult to find out whether any other instructional approach was having an effect on underlying processes.

Classroom applications of goal concretization (through the use of ending sentences) have been the subject of recent studies carried out by Valerie Anderson. It appears that merely having students write to ending sentences is ineffective. Students quickly adapt to the task so that they are able to carry it out with no apparent modification of their normal ways of generating text. (According to Tetroe's findings, discussed in Chapter 3, this could have been accomplished by adopting a serial strategy of dealing with one ending sentence constraint at a time.) In short, as we emphasized in the preceding section on goal construction, it seems essential to enlist children's active support in the educational effort and to communicate to them as much as possible what the cognitive goal is that they should be striving to attain. Later classroom replications in which this was done appear to be yielding results. A second conclusion is that use of ending sentences appears to be useful in the context of introducing students to new genres. One instructional experiment focused on reflective essays—a genre that is usually foreign to children because, as far as we have been able to make out, reflective essays aimed at young readers are essentially nonexistent. Ending sentences like "It seems funny when you stop and think about it," served to keep students oriented to the distinctive character of reflective writing and to keep them from slipping into the more familiar genre of argument or personal narrative writing. This result is especially encouraging because it suggests a way that goal concretization may be used to set in motion rethinking processes that are essential to a knowledge-transforming process in writing.

Research on construction and use of goals in writing is currently under investigation in doctoral thesis research by Pamela Paris. In this research, procedural facilitation in the form of sets of possible goals and subgoals to choose from is being used as both a research and an instructional tool. The experiment on teaching reflective processes in writing, reported in Chapter 12 of this book, also involved efforts to facilitate and encourage goal construction. One of the interesting findings from that study is that students began taking goals seriously when they had managed, through other kinds of facilitation, to begin generating more content than they could use in their compositions. This makes perfect sense. People on a subsistence diet have little reason to be interested in meal planning. Similarly, the elaboration of goals for a composition presupposes that the writer has a range of content possibilities to choose from. But that in turn requires efficient memory-search procedures. Thus are we reminded once again of the interdependence of different parts of the composing process.

Chapter 11
Fostering Evaluative, Diagnostic, and Remedial Capabilities

PREFACE

The several studies reported in this chapter and in the postscript to it illustrate a progression from (1) basic research into a cognitive process to (2) extension of this research to the testing of a more powerful instructional intervention and finally to (3) an instructional experiment testing a practical classroom application. The main body of this chapter is devoted to a study using procedural facilitation to uncover students' ability to carry out mental processes hypothesized to underly revision. It starts with a model of these hypothesized processes, then presents a complex procedural facilitation of these processes. The facilitation was designed to tell us as much as possible about students' competence, not to be as facilitating as possible. The postscript to this chapter reports two studies that focus increasingly on issues of teachability of the processes examined in the first study.

11

The study to be reported in this chapter examines how various cognitive processes interact during evaluation and revision. These processes include (1) language production, (2) evaluation, (3) tactical decisions (such as whether to delete or rewrite), and (4) executive control of the overall process (allocating resources to the various subprocesses and switching from one to another).

The study deals with what we call the CDO process (COMPARE, DIAGNOSE, OPERATE), a part of the composing process that is involved in revising text and in rethinking rhetorical choices.

Figure 11.1 is a diagrammatic representation of the CDO process as we currently conceive of it. During the course of composition, two kinds of mental representations are built up and stored in long-term memory. These are a representation of the text written so far, and a representation of the text as intended, which includes the whole text, not just parts already written. The CDO process is initiated by a perceived mismatch between these two representations.

We conceive of the CDO process as an interruption to other composing processeses, so that it ends with a return to the interrupted process, whatever that might be (reading, planning, generating, etc.). Figure 11.1 does not show how the process starts, how the initial comparison between written and intended text is instigated. That is a matter of considerable uncertainty, and one that is by-passed in the present investigation by using a facilitating procedure that routinely starts the process.

The model in Figure 11.1 is a simple feedback loop, similar to a TOTE

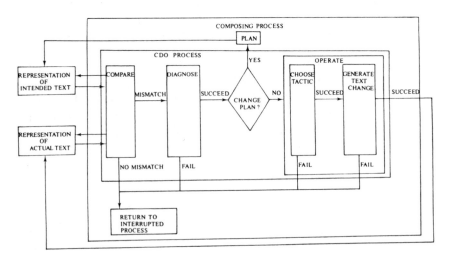

Figure 11.1.   Model of the CDO (COMPARE, DIAGNOSE, OPERATE) process in composition.

unit (Miller, Galanter, & Pribram, 1960). When COMPARE detects a mismatch, attention shifts to DIAGNOSE, which may involve search of the text and a search of rhetorical knowledge stored in long-term memory for a possible cause of the detected mismatch. One possible outcome of diagnosis is a decision to alter intentions rather than to alter the text. In terms of the present model, this means exiting from the CDO process. A more elaborate model could incorporate not only this route to resolving the mismatch but also the more complex possibility of a "negotiated settlement" in which both the actual and the intended text are altered. Figure 11.1 traces the more common and simple route by which the text alone is altered in order to remove a perceived mismatch with intentions. The OPERATE phase has two components. In CHOOSE TACTIC, a general kind of text change is elected, such as changing wording, deleting, or adding on. The writer may also elect to leave things as they are and exit here, but if the tactic chosen involves changes to the text, the writer will move on to the GENERATE CHANGE phase, where a specific enactment of the chosen tactic is made. This leads to a modified text representation, and a new COMPARE, which leads to a new CDO cycle. The process keeps cycling until either removal of the mismatch or a failure at some point causes control to return to the interrupted process.

Although the model purports to show what goes on in revision, it is important to keep in mind that the CDO process may go on even though revision does not occur. The process may fail to result in the text being changed for a number of reasons. It may also result in text changes that we would not normally call revisions. The latter occurs if a CDO process is initiated during original composition and the chosen tactic for removing the mismatch is to take care of the problem through what is written next, rather than alter existing text.

Children notably do very little revision, and what they do usually consists of minor changes to conform to conventional usage (Nold, 1981). It therefore seemed that the CDO process might be a fertile object of inquiry in trying to understand the development of writing competence, and particularly the interaction of competence and performance factors. Children's weaknesses in revision have often been attributed to an inability to see their texts from the reader's or an objective point of view (Kroll, 1978). This would imply a defect in the COMPARE stage of the CDO process, such that other parts of the process never get activated. But the problem could as well lie elsewhere; in the inability to diagnose, in poor choice of tactics, or in a failure to generate adequate remedies. On the other hand, it could be that the problem is not with elements of the process at all, but in organizing those elements and in incorporating the CDO sub-process as a whole into the larger composition process. The problem, in other words, could be a problem of executive control. Children might have the necessary competence to carry out the CDO process but they cannot, in a sense, *afford* to do so, because the executive burden might be too great and would threaten to disrupt the whole composing process.

Research into these intriguing possibilities is normally hampered by the invisibility of the CDO process. In this study, procedural facilitation (see Chapter 10) was used both to bring normally hidden parts of the process into the open and to lessen the executive burden of implementing the CDO process. When used during original composition the procedure went like this: After writing a sentence, the child selected one of eleven possible evaluations that best characterized the preceding unit of text. This task corresponded to COMPARE in the process model. The child then had to explain orally how the evaluation applied (DIAGNOSE). Following this, the child chose one of six directives indicating possible tactics to employ (CHOOSE TACTIC). These tactics ranged from leaving things as they were, to adding more information, to scrapping a sentence and writing a new one. Unless the child elected to leave things, this step was followed by some alteration of the written text (GENERATE REVISION). This procedure was repeated as each additional sentence of text was produced.

For simplicity, we shall call this the Alternating Procedure. The name highlights its main facilitating feature. Instead of leaving the CDO process to occur spontaneously, sporadically, or perhaps not at all, it occurred in a regular way, alternating with text generation. Movement from step to step within the process was also part of the routine, and the executive burden was further reduced by limiting COMPARE and CHOOSE TACTIC to finite choices rather than leaving them as open-ended tasks that might entail heavy processing loads in their own right.

There are two ways in which the experimental procedure falls short of fully representing the process depicted in Figure 11.1. First, the CDO process as represented there is an iterative process that may go through several cycles before a particular mismatch is removed. In the present study, in order to keep children's working time within a reasonable limit, the children went through only one cycle at each step. At the end of the chapter, however, we shall mention interesting preliminary findings about what happens when children try successive CDO cycles.

The second limitation has to do with the level of mismatches dealt with. The CDO process is conceived of as a very general one that may respond to any kind of perceived mismatch from a doubtful spelling to a general feeling that an essay is not turning out right. There is no assurance, of course, that a person will have equal competence in handling mismatches at all levels. That will depend, among other things, on the availability of relevant rhetorical knowledge. To keep the scope of the present study within reasonable limits we focused on a range of mismatch possibilities that was above the level children were known to attend to and yet not at such a high level that it might be altogether baffling to them. We concentrated on relatively simple considerations of appropriateness, coherence, and audience response, and excluded evaluation cues at the level of mechanics (spelling, punctuation, etc.).

The Alternating Procedure may be thought of as a reduced and somewhat simplified *working* model of the CDO process. It is simpler than the conceptual model shown in Figure 11.1, which in turn is simpler than we believe the actual process to be. Simplifications of this kind are inevitable in theoretical research and they are most pronounced in the early stages of theory development, where first approximations are being sought. The trick, always, is to introduce simplifications that will highlight main principles and to avoid simplifications that nullify them. We believe that the results of this first experiment show the Alternating Procedure to be quite promising in this regard. It appears to set in motion a cognitive process that is new for most children, to bring into view some surprising competencies, and also to render certain handicaps of young writers more understandable than they were before.

DESCRIPTION OF THE EXPERIMENT

An experiment was conducted in which elementary-school children at three grade levels composed and revised short opinion essays. Ninety children were involved, 30 in each of grades 4, 6, and 8 (ages approximately, 10, 12, and 14 years). They came from schools in a predominantly middle-class area of Metropolitan Toronto.

Half the children in each grade used the Alternating Procedure in the way that has already been mentioned, and that will be described in more detail below, a way which called for them to go through a CDO cycle after each sentence was composed. The other half of the students wrote their compositions first and applied the Alternating Procedure afterwards, sentence by sentence. We shall call the first group the "on-line" group and the second group the "evaluation after" group.

In order to teach children the on-line procedure, the experimenter demonstrated it by composing a short paragraph herself, using the Alternating Procedure. Writing on the topic, "Is it better to be an only child or to have brothers or sisters?", she wrote the following first sentence:

Yes, it's better to have both.

Then she stopped and turned to the list of evaluations at her side, each of which was written on a separate slip of paper. After reading her first sentence over, she started thinking aloud, demonstrating how to use the evaluations as an aid to thinking. For instance, pointing to evaluation number 9 (shown in Table 11.1), she remarked, "It says I'm getting away from the main point. . . . No, that's not a problem I have to think of yet. I'm just trying to get to my main point. So this won't help me." Moving evaluation number 9 aside, she turned to number 8, saying, "Now here's one that says I could have said what I said more clearly. That's for sure! I'd better keep this one here and think more about it." In this way the experimenter considered each evaluation, moving it aside if it was judged irrelevant, and keeping it if it was judged relevant. Then she looked for the most appropriate among the relevant evaluations, asking herself, "Now, what's the main problem?"

Having selected an evaluation, she turned to the directives (listed in Table 11.2), which were printed on differently colored slips of paper. She went through the same thinking-aloud process as with the evaluations, considering each directive as to its relevance and chose the most promising of the relevant ones. In considering the relevance of directive 5, for instance, she would say something like: "Let's see, this says I'd better say more. I don't really think saying more would help. I've got to get this part right before I say more." Finally, depending on the directive chosen, she revised her sentence in accordance with her evaluation or left it alone.

After this activity was completed she wrote her next sentence and went through the entire cycle again. For each new sentence the evaluation and directive cards were shuffled and run through, to stress the point that there was no special order in which they were to be used. (Evaluations and

Table 11.1   Evaluations Used to Facilitate COMPARE Operations

Evaluative Phrases

1. People won't see why this is important

2. People may not believe this

3. People won't be very interested in this part

4. People may not understand what I mean here

5. People will be interested in this part

6. This is good

7. This is a useful sentence

8. I think this could be said more clearly

9. I'm getting away from the main point

10. Even I am confused about what I am trying to say

11. This doesn't sound quite right

Table 11.2 Directives Used to Facilitate TACTICAL CHOICE

Directive Phrases
1. I think I'll leave it this way
2. I'd better give an example
3. I'd better leave this part out
4. I'd better cross this sentence out and say it a different way
5. I'd better say more
6. I'd better change the wording

directives were not numbered on the experimental materials, and children were explicitly urged not to treat them in a fixed order but to arrange them in any way that helped them think.)

Proceeding as described, the experimenter produced a nine-sentence paragraph in approximately 15 minutes. Although the experimenter's thinking aloud was not fully scripted, it covered essentially the same ideas when performed in individual sessions with each of 45 students. Care was taken to model the use of each evaluation and directive with approximately equal frequency. The amount and kind of thinking modeled varied, however, according to the evaluation being considered, from a quick, impressionistic judgment in the case of "People will be interested in this part," to a high-level review of the whole text in the case of "I'm getting away from the main point."

After the procedure was demonstrated, the children were put through a short check-out phase. Given the topic "Is winter the best season?", the experimenter wrote the first sentence and the children applied the Alternating Procedure to it. The sentence given was "Winter is it.", a sentence chosen for its susceptibility to a variety of evaluations and directives. (It could be judged satisfactory and left as it was; it could be judged unclear and reworded, expanded, or replaced.) After executing the Alternating Procedure on this sentence the child was asked to compose the next sentence and to apply the procedure to it. The purpose of this check-out phase was to eliminate children who could not handle the mechanics of the procedure (the quality of their choices was not a consideration). No children had difficulty with the procedure, however, and so all proceeded to the next, independent composition phase.

In the next phase children wrote original compositions. For purposes of comparison, they wrote on a topic we had used in several previous studies, "Should children choose the subjects they study in school?" The Alternating Procedure was applied after writing each sentence. The experimenter recorded each selection and placement of the evaluations and directives. She also asked children to justify their choices, recording their responses on audio-tape. The experimental session was concluded with an interview in which children were questioned on their experience and how it compared with their usual writing experience. The entire session lasted about 90 minutes.

Procedures for children in the "evaluation after" group involved a simple modification of those just described. The day before the experiment, these children wrote in class on the prescribed topic. In the experimental sessions, which were again conducted individually, they revised these previously written compositions. The experimenter's demonstration was modified to suit the "evaluation after" procedure. She presented an already-written composition and went through it sentence by sentence, thinking aloud as she applied the evaluation/revision procedure. The content of the demonstration, however, was identical to that used in demonstrating the "on-line" procedure, so that children in both conditions were exposed to the same original text, the same revisions, and the same verbalized thought leading up to the revisions. Children went through the same two-sentence check-out procedure as in the "on-line" group (and again all children succeeded in handling the procedure). They then applied the procedure to their own compositions and finally went through the same interview as children in the other group.

These two variations in procedure, the "on-line" and the "evaluation after," were chosen for their naturalistic and theoretical interest. They represent two of the ways that evaluation and revision go on in writing: as part of the composing of an original draft and as a separate process applied to a completed draft. The two approaches differ in their cognitive demands. On-line revision poses the problem of keeping plans for future text in mind while pausing to reconsider text already written. It has, however, a potential compensating advantage for text generation, in that on-line evaluation may have forward-acting effects such as suggesting additional things to write. Revision afterwards presents less threat of losing hold of plans and intentions, but it makes the task of revision more constrained, since revisions must be fitted to following, as well as to preceding, text. Thus, if one procedure were found to be more facilitating than the other for children of a certain age, this might give us clues as to what parts of the writing task were commanding their attention. We could consider, for instance, to what extent they were concerned with hanging on to plans as compared to thinking of new material to include in their compositions.

FINDINGS

The key assumption underlying this experiment was that providing children with a simplified executive routine for sentence-by-sentence evaluation and revision would reduce executive control problems and thereby give latent evaluative, tactical, and language-production abilities of children an opportunity to reveal themselves. Let us therefore look first at evidence bearing on this assumption. First, it is relevant to note that none of the 90 children from grade 4 to grade 8 were unable or unwilling to use the Alternating Procedure, in spite of its apparently cumbersome nature. Children in grades 4 and 6 in the "on-line" condition, who had to go through the procedure on each sentence before composing the next, nevertheless produced compositions of the same average length as the "evaluation after" group, who wrote their compositions under normal classroom test conditions. Grade 8 children did produce significantly less in the "on-line" than in the "evaluation after" condition. Since this effect did not appear with younger children, however, it cannot reasonably be attributed to inability to handle the procedure. A behavioral indicator of difficulty with, or reluctance to go through, the procedure, is the choice of evaluative and directive statements that allow one to "by-pass" the revision task. By choosing favorable evaluations and/or by choosing the directive, "I think I'll leave it this way," a student could largely circumvent the procedure and proceed through the composition with little extra effort. Only six of the 90 children consistently chose a "by-pass" strategy; four of these were in the youngest group.

In follow-up interviews, children were unanimous in declaring that the procedure helped them do something they did not normally do and had found difficult, namely, evaluating their writing in detail. Seventy-four percent, in fact, declared that the procedure made the whole process of writing easier. They usually explained this on the basis of mental activity stimulated by use of the "cards" (evaluative and directive statements):

> "Easier, because I don't usually ask myself those questions. It made me able to correct sentences; it was a good guide."
> "Easier. You're kind of answering the kinds of questions a teacher would ask when she is marking your paper, so it helps you correct mistakes before she marks."
> "Yeah, made it easier. If there were cards like that in class everyone would get it done fast."
> "They gave me a little bit more thinking. They made me think more about what I wrote."
> "Much easier, because they helped me look over the sentence, which I don't usually do."
> "I guess it's a little easier You can use the cards to realize what

you're saying. After a little while . . . you wouldn't have to use the cards but could get it in your head and it would be faster. Right now I'd need to use the cards because I don't think of those questions."

The 12% who thought the procedure made writing on the whole more difficult referred either to the need to think more carefully or to the time it required:

> "I never thought closely about what I wrote. I thought about it and if it was good I wrote it down, but I never went sentence by sentence."
> "Takes more time when you're using the cards, so it's probably harder; but it makes your writing better."

The remaining children judged the procedure to make writing harder in some ways, easier in others, citing factors similar to those noted by the other children. In summary, it appeared that the procedure was working as intended. It provided children with an executive routine that they generally experienced as facilitating. It also made it possible for them to incorporate activities into their writing that they already knew something about but that they usually omitted. According to the children's reports, the Alternating Procedure had a marked effect on their composing processes. Before probing more deeply into the nature of this effect, we must see what, if any, effect carried through into the written products.

Effects of the Procedure on Written Products

Judging from norms of the National Assessment of Educational Progress (1977), children in this study revised more than normal. In the National Assessment study, children were asked to look over compositions they had just written to see if they wanted to change anything, ample time being allowed to make changes. At grade 4, 40% of the children made no changes; in the present study the corresponding figure was 20%. At grade 8, 22% of the National Assessment sample made no changes, compared to less than 7% in the present study.

In this section we consider the effects of this revision activity on children's texts. Before pursuing such effects, however, it is helpful to consider how successful children in this age range are in revising essays on this same topic when left to their own devices. Data are available on this from an earlier study we conducted (Bracewell, Scardamalia, and Bereiter, 1978). Here we found that among grade-4 children there was no discernible tendency for them to make compositions better or worse by revision (and little agreement between raters as to whether changes were for better or worse). Raters did begin to agree on the revisions made by grade-8 students, but they agreed that the tendency was for compositions to be made worse by revision! Thus, any tendency for children to make changes for the better in the present study could be taken as showing beneficial effects from the experimental procedure, since baseline performance is to produce changes that are neutral or negative. It is also informative to note that, whereas children were nearly unanimous in believing that the Alternating Procedure had a positive effect on their composing processes, they were far from unanimous in believing that the resulting compositions were better than what they usually produced. Children expressed concern about offsetting factors such as newness of the procedure and difficulty with the topic.

Against this background of acknowledged difficulties, we will consider first how well children coped with individual revisions, then see how successful they were in improving the overall quality of their compositions.

Ratings were made of each individual change that children elected to make. Raters were given original and revised versions of texts with all the differences underlined but were not informed which was the original and which the revised. Instead, one composition in each pair was randomly designated to be treated *as if* it were the original; the raters then judged whether each discrepancy noted on the other version constituted a change for the better, a change for the worse, or a change that made no difference in quality.

Two raters, one an editor and one a former junior high school English teacher, judged each separate change. The score finally assigned to a composition was the number of changes judged to be for the better minus the number judged to be for the worse. Although the two raters did not agree at all closely in their judgments (r for scores assigned to compositions = 0.24), they agreed in assigning scores of a positive tendency to all grades and conditions. The grand means of $+0.83$ based on one rater and $+1.16$ based on the other rater are both significantly different from zero at beyond the 0.001 level ($t(87)$ = 3.71 and 4.19). An analysis of variance showed no significant difference between grades or conditions. Thus there was a pervasive tendency for changes for the better to outnumber changes for the worse.

We now turn to the question of whether these changes added up to revised texts of significantly higher quality than the original. The answer is no, at least in so far as we can tell from the following analysis. The final 30 compositions written in either condition by students at each age level were rank-ordered on the basis of overall impression of quality. On the basis of these rankings the top-ranked child in the "on-line" condition was matched with the top-ranked child in the "evaluation after" condition, the second-ranked with the second-ranked, and so on. Thus 15 pairs of essays roughly matched for quality were formed. The original essay of the child in the "evaluation after" condition was then added to the set containing that child's revised essay. The final compositions produced in both the "on-line" and "evaluation after" conditions were compared to this "original." This procedure was used to get around the problem that there were no intact original essays for the on-line condition against which final compositions could be compared. Original and revised compositions were presented in pairs to raters, with the order varied randomly so that raters did not know which was which. At no age level, for either condition, was the final composition judged to be significantly different from the original.

There is a seeming paradox in children's ability to make individual changes for the better but not to have these amount to any overall improvement. The paradox is removed, however, if two additional factors are considered. The first is the level of evaluation and revision carried out. There were two evaluative phrases children could select that would suggest they were directing their attention to overall text concerns when they made the revision. These two phrases were "I'm getting away from the main point" and "Even I'm confused about what I'm trying to say." These two phrases were seldom used at any age level. Generally, children were concerned with small units of language, as we will discuss in greater detail later, and they evaluated these only in relation to local context. A second fact accounting for the seeming paradox is that while positive changes outnumbered negative changes, they did not outnumber them by very much. The average revised text contained one more change for the better than changes for the worse. This was a statistically significant advantage, but not one that could be expected to influence overall impressions of text quality.

To summarize the results so far, we find that, when children use the Alternating Procedure, they experience it as helping them to incorporate evaluation and revision phases into their composing and that they do make changes that are mostly judged to be in a positive direction. Many negative changes are also made, however, and the overall result is that compositions are not improved. These results, taken at face value, are not incongruous. If, in fact, children had seldom previously evaluated and revised what they wrote, then it stands to reason that they might lack some of the competencies necessary to do so effectively. Among the possibilities to be considered is that they are unable to judge the effect of what they write, that they are unable to diagnose the sources of trouble, that they make unwise decisions about the general kind of change to undertake, or that they lack the sentencing skills needed to bring off the changes they intend. We shall turn now to examining each of these possibilities in turn.

Quality of the Evaluations

A semi-professional writer went through each text and after each sentence chose the evaluative statement from Table 11.1 that corresponded best to her own evaluation. The phrase actually chosen by the child was then judged according to whether it was the same one chosen by the rater, different but also appropriate, somewhat appropriate, or not fitting at all. The percentages of students falling into the different categories are shown in Table 11.3. (The scores of three students in two different cells are missing due to audiotape difficulties.) It can be seen from Table 11.3 that in grades 6 and 8 the children's choices of evaluations corresponded very closely indeed to the choices of the semi-professional writer. Even at grade 4, most of the choices are either exactly the same or ones that the rater judged to be appropriate. Only 10% of the grade-4 children *ever* made a choice judged altogether inappropriate; 5% of grade-6 children did so, and no grade-8 children did. Children at all grades would thus appear to be surprisingly capable when it comes to making evaluations of their writing.

The first four evaluations shown in Table 11.1 are criticisms expressed in terms of reader reaction ("People may not believe this", etc.). The last four are criticisms expressed either as unqualified assertions or as personal opinions ("I think. . . . "). This distinction was built into the list with the thought that it might reveal a developmental trend toward more reader-related criticisms. Such tendency as did appear, however, was in the opposite direction. Excluding instances in which positive evaluations were chosen, the proportion of reader-related criticisms went from 47% in grade 4 to 35% in grade 6 and 30% in grade 8. Thus, older students were attributing more problems with their writing to personal dissatisfaction than to anticipated dissatisfaction of the reader.

Table 11.3 Appropriateness of Evaluations: Percentage of Subjects in Categories Based on Mean Appropriateness Ratings

	Grade					
	4		6		8	
Rating category	On-line	After	On-line	After	On-line	After
Same as expert picked	23	47	60	93	71	67
Not same, but appropriate	62	47	33	7	29	33
Somewhat appropriate	15	6	7	0	0	0
Not appropriate	0	0	0	0	0	0

Quality of Diagnoses

The same semi-professional writer who judged the evaluations also judged the children's explanations of their evaluations. Again, the standard was how closely the child's judgment corresponded to that of the expert. Some responses could not be classified according to this standard. Either the student (a) gave a justification, the intent of which was not clear; (b) repeated the evaluation phrase instead of constructing a justification; or (c) could not elaborate on the evaluation. Percentages of students giving such unclassifiable responses, responses that generally can be taken to indicate difficulty with the task, are shown in the unclassified category at the foot of Table 11.4. This table also shows how the remaining responses were classified against the expert standard. Evidently, children showed much less accord with expert judgments when it came to justifying their evaluations. Mean ratings on the 4-point scale (unclassified responses were not included) go from 2.00 at grade 4 to 2.56 at grade 6 to 2.98 at grade 8. Thus, it is only at grade 8 that the explanations are judged, on the average, to be appropriate.

A reading of the transcripts of children's explanation shows why they end up with ratings that do not correspond closely to those an expert would make. For the most part, children focus on overly specific details. Thus, while the expert is dealing with issues at the text level, tracking meaning and finding the intent of a sentence confusing, the child is concerned about the effect of a certain word or phrase in that sentence. Another way in which they fail to construct an expert diagnosis is to give up on a perceived problem too soon. They manage to criticize a sentence, often astutely pointing out some critical reader response that it is likely to provoke. Then they ignore this insight and proceed with a justification of the sentence based on why it was written in the first place.

It would thus appear that, although children show an ability to form

Table 11.4 Appropriateness of Diagnosis: Percentage of Subjects in Categories Based on Mean Appropriateness Ratings

	Grade					
	4		6		8	
Rating category	On-line	After	On-line	After	On-line	After
Same as expert picked	0	0	0	27	21	20
Not same, but appropriate	23	27	47	20	43	60
Somewhat appropriate	31	20	13	20	0	13
Not appropriate	8	13	13	7	0	7
Unclassified	38	40	27	26	36	0

accurate impressions of the effectiveness of their writing, they do not identify accurately the source of the difficulties they perceive.

Choice of Remedial Tactics

The tactical choices represented by the directives in Table 11.2 are of a very general sort and one can seldom assert with confidence that, in a particular instance, a particular choice is good or bad. Such choices as altering the wording or saying more are often difficult to evaluate without knowing what sort of change of working or addition the writer has in mind. On the other hand, when a sentence has been evaluated as unclear and the sentence itself is garbled, adding more information is not the most promising way of trying to clear matters up. We asked the same rater who had judged the choices of evaluations to judge the choices of directives. In this case, however, the judgement was simply whether the chosen tactic was a high-probability choice or a low-probability choice for dealing with the problem that the child had identified. The percentage of tactics judged to be of high probability increased from 50% at grade 4 to 74% at grade 8. (Chance level cannot be computed, although it is necessarily at least 17% and is unlikely to be as high as 50%.) There is thus evidence of a developmental trend toward the choice of more promising ways of responding to evaluations.

Table 11.5 shows the distribution of choices of directives for the several grade levels and the two treatment conditions. There is little indication of any difference between grade levels. This implies that the improvement with age in the quality of tactical choices is due to a better fit between tactic and problem, not to a change in the popularity of the various choices. It is especially noteworthy that the choice to leave the text the way it is shows no dramatic change with age, although the fourth-graders in both conditions choose it more frequently than the older children.

There is an interesting difference between treatment groups. Decisions to say more or to give an example account for only 6 to 8% of the choices at each grade level in the "evaluation after" condition, but account for 18 to 20% of the choices at each grade level in the "on-line" condition. It seems that in the on-line condition, children frequently used the evaluation to suggest additional material to include in their compositions. For children who have already completed a draft, evaluation seldom results in material being interpolated.

The data do not permit us to draw firm conclusions about the competence of children to select promising general tactics for revision. The data suggest, however, that such choices may not be very well attuned to perceived problems at grade 4 and that substantial progress is made in the following 4 years.

Table 11.5   Percentage of Times Each Directive Was Chosen

Condition	Grade	I think I'll leave it this way	I'd better give an example	I'd better leave this part out	I'd better cross this sentence out and say it a different way	I'd better say more	I'd better change the wording
On-line	4	68.3	12.2	0	0	7.3	12.2
	6	54.5	12.7	1.8	10.9	5.5	14.6
	8	63.5	9.5	3.2	0	9.5	14.3
Evaluation After	4	60.6	3.0	3.0	9.1	4.6	19.7ˉ
	6	50.0	2.1	0	20.8	6.3	20.8
	8	49.5	1.9	3.7	6.5	3.7	34.7

Effectiveness of Execution

The most pertinent evidence we have of children's ability to carry out intended changes in their compositions is the high frequency of changes that raters judged to be for the worse. Since the children demonstrated ability to evaluate their texts in ways that conformed to expert judgments, the frequency with which their changes made things worse would seem to reflect serious difficulties in managing written language. The flavor of these difficulties can be gained from examining those instances in which children elected to strike out and replace an entire sentence.

There were 30 instances of children choosing this tactic. In 11 of these 30 instances the child was unable to come up with a recast sentence and instead rewrote the original sentence with some minor word or phrase change. For example, an eighth-grader elected to cross out and rewrite the following sentence:

> The reason they wouldn't do well is because if the subject chosen by the teacher is one the student hates, the student won't try, and will do badly.

The student eventually rewrote the sentence exactly as before, except for changing the last word to "poorly"!

At the other extreme, we have five instances in which children replaced a sentence with one that said something entirely different. In changing their minds about what they wanted to say, these children may have been demonstrating an important effect of the Alternating Procedure, but in changing the content they by-pass the problem of finding alternative means of expressing an idea.

In the remaining 14 sentences some more or less major overhaul was attempted, while preserving the idea of the original version. The most successful of these attempts was the following:

> *Original version:*
> I think we shouldn't because when we have math or any subject we might pick something that would be too easy and also teachers teach us math or any subject.
> *Revised version:*
> I think students shouldn't get to pick out any subject because we might pick out some work that's too easy for us.

This is an example of cleaning up a sentence that badly needed it. Note, however, that the basic plan of the sentence remains intact. All the successful examples were of this kind. They preserved the original sentence plan in the revised version, altering it by the addition or deletion of material, or by splitting it into shorter sentences. The four instances of children trying to make a fresh start at expressing an idea are all clear failures. In the following attempt, for instance, the child appears to hold on to the original idea, but one version is as elliptical as the other:

> *Original version:*
> The school gives him maths and sciences how is he going to be a carpenter.
> *Revised version:*
> There are some jobs that you don't need some classes like history.

In the next example the child, apparently trying to expand on the point made in the original, loses hold of the original point altogether and produces a statement that is less coherent than the original.

> *Original version:*
> Teachers are very important because a child has to learn something before they could go on to something else.
>
> *Revised version:*
> A child shouldn't choose his or her subject because the teacher might not know if the child knows how to do it or not.

The task of reformulating a sentence in order to accomplish some objective more successfully would appear to be a very complex task. It presents executive problems and competence demands of its own, quite apart from those involved in getting up to the point of attempting such a reformulation. Most children in the sample avoided the task altogether. When they attempted it they seemed to be successful only if they preserved the plan of the original sentence.

INTERPRETATION

Let us now reconsider the CDO model sketched at the beginning of this chapter in the light of experimental findings. Judging from self-report and textual evidence, we must conclude that under ordinary circumstances the CDO process is not run through by children at all. With support from the Alternating Procedure, however, children were able to carry out the steps of the process as depicted in Figure 11.1, and to do it with some measure of effect even on their first attempt. Although they recognized the process as different from their usual procedures, they accepted it as reasonable and helpful.

This constitutes significant support for the model of the CDO process depicted in Figure 11.1. In computer simulation, a test of a model's completeness and validity is that the model can actually be run on a computer and that it yields traces compatible with those that are obtained from human participants. In the present *simulation by intervention* the model was shown to "run" on human participants who are not already "programmed" to run that way. The simulation yielded traces compatible with those of an expert writer whose performance is taken as criterial. Beyond that, our human participants can do something the computer cannot, which is tell us about the experience. This provides an important kind of evidence on psychological validity in addition to the purely formal evidence of fit between "simulated" and natural traces.

Two previously noted limitations on the scope of the experiment are relevant at this point. First, the CDO process as depicted is an iterative process that keeps cycling until a mismatch has been removed or until failure occurs at some point. This iterative aspect of the model was not tested. We have done some research with an iterative revision procedure (Scardamalia, Cattani, Turkish, and Bereiter, 1981). Although only two iterations were used, it was clear that for some children the process was divergent; instead of progressively changing the text toward some desired goal, they shifted focus from one cycle to the next and sometimes undid what they had accomplished on the previous cycle. Iterative refinement of text would seem to call for a top-down control not represented in the model (and not provided for in the Alternating Procedure), a control which ensures that successive changes are related to the same goal. The second limitation is that the present experiment dealt with a kind of middle level of mismatches between text and intention. The model assumes that the process remains the same for mismatches at all levels from proofreading to detecting major structural problems. This assumption remains to be tested, and we can only say of the present study that it gives us no reason to doubt it.

A third limitation of the Alternating Procedure is that it depends on routinely triggering the CDO process instead of leaving it to be triggered spontaneously by perceived problems. What difference this might make in the functioning of the CDO process is not obvious, however. Some adults, on learning of the Alternating Procedure, have proclaimed that they could not tolerate using such a procedure themselves. While we suspect that these people underestimate their adaptability, they no doubt have a point. In mature writers the Alternating Procedure would be running in parallel with a well-developed natural CDO process, so the routine triggering would be redundant and occur too frequently, especially since adults likely plan text in much larger units than young children do. Adults might also be reacting to the limited range of evaluations available. This does not mean, however, that the applicability of the CDO model for adults is being called into question, only the simplifications that were introduced in order to activate the process in children. None of the children interviewed gave even a hint about such interference, either from the routine triggering or from the limited set of evaluations available. The only evidence that might suggest interference is the reduction in amount of text produced by grade-8 children in the "on-line" condition. For the younger children all indications are that the Alternating Procedure filled a void, initiating cognitive operations that were not otherwise occurring.

If we accept the Alternating Procedure as at least a rough working model of the CDO process, then we can use children's performance in the experiment as a source of information about their competencies with respect to various aspects of the CDO process.

As a start on pulling findings together, we shall go through one complete protocol. This is from a grade-8 student who produced one of the lower-rated compositions for that grade. (Numbers are added for reference.)

Original version
(1) I think students should choose their own subject because only they know what they want to be or do. (2) This way student will choose a subject so that is more fun and he or she

will enjoy school. (3) This way student could not say that he doesn't like the subject. (4) And he will be forced to do a better job. (5) This way student learns just the things he needs to learn.

Revised version
(1) I think students should choose their own subject because only they know what they want to be or do. (2) This way student will choose a subject so he or she will enjoy school. (3) This way student could not say that he doesn't like the subject. (4) And not do good job. (5) This way student learn just the things he need to learn.

Of two raters who compared these versions, not knowing which was which, one rated them as equal in overall quality and the other rated the original as slightly better. The changes are, in fact, slight and they seem unrelated to major problems with the text. Thus, on the surface, we have what is typical at this grade level (cf. Bracewell et al., 1978), little revision activity and what there is tending to make things worse. When we follow the writer through the steps in the CDO process, however, we see quite a bit of relevant mental activity going on.

> *First sentence:* I think students should choose their own subject because only they know what they want to be or do.
>
>> COMPARE: This is a useful sentence. (MATCH: GO TO NEXT SENTENCE.)
>> (Comment: Child added that it was a useful sentence "because it says what I think is right".)
>
> *Second sentence:* This way student will choose a subject so that is more fun and he or she will enjoy school.
>
>> COMPARE: This doesn't sound quite right.
>> DIAGNOSE: It doesn't sound clear.
>> CHOOSE TACTIC: I'd better change the wording
>> GENERATE CHANGE: Deletes "that is more fun and".
>> (Comment: DIAGNOSE does not proceed to the point of identifying what sounds wrong. Instead it restates but actually shifts the identification of the mismatch. The change generated does not follow the chosen tactic. Nevertheless deletion, a fairly uncommon practice in students of this age, was successfully accomplished and resulted in a more grammatical sentence. Possibly deleting the indicated clause was the only substantial change the child could find that did not conspicuously worsen the sentence.

This would suggest that the child may have covertly gone through several CDO iterations before coming up with the overt change.)

Third sentence: This way student could not say that he doesn't like the subject.

COMPARE: This is good (MATCH: GO TO NEXT SENTENCE)
(Comment: Given the child's overall language skills, an accurate evaluation.)

Fourth sentence: And he will be forced to do a better job.

COMPARE: Even I am confused about what I am trying to say.
DIAGNOSE: I was confused. I couldn't write what I meant. I shouldn't put 'force' here. If you're responsible you shouldn't have to be forced.
CHOOSE TACTIC: I'd better leave this part out.
GENERATE CHANGE: Replaces sentence with "And not do good job".
(Comment: The child claims that the sentence does not convey the meaning he is after. The effort to diagnose the problem goes awry, however, when the child's attention is captured by a single word, 'force', that to him seems incongruous with the general idea he is trying to develop. Remediation then focuses on the troublesome word rather than on developing the idea more fully. Removing the word 'force' results in removing the one main clue to the writer's idea, that students must develop self-defined constraints on their behavior.)

Fifth sentence: This way student learns just the things he needs to learn.

COMPARE: This is a useful sentence. (MATCH: EXIT)

This protocol is typical in showing initial reactions, at the COMPARE stage, that are reasonable and that, if appropriately followed up, would lead to an improved text. Serious troubles arise at the DIAGNOSE stage, however. This protocol illustrates one of the most prevalent troubles. Children may sense a difficulty at an abstract level, as in the case of the fourth sentence cited above. As soon as they start searching for the cause, however, their attention is captured by some salient concrete element and they lose hold of the higher-level goal that was motivating the search. We have discussed elsewhere this stimulus saliency problem as it affects control of attention in composing (Chapter 3) and in logical problem-solving (Scardamalia, 1973, 1975). An elaborated CDO model would show a complex search process within the DIAGNOSE box. The executive demands of this sub-process are probably high and, without procedural support, children will tend to lose hold and fall back upon simple diagnostic procedures that have minimal information-processing demands. Identifying a concrete element as the source of the problem would be one of these.

Another problem which appears at the diagnostic stage is simply faulty knowledge. This appears most commonly when children replace a perfectly good informal expression with a stilted or even unidiomatic formal-sounding one. The problem starts at the diagnostic stage with identifying the informal expression as not sounding right. The same problem appears at the semantic rather than stylistic level in the current protocol, with the child's concern about the word 'force'. The child's original use of the term was quite appropriate, if we accept the following gloss on sentences 2 to 4 of his text:

> If students can choose their own subjects, then a student can
> no longer excuse poor work by saying that he doesn't like the
> subject. This will force him to do better work.

Here "force" refers to an internal compulsion resulting from circumstance. In judging the word to be inappropriate, however, the child seems to be using a more restricted sense of the word that means a direct external compulsion.

Children who edit out an acceptable informal expression may be assumed to have generated that expression out of their unconscious rule systems and then applied inadequate conscious rules which wrongly classify the expression as inappropriate in writing (cf. Krashen, 1977). Such inadequate rules are to be expected in children relatively new to written language, of course. In the DIAGNOSE phase these inadequate rules are brought into confrontation with text generated according to a different rule system. In a skilled writer the consciously available rules will normally serve as an aid in discovering the source of intuitively sensed inadequacies. Thus they serve as powerful tools in diagnosis. For children, however, consciously available knowledge seems as likely to be an obstacle as an aid to accurate diagnosis.

While there is much that we do not yet understand about children's difficulties in the DIAGNOSE and OPERATE phases of the CDO process, we can in a very broad way attribute them all to lack of practice; to lack of practice, that is, in the CDO process itself. Further writing experience may or may not include practice of this sub-process. It seems possible therefore that a person might grow up to be a fluent and prolific writer without ever developing much skill in diagnosing text problems and remedying them.

This brings us to the question, untouched by the present experiment, of what it takes to activate the CDO process spontaneously, and of why it is that the process does not seem to be activated in children. Many conjectural explanations are possible, but the present experiment contributes one finding which limits a free range of conjecture. This is the finding that children are quite apt at detecting mismatches between intended and actual text, when prompted to look for them. This ability must surely have arisen from experience and practice of some kind.

Our own conjecture on these points, based on a variety of empirical observations but certainly not firmly grounded on evidence, is that children frequently execute the COMPARE phase of the CDO process but go no farther. They detect mismatches between actuality and intention just as they detect mismatches between the general quality of their texts and the texts they read. Instead of proceeding to diagnose and operate, however, they return to the interrupted procedure. They retain, though, some trace of such mismatches in long-term memory where they contribute to a growing data file on their shortcomings as writers. Hence the widespread belief of children that they are incompetent in writing. This belief is commonly blamed on teacher criticisms, but, in our view, it is much more deeply rooted in children's writing and reading experience than that (see also Bracewell, 1980).

This short-circuiting of the CDO process may have several contributing causes. One likely cause is incompletely developed mental representations of actual and intended texts. These representations may be developed to the point where the child can detect that something is amiss, but not far enough for the child to discover what it is. This is analogous to the experience one may have in traveling somewhere over an indistinctly remembered route. One senses that things do not look right and therefore begins to suspect that one has taken a wrong turn, but the mental representation of how things should look is not sufficiently clear to indicate where the wrong turn might have been made, or even to establish definitely that one is off course. A common response in the travel situation is just to keep going and hope things will become clearer. This is what children seem to do in writing.

Another possible contributing cause could be a prior history of failed attempts at remediation. As we have observed, children's attempts at remediation are frequently not successful and they often amount to little overt change at all. If children's occasional ventures into the CDO process have yielded only negative results, then it makes sense that they should learn to by-pass it.

There is another kind of short-circuiting observable in children's protocols which seems to occur in mature writers as well. This is a direct jump from COMPARE to GENERATE CHANGE. In these cases the mismatch first comes to consciousness in the form of a perception that some other word would be better, that a comma is missing, etc. This very rapid procedure, which seems to be mainly of value in catching slip-ups, may be enough to keep a COMPARE process going during composition. However, it would not develop the knowledge and skills necessary to deal with mismatches that require diagnosis and deliberate search for alternatives.

Finally, we must consider the possibility that children avoid the CDO process normally because it threatens loss of hold on the composing process as a whole. We know from questionnaire evidence (Keeney, 1975) that school-age writers are concerned about external distraction that may cause them to forget what they intended to write. The CDO process represents an internal diversion of attention which they might wish to avoid for the same reason.

The Alternating Procedure offers promise as an instructional device because its routine alleviates some of the danger of losing hold of the composing process. It also leads children into the DIAGNOSE and OPERATE phases of the CDO process, which they normally miss. Thus it has the potential of boosting the amount of experience through which skills in diagnosis and remediation may be developed. Finally, however, the CDO process must come to be triggered spontaneously, not through routine cuing. We cannot expect that practice with the Alternating Procedure would lead to a greater tendency for the system to respond spontaneously in an appropriate way. If we are correct, however, in our conjecture that spontaneous activation of the CDO process depends on refined development of mental representations of text, (an idea that is pursued further in Chapter 14) then it is clear that whole other dimensions of writing development are involved. The ability to plan, the ability to apprehend and elaborate rhetorical problems, the ability to encode large linguistic units in mentally manipulable form, these are some of the other aspects of writing development that impinge on the starting point of the CDO process. They also suggest the larger context of composing operations in which the CDO process plays its significant and revealing part.

POSTSCRIPT

The preceding study was primarily an investigation of children's competence and only secondarily an instructional study. However, its results were sufficiently encouraging from an instructional standpoint that two additional studies were conducted to see whether the general approach could be extended to produce improvements in all aspects of the CDO (COMPARE–DIAGNOSE–OPERATE) process. For ease of reference we will call the study already reported the COMPARE study, since it mainly concentrated on facilitating the COMPARE phase. The second study will be called the DIAGNOSE study, for it concentrated on facilitating the DIAGNOSE phase. Finally, the OPERATE study included procedural facilitations similar to those used in the preceding studies but added instruction in procedures that could be applied during the OPERATE phase.

The COMPARE study had shown young writers to be surprisingly capable at evaluating their own writing, but to be considerably less capable at diagnosing causes of detected inadequacies and at carrying out remedial operations. The DIAGNOSE and OPERATE studies were intended to see whether students would demonstrate further capabilities if they were provided with procedural and instructional support in these later phases of the CDO process. We will briefly describe these two additional studies and their results.

THE DIAGNOSE STUDY

This study, conducted by Clare Brett as an honors thesis, differed from the COMPARE study in two ways. First, as indicated above, it gave prominence to the DIAGNOSE component of the hypothesized three-component COMPARE–DIAGNOSE–OPERATE model of the revision process. Second, it specifically directed students' attention to both whole-text and to local-level problems. In the previous study the alternating procedure by which students' attention was shifted from content generation to problem detection was initiated routinely at the end of each sentence. In the present study a more global means of initiating problem detection was attempted. This will be described shortly.

Method

The study involved 20 students from grade 6 (10 experimental and 10 control) and 16 from grade 12 (8 experimental and 8 control). Students were from urban schools serving primarily middle-class families. Students were interviewed individually and assignment to experimental and control groups was random.

Each student diagnosed five essays. One of these was an essay previously written by the student. The other four essays were drawn from a pool of nine grade-6 essays selected for the number, variety, and representativeness of the inadequacies they contained. Of these four essays, one was the same for all students and was presented last. The others were selected randomly and presented in counter-balanced orders, along with the self-written essay, which was placed in either the second or fourth position. In addition to diagnosing problems, the students suggested revisions for two of the essays—their own and the final essay.

COMPARE–DIAGNOSE–OPERATE procedures.

In the COMPARE phase, students read through an essay as many times as they wished, placing markers in the margin wherever they sensed a problem—a green marker if they were sure what the problem was and a red marker if they were not.

The DIAGNOSE phase was handled differently for experimental and control groups. Control students were simply asked to identify and explain all the problems they had detected. Experimental students were provided with 13 cards corresponding to phrases indicated in Table 11.6. Experimental students were asked to consider each card in turn and to judge whether it applied and if so where—whether to the text as a whole or to a specific part.

A comparison between the diagnostic phrases used in this study and the evaluative phrases used in the COMPARE study (see Table 11.1) will help to clarify the difference in emphasis between the two studies. In the COMPARE study evaluative phrases were aimed at general analyses of text: was the text interesting, believable, important, understandable? For example, students were encouraged to monitor clarity by considering whether the phrase "People may not understand what I mean here" applied. It was at this general level of problem detection that they were found to exhibit considerable competence. In the present study students were encouraged to be more specific about why a person might have difficulty understanding their text. Rather than a global "People may not understand" judgment the diagnostic

Table 11.6   Cues Used to Facilitate DIAGNOSE Operations

---

1. Too few ideas.

2. Part of the essay doesn't belong with the rest.

3. Idea said in a clumsy way.

4. Incomplete idea.

5. The writer ignores the obvious point someone would bring up against what they were saying.

6. Weak reason.

7. Example doesn't help to explain the idea.

8. Choppy—ideas aren't connected to each other very well.

9. Hard to tell what the main point is.

10. Doesn't give the reader reason to take the idea seriously.

11. Too much space given to an unimportant point.

12. Says something that's not believable.

13. The reader will have already thought of this.

---

phrases focused on specific features of a text that might impede understanding—for instance, "The example doesn't help to explain the idea," "Choppy—ideas aren't connected to each other very well," "Part of the essay doesn't belong with the rest."

In order to limit task time, the OPERATE phase was reduced to having students suggest revisions, without actually carrying them out. For the final essay, experimental students worked without diagnostic cards. Thus the final essay constituted a transfer task in which experimental and control conditions were the same.

Results

Each of the essays was diagnosed by a professional editor, who produced a list of diagnostic statements for each essay. Two independent raters then evaluated the degree of correspondence between diagnoses made by students and each item on the expert's list (the professional editor's list was generated without reference to the diagnostic statements found in Table 11.6). A score of 3 indicated that the student identified the identical problem that the editor did and a score of zero indicated that the student's diagnosis did not mention the problem diagnosed by the editor. An analysis of variance on the combined ratings for all five essays revealed significantly better diagnoses for the grade-12 group ($F(1,34)$ = 17.12, $p < .001$) and for the experimental groups ($F(1,34)$ = 12.05, $p < .01$).

When only the final essay is considered, the essay on which the experimental group had to work without diagnostic cards, it is found that there was again a significant treatment effect, but it is entirely accounted for by the grade-12 group (F for the treatment effect = 5.59, $p < .05$; F for grade-by-treatment interaction = 7.97, $p < .01$). Thus it appears that students at both grade levels made superior diagnoses when assisted by the diagnostic cards, but only the grade-12 students showed transfer to diagnosis without cards.

Quality of suggested revisions was rated by two independent raters using a 5-point scale, with the top rating indicating a revision that the rater would also have chosen to make and the lowest rating indicating a revision that would be expected to make the composition worse. When combined ratings for their own and for the final essay were used, significant grade and treatment effects were again found, with the advantage for the experimental group tending in this case to be greater at grade 6 (mean rating for experimental and control groups = 2.91 versus 2.04 at grade 6; 2.94 versus 2.69 at grade 12). When only the final transfer essay is considered, however, a significant effect for quality of suggested revisions is found only at grade 12 (mean rating for experimental and control groups = 3.12 versus 2.64, $p < .05$), although the trend at grade 6 also favors the experimental group (mean = 2.79 versus 2.51).

There were also indications that the experimental treatment served to direct attention to higher-level text units. Among experimental students, approximately 79% of diagnoses were directed toward sentence, paragraph, or whole-text levels, whereas this was true of only 55% of diagnoses among control students.

Conclusion

Procedural facilitation of diagnosis through the use of diagnostic cards appears to be a helpful and practical instructional strategy. After only an hour of experience with the cards, grade-12 students showed a gain in diagnostic abilities even without cards. Although grade-6 students did not show such transfer, the fact that they were able to use the diagnostic cards to advantage suggests that learning could occur, either from more extended experience or from more direct coaching in making independent use of the diagnostic concepts. It is especially noteworthy that the experimental treatment had an effect on the quality of students' suggestions for revision. The gains in quality of diagnoses might be explained simply as the result of providing students with more precise expressions for stating what they thought was wrong; but if this were the sole effect (which, in itself, is not minor), it seems unlikely that it would carry over into making better recommendations for revision. We do not know, of course, how successful students may have been in carrying out revisions. We turn to this issue in the next study. It is important to appreciate, however, that there could be considerable loss between intention and execution and this would not detract from the present finding, but only strengthen a general conclusion we have stressed throughout this book and to which the present findings contribute: Student writers have varieties of relevant knowledge and competence that are not brought into play in composition because they lack executive procedures for bringing these, or for bringing related competencies (such as deliberate language manipulation) into play. The present study indicates that this is true of diagnostic competencies—that they are considerable, but are not brought into play without initial external support.

THE OPERATE STUDY

This study, conducted by Ellen Cohen as an honors thesis, was designed to determine whether diagnostic operations, found in the preceding study to lead to profitable suggestions for text revisions, could lead in fact to remedial action. Students were shown a simple notation system for indicating insertions and deletions to texts, and received practice in remedying diagnosed problems on texts written by themselves and by others.

Method

Participants in this study were 30 grade-6 students from a middle-income area in metropolitan Toronto. The experiment consisted of nine days of group instruction, plus three days of testing. The data reported are on the 21 students who were present on each of the data-collection days. Prior to instruction, each student wrote and revised an essay. After instruction, students were given copies of their original essays and asked to revise them again. Results are based in comparisons of these three essays—original, revision 1, and revision 2.

Instructional procedures

During instruction students were introduced, at the rate of one or two a day, to the diagnostic phrases. Seven of the phrases are essentially the same as the first seven listed in Table 11.6. Two additional phrases were introduced to accommodate special concerns of the instructor—"Introduction does not explain what the essay is about" and "Conclusion does not explain ideas."

The following procedure was used to introduce each diagnostic phrase. The phrase was read aloud to the class, then students were shown an essay specially written to demonstrate the kind of difficulty indicated by the diagnostic phrase. The essay was presented on an overhead projector, the diagnostic phrase on the blackboard. Students engaged in group discussions about how the diagnostic phrase on the blackboard applied to the essay—for example, why part of the essay did not belong with the rest. They then suggested revisions to remedy the problem and watched as the instructor carried out their suggested change. For example, the instructor would cross out the statement a student claimed did not belong. This generally led to students noting that some information needed to be inserted in its place and students would suggest information to be inserted. The instructor would make the change in accordance with suggestions and the class would then discuss the effectiveness of the change. Frequently, through their own or the instructor's suggestion, they would reconsider the remedial action taken, returning to a copy of the pre-revision essay and discussing the relative merits of alternate suggestions. Suggestions were not limited to the diagnostic phrase under immediate consideration, although a minimum of one revision was devoted to that particular source of difficulty.

In addition to group revision of specially prepared texts, students worked individually. Before the day's instruction each student wrote a short essay. After the group instruction they revised their essay, with special emphasis on the diagnostic phrase or phrases introduced that day. During the last three of the nine instructional sessions students took over the instructor's role in guiding the class discussion of diagnoses and revisions (cf. Palincsar & Brown, 1984, on reciprocal teaching).

Results

Holistic ratings of original, revision 1, and revision 2 essays were conducted by two raters, using a 5-point scale. All 63 essays (3 by each of 21 students) were randomly presented so that raters did not know which version any particular essay represented. An analysis of variance showed significant differences between the three essays ($F(2,38) = 10.62$, $p < .001$). Post hoc analyses showed that revision 2 was judged significantly superior to both the original essay ($F(1, 19) = 12.71$, $p < .01$) and to revision 1 ($F(1, 19) = 10.31$, $p < .01$), but that revision 1 was not judged significantly different from the original essay.

Comparisons of individual changes to essays were also conducted. Each alteration to the original text was classified as being a mechanical, word, phrase, single sentence, or multiple sentence revision. The number of students making high-level revisions increased significantly from revision 1 to revision 2 (McNemar's test, with Yates's correction $= 15.05$, $p < .001$). Finally, each revision that involved an idea change was categorized as one that added, altered, or deleted information. There were only four idea changes of any kind in revision 1. In revision 2 there were 40 idea changes, of which 28 (70%) consisted of added information. Every student made at least one idea change in revision 2, and all but two of the students made idea changes that were judged to be improvements.

Discussion

The DIAGNOSE study found that, as a result of procedural facilitation, students were better at diagnosing texts and at offering suggestions for revising texts. The current study shows that students can operate successfully on diagnoses and thereby significantly improve the quality of their texts. It is of note that the students in the present study received group instruction rather than individual instruction and that the instructional effort was not a very complex or lengthy one. Basically, instruction amounted to giving children insight into specific problems calling for revision, and providing guided practice in trying out and evaluating revisions.

It should be noted that, whereas conventional school practices treat revision itself as the focal point—what changes would improve the text?—the approach that we have taken treats revision as the last step in a series of analytic activities which begin with sensing something wrong, move to identifying the source of the trouble, and then proceed to considering possible actions. The conventional view is implicit in the current wave of enthusiasm for word processors in school writing instruction. Revision is treated as a significant activity in its own right, one that is impeded by the technical problems of the pen-and-paper medium. The approach we have taken, on the other hand, presumes that revision is of little significance in and of itself, and that students avoid it not so much because of technical difficulties but because they have trouble marshalling and applying the several kinds of knowledge required for successful revision. We attribute the success of the preceding studies in promoting effective revision to the use of procedural facilitations that help young writers identify causes of reader difficulties and to the provision of practice in detecting and remedying perceived problems.

We would not claim that the instructional interventions employed in these studies have succeeded in moving students from a knowledge-telling to a knowledge-transforming strategy, but that they have achieved progress in that direction. Both the extent and the limits of the progress achieved are suggested by the kinds of revisions students were found to make after instruction in the OPERATE study. All of the students had begun to make revisions at the idea level—an important advance over typical elementary student performance—but the majority of the changes consisted of adding ideas. Regardless of whether students diagnosed the text as choppy or as including an idea that did not belong, their preferred means of coping was to add material that would provide a more suitable link or context for an idea.

When we consider such results in light of knowledge-telling and knowledge-transforming operations we see an interesting combination of both kinds of activity. The problem-detection operations encouraged by the facilitation—the identification, for example, of choppiness and ideas that do not fit—are clearly distinct from content generating activity. That is, the student moves into a backward-looking, problem-detection mode as opposed to a forward-looking content-generation mode. In this sense we see knowledge-transforming as opposed to knowledge-telling mechanisms in operation. On the other hand, the "add on" remedial tactic suggests that the backward-looking or analytic operation brought to mind additional, or in some cases alternative things to say. These new ideas clearly provide more information and are helpful to a reader. But it is important to appreciate that they are not transformational in the sense of reworking the original ideas.

Our experience suggests that the changes to text young children make generally fall into the "thinking of something different or more to say" category rather than in the identification of inadequacies or fallacies leading to reassessment of prior knowledge. Nonetheless, the ability to pinpoint difficulties such as poor connections between sentences and missing or inappropriate ideas is surely a precursor to the second-order operations by which such perceived difficulties are remedied. It is also significant that on the posttest these young writers demonstrated skills at problem detection as well as remediation, and that they were able to exercise these skills without help from either teacher or peers.

The three studies on revision each demonstrate that while children do not appear spontaneously to shift attention between content generation and problem identification they can be enabled to do so with appropriate procedural facilitation. Even in the COMPARE study, where the student's train of thought was interrupted after every sentence, there was no perceivable decline in performance. To the extent that such shifting of attention created change, the change was positive. As we clarify and redefine our understanding of the underlying operations and manage to convey them to children, even more effective executive procedures should be teachable.

The present work encouraged us to believe that a similar approach might be successfully applied to facilitating composition planning. Mature writers do a good deal of revising in their heads, and this tends to be labeled planning rather than revision. But surely, at the level of mental processes, revision of ideas on paper and revision of ideas in the head must be similar, even though the latter may create a greater demand on working-memory capacity and thus require more sophisticated executive procedures. We therefore reasoned that if we could design procedural facilitations for operating on thoughts not yet committed to writing, we might be able to create the executive support required to foster planning and also help students conserve resources by breaking the complex task of planning into manageable subtasks. It is to this effort that we turn in the next chapter.

Chapter 12
Fostering Reflective Processes

PREFACE

The study reported in this chapter was a direct attempt to promote a shift from a knowledge-telling to a knowledge-transforming process in composition. The crucial difference between knowledge telling and knowledge transforming, as these were described in Chapter 1, lies in the problem-formulating and problem-solving activities associated with the latter. In particular, it was postulated that knowledge transforming involves parallel activity in two problem spaces, a content space and a rhetorical space, with interaction between the two spaces so that results obtained in one space may be translated into problems to be solved in the other space. Instructional effort in the present study was concentrated on fostering such a back-and-forth or reflective process.

A model of the reflective process is presented, which is simply that portion of the knowledge-transforming model (see Figure 1.2) that encompasses the two interacting problem spaces. It was expected that it would not be a quick or easy matter to get students to start formulating and solving problems in composition and to respond to what they had produced by formulating further problems. Consequently an extended program of instruction was carried out, making use of not only procedural facilitation but also explanation and modeling of thinking.

12

Most modern approaches to composition instruction give an important place to reflective processes, in contrast to the linear procedures often espoused in older composition textbooks (Rose, 1981). Not only is reflection valued as an aid to writing, but writing is valued as an aid to reflection (Murray, 1978; Nystrand & Wiederspiel, 1977; Wason, 1980). Reflection is here viewed, following Piaget (1980), as a dialectical process by which higher-order knowledge is created through the effort to reconcile lower-order elements of knowledge. Reflective processes figure in the instructional approaches based on "heuristics of discovery" (Young et al., 1970) and those based on dialogue between teacher and student concerning the content or form of what the student has written (Graves, 1983; Staton, 1980). In the latter approaches there seems to be an underlying assumption that the dialectical process carried on between teacher and student will eventually be internalized by the student, who will then be able to carry it on independently. This assumption remains largely untested, however.

The present study addresses the question of whether elementary-school children can be enabled to sustain reflective processes in composition independently. Planning episodes of experts thinking aloud while writing (Flower & Hayes, 1980a, 1981) are replete with evidence of reflective activity—elaborating and reformulating goals and plans for achieving goals, critically examining past decisions, anticipating difficulties, reconciling competing ideas, etc. Such activity is almost completely absent from the protocols of school-age writers (see Chapter 8).

As we indicated in the opening chapter of this book, and as will be argued more fully in the final chapter, there is a variety of collateral evidence that this lack of reflective statements in the protocols of young writers is not an artifact, that immature writers do indeed follow a procedure that permits them to generate texts through primarily linear, nonreflective processes. This is the procedure we have been calling the "knowledge-telling strategy." In brief, it consists of reducing writing assignments to topics, then telling what one knows about the topic. The knowledge-telling strategy takes account of semantic and structural constraints, but it does not involve operating upon representations of goals for the text. It thus permits novices to reduce writing to a routine. Primary concerns in this routine are what to say next and how to put it into appropriate language—fairly local considerations that allow writers to deal with problems singly or in small units rather than needing to work out implications of multiple constraints simultaneously.

Although, as noted, there has been considerable effort to foster reflective processes in school children through various types of dialogue, the question of the extent to which children can learn to carry on such processes independently does not seem to have been investigated. The question is important, not only from the standpoint of instructional psychology but from the standpoint of understanding the emergence of more complex structures in cognitive development (cf. Piaget, 1980). We had previously conducted short-term experiments of limited focus on this question (Scardamalia & Bereiter, 1985a). The present study is an extension of that work into a substantial instructional intervention.

A DUAL PROBLEM
SPACE MODEL OF REFLECTION

A principled approach to teaching reflective processes in writing requires some assumption as to how such processes are carried out in the mind of the solitary writer. One attractive notion has been that reflection takes the form of an internal dialogue, as between writer and imagined reader (Widdowson, 1983). At least one instructional approach is based on teaching students to carry on such dialogue explicitly (Gray, 1977). The informal approaches referred to in the preceding section, which make use of teacher-student or student-student dialogue, appear tacitly to assume such an internal-dialogue model of reflection. However, in the body of protocol research on skilled writers running from Emig (1971) to Flower and Hayes (1981) we are not aware of a shred of evidence to support the internal-dialogue model. We take the absence of evidence to be severely damaging, since if internal dialogue were the main vehicle for reflective thought in writing, one would expect it to be so salient in the thinking-aloud protocols of skilled writers that it would have been noted even by those not specifically looking for it. (This does not mean that instructional approaches based on the internal-dialogue model are necessarily ineffective; but it does mean that their effects would have to be explained on the basis of something more complex than mere internalization of a form of interchange between writer and reader).

The thinking-aloud protocols of expert writers do not look anything like dialogues, but they do look a great deal like problem-solving protocols (Hayes & Flower, 1980). There is a great deal of soliloquy of the "where am I?" variety, virtually no colloquy of the "where are you?" variety. Starting from the notion of composing as a form of problem solving, and making use of Newell's generalization of the concept of problem spaces (1980), we may construct a somewhat more plausible model of reflective processes in writing. We may conceive of composition planning as taking place in two types of problem spaces. One type, the *content space,* is made up of knowledge states that may be broadly characterized as *beliefs.* It is the kind of space in which one works out opinions, makes moral decisions, generates inferences about matters of fact, formulates causal explanations, and so on. Content spaces thus have wide use in daily life and are by no means limited to composition planning.

The other type of problem space, the *rhetorical space,* is specifically tied to text production. The knowledge states to be found in this kind of space are *mental representations of actual or intended text*—representations that may be at various levels of abstraction from verbatim representation to representations of main ideas and global intentions (Beaugrande, 1984b; Chapter 4). Collins & Gentner (1980) provide a succinct analysis of types of problems dealt with in a rhetorical space and kinds of operators that may be applied. Whereas the goal states in the content space are knowledge (in the sense of warranted beliefs), the goal states in the rhetorical space are plans for achieving various purposes in composition (Flower & Hayes, 1980a).

Something like this notion of two types of problem space is implicit in most cognitive descriptions of the composing process. Collins and Gentner (1980) say, for instance:

> It is important to separate idea production from text production. The processes involved in producing text, whether they operate on the word level, the sentence level, the paragraph level, or the text level, must produce a linear sequence that satisfies certain grammatical rules. In contrast, the result of the process of idea production is a set of ideas with many internal connections, only a few of which may fit the linear model desirable for text. (p. 53)

The obvious way to think of the connection between these two spaces is to think of output from the content space serving as input to the rhetorical space. The model illustrated in Figure 12.1, by contrast, shows operations working in both directions. These may be thought of as productions, or condition-action pairs, some of which take beliefs as conditions and convert them to rhetorical goals, some of which take rhetorical problems and convert them to subgoals to be satisfied in the content space—that is, through operations on beliefs.

Our contention is that this interaction between the two problem spaces constitutes the essence of reflection in writing. There may, of course, be reflective thought that goes on wholly within the content space or within the rhetorical space. (Considering different schemes for organizing a text might be an occasion for the latter.) But the peculiar value that many have

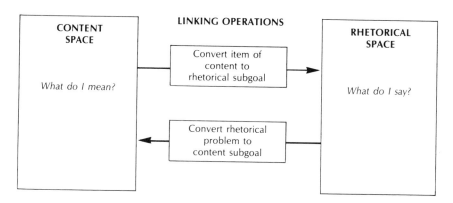

Figure 12.1. A dual-problem space model of reflective processes in written composition.

claimed for writing as a way of developing one's understanding (Murray, 1978) cannot inhere in either of these problem spaces separately. Thought carried out solely within the content space is not distinctive to writing, and thought carried out solely within the rhetorical space would be expected to develop craft but not wisdom or world knowledge. (In Plato's *Gorgias* Sophocles objects to rhetoric for this very reason.)

The key requirement for reflective thought in writing, according to this model, is the translation of problems encountered in the rhetorical space back into subgoals to be achieved in the content space. For instance, recognition that a key term will not be understood by many readers gets translated into a call for a definition; search within the content space for semantic specifications leads to a realization by the writer that he or she doesn't actually have a clear concept associated with the term, and this realization sets off a major reanalysis of the point being made. (See Scardamalia & Bereiter, 1985a, for additional examples.) Very similar interactions occur in conversation—e.g., the query "What do you mean by X?", coming from a conversational partner, may set off the same reanalysis referred to above. It is accordingly not surprising that in trying to represent a mechanism for reflective thought in writing, people have been attracted to the internal dialogue model. What we propose instead is that the dialectical process that in conversation is sustained by the alternation between speakers and their respective points of view is sustained in writing by the alternation between problem spaces with their different but related knowledge states.

The model presented in Figure 12.1 provides a simple way to account for a variety of expert-novice differences in writing. The explanation is that the novice possesses productions for transferring information from the content space to the rhetorical space, but lacks productions for the return trip. The result is a think-say process of composition, reflected in such commonly noted tendencies as that of making the order of presentation correspond to the order of idea generation (Flower, 1979) and limiting revision to cosmetic improvements (that is, to improvements that can be worked out entirely within the rhetorical space). The expert, on the other hand, carries on a two-way process of information transfer, which results in the joint evolution of the composition and the writer's understanding of what he or she is trying to say—what Murray (1978) calls "outer" and "inner" revision.

This dual-space model led the authors to take a different approach to teaching reflective processes in writing from those currently popular. Approaches that make use of "discovery" heuristics concentrate on operations within the content space, resulting in a richer body of content to carry over into the rhetorical space. Dialogue approaches rely on the teacher to provide the linking operations between the two composing spaces, with the tacit assumption that these operations will eventually be taken over by the student. The approach taken by the present authors could be described as *assisted monologue* rather than dialogue. The focus is on the covert or overt monologues students carry on while planning a composition, and the instructional interventions consist of efforts to introduce and support in such monologues the two-way flow of information shown in Figure 12.1.

Method

Experimental and control groups were two intact classes constituting the sixth grade in a public school serving a middle to high income urban area. Assignment to classes was reportedly random, as further suggested by pretest results. There were 30 students in the experimental class, 32 in the control class.

Instruction for the experimental class consisted of two 50-minute periods a week for 19 weeks, conducted by one of the authors and a research assistant. The first 10 weeks focused on the opinion essay and the remaining weeks on factual exposition. Several distinctive components were woven together in the instruction:

   1. *Procedural facilitation.* Scardamalia & Bereiter (1985a) had found that use of cues that stimulated self-questioning during composition planning resulted in essays scored as showing more evidence of thought. In the present experiment students were taught to incorporate phrases such as "An important point I haven't considered is. . . . "

and "Someone might think I'm exaggerating because. . . ." into thinking-aloud planning episodes. Initially, thinking aloud was conducted by instructors, then by student volunteers. The person thinking aloud would stand before the class and start thinking about plans for an essay on some assigned topic. At points of stuckness the planner would select a card from a deck of planning cues, insert the selected phrase into the monologue, and continue as if that phrase had come to mind spontaneously.

Once this basic format was established the method was refined by encouraging students to make selections based on rational choice of the *kind* of thinking they needed to be carrying out. To aid them, cues were grouped into categories according to function (see Tables 12.1 and 12.2) and students were taught to consider first what kind of cue they needed, and then to select a cue from within that category. Both the selection of such planning cues and responses to them were under the student's control. No adult assistance was provided.

Public demonstrations of planning were followed by students' individually planning compositions at their seats, using individual sets of cue cards, but carrying on the planning monologue subvocally.

Table 12.1 Planning Cues Used for Opinion Essays

New Idea	Elaborate
An even better idea is . . .	An example of this . . .
An important point I haven't considered yet is . . .	This is true, but it's not sufficient so . . .
A better argument would be . . .	My own feelings about this are . . .
A different aspect would be . . .	I'll change this a little by . . .
A whole new way to think of this topic is . . .	The reason I think so . . .
No one will have thought of . . .	Another reason that's good . . .
	I could develop this idea by adding . . .
	Another way to put it would be . . .
Improve	A good point on the other side of the argument is . . .
I'm not being very clear about what I just said so . . .	Goals
I could make my main point clearer . . .	A goal I think I could write to . . .
A criticism I should deal with in my paper is . . .	My purpose . . .
I really think this isn't necessary because . . .	Putting It Together
I'm getting off topic so . . .	If I want to start off with my strongest idea I'll . . .
This isn't very convincing because . . .	I can tie this together by . . .
But many readers won't agree that . . .	My main point is . . .
To liven this up I'll . . .	

Table 12.2   Planning Cues Used for Factual Exposition

New Idea	Elaborate
An important distinction is . . .	I'm impressed by . . .
A consequence of (this is) . . .	I sometimes wonder . . .
The history of this is . . .	An explanation would be . . .
Something that is similar is . . .	My own feelings about this are . . .
Its features remind me of . . .	An example of (this is) . . .
One thing that makes this different from other things like it is . . .	This results in . . .
	My own experience with this is . . .
A cause of (this is) . . .	
A practical benefit is . . .	**Goals**
A way to improve the use of this is . . .	A goal I think I could write to . . .
I might explain a method used to . . .	My purpose . . .
Improve	**Putting it Together**
I could describe this in more detail by adding . . .	If I want to start off with my strongest idea I'll . . .
I could add interest by explaining . . .	I can tie this together by . . .
This isn't exactly how it is because . . .	My main point is . . .
I could give the reader a clear picture by . . .	
This isn't true of all . . .	
To put it more simply . . .	
Readers will find it boring to be told . . .	

2. *Modeling thought.* Earlier, one-shot applications of modeling planning did not produce encouraging results with elementary students (Chapter 8). In the present study, however, modeling was used frequently, both with the instructor as model and with students modeling for each other, with and without cue cards, and with follow-up discussions of the thinking strategies exhibited. Such more extensive use of modeling thought, coupled with direct instruction, had been found effective by Bird (1980) in promoting the use of expert-like reading-comprehension strategies by elementary school students.

3. *Direct strategy instruction.* The idea of dialectic was explained to students (in suitably simplified terms) and students were explicitly urged to pursue a strategy of looking for high-level ways to reconcile inconsistencies. Dialectic was explained as a matter of trying to "rise above" opposing arguments by producing an idea that preserves what is valid on both sides. In examining the complexity of arguments in children's opinion essays, we have found (Chapter 6) that when elementary students tried to cope with opposing arguments they tended either (a) to juxtapose them, with no effort at resolution, (b) to choose one and reject the other, or (c) to find some compromise position which took account of the opposing sides but did not take account of the reasons supporting those sides. In only one out of 80 compositions did we find evidence of successfully reconciling thesis, opposing argument, and supporting argument. This is what students were urged to do in the present study. It was explained that the strategy of rising to a plane above the conflict applies not only to conflicting content but to conflicts of any sort that may occur during composition—for instance, the conflict between the wish to include a certain point and the wish to hold to a neat structural plan.

Formal assessment was based on the following: Each student produced pretest and post-test opinion essays and topical expositions, with assigned topics counterbalanced as to order. Six randomly selected students from each class were taperecorded as they thought aloud while planning each of these four essays. During the term, experimental and control students also produced a major topical essay, on a self-chosen topic, written during class time, with up to four periods allowed for preparation and writing. Four periods was the length of time experimental children worked spontaneously. The control teacher agreed to set aside an equal amount of time and to encourage children to use the time to plan and to take notes. For this essay students were allowed to consult library materials, and experimental students were allowed to use planning cue cards if they wished. For the pre- and post-test essays no external aids were permitted.

Results

Planning. Thinking-aloud planning protocols were blind coded, using categories based on Hayes and Flower's division of the planning process into generating (primarily generating content), organizing, and goal setting (Hayes & Flower, 1980). In addition, coders marked any statement they judged to indicate reflective thinking. As in other studies of composition planning in young writers (Chapter 8), the great majority of statements consisted of content generation. The frequency of other types of statements varied so greatly both within and between students that no attempt was made to extract measures of central tendency.

Consistent effects did appear, however, in the number of protocol statements coded as "reflective." Experimental students went from a pretest mean of 3.67 to a post-test mean of 5.17; control students went from 4.33 to 2.42. The difference between groups on the post-test is significant both by analysis of variance $(F(1,10) = 6.66, p < .05)$ and by analysis of covariance, adjusting for pretest scores $(F(1,9) = 11.33, p < .01)$.

Major Essay.   Two raters rated these essays on a global scale ranging from knowledge telling ("reads like an encyclopedia article") on one extreme to reflective ("like what you would expect to find in a magazine or collection of essays") on the other. Note that this was not a good-bad dimension. Good writing might be found at either extreme, but of different sorts. (A magazine article on bears, for instance, might be expected to differ markedly from an encyclopedia article on the same subject. While the encyclopedia article presents organized facts, the magazine piece might adopt a personal point of view, develop a single interest-holding theme, and perhaps include elements of speculation.)

On a 9-point scale, with a score of 9 being the most reflective, the experimental group averaged 5.43, compared to a control group mean of 3.35. The difference is statistically significant beyond the .05 level ($t(38) = 2.57$). Only students who had been present for the full four days of work on this essay were included in the analysis.

Changes Between Pretest and Post-test.   Pretest and post-test essays were subjected to a more detailed comparison using criteria listed in Tables 12.3 and 12.4. Raters assigned difference scores of 0 to 3 points to paired essays, not knowing which was the pre- and which was the post-test essay. This resulted in a 7-point scale, once direction of difference was taken into account. Difference scores aggregated over all the rating dimensions showed a significant advantage for the experimental group on the topical essay ($Z = 2.14$, ranks-sums test, $p < .05$). Aggregated difference scores also favored the experimental group on the opinion essay, but not to a degree approaching statistical significance.

Mean difference scores on the separate rating dimensions are shown in Tables 12.3 and 12.4. An examination of the scores in Table 12.3 suggests that the strong points of topical articles written by the experimental group students lay in their having the character of personal essays that revealed normal personal involvement in the topic (items 1, 2, and 9) and an effort to involve the readers as well (items 3, 7, and 8). Pre- and post-test essays by an experimental group student, shown in Table 12.5 illustrate such a shift toward essay-like character.

Table 12.4 indicates that the same rating dimensions are among the stronger points of the opinion essays as well, but that the control-group students also made gains on these dimensions. In light of the effort to teach a dialectic, "rise above it" strategy, it is interesting to note that the largest advantage of the experimental group over the control group on opinion essays was on the criterion, "Attempts to resolve opposing points instead of simply noting pros and cons." On the other hand, where experimental students did worst in comparison to control students was on items 10 and 11, which have to do with developing a coherent and well-thought-out

Table 12.3   Mean Differences Between Pretest and Post-test Factual Expository Essays

Rating Dimension	Group	
	Experimental	Control
1. Suggestion of personal involvement or interest in topic, not limited to the relating of personal experiences.	+.59	−.36
2. Essay-like character, as opposed to having the character of an encyclopedia article.	+.52	−.34
3. Use of attention-getting expressions of points, especially in opening or closing sentences.	+.41	+.12
4. Adherence to requirements of the assignment—i.e., to focussing on *one* animal or occupation and dealing with its interestingness.	+.02	−.23
5. A distinctive viewpoint on the topic.	0	+.20
6. A distinctive manner of presentation.	−.13	+.11
7. Content selected to convey the point of the essay, not simply because of its connection to the topic.	+.43	−.11
8. Attempt to communicate interestingness of topic to the reader, rather than taking the reader's interest for granted.	+.54	−.36
9. Indications of uncertainty, questioning, or speculation.	+.67	−.02
10. Statement of a theme or purpose or delimitation of topic.	+.26	−.37
11. Focus on a central theme or point or aspect of topic, as opposed to unfocussed collection of sub-topics.	+.14	−.21

Note: Positive score indicates post-test higher than pretest. Maximum difference = ±3.

position on the opinion essay topic. This suggests a gap between attempt and execution, which will be expanded upon in the next section.

INFORMAL OBSERVATIONS

The quantitative results point to some overall change in the direction of reflectivity having taken place in the experimental group. The following informal observations are intended to offer suggestions—of a necessarily

Table 12.4   Mean Difference between Pretest and Post-test Opinion Essays

	Group	
Rating Dimension	Experimental	Control
1. Balanced use of personal experience and feelings integrated with more objective information; personal biases recognized as such.	+.36	+.19
2. Essay-like character, as opposed to having the character of knowledge telling or egocentric self expression.	+.36	+.21
3. Use of attention getting facts, ideas or expressions, especially in opening or closing sentences.	−.16	+.07
4. Adherence to requirements of the assignment—i.e., to dealing with *influence* of TV as a *whole* or with relative merits of the two designated ways of handling allowances.	+.34	+.23
5. A distinctive viewpoint on the topic—in contrast to reporting conventional wisdom, typical personal reactions, or familiar scenarios.	+.04	+.10
6. A distinctive manner of presentation.	0	−.13
7. Content selected to convey the point of the essay, not simply because of its connection to the topic.	+.20	+.04
8. Attempts to persuade or get reader to think, rather than relying on unsupported statements of opinion.	+.28	+.22
9. Indications of uncertainty, questioning, or speculation, suggesting an effort to get at the truth of the matter or to resolve problems involved in the issue.	+.36	+.37
10. An elaborated statement of position as opposed to simple "it depends," "it's good," "it's bad," "they should," "they shouldn't."	+.12	+.27
11. Definite line of thought (even if rambling) runs through text, as compared to a list structure.	−.02	+.19
12. Avoidance of polemic, overstatement, and dogmatic, simplistic arguments.	−.02	−.10
13. Attempts to resolve opposing points instead of simply noting pros and cons.	+.44	+.23

Note: Positive score indicates post-test higher than pretest.
Maximum difference = ±3.

more subjective and speculative nature—on what the underlying cognitive changes may have been that were reflected in the quantitative gains.

1.   Enjoyment of planning as an activity. Although the experimenters had qualms about asking students to plan aloud in front of their

Table 12.5   Sample Pretest and Post-test Factual Essays by an Experimental Group Student

---

(Pretest)
Job or Occupation

An interesting job or occupation is being an airline stewardess. I think airline stewardesses have an interesting job because they get to travel all over the world and meet new people. I know because my friend is an airline stewardess and travels a lot. I would like to be an airline stewardess when I grow up.

(Post-test)
An Interesting Kind of Animal

All animals are interesting, but sometimes you may find a person that may like an animal better than you. That proves that all people are different. I think an interesting animal is a tiger because of its fierce and gentle sides makes it exquisite. Most people think it is only fierce and only hurts people but that isn't so. The tiger has so much grace in his walk it almost looks as if he puts a lot of thought into it, and his fur coat is so unique I think it's one of a kind, and nothing could be better or more beautiful than that striped coat to me. That is why I think the tiger is the most interesting animal.

---

classmates, this proved to be an extremely popular activity with most of the students, who clamored for a chance at what they came to call "soloing." No doubt a good part of the enjoyment was simply the pleasure of being at center stage, but it is nevertheless noteworthy that these students seemed to find planning a significant enough skill that they were eager to display their ability under conditions in which even the most talented were likely to display effort and difficulty, not flair.

2.   Increased ability to monitor and analyze thinking. This was revealed mainly in the sessions in which students took turns planning aloud in front of the class. Students appeared to become increasingly careful in monitoring the thinking of the "soloist." They began to notice discrepancies between goals and plans—for instance, a discrepancy between an author's stated intention of getting readers to appreciate the difficulties of modern dance and a plan that consisted mainly of description of types of modern dance.

3.   Recognition of problems at the planning level. The monitoring and analysis described above often resulted in problems being posed which the author did not know how to solve, with an ensuing discussion of possible solutions and inquiries as to how expert writers would handle such problems.

4.   Understanding the function of planning cues. The division of planning cue cards into functional types, as shown in Tables 12.1 and 12.2, was done in collaboration with the students. This activity, which had been intended to occupy one class session, ended up

taking three sessions to complete because of the amount of discussion about what functions various cues could serve in planning. For instance, students would argue that the cue, "My main point is . . . ," could serve either for figuring out one's goal or for putting the text together. By their own reports, however, students had never previously thought of ideas in terms of their functions in texts. Further indications of understanding cue functions came from the planning-aloud sessions, in which students gave clear indications of considering what type of cue they needed to guide their thinking at different points during planning.

5.   Using goals as criteria for selecting ideas. From the beginning of the course, the experimenters encouraged students to state goals for their compositions as an aid to planning. The students showed little indication of making use of such goal statements, however, until they reached the point where they were generating more content ideas than they could use. As we have indicated in previous chapters, generating sufficient content to complete an expository writing assignment is a common problem with elementary school students. By using the planning cues, however, students were soon able to generate more ideas than they could appropriately incorporate in the intended composition. Once the problem of excess ideas arose, students began to use goals as a basis for selection. Thus, for instance, if they established the goal of making their composition amusing, they could assess ideas on their potential for being amusing. Such assessment in turn led to thinking of rhetorical strategies for achieving goals—for instance, making a fact about a penguin at a zoo dying from swallowing tossed coins amusing by comparing the penguin to a piggy-bank.

6.   More mature notemaking. Research reported in Chapter 8 showed a developmental progression in notemaking during composition. From listing content more-or-less in the form that it would appear in the finished composition, students moved on to sketching ideas at different levels, increasingly producing plans that differed both in content and arrangement from the eventual compositions. During the course of the experiment, students began to display many of the more adult-like characteristics in their notemaking—for instance, listing ideas for and against in separate columns, or separating statements of personal feeling from factual statements. They also started to use arrows and other graphic devices to indicate how ideas needed to be reorganized. (One lesson of about 20 minutes was given on notemaking; however, most of the devices used by the students were of their own invention.)

7.   More reflective use of information sources. The behavior of

experimental-group students during four days of planning their major essays showed signs of the back-and-forth movement between content and rhetorical spaces depicted in Figure 12.1. They tended to generate some initial plan for a paper, then go to library resources for particular information that they found they needed, recast their plan in light of new information gained, and so on. By contrast—to judge from planning notes, reports by their teacher, and the compositions themselves—control-group students proceeded in the one-way manner more typical of novices. They first extracted material from encyclopedias and similar source books, and then developed a composition from it, allowing the information sources to dictate both the type of content and the general form of their essays.

8. Ability to sustain planning. In preparing their major essays, experimental-group students spontaneously took four days to plan and write them (some using all the time for planning and doing the writing at home). By contrast, it took a great deal of encouragement and support from their teacher to get the control group to spend four days on the project, and the most common use these students made of their time was for extracting additional information from books to insert in their essays. In this connection, it may be noted that the pre- and post-test essays were written under time constraints (30 minutes), which allowed only minimal time for planning. While this time allotment may have been ample for the kind of planning students normally do (Applebee, 1981; Chapter 8), it obviously did not allow the extended plan-development that experimental-group students had been learning to do, but at which they had not yet developed much facility. This might help to explain why experimental-control differences were more pronounced on the major essay than on the pre-post comparisons.

9. Beginnings of a dialectical process. In full-fledged reflective planning, dialectical processes may be thought of as going on at two levels. At a lower level, individual ideas are being reconsidered and modified as a result of the interaction between rhetorical and content-related concerns. At a higher level, goals and general point of view are being transformed through this interaction (Scardamalia & Bereiter, 1982). It is at this higher level that what we have called the "rise above it" strategy applies. There are clear indications that gains in reflective planning at the lower of these levels took place. The increased incidence of protocol statements scored as showing reflective thought is the most definite evidence. Informal observations of students "soloing" bear out the conviction that with the help of planning cues they engaged in substantial reconsideration of ideas.

What was not evident, except in scattered instances, was reflection at the higher level, involving major goals or viewpoints on a topic. Although, as noted in point 4, students did begin to make use of goal statements, analyses of the post-test planning protocols indicated that the modal number of goal statements per protocol was one. When such solitary goals are compared to the complex goal networks found by Flower and Hayes (1980a, 1981) in the protocols of expert writers, it is not surprising that little dialectical activity involving goals was observed to take place. Another indication of the lack of high-level reformulation of plans is that when doubts, questions, or alternative ways of looking at a topic occurred in planning, they tended to be expressed directly in the text rather than to modify the overall plan of the text. This may explain why the data in Table 12.4 show the experimental-group students to have gained in efforts to reconcile opposing viewpoints but not in ability to present a coherent and balanced argument.

There was, however, some indication of movement toward higher-level reflection. These indications came mainly from the kinds of help students sought while they were working on compositions. Increasingly their problems had to do, not with a particular sentence or idea, but with the reconciliation or synthesis of different ideas—different intentions, different statements, different plans of attack, etc. Thus the basis for dialectic appeared to be taking shape—"the splitting of a single whole and the cognition of its contradictory parts" (Lenin, 1915/1977, p. 381)—but the ability to carry it through apparently remained to be developed.

CONCLUSION

The question that motivated this study was whether elementary-school children could be enabled to sustain reflective processes in writing independently. The answer, as furnished by this initial study, is affirmative but with qualifications. There are indications from the extent of planning and from the presence of reflective statements in thinking-aloud protocols that some two-way traffic between content space and rhetorical space had been established. This conclusion was further supported by ratings on reflectiveness of the essays produced. Reflection appeared to be mainly at a local level, however, focused on individual ideas. Reflection having to do with the reshaping and elaboration of goals and central ideas, so noticeable in expert writers, had yet to gain a secure foothold in their composing processes. However, all indications were that progress was in the direction of a knowledge-transforming approach to writing. It is also significant that what children were able to do by the end of this experiment they were able to do independently. Most of the informal educational research related to children's composing permits no such judgment.

POSTSCRIPT
FURTHER STUDIES ON
TEACHING REFLECTIVE PROCESSES

With a view to eventually integrating procedural facilitation with word processing, a computer program was written that allowed students to call up planning cues according to the categories shown in Tables 12.1 and 12.2. Trials were run with 6 experimental- and 6 control-group children who had participated in the previous study. Both groups of students made substantial use of the cues while composing. Experimental-group students, however, used a greater variety of types of cues. These results, although uninformative as to effectiveness, suggest that computerization of planning cues is feasible but that it may well need to be accompanied by instruction to help students make full use of the facilitation.

Burtis and Scardamalia (1983) investigated the use of planning cues in narrative writing. In a previous study, comparing the narrative-planning protocols of graduate students and elementary-school students, Burtis (1983) had found that graduate students were the only ones to show any evidence of trying to find a central idea or point to build the story around (cf. Wilensky, 1983). All of the younger students (as well as a number of the adults) proceeded in a more linear fashion to generate a chronological sequence of events.

In order to see whether more sophisticated planning could be fostered in children, Burtis and Scardamalia constructed planning cues analogous to those shown in Tables 12.1 and 12.2, but oriented toward narrative. One difference was that some cues were specific to the assigned topic, which happened to be "The Kid Who Lost Things." One category of cues was concerned simply with generating story content—for example, "Something the kid loses could be. . . ." Another category of cues was designed to elicit the kind of thinking observed in adult protocols concerned with developing a story point—for example, "I could make my story special by having. . . ." The final category of cues was designed to elicit review, another behavior found only in adults—for example, "So far my story says. . . ."

This use of planning cues did not turn up any evidence of effect on students in grades 4 and 6, but there was evidence in grade 8 of experimental-group stories having more "interesting or dramatic point." Whereas the knowledge-telling model can easily account for production of coherent or well-formed narratives, it would seem that some more goal-oriented procedure is needed in order to create a story having a central point. Thus these results are encouraging about the possibility of facilitating goal-directed procedures in narrative planning, at least with adolescents. Whether younger students would profit from a more extended or intensive instructional treatment remains to be investigated.

The final instructional study is a single-case study carried out as a course project by Clare Brett. She worked with a grade-4 student who showed something like a knowledge-telling strategy in computer programing. That is, he would proceed in a straight-ahead fashion, concentrating on what to say next, with little indication of subgoal setting or problem solving. Hearsay has it that this is not at all uncommon among young programers (see also the research by Woodruff and Scardamalia reported in the postscript to Chapter 9).

Brett provided planning cues designed to elicit more sophisticated planning moves, such as formulating goals, identifying obstacles, and reviewing (e.g., "What is my program doing that is right?"). Over the course of several programming tasks using the planning cues, the student showed marked progress toward greater use of intelligent planning.

These small studies suggest that the general approach taken in the main experiment can be extended to promote a more reflective approach in other areas. More important than the question of breadth, however, is the question of depth: How profound a shift is it possible to bring about in students' composing processes? Can the knowledge-transforming process be, in some sense, taught? The present studies are encouraging but must be considered preliminary to a sustained program of research into this issue.

Chapter 13
Helping Children Gain Insight into Their Own Cognitive Processes

PREFACE

This chapter does not present new findings but takes a different slant on the research that has been reported in previous chapters. The slant is that of considering what taking part in such research can do for the student. Obviously not all cognitive research is illuminating to the participants who take part in it. If you are the participant in a reaction time or a gaze duration experiment (e.g., Just & Carpenter, 1980) you may be providing data that are ultimately of great theoretical importance, but the variations in behavior that produce these data are probably too minute for you to detect and, unless you were versed in the underlying theory, you would not know what to make of the variations if you could detect them. But the participants' situation is quite different in research that requires them to judge, predict, justify, or to verbalize their thoughts. Here participants can monitor their own behavior and may be surprised, puzzled, or enlightened by what they observe. Moreover, what is enlightening to the participant is likely to be enlightening to the researcher, and vice-versa. Thus there is the possibility of a kind of collaborative investigation that is beneficial to all parties.

Gaining insight into the cognitive processes of writing is seen as especially important as a basis for changing from knowledge telling to knowledge transforming. The preceding chapters indicated ways that procedural facilitation could help new executive strategies to get a start. The hope in fostering insight into relevant cognitive processes is that students will be able to take a more active, intentional role in development of their cognitive strategies. This requires self-awareness of strategies and goals—what is loosely referred to as metacognition. Productive ways of developing such awareness are the focus of this chapter. As the preceding studies suggest, procedural facilitation itself is a valuable medium for developing metacognition. In the present chapter that role is elaborated upon. We also present a variety of other less formal means of coinvestigation that could be used on almost a day-to-day basis in teaching.

13

This chapter is based on a simple premise—that children's metacognitive development may be aided by giving them greater access to data arising from their own cognitive processes. It seems to be generally agreed that children are less aware of their cognitive processes than adults. (Brown, 1978; Flavell, Speer, Green, & August, 1981; Flavell & Wellman, 1977; Paris & Lindauer, 1982). Certainly one important factor retarding the growth of metacognitive knowledge is the limited availability of data from which such knowledge may be constructed. Not only are the data elusive because of the rapid and fleeting nature of mental events, but also because when people are engaged in mental activity their attention is normally taken up with the task at hand or with the content of cognition rather than being directed toward the process itself.

We are assuming, as others have assumed (Brown, 1977; Flavell, 1979; Paris, Newman, & McVey, 1982), that metacognitive knowledge must be constructed like any other kind of knowledge. Insight into one's own mental processes does not occur because of a window opening on the mind but because in the course of long experience one manages to piece together some kind of coherent knowledge on the basis of fragmentary data.

A corollary to this premise is that not all experiences are equal in their ability to provide data for the construction of metacognitive knowledge. Activities may differ not only in the kinds of cognitive processes they elicit but also in the extent to which the cognitive processes that are brought into play yield instructive data. Let us consider an obvious example. The person solving a problem silently and the person solving a problem while thinking aloud are carrying out some of the same cognitive processes (no need to argue that they are altogether the same). The person thinking aloud, however, generates data that cognitive researchers will often find to be more informative than the data yielded by the silent problem-solver (Ericsson & Simon, 1980). Is it not reasonable to suppose that thinking aloud might also yield data helpful to the thinker in understanding his or her own cognitive process, bringing events to light that might otherwise pass unnoticed? Thinking aloud is one among a variety of ways that cognitive researchers try to get cognitive behavior to yield more informative data. In setting out to devise ways of giving children greater access to data on which they could base metacognitive knowledge, therefore, a good starting place might be the kinds of activities that have proved illuminating in cognitive research.

The preceding chapters have described a large variety of procedures that we have used for probing mental processes in young people's writing. A frequent side effect has been that the children themselves became actively interested in what the experimental procedures were allowing them to discover about their mental processes. For the most part we have employed experimental designs that permitted us to inform students about the purpose of the inquiry and to discuss matters freely with them as we proceeded. This allowed children, in effect, to participate as coinvestigators—to function not only as sources of data but as seekers and interpreters of data as well. Involvement and enthusiasm have generally been high. Students who have not liked writing have nonetheless enjoyed analyzing the task and the process.

This chapter describes a variety of techniques that we have found helpful for getting children profitably involved in inquiry into their cognitive processes. They are divided into two groups. Those under the heading of *open inquiry* are techniques that can be applied freely to explore cognitive processes and strategies. Those under the heading of *model-based inquiry* require some theory of the process being explored. These potentially more powerful kinds of inquiry are especially pertinent to helping students grasp new models of cognitive behavior. Thus they are especially relevant to helping students progress from knowledge telling to knowledge transforming.

The techniques discussed are only techniques for making data from cognitive processes more accessible. What is done with the data—what kinds of discussions, comparisons, analyses, and planning of further explorations might ensue between teacher and child—remains an open question. Simply getting cognitive data out into the open where it can be dealt with is no small accomplishment, however, especially when the data in question come from children who have had little experience in contemplating or consciously regulating their mental processes. We hope that the development of techniques for bringing cognitive behavior out into the open will create educational possibilities of exciting and unforeseen kinds.

WHERE COGNITIVE INQUIRY MAY HELP

It is possible to agree with the points made in the preceding section and nevertheless question the advisability of encouraging children to focus attention on their own cognitive processes. Most intellectual skills, after all, are taught reasonably successfully without any need for the learners to investigate what is going on in their own minds. Most of us probably have very little idea of how we read, for instance, and we probably had even less idea at the time we were learning; yet we do not feel that our capacity for intelligent reading has been hampered. Apparently, through practice and self-monitoring, we gain sufficient insight to hold us in good stead.

The normal processes of acquiring procedural knowledge or "know-how" include observation, practice, and rule learning. The problem in acquiring many cognitive strategies, however, is that observable behavior gives only a limited and sometimes misleading basis for reconstructing the underlying mental operations.

An anecdote provided by a colleague illustrates the problem. Her young son one day announced that he had learned to revise. He proudly showed her an essay with sentences crossed out and with arrows directing the reader to insert chunks of text and to reorder different parts. The trouble was that the revised draft did not make sense, so she asked her son what he was trying to accomplish. What he was trying to do was make his papers look like a manuscript she was working on. He mimicked the observables of the revision process but not the accompanying mental operations that gave purpose to the observables.

We should not underestimate the value of such observational learning. It provides a concrete framework to which the more elusive mental operations may be attached. Thus, we would expect this colleague's son to be at a considerable advantage compared to many young students with whom we work, whose only concrete model for revision is the production of a clean copy. Observational learning may also be helpful in creating a motivational context for cognitive-strategy learning. Although not yet grasping what revision was for, our colleague's son must have sensed that it was a valued activity and one worth emulating. Similarly, children who observe their parents reading may not thereby learn much about the process of reading, but they are likely to learn something about its place in life.

As we see it, the observable manifestations of cognitive behavior provide an excellent starting point for coinvestigation of the process, for adult and child to discover, for instance, what is different in the ways they decide what to cross out and where to draw the arrows in revising a manuscript. But if children are left too much on their own to fill in the mental activities lying behind observables, there is a danger that they will remain dominated by what they observe. Thus, in writing, we find children's composing processes to be dominated by the observable part of the process—the manuscript. As indicated in previous chapters, when asked to plan texts aloud, they yield protocols that are little different from what we receive if we ask them to dictate essays. Expert writers, on the other hand, display a large and varied amount of thinking during composition that is relevant to but never appears as part of the manuscript (Hayes & Flower, 1980). In order for children to grasp these other kinds of thinking, they need sources of information beyond ordinary observation.

One of the ways that instructional researchers have tried to overcome the limitations of ordinary observation has been by rendering more of the cognitive process observable, often through the use of thinking aloud while modeling (Bereiter & Bird, 1985; Brown, 1978; Chapter 8 of this book). Studies so far reported all seem to indicate that cognitive modeling, unless it is supported by more active instructional procedures, is not effective in changing children's strategies.

In the case of highly specific skills such as high-jumping or playing chess, learners can have from an early stage a fairly clear idea of what they are trying to achieve. If they are motivated to achieve it, then they will likely make the most of the opportunities offered by observation, practice, and rule learning, and show progress to more sophisticated strategies even when the learning conditions are far from ideal.

In the case of more general intellectual skills such as composition, however, students who have not yet achieved a sophisticated strategy are not in a good position to appreciate what the strategy could do for them. Consequently, as we discussed in Chapter 10, there is a serious motivational problem, not in the sense of students' unwillingness to exert effort but in the sense of their not having a clear notion of what their efforts are supposed to yield. In the absence of such a notion, it is natural for students to stick with the cognitive strategies they have and to assimilate new learning to them. We have repeatedly found that our efforts to guide students to more complex composing strategies are thwarted unless we can convey to the students some sense of cognitive outcome to strive for. Coinvestigation of cognitive strategies has so far appeared to have its most significant function in this motivational context. It gives children an opportunity to grasp the potentialities of cognitive strategies that they have not yet mastered, and this allows them to engage in strategy-learning activities with a greater sense of purpose.

OPEN INQUIRY

The techniques discussed in this section are general-purpose techniques for bringing cognitive events out into the open in working with children. Although children may be as mentally active as adults, and often even more willing to expose their mental activity to scrutiny, it is usually more difficult with children than with adults to bring forth information on their cognitive processes. This is partly because children are less accustomed to paying attention to their mental processes and consequently lack some of the metacognitive skills needed to extract metacognitive knowledge. Also, they lack the large repertoire of terms relating to mental processes that the sophisticated adult possesses, and this limits their ability both to understand questions and to formulate statements related to cognitive events. This does not make cognitive inquiry with children any the less rewarding, either for the adult or for the child; it only means that the adult must come equipped with appropriate techniques for helping children surmount the obstacles to inquiry and communication.

The simplest way to engage children in collaborative interchange is to have them introspect—simply talk to you about how they typically do something or try to monitor their mental activities as they engage in some activity. In our experience with such techniques, major difficulties in employing them come not so much from limitations in what children can contribute, as from the adult's misunderstanding of what the child can be expected to contribute.

It is true that the child cannot keep up as active an interchange as an adult coinvestigator can. Adult coinvestigators have a good deal of sophistication in making points clearly, coming back to points not made clear on first go-around, noting when there is a mismatch between what has been conveyed and what is intended, and so on. A rule of thumb we seldom find ourselves regretting having followed is to assume that when a child is telling us something that seems either insignificant or very confused, we are probably missing something important. Also, the child is probably struggling to explain something at the edge of current awareness. This is precisely the point at which we must try harder to make sense of what is happening.

What follows is a list of techniques for supporting discussion under such circumstances. Before proceeding with this list, however, a list that might make it appear that the adult is not assuming the role of coinvestigator so much as the role of coach, we would like to clarify the sense in which the effort is a collaborative one, with mutual benefits for investigator and child.

It is important to remember that the adult is involved in the first place because the kinds of complex activities being dealt with are not well understood. If the adult knew the procedures underlying the phenomena in enough detail to model them clearly or reduce them to specific rules, then the problem would not be so difficult. The truth of the matter is, however, that adults are novicelike in this respect and are trying themselves to understand procedures being used. In interchange with children we typically start by explaining that our purpose for being there is that we would like to learn more about how people write. It is precisely because this process is not well understood that we seek their help. We believe they have important knowledge to contribute about how children their age do things. The message is a sincere one, because it is true, and it establishes their legitimacy as coinvestigators.

a. *Teach Children to Think Aloud.* The purpose behind teaching the child to think aloud is that the thinking-aloud experience itself provides data for comment. That is, it appears to make normally covert processes more accessible to the person doing the thinking aloud, as well as to the person listening.

However, we have found that young children find thinking aloud a more difficult task than adults do. Adults, asked to say aloud all the things that naturally occur to them as they engage in some task, can proceed with little additional instruction. In contrast, younger children tend to need someone beside them to provide encouragement and to ask questions when they fall silent (see sections d and e). Practice also seems to help, as does learning to think aloud while doing some nonverbal activity such as drawing a picture.[17]

The rewards of engaging students in think-aloud experiences are substantial. The following discussion took place in a class of grade-10 students who had just completed one session of thinking aloud while reading. First one student put up his hand: "I think that when you have to read out loud you slow down the whole process of reading. I read much faster when I read to myself. Don't you think that if information goes into your head faster that better things might come out?" This child seems to have some insight into the concept of coding efficiency as currently represented in the literature (Perfetti & Lesgold, 1977). Another student put up her hand in response and said: "Well, I think it's not the speed that's the big thing. I think it's the fact that when you make me say everything out loud I'm using up a lot of what's in my head to do the job of thinking aloud so I don't have so much [mental working space] left to do the thinking about what I'm reading." (This student appears to have some insight into limited capacity information-processing models). Another student, in a tone suggesting embarrassment, confessed: "I have a problem. When I read, I like to read the last paragraph first. That way when I start again from the beginning, I have some idea of what's going to happen." She seemed delighted to discover that we thought

---

[17]The use of nonverbal tasks in series with verbal tasks was investigated by Tetroe (1981).

her strategy was a sophisticated one, and other children seemed interested in the possible advantages and disadvantages of this strategy.

The point of these examples is not that students have sophisticated ideas about cognitive processes, although they sometimes do. The point is that they are very interested in analyzing their cognitive processes, and that they are interested in them in much the same way as cognitive psychologists are.

b. *Give Students Something Concrete to Talk About.* Vague questions such as "How do you decide what to write when you're given a writing assignment?" are likely to result in vague or stereotyped answers. We find, in fact, that questions of this broadly "metacognitive" kind make for a tense interview. The student wants to be cooperative but is never quite sure what you are trying to get at. It is much better to give the students something to do—moving things, underlining, searching, etc.—and then discuss what they are doing as they do it. In studying text comprehension, for instance, we have found that the task of arranging sentences described in Chapter 9 provides the basis for a richer discussion of comprehension strategies than does ordinary reading, because the task involves discrete decisions that can be questioned and justified.

Hayes-Roth & Hayes-Roth (1979) have a task they use to study planning that illustrates the advantages of tasks that are not strictly dependent on verbal report. Participants are provided with a shopping list and a city map and are asked to plan a day of shopping in which they try to accomplish many things in limited time. The nice feature of the task for purposes of uncovering planning procedures used by young children is that their planning strategy shows up concretely in the way they track things on the map and refer to the shopping list. What an experimenter can see from observing such activity is that whereas adults get themselves oriented to the map as a whole, determining sections of the city where with little travel they can get much accomplished (Hayes-Roth & Hayes-Roth, 1979), by comparison, young children get themselves located at one point on the map, see if the building next to it is one where they can accomplish any one of the specified tasks. If not, they move to the next building and repeat the same procedure. Planning, with this task, becomes something like a board game, making it possible to discuss and compare strategies as one might, for instance, with a game like checkers.

Tasks that manage to uncover strategies for adult investigators tend also to provide children with data they need to understand their own activity. Children frequently can describe their activity after such an exercise, although they would not do so before. Further, seeing an adult do the task after they have themselves had the opportunity to "see" how they perform, appears to create interest in and appreciation of the adult strategy.

In one study we wanted to investigate children's conceptual knowledge of written genres. Questions like "What kinds of things would you include in a story?" obtained results from high-school students, but elementary-school children did not know what to make of the question. In this case giving them an actual story to talk about would only serve to focus attention on specific story content rather than on general properties of the genre. What finally worked was to show them an actual composition but not let them read it, saying, for instance, "This is an essay I wrote trying to convince somebody of something. What kind of thing do you think I probably said at the beginning, in order to make this a good essay?" Although getting children to discuss abstract characteristics of text was still not easy, this minimal amount of concretizing at least made it possible (see Chapter 3).

   c. *Have Students Prescribe Rather than Describe.* Students who are inarticulate in trying to describe how they go about doing some mental task often come forth with clear statements of procedure when asked to give advice to another student, particularly a younger one, for carrying out the task. Even formulating instructions for themselves can be helpful, as Meichenbaum (1973) has shown. The benefits that peer-tutoring has been found to yield for the child doing the tutoring (Cloward, 1967) may be partly due to this effect. Children seem to have a better vocabulary for prescribing than for describing. It is also possible that the task of prescribing gives better direction to their search of long-term memory than does a task of describing.

   d. *Attend to Nonverbal Cues and Use Them as Points for Discussion.* Here are some examples of observable behavior and related questions:

Observable Behavior	*Possible Question*
Eye Shift	You just noticed something, didn't you?
Change in rate	You're going faster now. Is this part easier?
Discouraged look	You look discouraged. Is something particularly hard here?
Satisfied look	Did you just figure something out?
Long pause	What's going on in your mind now?

   e. *Enlist the Student's Help in Getting You to Understand.* When a child makes an unclear statement, novice interviewers tend to err in either of two ways. They either take the statement at face value, which means the child gets classified as the one who doesn't understand, or they resort to courtroom procedures of insistent questioning, which often confuses or intimidates the child. In coinvestigation, however, adult and child should be trying equally to help each other understand what is going on.

   We have found conversational moves like the following to be useful in getting students to take an active role in helping us to understand, rather than responding passively to the questions they are asked:

   Ask student to fill in gaps: You've lost me here. How did you get from thinking about X to thinking about Y? Did I miss something?

Ask student to restate more slowly: "Wait, you're going too fast for me. Could you say that a little slower so I can write it all down?" (This often leads to restatement in different terms, yielding more clues for understanding.)

Confess incomprehension: "I just don't get it. If this is so hard that you can't do it, then how did you know to write down what you've written so far?"

Check distortions: "I think I got something wrong here. I wrote down _____ but I don't think that's quite what you said." (By getting a chance to correct misstatements children not only clarify what they said originally, but they begin to feel free about correcting the adult and consequently may begin to do so when the adult isn't aware of a need to be corrected.)

With all the foregoing statements, the essential thing to convey is that it is you, the adult, who has a problem with the verbal interchange—not the child. That is, you are failing to get some piece of information that you believe is quite important. When children clearly get this message we find them taking on more assertive roles, correcting the adult's misconceptions, asking the adult to rewrite something because it is not quite right, and we've even had children suggesting to us questions we might ask them if we really wanted to know what they were thinking.

f. *Arrange a Series of Tasks in an Order of Increasing Complexity.* Because change is usually more salient than constancy, children can often gain awareness of cognitive strategy features by noticing what things get harder to do as a task increases in difficulty. The task sequence must be carefully designed, of course, so that changes are clear-cut and psychologically interesting. One would not, for instance, derive much from presenting students with a sequence of miscellaneous reading passages selected so as to be graded in readability level. They would differ in too many ways at once, and some of the major factors in difficulty, such as vocabulary, are probably not very fruitful ones for coinvestigation.

A simple task sequence that we found productive for studying composing processes was a sequence that involved planning a paragraph that would incorporate two given sentences (Paris, Scardamalia & Bereiter, 1982). At the easiest level the two sentences contained common topical words. At an intermediate level they contained related but not identical topical words. At the most difficult level the two sentences did not directly suggest a common topic at all, so that the student had to invent a unifying theme. Task sequences suitable for coinvestigation of cognitive strategies can be found scattered throughout the experimental cognitive-developmental literature; see for instance the balance-scale tasks in Siegler (1981), and the equivalent-fraction tasks cited by Case (1985a).

For use in coinvestigation it is important that the tasks start at an easy enough level that the students can build confidence in their basic ability to handle the type of task, and they should if possible increase in difficulty by steps sufficiently fine that students can experience points that give them real difficulty, short of total failure.

Again, it is vital for children to understand that the point of the activity is not successful or unsuccessful task performance but rather understanding the mental processes involved in the task. Once children catch on to the idea that each step in task difficulty means an interesting new phenomenon to investigate, they seem to lose their anxiety about success and failure and can even begin to regard failure, when it comes, as itself an interesting phenomenon to be explained. A further possible benefit from this kind of activity is metacognitive awareness by students of their own capabilities, with an accompanying ability to predict what will and will not cause them difficulty.

g. *Turn the Task the Child Must Work on into a Discrimination or Comparison Task.* Rather than requiring students to describe the strategies they use to solve a task, ask them to evaluate some strategy that you propose or demonstrate.

We have found three different presentation formats useful. Each assumes that the child has worked previously on the task and therefore has something with which to compare the adult's procedure.

The first is the most straightforward. Simply think aloud while you do the precise task the child was just asked to do. Then ask the child if what you did was anything like what he or she did.

One child we had been working with struggled for a long time trying to figure out which of several stories fitted a particular proverb. His strategy, as far as could be determined from what he did, was to find a topic that the proverb and story shared, and match proverb to story on this topical basis (i.e., they are both about monkeys), rather than on the basis of underlying meaning. We then modeled how we went about the task, matching elements in the story with elements in the proverb and checking to see whether the story elements could fit into the proverb and still make sense. Upon seeing this (the strategy was not described to the child, the child just looked on while the adult talked aloud) the child proceeded to describe accurately the adult's strategy, compare it with his own, and consider how he might go about the task differently in the future. Prior to this the child had seemed neither to be able to describe his own strategy nor to appreciate what the adult was saying about how he might do things differently.

Another format is to lead students through the execution of a different strategy themselves and then have them compare it to what they normally do. This only works, of course, with procedures that are straightforward enough that one can coach students in carrying them out. But a variety of important cognitive strategies are of this kind, such as those involving rehearsal, review, apportionment of study time, and elaboration in memorizing (Brown, 1978; Paris, Newman, & McVey, 1982; Rohwer, 1973).

The third format, easiest for the child, requires the most work on the part of the adult. The adult identifies cognitive procedures that the child appears to be using and puts these in a list along with other procedures that the child does not appear to use. Some of these other procedures reflect less mature strategies, some of them more mature strategies than the child appears to employ. This method has been employed by Paris and Myers (1981) to identify reading strategies. We have found it useful from the child's point of view for gaining insight into strategic choices related to more and less successful task performance. One child, for instance, had been working on revising stories to accommodate new information. When presented with a list of procedural rules, he could identify procedures he once followed but no longer did (keep the story the same and add the new information at the end), as well as identify useful procedures that he had not previously thought of (e.g., think of different ways the ideas already in your story and the new idea can fit together, then choose the one that makes most sense).[18]

The methods of open inquiry described in this section are all ones that can be used without any great deal of formal psychological knowledge. This fact naturally raises a question of validity. If one were proposing student inquiry in physical science, one would want to be sure it didn't result in the learning of a lot of wrong principles. What is to prevent coinvestigation of cognitive processes from resulting in a lot of false psychological knowledge?

False knowledge is not likely to be a problem so long as the responsible adult tries to keep attention focused on strategy description and evaluation, avoiding the temptation to formulate general laws about how the mind works. The cognitive inquiry we have been talking about is largely a matter of observing events and trying to relate them coherently to one another. Naturally the observing and the relating will both be limited, but that would be true for any other kinds of events. In discussing a field trip, for instance, students will have failed to see much of what was there to be seen, will have misperceived some things, and will interpret events in ways that reflect their lack of background knowledge and concepts. The teacher, furthermore, will often not be an expert in the area pertinent to the field trip. But those are not reasons to avoid field trips and much less are they reasons to avoid describing and discussing what was observed. On the contrary, it is through just such experiences that one hopes to build the experiential basis that will give meaning to later, more disciplined study.

---

[18]This procedure was devised by Sonja Dennis in course work at the Ontario Institute for Studies in Education, and the example is from her report.

MODEL-BASED INQUIRY

Techniques of open inquiry, such as those described thus far in the chapter, serve mainly as a way of putting children in touch with the cognitive strategies they presently use. Another dimension of metacognitive knowledge, however, is awareness of strategy change—being aware not only of one's current cognitive behavior but of developments that lie ahead. Again, some of this knowledge can be imparted by conventional means—by demonstrating or explaining more advanced strategies, for instance. Although these didactic approaches, if based on sound knowledge, can be extremely valuable, we believe the ideal circumstance for learning would be one in which students can actually experience strategy change. In other words, although it may be very useful to understand "This is how I do it and this is how an expert does it," a sizable increment in self-knowledge occurs if the terms can be shifted to "This is how I usually do it and this is how it feels to do it like an expert." Needless to say, such a foretaste of expert competence can also be expected to have a strong motivating effect.

But how does one get a child to experience expertlike performance, short of turning the child into an expert? The answer may lie in a technology that has only recently begun to take shape among instructionally oriented developmental psychologists—a technology that we have called *simulation by intervention* (Chapter 2; see also, Brown & Campione, 1981; Butterfield et al., 1980). In scientific applications, simulation by intervention involves testing theoretical notions about cognitive development by experimentally introducing either facilitations that the theory predicts will cause younger students to act like older ones, or impediments that the theory suggests will cause older students to act like younger ones (see, for instance, Case et al., 1982). Simulation by intervention thus requires a fairly strong model of the cognitive process under investigation, in order to have a basis for making and testing predictions.

Educational applications of simulation by intervention also require a fairly strong model of the process in question, which is why we have labeled this section "model-based inquiry." The idea is to intervene in children's typical cognitive processes in such a way as to induce cognitive behavior that formally resembles or contains significant elements of more mature cognitive behavior. Because students find themselves involved in mental activities that are new to them, the situation is a natural one for coinvestigation of cognitive processes.

In this section we discuss and illustrate three approaches to model-based inquiry. Whereas in the section on open inquiry we could discuss a variety of detailed techniques that are applicable in a wide range of activities, model-based inquiry tends to require different techniques, depending on the model employed. Consequently the material in this section is intended mainly to suggest general ways of going about model-based inquiry.

a. *Induce a Simplified Version of the More Advanced Strategy.* This approach, which we have termed procedural facilitation, has been described (Chapter 10) and illustrated with several examples (Chapters 11 and 12). The point of relevance in the current context is that an advanced strategy may be simplified by reducing open-ended decisions to choices among a few alternatives and by establishing routines that bypass certain difficulties. The child is helped to execute the strategy by the use of externalized procedures and cues. However—and this is a key point as far as coinvestigation of cognitive processes is concerned—the child still has to do all the productive thinking. Procedural facilitation simply helps to structure the process. Hence, children find themselves engaging in mental activities that are new to them, and this frequently fascinates them, providing a natural focal point for coinvestigation. By providing an explicit contrast to routine procedures such methods tend to highlight two kinds of data: (1) how one typically goes about the task—information that naturally arises out of the child's efforts to cope with changes forced by the new routine; and (2) the nature of more sophisticated performance—information that follows from what the routine enables the child to do that is in advance of normal procedures.

One of the most elaborate procedural facilitations we have tried (Chapter 11) was concerned with getting students to evaluate, diagnose, and revise their texts. With the induced procedure students made more adultlike revisions. Moreover, they unanimously reported that the procedure had taught them to do things they didn't normally do—consider the coherence of consecutively presented ideas, consider how an idea might confuse a reader—and to stop doing things they normally did. The procedure stood directly in the way of their carrying out typical revision activities of producing clean copy, and most children claimed it was the first time they had any idea *how* one might go about doing things in ways other than those they were accustomed to, even though they knew all along that they should.

The same principles of coinvestigation apply here as with the more informal procedures discussed in the preceding section. Purposes need to be open and shared. Students need to feel that the emphasis is on mutual understanding of the mental phenomena, not on successful performance. And the same methods for achieving fruitful discussion are applicable. The difference is that procedural facilitation opens up rich possibilities for turning the spotlight of coinvestigation on mental growth itself.

b. *Use Tasks that Transfer Existing Strategies to New Domains.* In writing, as in a variety of intellectual tasks, children fail to evidence capabilities they evidence in more practical contexts. For example, although in their daily lives children clearly demonstrate planning toward goals, they rarely show evidence of explicit goal-directed planning in composition. There are some profound reasons, as we have indicated in Chapter 10, why composition goals should be harder for children to get a fix on than many other kinds of goals. But by altering the composition task somewhat, as we have done with ending-sentence tasks (see Chapters 3 and 10) it is possible to get students to apply their already existing abilities in goal-directed planning to writing.

In order for interventions of this kind to have a lasting effect, it seems essential that students gain as much insight as possible into what they are doing. Planning to reach an ending sentence is not the same as the planning mature writers do to achieve a rhetorical goal, but it has similarities that students may be able to recognize through discussion and reflection—through considering, for instance, why the ending-sentence task is harder than the typical writing task and what it is that they do differently in coping with it. In this particular case the task enabled children to distinguish between their "what next" approach to text production—thinking of an idea and then considering what they should say next—and the strategy of considering multiple task constraints simultaneously—the strategy that writing to an ending sentence encourages.

An extensive collection of writing tasks that use concrete goals to mobilize strategies that students do not spontaneously apply to writing is presented in Scardamalia, Bereiter, and Fillion (1981). We are not aware at this time of other domains in which strategy-mobilizing or strategy-transferring tasks have been devised.

c. *Have Students Provide Procedural Support for Others.* In the "Open Inquiry" section we mentioned the benefits for cognitive inquiry of having students prescribe procedures for others. A more refined version of this approach is one in which children administer procedural facilitations to an adult or to other children. This approach has the significant advantage that it permits the child to participate in or actually to induce in someone else a cognitive strategy that the child himself or herself has not yet mastered.

We have tried this with children providing procedural support to someone else who is planning a composition. The child is provided with a list of sentence openers like those listed in Tables 12.1 and 12.2 ("An even better idea is . . . ," "I could make my main point clearer if . . . ," and "But many readers won't agree that . . . ," etc.). The child's task was to use these planning cues to help an adult plan a composition. The adult planned out loud and the child was to listen closely and hand the adult a planning cue whenever the adult was stuck or when it seemed appropriate to help the adult think harder or more completely about the composition. When handed a planning cue, the adult was supposed to start the next planning sentence (not text sentence) with it, if possible.

What we find consistently, even with children of age 8 who use this procedure, is such close monitoring of what the adult is saying that the cards, selected at "stuck points" are those the adult might well have selected were she conducting the procedure herself. The data the child is made privy to under such conditions should serve both to illuminate the nature of mature processes and to provide the child with a means of entering into the mature process.

Children can be shown to produce thought judged more reflective than that produced by children not using the cards under conditions in which roles are reversed—where the adult is handing cards to the child (Scardamalia & Bereiter, 1985a). This suggests once again that, given insight into more mature processes, children will make use of that insight (see also Paris, Newman, & McVey, 1982).

One distinct advantage of having a child provide procedural support for someone else is a division of mental labor. When students tried to use planning cues by themselves they usually found this more difficult. As one 11-year-old put it, "You've asked me to both think of ideas and to look at them at the same time! I can't do that. And if I think of the idea, then stop to think about it, I forget what I'm supposed to be thinking of." By dividing cognitive tasks and switching roles, students have the opportunity to see a process from different viewpoints and to avoid cognitive overload while doing so. They also get a picture of why the task they are being asked to perform is so difficult.

Model-based inquiry clearly has advantages in directing inquiry toward the growing edge of the child's competence rather than toward the child's habitual practices. It is clear, however, that one needs to make strong assumptions about the nature of this growing edge and where it is growing to in order to design procedural facilitations and other model-based interventions.

Two concerns might occur to the reader. One is, what if the model is wrong? That is, what if the supposedly more mature strategy that we are trying to give children a feeling for isn't really the way mature people function but is instead some psychologist's mistaken idea of how they function? In our experience this problem has seemed to be self-correcting. If we try to persuade children to use a poorly conceived procedure, they either can't do it, find it silly or unnatural, or—which is most frequent—transform the procedure in such a way as to make it work within their existing strategies. Fortunately, a model-based procedure can be satisfactory even though the model it is based on is only a very rough approximation. So long as the procedure leads children somewhere into the neighborhood of a more mature process, they can start to have experiences that open their eyes to possibilities for further growth and learning.

Students need to realize that they are experimenting with ways to extend their mental capabilities. They are not experimenting with neat tricks to make work easier, but rather with procedures that involve thinking more deeply about more things. In our experience students respond marvelously well to this kind of opportunity, provided they are supplied with procedures that enable them to act. It is being asked to think harder when they have no available means for thinking harder that makes students retreat from intellectual challenges.

CONCLUSION

In the preceding sections we have presented a number of specific techniques whereby adult and child can collaborate in the investigation of cognitive activities. Our emphasis has been on techniques the adult may use to facilitate communication and to bring into the open the kinds of phenomena that will make coinvestigation fruitful. In concluding, however, we want to reemphasize the mutual nature of the investigative enterprise and take a broader view of its purpose.

One of the reasons that inquiry learning in the schools may not live up to the glowing words in which it has been advocated is that, for the most part, children are finding out things that the teacher already knows. The result is that the teacher can, at best, share vicariously in the children's curiosity and joy of discovery. At worst, inquiry turns into puzzle solving, in which the teacher knows the answer and the children's job is to find out what it is.

Inquiry into people's own cognitive processes is a different story. Here, teachers and students can work as genuine partners in inquiry. Partly this may be because everyone is rather ignorant about how the mind works. But there is more to it than that. We have perhaps done more cognitive research on children's writing than anyone else has or will ever care to, yet we have experienced no decline in the amount of new insight we can gain by sitting down with a child and engaging in one of the kinds of shared inquiry described in this chapter. Quite the contrary. The more we understand the composing process, it seems, the more we can learn and the more we can help a child to learn.

The crucial thing seems to be that we are learning about ourselves (and we, the experimenters, always are learning about ourselves in coinvestigation, as well as learning about the children—and the children, also, are learning about us as well as learning about themselves). Understanding of self and others appears to be nonterminating, and this is probably because it aims to be holistic. Consequently every new detail is a potential challenge to our understanding of the whole.

The principal value that we see in acquiring personal (as contrasted with theoretical) knowledge of cognitive processes is that it enables students to take a more self-directive role in their mental development. Cognitive development in young children is largely unintentional. As Montessori (1967) pointed out, the young child does things that result in learning, but does not do them in order to learn. Cognitive development is a natural consequence of activity carried out for other purposes. The child's actions may be driven by curiosity, but the curiosity is "aroused" by external events. Later we begin to see the emergence of what we have elsewhere analyzed in detail as *intentional cognition* (Bereiter & Scardamalia, 1983b).

In its largest sense, intentional cognition means having a *mental life* that is carried on consciously and purposefully, just as one's outer life is, but that is not simply a projection of that outer life. Rather, mental life has purposes and activities of its own, which are primarily concerned with the active construction of knowledge. Knowledge-transforming processes in writing are one important way in which the purposes of a mental life can be pursued. Perhaps the most far-reaching consequences of developing a self-directed mental life is that meaningfulness ceases to be a property that is "found" or not "found" in external activities and contexts. It becomes a property that people invest activities with, by virtue of assigning them a role in their mental lives.

Coinvestigation appears to hold promise at two levels. One is at the level of cognitive strategy acquisition. As we indicated earlier, coinvestigation is most applicable for cognitive strategies that cannot reliably be acquired through observation, practice, and the learning of explicit rules. Strategies involved in the construction of personal knowledge are preeminently of this kind—remote from observation, inaccessible to assigned practice, and difficult to formalize under rules.

The other level is the level of direction and purpose. Students cannot be expected to take a self-directive role in their cognitive development unless they themselves, and not just the teacher, have a sense of where development is heading—where the growing edge of their competence is and what possibilities lie ahead. Studying theories of developmental psychology is not likely to give students such knowledge in a usable form. Active investigation of their own cognitive strategies can do so, however—especially if it is done in collaboration with an adult who can help them recognize and reflect upon what is happening and help them experiment with possible next stages in development.

Part V
Conclusion

Chapter 14
Knowledge-Telling
and Knowledge-Transforming
Differences: Their Psychological
and Educational Implications

14 In this final chapter we want to return to a focus on the knowledge-telling and knowledge-transforming models themselves, their validity and their implications. Talking about models is much different from talking about people, even though it is easy to lose sight of the difference. Because most of the studies involve having people carry out some writing task, it is easy to lapse into regarding the studies as nothing more than comparisons of different kinds of writers or different kinds of writing conditions (cf. Horowitz, 1984). At times in the preceding chapters we ourselves have lapsed into referring to people as "knowledge-tellers" or "knowledge-transformers" rather than sticking to such clumsy but more accurate expressions as "people whose composing processes more nearly conform to the knowledge-telling model."

If we say, for instance, that the knowledge-telling model contains no provision for strategic pursuit of goals, this is literally true and is easily confirmed by examining the model as portrayed in Figure 1.1. On the other hand, to say that a given person or group of people is incapable of strategically pursuing goals in writing would be foolhardy. We cannot imagine any way of validating such a claim, and we hope the reader has not interpreted anything in the preceding chapters to be claims of that sort.

What can be shown is that some people exhibit very little evidence of goal-directed planning in writing. The job of the knowledge-telling model in this context is to explain how it would be possible to produce a normal-appearing composition without any more planning than such writers exhibit. Similarly, the knowledge-transforming model is not intended to assert anything about the cognitive behavior of an identifiable group of expert writers. Its explanatory job is to show (a) how the process of writing can lead to growth in knowledge, as many expert writers claim it does, and (b) how writing could be such hard work for some people, even though they are highly skilled at it.

Nevertheless, there is an issue of psychological reality to be addressed. We want to be able to say that there are processes going on in the minds of real people of which the knowledge-telling and knowledge-transforming models are idealized descriptions. Furthermore, we want to be able to say (this was the gist of Chapter 1) that psychological reality requires both models, one to provide an idealized description of what is common to the processes of many immature and inexpert writers (although the processes are by no means absent in expert writers) and one to provide an idealized description of what is distinctive about the composing processes of more expert or thoughtful writers.

It may not be obvious what virtue there is in idealized models as opposed to careful descriptions of real people doing real things. The virtue lies in the possibility of making scientifically or educationally worthwhile generalizations. Naturalistic descriptions leave one with the options of either not generalizing at all or else generalizing by averaging over cases. Neither option is at all satisfactory. Each individual case presents innumerable unique, idiosyncratic or incidental details. Even if the case is chosen as representative, there is bound to be much about it that is not representative and which anyone would be foolish to generalize. As a result, investigators who use naturalistic case methods (e.g., Graves, 1983) almost always end up formulating idealized descriptions, albeit informally. That is, they try to state essential truths, which would have to be qualified in order to fit any actual case. If one is going to go in for such ideal generalizations, there is obvious value in doing it formally, by creating models or theoretical propositions, so as to get a better hold on inconsistencies, gaps, and implications that need to be tested.

The other way to generalize is empirically, by extracting some kind of average from the individual cases. It does not matter whether the averaging is done quantitatively or whether it is done impressionistically, through statements of the "What we usually find. . . ." type. There remains a fundamental obstacle, which was stated most succinctly by Newell (1974): We must not average over methods. We can determine the average amount of time writers devote to one activity and another. We can determine the average number of thinking-aloud protocol statements of one type and another. But there is no way that these results can add up to a description of something that can be called "the average writing process." If different writers are going about the task differently, the averaged results will not only fail to reveal these differences but will probably also fail to reveal whatever underlying similarities these methods may have.

Seemingly the only way to make worthwhile generalizations about a process is to formulate an idealized model of the process and then investigate its validity. This means seeing how well it fits with known facts and testing its implications on new kinds of data. Also, when one is interested in a model's usefulness, it means testing its practical implications. These are the matters that will concern us in the remainder of this chapter.

Our initial focus will be on the knowledge-telling model. It is clearly the more controversial of the two models. If the knowledge-transforming model, with its dual problem spaces for dealing with content and rhetorical problems, were proposed as a general model for all written composition, there would probably not be much argument. Differences in writing skill would be accounted for by differences in how the various subprocesses are carried out or by differences in amount of problem-solving activity. We take it, therefore, as a nontrivial matter to show that there is reason to suggest a radically simpler model, the model of knowledge telling, to account for the composing behavior of many writers.

Accordingly, we shall first turn to reviewing the knowledge-telling model and the evidence relating to its psychological reality. Then we turn to the psychological implications of the proposed two-model view of writing processes. Here the focus will be on what these two models imply concerning the sorts of mental representations writers work with. The knowledge-telling model has a role for only a very limited range of representations, whereas the knowledge-transforming model implies a large and interconnected set of mental representations involved in composition. Several experiments will be reviewed that support these implied differences in mental representation.

Finally, we will turn to educational implications. On this account, the most important implication arises from the fact that the knowledge-transforming model is not simply an elaboration of the knowledge-telling model. Rather, it is a different kind of model—essentially a problem-solving as opposed to a task-execution model—which incorporates the simpler model as a subroutine. This implies that helping students move from a knowledge-telling to a knowledge-transforming approach to writing is not a simple matter of promoting growth and elaboration of skills. It is a matter of bringing writing under the control of a problem-solving executive that does not initially control it. What this implies for educational strategies is the subject of the final section of this chapter.

ORIGIN OF THE KNOWLEDGE-TELLING MODEL

The knowledge-telling model grew out of the effort to make sense of a growing body of facts about novice's composing. Regardless of how the model itself fares, the body of facts still needs to be explained. Consequently it seems worthwhile to review the thinking that led up to the model, of what we thought needed explaining and of how we came to explain it the way we did.

One starts out looking at the writing process from one's own perspective, which in our case is that of adults who experience much of their most strenuous wrestling with the complexity of ideas and the limitations of their own capacities while trying to put thoughts into writing. Thinking-aloud protocols have borne out the notion that for people in our walk of life writing is a form of very complex, ill-defined problem solving (Flower & Hayes, 1980a, 1980b). If one thinks of children and novices as engaged in basically the same kind of problem solving, but less well equipped to cope with its demands, then one expects to find the composing process continually breaking down or on the verge of doing so for such people. But obviously that is not the way it is. To us, a task such as writing the present chapter is close to overwhelming because of the abundance of information that needs to be considered, the variety of sometimes incompatible goals we would like to achieve, and behind all that, the spectral legions of questions not yet answered or even fully formed, the doubts, the inklings, the yearnings after something not yet identified. But as far as we have been able to ascertain, such problems are side-stepped by novices. As we have seen repeatedly (especially Chapters 3 and 4), when young writers do have problems composing, these tend to be problems of finding too little rather than problems of finding too much to say.

Now if one persists in the adult perspective, one starts immediately to form a proposition that begins, "The reason young writers have trouble finding enough to say is. . . ." Almost invariably, this line of thought seems to lead to identifying situational determinants of children's differences from us—the artificial nature of school tasks, the lack of audience, etc. Such a line of thought may lead to significant conclusions about how to improve educational conditions, but it advances us nowhere in understanding how immature writers do what they do.

We chose to take a more positive approach, by looking at what the children we have studied are able to do in writing and trying to explain how it is possible for them to do so. We first looked at completely unassisted writing, the kind discussed in Chapter 6—an assigned topic, no preparation, no time or length specifications. The one thing that seemed to be achieved in every case (at least by children of age 10 and up) was local coherence, a meaningful connection of the sentence to the topic or something preceding (McCutchen & Perfetti, 1982). This is what is called Level 1 coordination in Chapter 5. Initial efforts to account for such an achievement gave rise to the idea of associative writing (Bereiter, 1980). The idea was that by processes much like those involved in free association, the topic would give rise to a first utterance, something in the first utterance would provide a cue for a second, and so on.

Although there are examples of immature writing (for instance, some of the Level 1 productions described in Chapter 6) that appear to be explainable by a purely associative model, it quickly became apparent that such a model was too simple to do justice to all that beginning writers can do. Associative writing could not, for instance, account for children's producing well-formed stories, something which even primary-grade children appear able to do (Stein & Trabasso, 1982). Furthermore, even the least developed compositions illustrated in Chapter 6 exhibit an appropriateness to the genre—in this case the opinion essay. Something beyond topical associations had to be guiding the children to give opinions and reasons rather than, say, fragments of autobiography.

Granting that children have some kind of knowledge of literary forms (see Chapter 3), the problem then becomes to explain how this knowledge is brought into use in writing. One way could be by deliberate planning, within constraints imposed by genre requirements. But although such planning could be observed in the protocols of mature writers, it has not been found with young children (Chapter 8). Deliberate planning also seemed unlikely because of its heavy information processing load, caused by having to hold constraints in mind while searching for content to meet them. To be realistic, a model of immature composing would have to show a way that knowledge of literary forms could function without a high processing load.

The key idea for meeting this requirement was the idea that knowledge of literary forms could function as a source of prompts for retrieving content from memory. To get an idea of how this might work, imagine that you are a 12-year-old who has gotten stuck while composing an essay on why students should learn foreign languages. Suppose that from somewhere (from the outer world or some vagary of memory) comes the suggestion, *world peace.* Immediately this brings forth an idea connecting foreign languages with world peace, and you are off and running again. That is the kind of association based on simple topics that was assumed to form part of the composing process. But suppose that instead the suggestion was *reason on the other side.* This suggestion might also bring forth an idea, which would set you off on stating and responding to some argument against studying foreign languages. The prompt in this case is of a more abstract kind, but it seems to work in much the same way as a topical prompt.

The basic structure of the knowledge-telling model, as it was set forth in

Chapter 7, depends on the processes of retrieving content from memory on the basis of topical and genre cues. With these as the processes that drive composition, it is possible to account for children's ability to generate coherent and well-formed texts without attributing to them the resource-demanding planning or problem-solving processes that make writing difficult even for highly skilled writers. To be more precise, however, these processes account for children's ability to produce texts that *tend* to be coherent and well-formed. Retrieval cues cannot be expected to work perfectly. Consequently, there will be a probability of generating content that strays from the topic or is inappropriate to the genre. To account for the level of coherence we have typically found in children's compositions, it seemed necessary to hypothesize a testing function applied to retrieved content that rejects content which happens not to match the topical and structural probes. With the addition of this testing function to the cuing functions, we have essentially the knowledge-telling model as shown in Figure 1.1.

VALIDITY OF THE
KNOWLEDGE–TELLING MODEL

Let us briefly review evidence that supports the knowledge-telling model:

1. Texts written by inexpert writers tend to have
characteristics derivable from the knowledge-telling model

a. *Topical coherence.* According to the model, topical coherence is achieved by the use of topical cues drawn from the assignment and from already-generated text. This should result in texts that tend to stick to their simple topics but that do not necessarily conform to the requirements of an elaborated topic. For instance, a text on the topic of whether television is a good or bad influence on children would be expected to deal with television watching and children, but would not necessarily address the issue of television's influence. In keeping with this expectation, McCutchen and Perfetti (1982) found that in fourth-grade texts the simple topic was usually the only reference for given (as opposed to new) information, so that sentences were coherent with the topic but not with each other, as they would be in a more carefully planned treatment of an issue.

b. *Well-formedness.* The model presupposes that the writer has a structural discourse schema, which can also serve as a source of cues for retrieving content from memory. This should tend to result in texts that are well-formed in the sense of conforming to the structural requirements of literary forms. Such texts would not necessarily be successful in fulfilling the functions of the literary form, however, because that would often require problem-solving capabilities not available in knowledge telling. A written argument, for instance, might meet the requirements of stating a position and supporting reasons, but fail to develop a convincing line of argument. This, in fact, proved to be the modal type of persuasive essay produced by both 13-year-olds and 17-year-olds in the National Assessment of Educational Progress (1980a, 1980b) evaluations of persuasive writing. Similarly, in narrative writing, almost a third of the stories produced by 17-year-olds were judged to fall short of developing a plot, even though they conformed to the basic structural requirements of narrative (National Assessment of Educational Progress, 1980a, p. 14). The basic structural requirements of narrative, in fact, appear to be met by most children by the second year of school (Rentel and King, 1983).

c. *Weak adaptation of content to audience.* Although the knowledge-telling model provides means for generation of text content appropriate to topic and to text type, it does not provide means for finding and organizing content with the reader's needs in mind. (Note that the model does not imply anything one way or another about writers' ability to adapt language to an intended audience.) Flower (1979) has identified a pervasive kind of student writing that is distinguished by the very weaknesses implied by the knowledge-telling model. "Writer-based prose," as Flower calls it, presents content that is salient in the mind of the writer but not necessarily sufficient or relevant for the reader. The arrangement of this content tends to reflect its chronology in the experience of the writer and therefore is often not in an order suitable to gain the interest or comprehension of the reader.

2. Self-reports of immature writers are consistent with the model

Interview statements by elementary school students presented in Chapter 1 indicated that they saw writing as primarily a matter of recalling what they knew about a topic and writing down either all their ideas or the best of those they had retrieved. Although self-reports of cognitive processes are not convincing evidence in their own right, when combined with other evidence they contribute to confidence in the psychological reality of the model.

3. Thinking-aloud protocols of immature writers show little evidence of goal-setting, planning, and problem-solving, except at a local level

This finding, which is discussed in Chapter 8, accords with the lack of provision for such operations in the knowledge-telling model. As noted in Chapter 8 and elsewhere, absence of protocol evidence is not conclusive, since it could mean that immature writers carry on processes covertly that are more overt in mature writers. The objection is not very compelling, however, because skill acquisition normally works in the opposite way presupposed by this objection—that is, procedures become more automatic (and therefore less reportable) in the later stages of skill development (Anderson, 1982). Consequently, protocol evidence cannot be dismissed.

4. Start-up times of immature writers are unrelated to time and length constraints

This finding, discussed in Chapter 1, argues against any composing process that involves a great deal more deliberation than is hypothesized by the knowledge-telling model. Correspondingly, the fact that more mature writers do vary their start-up times according to the amount of writing time available and the amount to be written suggests a process involving more planning.

5. Novice revising behavior is consistent with a knowledge-telling way of generating content

One of the strongest points of the model is that it makes students' avoidance of revision, and their tendency to confine revision to cosmetic language changes, predictable from the way they write rather than treating them as additional phenomena in need of special explanation (and special treatment). Whereas the knowledge-transforming writer can use text already produced as a basis for problem identification and clarification of goals to be achieved through revision, to the knowledge teller existing text serves mainly as a source of cues for retrieval of additional content—so that, at best, revision is likely to consist of adding content rather than replacing or overhauling it. As noted in the postscript to Chapter 11, revision can be fostered in young writers, but results demonstrating knowledge-transforming operations are virtually nonexistent.

6. Immature reading comprehension
follows procedures similar
to knowledge telling.

Chapter 9 presented evidence pointing to a comprehension strategy that, like knowledge telling, focuses on topic identifiers and functions without construction of high-level syntheses of content. This parallelism lends support to the knowledge-telling model, because, as van Dijk and Kintsch (1983, p. 262) remark, "It seems highly implausible that language users would not have recourse to the same or similar levels, units, categories, rules, or strategies in both the productive and the receptive processing of discourse."

Good writing
through knowledge telling

If the knowledge-telling model is to apply to writers ranging from elementary-school students to a sizable portion of the university undergraduate population it must obviously be compatible with a wide range of differences in the quality of performance. Many differences in writing quality can, of course, be attributed to differences in language skills, vocabulary, and so on, which are not directly related to the process by which content is generated. In addition, differences in the quality of written compositions can be attributed to differences in the two knowledge stores that form part of the knowledge-telling model: content knowledge and discourse knowledge. The older students' advantage in content knowledge to be drawn on in writing is obvious; it is also reasonable to assume that older students have more elaborate knowledge of discourse forms and conventions, which within the knowledge-telling model can serve to prompt more richly structured compositions. Another way in which experience may contribute to performance without altering the basic model, however, is by providing a more elaborate set of tests to be applied to content retrieved from memory. Some very immature writers may apply no tests at all, writing down whatever is retrieved via the topical and structural prompts. More sophisticated students may test not only for appropriateness to topic and text function but also for criteria such as clarity, plausibility, and interest.

Finally, the quality of texts produced by the knowledge-telling process may be enhanced by incorporating the process into a more sophisticated composing routine. Whereas the untutored elementary-school student may set the process in motion immediately upon receiving an assignment, and use it to generate an essentially finished version of the text, a more sophisticated knowledge-teller might begin by carrying out some form of prewriting exercise designed to generate high-quality content (Odell, 1974), and then instead of generating text directly, might use the knowledge-telling process to generate notes, which could later be culled, arranged, and added (see Chapter 8).

With all of these refinements to knowledge telling, one might ask whether it any longer makes sense to think of it as the same model as that which applies to the beginning writer. By the time it has incorporated tests of clarity, interest, and the like, and taken on prewriting, culling, and organizing procedures, has not knowledge telling evolved into a higher form? Has not the novice begun to write like an expert?

The answer to this question is purely analytic, since we are talking about the properties of models, not about the empirical data of writing behavior. From an analytic or design standpoint, it does not matter how many tests are added or what activities are tacked on before or after. The essential design features of the knowledge-telling model are that it generates content by topical and structural prompts, without strategic formulation of goals, subgoals, search criteria, and other components of problem solving. So long as these essential features remain, the composing process retains its knowledge-telling character and remains fundamentally distinct from the expert process described in Chapter 1 and characterized as knowledge transforming. With enough elaboration and supplementation, it is quite conceivable that the knowledge-telling process could produce texts of a quality difficult to distinguish from the products of a knowledge-transforming process. Even then, however, differences in the underlying mental operations could result in differences in what the writer gets out of the writing process.

PSYCHOLOGICAL IMPLICATIONS
OF THE TWO MODELS

The knowledge-telling and knowledge-transforming models have implications about how writers' minds work. These implications cannot be tested straightforwardly. The implications themselves must be interpreted theoretically to generate empirical predictions, thus adding a second level of uncertainty. But such psychological implications are crucial to explore if the models are to lay claim to being models of real processes.

Memory Search Procedures

One of the most formidable challenges to theories of language use is to explain how it is that skillful speakers and writers are able so quickly to think of material fitting multiple constraints. Theories of memory have quite a bit to say about how, for instance, one quickly comes up with the response *eagle* or *albatross* when asked to think of a large bird (e.g., Anderson, 1983). A contemporary explanation might posit a *bird* node in memory around which bird species are clustered, with the more typical birds closer to the center. Bird species are tagged by various attributes, including size. Search starts at the node and spreads out until a species is encountered that is tagged for large size. *Eagle* is likely to be encountered before *ostrich*, even though ostriches are larger, because eagles are more typically birdlike in appearance and behavior and are thus likely to be located closer to the node.

Suppose, however, that one is engaged in light conversation on the topic of birds and is seized by the impulse to say something clever. The normal constraints governing cleverness include the following: What is said must be relevant, not only to the topic but to the theme of the immediately preceding discourse; it must be amusing; it must be brief; and it must be within the bounds of taste likely to be tolerated by the company present. It seems altogether unlikely that one's bird knowledge contains nodes for potentially amusing information or that individual items of bird knowledge are tagged for amusingness and tastefulness the way bird species may be tagged for size. But it seems equally improbable that even the most slow-witted of conversationalists proceeds by retrieving items of bird knowledge at random and testing them until something is found that meets the constraints. Although one may try to think of something clever and fail, the rejected ideas are likely to be near misses, all of them meeting most of the constraints. There must be some method to the search.

Heuristic search refers to memory-search procedures that employ strategies for increasing the likelihood of finding what one is looking for (Newell &

Simon, 1972). In writing, the only heuristic search-strategy that has been examined to our knowledge is the strategy of elaborating constraints. Flower and Hayes (1980b) analyzed the protocols of expert and novice writers assigned the task of writing about their job for readers of a teenage magazine. Two things stand out from this analysis. One is that the expert writers realized they had a difficult problem, that the nature of the audience severely constrained their choices of what to say. The second is that they solved the problem by elaborating the implicit constraints until they were able to view the problem from a standpoint that suggested a way to proceed. This is typical in solving ill-structured problems (Greeno, 1978). The way it relates to memory search may be something like the following: The effect of elaborating problem constraints is to produce an increasingly integrated representation of the problem. Finally the representation becomes integrated enough to be recognizable as belonging to a certain formal class for which one already has available schematic representations of possible types of solutions. One might see the aforementioned writing problem, as one of Flower and Hayes's expert participants did, as a problem of finding a salient shared experience relevant both to the writer's topic and to the readers' interests. Such a reformulation of the problem becomes heuristic if it provides cues that activate appropriate nodes in memory. If the problem formulation serves as a source of prompts or probes, the writer can then start retrieving material that has a good probability of being appropriate for solving the writing problem. Thus, once the writer has identified the problem as being one of finding a shared experience, what might otherwise have been a futile search through an undefined space of possible things to say becomes a search of emotionally charged episodes related to work—a kind of search that probably every working person would find easy to carry out.

In place of heuristic search we propose that knowledge-telling searches are guided by topic and discourse probes derived from analysis of the assignment and from material already retrieved. Knowledge transforming also makes use of these kinds of probes—a similarity emphasized by having knowledge telling embedded as a module within the knowledge-transforming model (see Figure 1.2)—but they are augmented by analysis of the rhetorical problem, which produces heuristic probes likely to bring forth problem solutions.

The difference between these sources of memory probes was brought out vividly in a protocol study by Flower and Hayes (1981), who reported that 60% of the new ideas generated by the good writers were in some way responsive to the larger rhetorical problem (that is, they recognized the audience, the genre, etc., as well as the topic). By contrast, the poor writers generated over 70% of their new ideas in response to the topic alone or to the last element under consideration.

The knowledge-telling model, as we have indicated, does contain provisions for meeting rhetorical or audience-related constraints. Some provisions are contained within the genre schema itself—for instance, cues to the kinds of content suitable to writing an amusing essay. But a novel constraint, one not already taken care of by the genre schema, can only be met by tests that are applied to content after it has been retrieved from memory. This leads to certain predictions about the effect of imposing an additional constraint on a writing task. For writers following the knowledge-telling model, adding a further constraint should mean that content generation will be slowed down, because more material is being rejected, and content should be generated in less well-organized form, because there will be holes in it due to rejected material.

A study by Caccamise (in press) provides findings in accord with these predictions. Adults were assigned a topic and given the task of generating ideas to include in a pamphlet that was to present all the facts on the topic. Under one condition the audience was designated as adults. Under another condition the audience was designated as fifth-grade students who were to use the information in a planning project. Thus the second condition contained implied constraints on the level of sophistication and on the applicability of the information. Under the more constrained condition, there was less cohesion among ideas and there were more repeated ideas. The latter result would be expected if the effect of constraints was simply to cause repeated attempts at retrieval, without heuristic cues that would increase the likelihood of successful retrieval. Rate of idea generation was only marginally slower in the constrained condition, but ideas tended to be more at the same level, whereas in the less constrained condition there were more ideas related hierarchically. Caccamise interpreted these results as indicating that participants were not employing a problem-solving approach to the task but were instead retrieving ideas by association and then editing them out after the fact—the precise process hypothesized by the knowledge-telling model. The task instructions, which called for presenting all the facts on a topic, would be expected to encourage a knowledge-telling strategy even on the part of people who would not employ one in their normal writing. Clearly, further research along the lines of Caccamise's study is needed—research that directly contrasts expert and novice writers on content-retrieval tasks that do and do not call for problem solving.

Mental Representations of Text

Strategies need something to operate on. A chess-playing strategy, for instance, would typically operate on chess pieces and would consist of ways to achieve advantageous arrangements of those pieces. It is common to think of cognitive strategies as operating on mental representations. The idea of mental representation is not very well defined and is the subject of theoretical dispute (see, for instance, Pylyshyn, 1984, Chapter 2), but it plays an important role in understanding intellectual abilities. For in addition to having or not having certain cognitive strategies, people may or may not have appropriate mental representations for those strategies to operate on.

Suppose the chess player has no chess board or chess pieces available. The expert chess player might nevertheless be able to exercise chess-playing strategies, applying them to mental representations of a chess board and thus being able to work on chess problems entirely in the head. A less experienced chess player, however, might not be able to do this, even though fully capable of applying strategies when the actual pieces were present. Such a person may be said to lack adequate mental representations. This is not to say that the inexperienced player cannot, for instance, imagine what a pawn looks like or even picture, in a general way, a certain arrangement of pieces on the board. But the inexperienced player evidently lacks the repertoire of detailed representations of chess-board arrangements that the expert possesses (Chase & Simon, 1973).

In the case of writing, a variety of different mental representations may be operated on—representations of ideas, of goals, of structural features, and of language (see Chapter 4). During composition the physical text itself probably serves mainly as an aid to recalling these mental representations. Few composing strategies, in other words, operate on the physical text. Almost all operate on things in the mind, and so the availability of suitable mental representations is a significant issue in writing competence.

Thinking-aloud protocols of mature writers give evidence that they make use of a variety of abstract representations (Flower & Hayes, 1984). That is, they refer explicitly to specific language, to details and main ideas, to structural elements, problems, and goals. As was shown in Chapter 8, however, the protocols of immature writers consist almost entirely of references at a lower level, closer to the surface text. To judge from planning protocols, almost all the mental work of composing by young writers consists of operations involving discrete items of content or language.

It would be desirable, however, to have independent evidence of how text is represented in the minds of immature writers. When novice writers appear unable to apply strategies involving checking decisions against goals, for instance, is it that they lack adequate strategies or is it that their goals are too vague, too narrow, or too inaccessible or are represented in such a way that strategies cannot be applied to them? We say independent rather than direct evidence, because of course there is no such thing as direct evidence on mental representations. There is only inference based on paradigms. So what are needed are some experimental paradigms, besides analysis of thinking-aloud composing protocols, that permit inferences about writers' mental representations.

In recent research (Scardamalia & Paris, 1985) we have been experimenting with recall paradigms for investigating mental representation of text. Recall has played a major part in studying related issues in comprehension. What readers recall of a text, and in what order, have been used as grounds for inferring a hierarchical organization of memory for text (Meyer, 1977) and for inferring the existence of a story schema for organizing narrative text information (Stein & Trabasso, 1982). Memory for one's own text cannot be studied in so straightforward a manner, because each person is recalling something different. What is in the text in the first place and what is recalled are both clearly relevant to questions of mental representation and are not easily disentangled.

Whereas *what* people recall of their texts may be hopelessly confounded with what is in the texts, *how* they go about recalling it may be indicative of the kinds of text representations they have available in memory. Accordingly, we have asked people to think aloud as they tried to recall verbatim texts they had written or to answer difficult questions about their texts such as how many times they used a certain word or what proportion of the text was devoted to a certain purpose (Scardamalia & Paris, 1985). The assumption was that if people had available a variety of interconnected knowledge representations pertaining to their texts, then they would make use of these in recall—much as people trying to recall where they were at a particular time may make use of their knowledge of world events, of the season, of their life's preoccupations at the time, and so on. Recall-protocol statements by students in grades 6, 10, and graduate school were classified according to whether they referred to *language* (near verbatim restatement of a text segment), *structure* (references such as "second paragraph" or "section used to lead up to my reason"), *gist* (e.g., "I spent some time saying how that school time should be divided") and *intention* (reference to the intent or goal of some part or feature of the text).

It was found that references to language decreased with age, while the other three kinds of references increased significantly. Graduate student protocols contained about twice as many references to gist and 10 times as many references to intentions as did the protocols of the younger students. Adults used mediation (recalling one thing as a step toward recalling another) about twice as frequently as did younger students. They also used more extended chains of mediation, such as using intention to recall gist, gist to recall structure, and then structure to recall actual language. Among adults, 83% demonstrated at least one 3- or 4-link chain of mediated recall. These were almost non-existent among the younger students, two-thirds of whom showed a 2-link chain as their most elaborate mediation of recall.

These results are highly consistent with the two-models view of composing that has been advanced here. In keeping with the knowledge-transforming model, the graduate students generated goals for their compositions and engaged in problem solving involving structure and gist as well as verbatim representations. This activity makes available to them a richly interconnected set of text representations that they can appeal to in attempting to recall their texts from memory or to answer specific questions. The younger students, however, in keeping with the knowledge-telling model, devoted attention to specific items of content and to the language for expressing them; in remembering, therefore, they are restricted primarily to unmediated recall of what was actually said in the text.

It is noteworthy, also, that what mediation the younger students did engage in mainly involved structural representations. The knowledge-telling model implies that knowledge of text structures plays an active role in text production, but not in deliberate planning of the text's overall structure. It is therefore consistent with the model that immature writers should show an absence of explicit references to discourse structure in their composing protocols but should nevertheless have some representation of structural features of their texts.

A similar distinction between operating on a mental representation during the composing process and being able to construct it when called upon to do so applies to the gist or main propositions of a text. As we saw in Chapter 9, there was evidence that in reading and in sentence arrangement younger students did not construct the main propositions of the text. But when asked to summarize a text they could do so. The research of Brown, Day, and Jones (1983) indicates that children accomplish summarization by evaluating individual statements for importance, a procedure that results in creating a reasonable summary but that is quite different from the active gist-construction carried out by more expert readers as a part of the comprehension process.

In a recent study we tried to gain evidence on how main points are represented by asking students to judge alternative versions of the main points of compositions they had written (Bereiter, Burtis, Scardamalia, & Brett, 1983). After they had written essays on an assigned topic, students in grades 5 and 11 were asked to write down what they considered to be the main point of their essays. Later they were given statements of their main point to discuss. In various conditions they received either paraphrased versions of their own main-point statements, upgraded versions (attempts by the experimenters to provide a sharper statement than the student had provided), downgraded versions (in which a minor point had been elevated to main-point status), or sets including all three types. There was evidence of considerable development between grades 5 and 11 in the extent to which students seemed to have a firm grip on what their main points were. When presented with a single main-point statement, the younger students tended to accept it as valid, no matter which version it was, and when presented with all three versions at once they had trouble deciding and tended to judge on the basis of details. The grade-11 students were more discriminating, tending to make judgments in keeping with the characteristics the experimenters had tried to impart to the main-point statements.

Perhaps more revealing about mental representations, however, was the extent to which students appealed to their own intentions in justifying a main-point statement. If one's composing of an essay was guided by a definite idea of what one wanted to say (even if this idea took shape during the composing), then this intention would be expected to function as the criterion against which any suggested statement of main point would be judged. That is, regardless of what the text said—even if it could be recognized as lending itself to some other interpretation—the writer could still make an incontestable judgment on the basis of what he or she had intended to say. Only 20% of the grade-5 students made any appeal to their own intentions in justifying a main-point judgment, whereas 60% of the grade-11 students did so.

Research on mental representations is frustrating because the connection between data and conclusions is always tenuous enough that there is plenty of room for counter-interpretations. For instance, the main-point findings can easily be attributed to memory weaknesses on the part of the younger students or to their understanding the task demands differently. The only realistic prospect for improvement lies, not in methodological refinements, but in the gradual strengthening of theories to the point where they come to be felt as providing more parsimonious explanations than do the commonsense explanations that so readily leap to mind (cf. Heil, 1983).

We would argue that the knowledge-telling model does, in fact, provide a parsimonious explanation of the findings on mental representation in composing. It explains why some kinds of mental representations are referred to in young writers' text-processing protocols and others are not, why some are available for use in recall and others not, and why novice writers should behave the way they do when confronted with alternative statements of their main point. More importantly, however, it explains these results in a way that makes sense in relation to the large array of other things known about the composing processes of immature writers. Consequently, it may not be too rash to say that the model is strong enough to lend support to the findings on mental representation rather than arguing only that the findings on mental representation lend support to the model.

Interdependence of Strategies and Representations

From any reasonable theoretical standpoint mental operations and mental representations must be regarded as aspects of the same competence. The picture of mature writers that emerges from the preceding sections is that of people who can carry out purposeful, strategically guided operations on a variety of kinds of mental representations of the text or of the writing task. It is easy to see how, starting with that kind of competence, writers who keep at it can acquire extremely high levels of expertise. Through repeated experience trying to achieve similar goals and wrestling with similar problems, they evolve increasingly refined representations of goal types and problem types, as the following example illustrates.

One of our more talented university students, asked to plan an essay on whether people should be allowed to own guns, was initially at a loss as to how to proceed. Her first thought was that the task did not interest her—a simple reaction to the topic, much as one might expect from a novice writer. But her next verbalized thought was that her views on the subject would probably not be popular. It did not appear that at that point she had any definite opinion, but she had some representation of the anti-gun beliefs voiced by others and, contemplating this position, she sensed that she would not care to defend it. She was, accordingly, able to represent a gist, evaluate it against her beliefs, and recognize that she had an audience-related problem on her hands. This was a striking instance of the reflective process described in Chapter 12, involving movement back and forth between a content space, where problems of fact and belief are dealt with, and a rhetorical space, where problems are dealt with having to do with achieving objectives of the composition. A little later, after having elaborated her own ideas about guns and hunting, this same writer remarked, "I guess I'll make this a CBC [Canadian Broadcasting Corporation—Canada's government-owned radio and television networks] kind of thing." What she meant by this is not clear to us, but "CBC" evidently represented for her some sufficiently definite approach that she could begin to plan accordingly. Thus, while the novice writer might have an opinion essay schema that specifies statement of position, reasons, etc., and contains some global requirements for truth and reasonableness, this writer would appear to have a set of more specialized opinion essay schemata that represent different ways of having impact on an audience, different ways of leading into the topic, and so on.

It is also worth considering the possibility that the expert writer, rather than having a repertoire of more-or-less complete schemata for representing different kinds of texts, has a large collection of schema components, along with strategies for selecting and assembling a schema appropriate to the particular content and requirements of the task at hand (c.f. van Dijk &

Kintsch, 1983, pp. 310–11). This would represent a very close interaction indeed between strategies and representations.

On the one hand, having access to a variety of representations at different levels of abstraction makes planning and problem-solving possible. The novice writer has much less to plan and solve problems with. Forced to work with representations that are close to the physical entities involved—to near-verbatim representations of the assignment and of the actual or intended text—the novice writer is under immediate threat of information overload from any effort to deal with more than local problems of appropriateness and coherence. By constrast, the expert can deal with whole organizational patterns, strategies, or problem types as single entities and thus keep the number of informational chunks that must be dealt with simultaneously down to a manageable number.

But it is pointless to say that novices would be able to function like experts if only they had the expert's repertoire of mental representations. For, although there is much that we do not know about mental representations, we do know that they are not something you can go and pick up at a supply depot. It is hard to imagine how one would acquire a rich repertoire of plan or problem representations except through continued efforts to plan and solve problems. Undoubtedly much of the knowledge needed to represent text possibilities comes from reading rather than writing, but even this knowledge probably depends on what Smith (1982, p. 179) calls "reading like a writer"—an activity that presupposes an involvement in solving writing problems. Thus, one could equally well say that novices would acquire the mental representations they lack if only they would engage in the kinds of planning and problem solving that build up a useful representational repertoire.

In any complex system, of course, everything seems to depend on everything else. Therefore it is not saying anything very remarkable to assert that mental operations and mental representations are interdependent. The assertion takes on more force, however, if it is considered in relation to the hypothesis of two models of composing. The knowledge-telling model is a model of how composing can go on with only a limited range of mental representations. There needs to be a way of representing topic and text type and a way of representing individual items of content so that they can be tested for appropriateness to topic and text type. At a minimum that will suffice. What is more crucial, however, is that the model does not involve operations that would generate additional kinds of text representations.

This is the fundamental sense in which knowledge telling is self-limiting. When people are continually engaged in formulating and tackling problems, they develop representations of problem and solution types that render many situations no longer problematic (Chi, Feltovich, & Glaser, 1981). This frees mental capacity to pursue more advanced problems, which in turn generate representations that render problem solving unnecessary, thus permitting attention to shift to a still higher level of problem, and so on. Such a process seems to characterize expert writers, and is designed into the knowledge-transforming model. But no such process is built into the knowledge-telling model. Thus there is nothing in the knowledge-telling process *per se* that would induce the writer to formulate intentions, gists, or overall plans. That raises the question of how, if the model is realistic, knowledge tellers can ever become knowledge transformers.

EDUCATIONAL IMPLICATIONS

Traditionally, the teaching of writing has been a thankless task. For the writing instructor it has meant long, long hours of marking and commenting on student compositions, with little reason for confidence that this effort would have any positive effect. Starting around 1970, however, there have been waves of innovation and reform that have raised hopes for a brighter future in writing instruction. Some of the earliest and most successful innovations have involved changes in what is taught. These included transformational sentence-combining exercises designed to increase syntactic fluency (O'Hare, 1973) and "new rhetoric," which features methods of exploring and developing ideas before writing (Young et al., 1970). More recent developments, however, have had to do with changing the nature of the school-writing experience itself. These include encouraging children to start writing before they have learned to read, inventing their own spellings (Clay, 1975), encouraging large amounts of free writing, with children sharing their productions with one another, and the teacher playing a largely supporting role (Crowhurst, 1979; Graves, 1983), and the use of computers for word processing and for communication among writers (Quinsaat, Levin, Boruta, & Newman, 1983). These recent innovations all share the aim of making writing a more worthwhile and intrinsically satisfying activity for students.

   These innovations all took shape before there was any substantial research on the composing process. Knowledge of underlying cognitive processes should be valuable, however, in developing these innovations beyond their initial stages. At present, for instance, many educators are looking to computers to produce a breakthrough in the teaching of writing. This hope seems to be supported mainly by the dramatic motivational effects of word processors on young writers, and this alone may make them a worthwhile educational investment. But there is so far no indication that using a word processor causes students to adopt more sophisticated composing strategies.

There is much talk in computer circles about developing more interactive software that will in some fashion teach children to write better. Micro-computers do in fact show promise as a way of providing procedural support for more complex composing strategies and for directing attention to par-ticular aspects of the composing task (Woodruff, Scardamalia, & Bereiter, 1982). But the design of such software puts heavy demands on one's under-standing of the cognitive processes that the system impinges on. Some current software, for instance, merely provides utilities for taking notes, generating outlines, and the like. This can hardly be expected to have much impact on students who see no virtue in planning in the first place and whose composing strategies create no need for it. In fact, there is evidence that having a computer interact with students while they write can be disruptive to thought rather than facilitative (Woodruff et al., 1981). It seems that any really sophisticated piece of educational software in writing would have to be a virtual embodiment of a sophisticated theory of the writing process. The same, however, could probably be said of sophisticated versions of any of the currently popular approaches to writing improvement. Improvements in instructional methods can go some distance on the basis of bright ideas and enthusiasm, but further progress is likely to depend on basic understanding of the cognitive processes involved.

Knowledge Transforming as an Instructional Goal

The main educational implications of the present research, however, are not at the level of contributions to instructional know-how. They are at the level of altering what are seen as the principal goals and problems of instruction. To readers who have followed the progression of ideas through the preced-ing chapters, it will be evident that what began as a focus on writing abilities *per se* turned increasingly into a view of writing as a way of processing and developing knowledge. Coordinate with this change in research focus has been a shift toward seeing the central problem of writing instruction as that of altering the way students operate on their knowledge when they write. In short, the problem is that of shifting students from knowledge telling to knowledge transforming.

Such a view of the goal of writing instruction is not out of keeping with current thought among language arts educators. There is much talk about "writing as a tool of thought," about "language as a way of knowing," and about "writing as a process of discovery." Where the present research has import, therefore, is not in suggesting what writing may be good for. It is in suggesting what the problems may be in enabling students to achieve these cognitive benefits of writing.

The "Meaningful Task"

The popular view seems to be that writing is inherently conducive to personal knowledge. The contribution that a particular writing experience makes to the writer's knowledge development is seen as depending on contextual factors. An arbitrarily assigned topic, with an error-hunting teacher as the sole audience, may do little for the writer, whereas a topic the writer cares about and an audience responsive to what the writer has to say are the essential ingredients for a profitable experience. Hence the over-riding concern of the teacher becomes that of making writing a meaningful experience for the students (Graves, 1978a; Muller, 1967). The argument is extremely persuasive, and so there is little wonder that this "let them write" position occupies the high ground in any debate over pedagogy. There is hardly a point one can get hold of to disagree with. Yet there is a weak side to the position, and it is revealed in the phrase, "making writing a meaningful experience for the students." We must remind ourselves that mature writers are able to make writing tasks meaningful for themselves and *that this is part of their competence*. We must ask what this ability consists of, how it is acquired, and what effect different educational practices may have on its development.

Making a writing task meaningful for oneself is a matter of constructing a goal representation that takes account of external requirements (such as those imposed by a school assignment) but also includes goals of personal significance to oneself (Scardamalia & Bereiter, 1982). A goal that almost any writing task lends itself to is reinterpreting or reorganizing some part of one's knowledge. That seems to be what phrases such as "writing as a tool of thought" and "writing as a process of discovery" refer to. What our research on composing processes indicates, however, is that purposeful pursuit of such knowledge goals requires a knowledge-transforming executive structure.

Knowledge-telling, which involves stating what has previously existed in some less articulated form, is certain to have some knowledge-transforming effect—at times possibly even a major effect. The point is, however, that its effect depends on the topic and how it happens to connect to the writer's knowledge. It depends on the prescribed or chosen literary form. And it depends on transitory states of feeling and concern, on what the young writer has been thinking or learning recently, and so on. That, according to our analysis, is why students are so dependent on the teacher to provide a "meaningful context" for writing.

All of us are affected by context, of course. But the knowledge-transforming model provides resources for action that is not bound to context. It provides means for deliberately formulating and pursuing personally meaningful goals in writing, for recognizing and overcoming problems, and for assessing and revising choices made at a variety of levels. If it is acknowledged that young writers must develop these cognitive resources, then it must be asked whether the best environment for writing is one in which things are continually made meaningful by others.

The Larger Instructional Problem

We believe that knowledge telling is but one manifestation of a more general educational failing. It is the failure of education to promote intentional cognition (Bereiter & Scardamalia, 1983b). Intentional cognition may be briefly defined as the setting and deliberate pursuit of cognitive goals—goals to learn, to solve, to understand, to define, and so on. People do a great deal of learning, solving, understanding, etc., both in school and outside. But very little of it is intentional. Most of it is either spontaneous, evoked by things that capture their interest, or else it is incidental to achieving some more worldly goal, such as making the garden grow or getting a satisfactory mark on an assignment. The schools may be faulted for failing to promote the spontaneous, the incidental, and the emotionally guided as well, but that is not the point at issue here. It is failure on the intentional side that leaves students enchained by circumstance.

What we have called the knowledge-transforming model could be called a model of intentional writing. It involves the setting of goals to be achieved through the composing process and the purposeful pursuit of those goals. The knowledge-telling model lacks this intentional component, and thus represents a composing process that depends on evoked memories and emotions and on external assistance for its direction. Similarly, in reading (see Chapter 9) we can identify an intentional kind of process that sets goals of discovering the gist of a text and actively monitors attainment of those goals, and we can identify a more passive kind of reading that responds to the immediate saliency and plausibility of text elements and depends on external assistance to convert text propositions into knowledge.

Contemporary school practices of all kinds seem to encourage the more passive kind of cognition. One set of school practices favors passivity by continually telling students what to do. The opposing set of practices favors passivity by encouraging students to follow their spontaneous interests and impulses. Largely absent, scarcely even contemplated, are school practices that encourage students to assume responsibility for what becomes of their minds.

Symptoms of a lack of intentional cognition are to be found in the undeveloped thought content of student writing (see, especially, Chapter 6). They are equally to be seen in students' difficulties in learning from texts. Pearson and Gallagher (1983) report that it is common for elementary school teachers to restate the content of every text passage for students, on the assumption that many will have failed to grasp it. The failure of many adolescents to perform at a formal level on Piagetian tasks (Lawson & Renner, 1974) may also be taken as symptomatic, in so far as formal thought involves deliberate operations on one's knowledge. Recent evidence of the persistence of prescientific schemata in students who have studied physics (McCloskey, Caramazza, & Green, 1980) further bespeaks a failure of students to revise their existing cognitive structures in light of new information.

All of these findings can, of course, be interpreted in less damning ways, and it is not our intention to claim that the schools are failing utterly or even that there has been a decline. A much less contentious claim will suffice: namely, that there is room for improvement. But it is not improvement through doing better what the schools already do. It is improvement through rising to a higher level of educational objectives than are currently being pursued.

These higher-level objectives, which we have been trying to get at in the instructional experiments described in Part IV of this book, all involve imparting to the students those kinds of competence that have previously been reserved to the teacher. It has been the teacher who is expected to know what is worth learning and how it relates to what was learned previously. It has been the teacher's job to establish links between current activities and the student's needs and interests. It has been the teacher's job to recognize the spark of originality in the student's work and fan it into a flame. It has been the teacher's job to ask the probing question, to reveal the unexamined premise.

Writing, especially expository writing, offers an opportunity for students to work actively and independently with their own knowledge. They can clarify meanings, find inconsistencies, discover implications, and establish connections between previously isolated fragments of knowledge. In order to do this, however, they need to function according to a knowledge-transforming rather than a knowledge-telling model.

From what we know so far, it appears that for students to develop a knowledge-transforming model of composing is itself a major intellectual achievement. It is an achievement that seems likely to require more than simply a rich diet of relatively unrestricted writing experience. Drawing on the experiences described in Chapters 12 and 13, we would suggest the following as additional elements that ought to be present in writing instruction:

1. Students (and teachers) need to be made aware of the full extent of the composing process. They should understand that most of it does not involve putting words on paper but consists of setting goals, formulating problems, evaluating decisions, and planning in the light of prior goals and decisions. It needs to be constantly clear to

students that they should be working toward independence in managing the whole process.

2. The thinking that goes on in composition needs to be modeled by the teacher, who can thereby show the problem-solving and planning processes that students are often unaware of. The ability to model these processes needs also to be conveyed to the students, however, so that they can benefit from observing and discussing each other's mental efforts.

3. Acquiring higher levels of competence should be a clear goal in the minds of the students and not only in the mind of the teacher. One way of bringing issues of competence to the forefront in a constructive way is to involve students in investigations of their own strategies and knowledge. Ideally, students should see it as their responsibility to help each other develop their knowledge.

4. Although students need a supportive and congenial environment, they also need to experience the struggles that are part of the knowledge-transforming process in writing. This means pursuing challenging goals and not always writing what is most prominent in mind or what is easiest to do well.

5. The use of procedural facilitation—simplified routines and external supports—can help students through the initial stages of acquiring more complex executive processes. Students need to share in an understanding of the purpose, however, and to understand as much as possible about the nature and function of the process they are trying to acquire. Without such understanding, students are likely to adopt only superficial aspects of the complex process.

Writing is, of course, not the only medium for fostering the development of intentional cognition. Reading comprehension, especially insofar as it involves revising one's knowledge on the basis of what is read, is another area in which more active strategies need to be fostered. There are, in fact, promising instructional approaches to reading comprehension strategies that are highly congruent with the four principles suggested above (e.g., Bereiter & Bird, 1985; Palincsar & Brown, 1984). Pilot studies reported in the postscripts to Chapters 9 and 12 suggest that computer programing is also a medium in which strategies for more purposeful control of cognition might be taught. Finally, there is the growing body of evidence that science students accumulate new knowledge without revising the naive beliefs that they entertained before instruction (McCloskey et al., 1980). Helping students to develop independent knowledge-transforming skills in science and other subject matters is a problem that has scarcely been approached. But if students can develop powerful knowledge-transforming skills in writing, this should help them to become more active builders of their own knowledge in all domains.

References

Anderson, J. R. (1982). Acquisition of cognitive skill. *Psychological Review, 89,* 369-406.

Anderson, J. R. (1983). *The architecture of cognition.* Cambridge, MA: Harvard University Press.

Anderson, V. A., Bereiter, C., & Smart, D. (1980). *Activation of semantic networks in writing: Teaching students how to do it themselves.* Paper presented at the meeting of the American Educational Research Association, Boston.

Applebee, A. N. (1981). *Writing in the secondary school: English and the content areas.* Urbana, IL: National Council of Teachers of English.

Bachelder, B. L., & Denny, M. R. (1977a). A theory of intelligence: I. Span and the complexity of stimulus control. *Intelligence, 1,* 127-150.

Bachelder, B. L., & Denny, M. R. (1977b). A theory of intelligence: II. The role of span in a variety of intellectual tasks. *Intelligence, 1,* 237-256.

Bamberg, B. (1980). *Cohesive relations in written discourse at three age levels.* Paper presented at the meeting of the American Educational Research Association, Boston.

Bartlett, E. J. (1982). Learning to revise: Some component processes. In M. Nystrand (Ed.), *What writer's know: The language, process, and structure of written discourse* (pp. 345-363). New York: Academic Press.

Bartlett, F. (1958). *Thinking: An experimental and social study.* London: Allen and Unwin.

Beaugrande, R. de. (1980). *Text, discourse, and process.* Norwood, NJ: Ablex.

Beaugrande, R. de. (1981). *Modelling the operations of the writing process.* Paper presented at the meeting of the American Educational Research Association, Los Angeles.

Beaugrande, R. de. (1982a). Psychology and composition: Past, present, future. In M. Nystrand (Ed.), *What writers know: The language, process, and structure of written discourse* (pp. 211-267). New York: Academic Press.

Beaugrande, R. de. (1982b). The story of grammars and the grammar of stories. *Journal of Pragmatics, 6,* 383-422.

Beaugrande, R. de. (1984a). Learning to read versus reading to learn: A discourse-processing approach. In H. Mandl, N. L. Stein, & T. Trabasso (Eds.), *Learning and comprehension of text.* (pp. 159–191). Hillsdale, NJ: Lawrence Erlbaum Associates.

Beaugrande, R. de. (1984b). *Text production: Toward a science of composition.* Norwood, NJ: Ablex Publishing Corporation.

Beaugrande, R. de., & Colby, B. N. (1979). Narrative models of action and interaction. *Cognitive Science, 3,* 43–66.

Bellack, A., Kliebard, H. M., Hyman, R. T., & Smith, F. L., Jr. (1966). *The language of the classroom.* New York: Teachers College Press.

Bereiter, C. (1980). Development in writing. In L. W. Gregg & E. R. Steinberg (Eds.), *Cognitive processes in writing.* (pp. 73–93). Hillsdale, NJ: Lawrence Erlbaum Associates.

Bereiter, C. (1984). The limitations of interpretation [Review of Writing and the Writer]. *Curriculum Inquiry, 14,* 211–216.

Bereiter, C., & Bird, M. (1985). Use of thinking aloud in identification and teaching of reading comprehension strategies. *Cognition and Instruction, 2,* 131–156.

Bereiter, C., Burtis, P. J., Scardamalia, M., & Brett, C. (1983). *Developmental differences in mental representation of main point in composition.* Paper presented at the meeting of the American Educational Research Association, Montreal.

Bereiter, C., Fine, J., & Gartshore, S. (1979). *An exploratory study of micro-planning in writing.* Paper presented at the meeting of the American Educational Research Association, San Francisco.

Bereiter, C., & Scardamalia, M. (1978). *Cognitive demands of writing as related to discourse type.* Paper presented at the meeting of the American Educational Research Association, Toronto.

Bereiter, C., & Scardamalia, M. (1979). Pascual-Leone's M construct as a link between cognitive-developmental and psychometric concepts of intelligence. *Intelligence, 3,* 41–63.

Bereiter, C., & Scardamalia, M. (1983a). Does learning to write have to be so difficult? In A. Freedman, I. Pringle, & J. Yalden (Eds.), *Learning to write: First language, second language* (pp. 20–33). New York: Longman Inc.

Bereiter, C., & Scardamalia, M. (1983b). Schooling and the growth of intentional cognition: Helping children take charge of their own minds. In Z. Lamm (Ed.), *New trends in education* (pp. 73–100). Tel-Aviv: Yachdev United Publishing Co.

Bereiter, C., & Scardamalia, M. (1984). Learning about writing from reading. *Written Communication, 1,* 163–188.

Bereiter, C., & Scardamalia, M. (1985). Wissen-Wiedergeben als ein Modell für das Schreiben von Instruktionen durch ungeübte Shreiber [Knowledge telling as a model of instruction writing by immature writers.] *Unterrichts Wissenschaft, 4,* 319–333.

Bereiter, C., Scardamalia, M., Anderson, V. A., & Smart, D. (1980). *An experiment in teaching abstract planning in writing.* Paper presented at the meeting of the American Educational Research Association, Boston.

Bereiter, C., Scardamalia, M., & Turkish, L. (1980). *The child as discourse grammarian.* Paper presented at the meeting of the American Educational Research Association, Boston.

Bird, M. (1980). *Reading comprehension strategies: A direct teaching approach.* Unpublished doctoral dissertation, The Ontario Institute for Studies in Education, Toronto.

Black, J. B., Wilkes-Gibb, D., & Gibb, R. W., Jr. (1982). What writers need to know that they don't know they need to know. In M. Nystrand (Ed.), *What writers know: The language, process, and structure of written discourse* (pp. 325–343). New York: Academic Press.

Blalock, H. M., Jr. (1969). *Theory construction: From verbal to mathematical formulations.* Englewood Cliffs, NJ: Prentice-Hall.

Blass, T., & Siegman, A. W. (1975). A psycholinguistic comparison of speech, dictation and writing. *Language and Speech, 18,* 20-34.

Bobrow, D. G., & Norman, D. A. (1975). Some principles of memory schemata. In D. G. Bobrow & A. Collins (Eds.), *Representation and understanding: Studies in cognitive science* (pp. 131-149). New York: Academic Press.

Bracewell, R. J. (1980). Writing as a cognitive activity. *Visible Language, 14,* 400-422.

Bracewell, R. J., Bereiter, C., & Scardamalia, M. (1979). *A test of two myths about revision.* Paper presented at the meeting of the American Educational Research Association, San Francisco.

Bracewell, R. J., Fine, J., & Ezergaile, L. (1980). *Cohesion as a guide to writing processes.* Paper presented at the meeting of the American Educational Research Association, Boston.

Bracewell, R. J., & Scardamalia, M. (1979). *Children's ability to integrate information when they write.* Paper presented at the meeting of the American Educational Research Association, San Francisco.

Bracewell, R. J., Scardamalia, M. & Bereiter, C. (October, 1978). The development of audience awareness in writing. *Resources in Education,* (ERIC Document Reproduction Service No. ED 154 433).

Braddock, R., Lloyd-Jones, R., & Schoer, L. (1963). *Research in written composition.* Champaign, IL: National Council of Teachers of English.

Bransford, J. D. (1981). Social-cultural prerequisites for cognitive research. In J. Harvey (Ed.), *Cognition, social behavior, and the environment* (pp. 557-569). Hillsdale, NJ: Lawrence Erlbaum Associates.

Brewer, W. F. (1980). Literary theory, rhetoric, and stylistics: Implications for psychology. In R. J. Spiro, B. C. Bruce, & W. F. Brewer (Eds.), *Theoretical issues in reading comprehension* (pp. 221-239). Hillsdale, NJ: Lawrence Erlbaum Associates.

Britton, J. (1978). The composing processes and the functions of writing. In C. R. Cooper & L. Odell (Eds.), *Research on composing: Points of departure* (pp. 3-28). Urbana, IL: National Council of Teachers of English.

Britton, J., Burgess, T., Martin, N., McLeod, A., & Rosen, H. (1975). *The development of writing abilities (11-18).* London: Macmillan Education Ltd.

Brown, A. L. (1977). Development, schooling and the acquisition of knowledge about knowledge: Comments on chapter 7 by Nelson. In R. C. Anderson, R. J. Spiro, & W. E. Montague (Eds.), *Schooling and the acquisition of knowledge* (pp. 241-253). Hillsdale, NJ: Lawrence Erlbaum Associates.

Brown, A. L. (1978). Knowing when, where, and how to remember: A problem of metacognition. In R. Glaser (Ed.), *Advances in instructional psychology* (Vol. 1.) (pp. 77-165). Hillsdale, NJ: Lawrence Erlbaum Associates.

Brown, A. L., Bransford, J. D., Ferrara, R. A., & Campione, J. C. (1983). Learning, remembering, and understanding. In J. H. Flavell & E. M. Markman (Eds.), *Handbook of child psychology: Vol. 3. Cognitive development* (4th ed.) (pp. 77-166). New York: John Wiley & Sons.

Brown, A. L., & Campione, J. C. (1981). Inducing flexible thinking: A problem of access. In M. Friedman, J. P. Das, & N. O'Connor (Eds.), *Intelligence and learning* (pp. 515-529). New York: Plenum.

Brown, A. L., & Day, J. D. (1983). Macrorules for summarizing texts: The development of expertise. *Journal of Verbal Learning and Verbal Behavior, 22,* 1-14.

Brown, A. L., Day, J. D., & Jones, R. S. (1983). The development of plans for summarizing texts. *Child Development, 54,* 968–979.

Brown, J. S., & Van Lehn, K. (1980). Repair theory: A generative theory of bugs in procedural skills. *Cognitive Science, 4,* 379–426.

Bruner, J. S. (1983). *Child's talk: Learning to use language.* New York: Norton.

Burtis, P. J. (1983). *Planning in narrative and argument writing.* Paper presented at the meeting of the American Educational Research Association, Montreal.

Burtis, P. J., Bereiter, C., & Scardamalia, M. (1984). *Problems with integrating ideas.* Paper presented at the meeting of the American Educational Research Association, New Orleans.

Burtis, P. J., & Scardamalia, M. (1983). *Planning narratives: Children's problems in using adult-like strategies.* Paper presented at the meeting of the American Educational Research Association, Montreal.

Butterfield, E. C., Siladi, D., & Belmont, J. M. (1980). Validating theories of intelligence. In H. W. Reese & L. P. Lipsitt (Eds.), *Advances in child development and behavior* (Vol. 15.) (pp. 95–162). New York: Academic Press.

Butterworth, B., & Goldman-Eisler, F. (1979). Recent studies on cognitive rhythm. In A. W. Siegman & S. Feldstein (Eds.), *Of speech and time: Temporal speech patterns in interpersonal contexts.* (pp. 211–224). Hillsdale, NJ: Lawrence Erlbaum Associates.

Caccamise, D. J. (in press). Idea generation in writing. In A. Matsuhashi (Ed.), *Writing in real time: Modelling production processes.* New York: Longman Inc.

Case, R. (1974). Structures and strictures: Some functional limitations on the course of cognitive growth. *Cognitive Psychology, 6,* 544–573.

Case, R. (1975). Gearing the demands of instruction to the development capacities of the learner. *Review of Educational Research, 45,* 59–87.

Case, R. (1978a). A developmentally based theory and technology of instruction. *Review of Educational Research, 48,* 439–463.

Case, R. (1978b). Intellectual development from birth to adulthood: A neo-piagetian interpretation. In R. Siegler (Ed.), *Children's thinking: What develops?* (pp. 37–71). Hillsdale, NJ: Lawrence Erlbaum Associates.

Case, R. (1978c). Piaget and beyond: Toward a developmentally based theory and technology of instruction. In R. Glaser (Ed.), *Advances in instructional psychology* (Vol. 1.) (pp. 167–228). Hillsdale, NJ: Lawrence Erlbaum Associates.

Case, R. (1985a). A developmentally based approach to the problem of instructional design. In S. S. Chipman, J. W. Segal, & R. Glaser (Eds.), *Thinking and learning skills: Current research and open questions* (Vol. 2) Hillsdale, NJ: Lawrence Erlbaum Associates.

Case, R. (1985b). *Intellectual development: Birth to adulthood.* Orlando, FL: Academic Press.

Case, R., & Khanna, F. (1981). The missing links: Stages in children's progression from sensorimotor to logical thought. *New Directions for Child Development, 12,* 21–32.

Case, R., & Kurland, D. M. (1980). A new measure for determining children's subjective organization of speech. *Journal of Experimental Child Psychology, 30,* 206–222.

Case, R., Kurland, D. M., & Goldberg, J. (1982). Operational efficiency and the growth of short term memory span. *Journal of Experimental Child Psychology, 33,* 386–404.

Chafe, W. L. (1985). Linguistic differences produced by differences between speaking and writing. In D. R. Olson, N. Torrance, & A. Hildyard (Eds.), *Literacy, language and learning: The nature and consequences of reading and writing* (pp. 105–123). Cambridge: Cambridge University Press.

Chase, W. G., & Simon, H. A. (1973). Perception in chess. *Cognitive Psychology, 4,* 55–81.

Chi, M. T. H. (1977). Age differences in memory span. *Journal of Experimental Child Psychology, 23,* 266–281.

Chi, M. T. H., Feltovich, P. J., & Glaser, R. (1981). Categorization and representation of physics problems by experts and novices. *Cognitive Science, 5,* 121–152.

Chomsky, N. (1964). Formal discussion of "The development of grammar in child language" by W. Miller and S. Ervin. *Society for Research in Child Development Monographs, 29,* 35–39.

Chomsky, N. (1967). The formal nature of language. In E. H. Lenneberg (Ed.), *Biological foundations of language* (pp. 397–442). New York: Wiley.

Chomsky, N. (1980). *Rules and representations.* New York: Columbia University Press.

Church, E., & Bereiter, C. (1983). Reading for style. *Language Arts, 60,* 470–476.

Church, J. (1961). *Language and the discovery of reality.* New York: Random House.

Clark, H. H., & Clark, E. V. (1977). *Psychology of language.* New York: Harcourt, Brace, Jovanovich.

Clay, M. M. (1975). *What did I write: Beginning writing behaviour.* Auckland, New Zealand: Heinemann Educational Books.

Clements, P. (1979). The effects of staging on recall from prose. In R. O. Freedle (Ed.), *New directions in discourse processing* (Vol. 2.) (pp. 287–330). Norwood, NJ: Ablex Publishing Corporation.

Cloward, R. D. (1967). Studies in tutoring. *Journal of Experimental Education, 36,* 14–25.

Collins, A. M., & Gentner, D. (1980). A framework for a cognitive theory of writing. In L. W. Gregg & E. Steinberg (Eds.), *Cognitive processes in writing* (pp. 51–72). Hillsdale, NJ: Lawrence Erlbaum Associates.

Collins, A. M., & Quillian, M. R. (1969). Retrieval time from semantic memory. *Journal of Verbal Learning and Verbal Behavior, 8,* 240–270.

Collis, K. F., & Biggs, J. B. (1976). *Classroom examples of cognitive development phenomena.* Paper presented at the meeting of the Australian Association for Research in Education, Brisbane.

Committee on CCCC Language Statement (1974). Students' right to their own language. *College Composition and Communication, 25*(Special issue), 1–32.

Cooper, C. R., & Matsuhashi, A. (1983). A theory of the writing process. In M. Martlew (Ed.), *The psychology of written language: A developmental approach.* (pp. 3–39). London: John Wiley & Sons.

Cronbach, L. J. (1975). Beyond the two disciplines of scientific psychology. *American Psychologist, 30,* 116–127.

Crowhurst, M. (1979). The writing workshop: An experiment in peer response to writing. *Language Arts, 56,* 757–762.

Dickson, W. P. (Ed.). (1981). *Children's oral communication skills.* New York: Academic Press.

Donaldson, M. (1978). *Children's minds.* London: Croom Helm.

Duncker, K. (1945). On problem solving. *Psychological Monographs, 58* (5, Whole No. 270).

Elbow, P. (1973). *Writing without teachers.* London: Oxford University Press.

Emig, J. (1971). *The composing processes of twelfth graders.* (Research Rep. No. 13). Champaign, IL: National Council of Teachers of English.

Ericsson, K. A., & Simon, H. A. (1980). Verbal reports as data. *Psychological Review*, 87, 215-251.

Farrell, T. J. (1978). Differentiating writing from talking. *College Composition and Communication*, 29, 346-350.

Flavell, J. H. (1978). Comments. In R. S. Siegler (Ed.), *Children's thinking: What develops?* (pp. 97-105). Hillsdale, NJ: Lawrence Erlbaum Associates.

Flavell, J. H. (1979). Metacognition and cognitive monitoring: A new area of cognitive-developmental inquiry. *American Psychologist*, 34, 906-911.

Flavell, J. H., Speer, J. R., Green, F. L., & August, D. L. (1981). The development of comprehension monitoring and knowledge about communication. *Monographs of the Society for Research in Child Development*, 46 (5, Serial No. 192).

Flavell, J. H., & Wellman, H. M. (1977). Metamemory. In R. V. Kail & J. W. Hagen (Eds.), *Perspectives on the development of memory and cognition* (pp. 3-33). Hillsdale, NJ: Lawrence Erlbaum Associates.

Flower, L. S. (1979). Writer-based prose: A cognitive basis for problems in writing. *College English*, 41, 19-37.

Flower, L. S. (1981). *Problem-solving strategies for writing*. New York: Harcourt Brace Jovanovich.

Flower, L. S., & Hayes, J. R. (1980a). The cognition of discovery: Defining a rhetorical problem. *College Composition and Communication*, 31, 21-32.

Flower, L. S., & Hayes, J. R. (1980b). The dynamics of composing: Making plans and juggling constraints. In L. W. Gregg & E. R. Steinberg (Eds.), *Cognitive processes in writing* (pp. 31-50). Hillsdale, NJ: Lawrence Erlbaum Associates.

Flower, L. S., & Hayes, J. R. (1981). The pregnant pause: An inquiry into the nature of planning. *Research in the Teaching of English*, 15, 229-244.

Flower, L. S., & Hayes, J. R. (1984). Images, plans and prose: The representation of meaning in writing. *Written Communication*, 1, 120-160.

Flower, L. S., Hayes, J. R., & Swarts, H. (1980). *Revising functional documents: The scenario principle*. (Tech. Rep. No. 10). Pittsburgh, PA: Carnegie-Mellon University, Document Design Project.

Fodor, J. A., Bever, T. G., & Garrett, M. F. (1974). *The psychology of language: An introduction to psycholinguistics and generative grammar*. New York: McGraw-Hill.

Frase, L. T. (1980). *Writer's workbench: Computer supports for components of the writing process*. Paper presented at the meeting of the American Educational Research Association, Boston.

Frith, U. (Ed.). (1980). *Cognitive processes in spelling*. London: Academic Press.

Fromkin, V. (1971). The non-anomalous nature of anomalous utterances. *Language*, 47, 27-52.

Gazzaniga, M. S., & LeDoux, J. E. (1978). *The integrated mind*. New York: Plenum Press.

Gelman, R., & Gallistel, C. R. (1978). *The child's understanding of number*. Cambridge, MA: Harvard University Press.

Gold, A. P. (1978). *Cumulative learning versus cognitive development: A comparison of two different theoretical bases for planning remedial instruction in arithmetic*. Unpublished doctoral dissertation, University of California, Berkeley.

Goody, J., & Watt, J. (1963). The consequences of literacy. *Comparative Studies in Society and History*, 5, 304-345.

Gould, J. D. (1978). An experimental study of writing, dictating, and speaking. In J. Requin (Ed.), *Attention and performance VII* (pp. 299-319). Hillsdale, NJ: Lawrence Erlbaum Associates.

Gould, J. D. (1980). Experiments on composing letters: Some facts, some myths, and some observations. In L. W. Gregg & E. R. Steinberg (Eds.), *Cognitive processes in writing* (pp. 97–127). Hillsdale, NJ: Lawrence Erlbaum Associates.

Graves, D. H. (1975). An examination of the writing processes of seven-year-old children. *Research in the Teaching of English, 9,* 227–241.

Graves, D. H. (1978a). *Balance the basics: Let them write.* New York: Ford Foundation.

Graves, D. H. (1978b). Research update: Handwriting is for writing. *Language Arts, 55,* 393–399.

Graves, D. H. (1979). What children show us about revision. *Language Arts, 56,* 312–319.

Graves, D. H. (1983). *Writing: Teachers and children at work.* Exeter, NH: Heinemann Educational Books.

Graves, D. H., & Giacobbe, M. E. (1982). Questions for teachers who wonder if their writers change. *Language Arts, 59,* 495–503.

Gray, B. (1977). *The grammatical foundations of rhetoric.* The Hague, The Netherlands: Mouton Publishers.

Greeno, J. G. (1978). Natures of problem-solving abilities. In W. K. Estes (Ed.), *Handbook of learning and cognitive processes* (Vol. 5.) (pp. 239–270). Hillsdale, NJ: Lawrence Erlbaum Associates.

Halliday, M. A. K., & Hasan, K. (1976). *Cohesion in English.* London: Longman Inc.

Harpin, W. (1976). *The second "R".* London: George, Allen & Unwin Ltd.

Harrell, L. E. (1957). A comparison of the development of oral and written language in school age children. *Monographs of the Society for Research in Child Development,* Vol. 22(3).

Harste, J. C., & Burke, C. L. (1980). Examining instructional assumptions: The child as informant. *Theory Into Practice, 19,* 170–178.

Hayes, J. R. (1981). *The complete problem solver.* Philadelphia: Franklin Institute Press.

Hayes, J. R., & Flower, L. S. (1980). Identifying the organization of writing processes. In L. W. Gregg & E. R. Steinberg (Eds.), *Cognitive processes in writing* (pp. 3–30). Hillsdale, NJ: Lawrence Erlbaum Associates.

Hayes-Roth, B., & Hayes-Roth, F. (1979). A cognitive model of planning. *Cognitive Science, 3,* 275–310.

Hayes-Roth, B., & Walker, C. (1979). Configural effects in human memory: The superiority of memory over external information sources as a basis of inference verification. *Cognitive Science, 3,* 119–140.

Heil, J. (1983). Belief ascription, parsimony, and rationality. *Behavioral and Brain Sciences, 6,* 365–366.

Hidi, S., & Hildyard, A. (1983). The comparison of oral and written productions of two discourse types. *Discourse Processes, 6,* 91–105.

Hidi, S., & Klaiman, R. (1984). Children's written dialogues: Intermediary between conversation and written text. In A. D. Pellegrini & T. D. Yawkey (Eds.), *Advances in discourse processes: Vol. 13. The development of oral and written language in social contexts* (pp. 233–241). Norwood, NJ: Ablex Publishing.

Hildyard, A., & Hidi, S. (1980). *Resolving conflict in narratives.* Paper presented at the meeting of the American Educational Research Association, Boston.

Hirsch, E. D., Jr. (1977). *The philosophy of composition.* Chicago: University of Chicago Press.

Horowitz, R. (1984). Toward a theory of literacy. *Harvard Educational Review, 54,* 88–97.

Hotopf, N. (1980). Slips of the pen. In U. Frith (Ed.), *Cognitive processes in spelling* (pp. 287–307). London: Academic Press.

Hunt, K. (1965). *Grammatical structures written at three grade levels.* (Research Rep. No. 3). Champaign, IL: National Council of Teachers of English.

Inhelder, B., & Piaget, J. (1958). *The growth of logical thinking from childhood to adolescence.* New York: Basic Books.

Inhelder, B., & Piaget, J. (1969). *The early growth of logic in the child.* New York: Norton & Company, Inc.

Johnson, N. F. (1965). The psychological reality of phrase-structure rules. *Journal of Verbal Learning and Verbal Behavior, 4,* 469–475.

Jones, B. F., & Amiran, M. (1980). *Applying structure of text and learning strategies research to develop programs of instruction for low achieving students.* Paper presented at the meeting of the NIE–LRDC Conference on Thinking and Learning Skills, Pittsburgh.

Just, M. A., & Carpenter, P. A. (1980). A theory of reading: From eye fixations to comprehension. *Psychological Review, 87,* 329–354.

Just, M. A., & Carpenter, P. A. (1984). Reading skills and skilled reading in the comprehension of text. In H. Mandl, N. L. Stein, & T. Trabasso (Eds.), *Learning and comprehension of text* (pp. 307–329). Hillsdale, NJ: Lawrence Erlbaum Associates.

Keenan, E. O., Schieffelin, B. B., & Platt, M. L. (1976). *Propositions across utterances and speakers. Papers and Reports on Child Language Development, No. 12.* (Tech. Rep.). Stanford, CA: Stanford University, Committee on Linguistics. (ERIC Document Reproduction Service No. ED 161 298).

Keeney, M. L. (1975). *An investigation of what intermediate-grade children say about the writing of stories.* Unpublished doctoral dissertation, Lehigh University, Bethlehem, PA. (Order No. 76-5091).

Kintsch, W., & van Dijk, T. A. (1978). Toward a model of text comprehension and production. *Psychological Review, 85,* 363–394.

Kneupper, C. W. (1978). Teaching argument: An introduction to the Toulmin model. *College Composition and Communication, 29,* 237–241.

Krashen, S. D. (1976). Formal and informal linguistic environments in language acquisition and language learning. *TESOL Quarterly, 10,* 157–168.

Krashen, S. D. (1977). The monitor model for adult second language performance. In M. Burt, H. Dulay, & M. Finocchiaro (Eds.), *Viewpoint on English as a second language* (pp. 152–161). New York: Regents.

Kroll, B. M. (1978). Cognitive egocentrism and the problem of audience awareness in written discourse. *Research in the Teaching of English, 12,* 269–281.

LaBerge, D., & Samuels, S. J. (1974). Toward a theory of automatic information processing in reading. *Cognitive Psychology, 6,* 293–323.

Lakatos, I. (1970). The methodology of scientific research programmes. In I. Lakatos & A. Musgrave (Eds.), *Criticism and the growth of knowledge* (pp. 91–195). Cambridge, MA: Cambridge University Press.

Lakatos, I., & Musgrave, A. (Eds.). (1970). *Criticism and the growth of knowledge.* Cambridge, MA: Cambridge University Press.

Lawson, A. E., & Renner, J. W. (1974). A quantitative analysis of responses to Piagetian tasks and its implications for curriculum. *Science Education, 58,* 545–559.

Lenin, V. I. (1977). On the question of dialectics. In K. Marx, F. Engels, & V. I. Lenin (Eds.), *On dialectical materialism.* Moscow: Progress Publishers.

Lesgold, A. M., & Perfetti, C. A. (1978). Interactive processes in reading comprehension. *Discourse Processes, 1,* 323–336.

Levi-Strauss, C. (1963). *Structural anthropology.* New York: Basic Books.

Liu, P. A. (1981). *An investigation of the relationship between qualitative and quantitative advances in the cognitive development of preschool children.* Unpublished doctoral dissertation, University of Toronto, Toronto.

Loban, W. (1976). *Language development: Kindergarten through grade twelve.* (Research Rep. No. 18). Urbana, IL: National Council of Teachers of English.

Loftus, E. F. (1977). How to catch a zebra in semantic memory. In R. Shaw & J. Bransford (Eds.), *Perceiving, acting, and knowing: Toward an ecological psychology* (pp. 393–411). Hillsdale, NJ: Lawrence Erlbaum Associates.

Lowenthal, D. (1980). Mixing levels of revision. *Visible Language, 14,* 383–387.

Luria, A. R. (1973). *The working brain: An introduction to neuropsychology.* London: Penguin Books Ltd.

Luria, A. R. (1976). A neuropsychological analysis of speech communication. In J. Prucha (Ed.), *Soviet studies in language and language behavior* (pp. 191–207). Amsterdam: North-Holland Publishing Company.

Lyons, G. (September, 1976). The higher illiteracy. *Harper's,* pp. 33–40.

Macrorie, K. (1976). *Telling writing.* Rochelle Park, NJ: Hayden.

Maier, N. R. F. (1930). Reasoning in humans: Vol. 1. On direction. *Comparative Psychology, 10,* 115–143.

Mandler, J., & Johnson, N. S. (1977). Remembrance of things parsed: Story structure and recall. *Cognitive Psychology, 9,* 111–151.

Markman, E. M. (1979). Realizing that you don't understand: Elementary school children's awareness of inconsistencies. *Child Development, 50,* 643–655.

Markman, E. M. (1981). Comprehensive monitoring. In W. P. Dixon (Ed.), *Children's oral communication skills* (pp. 61–84). New York: Academic Press.

Matsuhashi, A. (1982). Explorations in the real-time production of written discourse. In M. Nystrand (Ed.), *What writers know: The language, process, and structure of written discourse.* (pp. 269–290). New York: Academic Press.

McCloskey, M., Caramazza, A., & Green, B. (1980). Curvilinear motion in the absence of external forces: Naive beliefs about the motion of objects. *Science, 210,* 1139–1141.

McCutchen, D., & Perfetti, C. A. (1982). Coherence and connectedness in the development of discourse production. *Text, 2,* 113–139.

McDonald, J. D. (1980). *Memory capacity and inferential abilities in five- and seven-year-old children.* Unpublished master's thesis, York University, Toronto.

McNeill, D. (1979). *The conceptual basis of language.* Hillsdale, N.J.: Lawrence Erlbaum Associates.

Meckel, H. C., Squire, J. R., & Leonard, V. T. (1958). *Practices in the teaching of composition in California public high schools.* California State Department of Education Bulletin, 27 (No. 5).

Meehan, J. R. (1976). *The metanovel: Writing stories by computer.* (Research Rep. No. 74). New Haven, CT: Yale University, Department of Computer Science.

Meichenbaum, D. (1973). Cognitive factors in behavior modification: Modifying what clients say to themselves. In C. M. Franks & G. T. Wilson (Eds.), *Annual review of behavior therapy: Theory and practice* (pp. 416–431). New York: Brunner-Mazel.

Mellon, J. C. (1969). *Transformational sentence-combining: A method for enhancing the development of syntactic fluency in English composition.* (Research Rep. No. 10). Urbana, IL: National Council of Teachers of English.

Mennig-Peterson, C., & McCabe, A. (1977). *Structure of children's narratives.* Paper presented at the meeting of the Society for Research in Child Development, New Orleans.

Meyer, B. J. F. (1977). What is remembered from prose: A function of passage structure. In R. O. Freedle (Ed.), *Discourse production and comprehension* (Vol. 1.) (pp. 307–336). Norwood, NJ: Ablex Publishing Corporation.

Meyer, B. J. F. (1984). Text dimensions and cognitive processing. In H. Mandl, N. L. Stein, & T. Trabasso (Eds.), *Learning and comprehension of text* (pp. 3–51). Hillsdale, NJ: Lawrence Erlbaum Associates.

Miller, G. A. (1956). The magical number seven, plus or minus two: Some limits on our capacity for processing information. *Psychological Review, 63,* 81–97.

Miller, G. A., Galanter, E., & Pribram, K. (1960). *Plans and the structure of behavior.* New York: Holt, Rinehart & Winston.

Minsky, M. (1980). K-lines: A theory of memory. *Cognitive Science, 4,* 117–133.

Mishler, E. G. (1979). Meaning in context: Is there any other kind? *Harvard Educational Review, 49,* 1–19.

Moffett, J. (1968). *Teaching the universe of discourse.* Boston: Houghton Mifflin.

Montessori, M. (1967). *The absorbent mind.* New York: Holt, Rinehart, & Winston.

Muller, H. J. (1967). *The uses of English.* New York: Holt, Rinehart & Winston.

Murray, D. M. (1978). Internal revision: A process of discovery. In C. R. Cooper & L. Odell (Eds.), *Research on composing.* (pp. 85–103). Urbana, IL: National Council of Teachers of English.

National Assessment of Educational Progress (1977). *Write/rewrite: An assessment of revision skills: selected results from the second national assessment of writing.* (Tech. Rep.). U.S. Government Printing Office. (ERIC Document Reproduction Service No. ED 141 826).

National Assessment of Educational Progress (1980a). *Writing achievement, 1969–79: Results from the third national writing assessment (Vol 1: 17-year-olds).* (Tech. Rep.). Denver, CO: National Assessment of Educational Progress. (ERIC Document Reproduction Service No. ED 196 042).

National Assessment of Educational Progress (1980b). *Writing achievement, 1969–79: Results from the third national writing assessment (Vol. II: 13-year-olds),* (Tech. Rep.). Denver, CO: National Assessment of Educational Progress. (ERIC Document Reproduction Service No. ED 196 043).

Nelson, K., & Gruendel, J. M. (1979). At morning it's lunchtime: A scriptal view of children's dialogues. *Discourse Processes, 2,* 73–94.

Newell, A. (1974). You can't play 20 questions with nature and win. In W. G. Chase (Ed.), *Visual information processing* (pp. 283–308). New York: Academic Press.

Newell, A. (1980). Reasoning, problem solving, and decision processes: The problem space as a fundamental category. In R. S. Nickerson (Ed.), *Attention and performance VIII* (pp. 693–718). Hillsdale, NJ: Lawrence Erlbaum Associates.

Newell, A., Shaw, J. C., & Simon, H. A. (1963). Chess-playing programs and the problem of complexity. In E. A. Feigenbaum & J. Feldman (Eds.), *Computers and thought* (pp. 39–70). New York: McGraw-Hill.

Newell, A., & Simon, H. A. (1972). *Human problem solving.* Englewood Cliffs, NJ: Prentice-Hall.

Nisbett, R. E., & Ross, L. (1980). *Human inference: Strategies and shortcomings of social judgment.* Englewood Cliffs, NJ: Prentice-Hall.

Nold, E. W. (1981). Revising. In C. H. Frederiksen & J. F. Dominic (Eds.), *Writing: The nature, development and teaching of written communication* (pp. 67–79). Hillsdale, NJ: Lawrence Erlbaum Associates.

Nystrand, M. (1977). *Language as a way of knowing: A book of readings.* Toronto: The Ontario Institute for Studies in Education.

Nystrand, M., & Wiederspiel, M. (1977). Case study of a personal journal: Notes towards an epistemology of writing. In M. Nystrand (Ed.), *Language as a way of knowing: A book of readings* (pp. 105–121). Toronto: The Ontario Institute for Studies in Education.

Odell, L. (1974). Measuring the effect of instruction in prewriting. *Research in the Teaching of English, 8,* 228–240.

Odell, L. (1980). Business writing: Observations and implications for teaching composition. *Theory into Practice, 19,* 225–232.

Odom, R. D., & Mumbauer, C. C. (1971). Dimensional salience and identification of the relevant dimension in problem solving: A developmental study. *Developmental Psychology, 4,* 135–140.

O'Hare, F. (1973). *Sentence combining: Improving student writing without formal grammar instruction.* (Research Rep. No. 15). Urbana, IL: National Council of Teachers of English.

Olson, D. R. (1977). From utterance to text: The bias of language in speech and writing. *Harvard Educational Review, 47,* 257–281.

Olson, G. M., Mack, R. L., & Duffy, S. A. (1981). Cognitive aspects of genre. *Poetics, 10,* 283–315.

Osgood, C. E., & Bock, J. K. (1977). Salience and sentencing: Some production principles. In S. Rosenberg (Ed.), *Sentence production: Developments in research and theory* (pp. 89–140). Hillsdale, NJ: Lawrence Erlbaum Associates.

Osherson, D. N. (1975). *Logical abilities in children.* Hillsdale, NJ: Lawrence Erlbaum Associates.

Palincsar, A. S., & Brown, A. L. (1984). Reciprocal teaching of comprehension-fostering and monitoring activities. *Cognition and Instruction, 1,* 117–175.

Papert, S. (1980). *Mindstorms: Children, computers, and powerful ideas.* New York: Basic Books, Inc.

Paris, P. (1980). *Discourse schemata as knowledge and as regulators of text production.* Unpublished master's thesis, York University, Downsview, Canada.

Paris, P., Scardamalia, M., & Bereiter, C. (1980). *Discourse schemata as knowledge and as regulators of text production.* Paper presented at the meeting of the American Educational Research Association, Boston.

Paris, P., Scardamalia, M., & Bereiter, C. (1982). *Synthesis through analysis: Facilitating theme development in children's writing.* Paper presented at the meeting of the American Educational Research Association, New York.

Paris, S. G., & Lindauer, B. K. (1982). The development of cognitive skills during childhood. In B. Wolman (Ed.), *Handbook of Developmental Psychology* (pp. 333–349). Englewood Cliffs, NJ: Prentice-Hall.

Paris, S. G., & Myers, M. (1981). Comprehension monitoring in good and poor readers. *Journal of Reading Behavior, 13,* 5–22.

Paris, S. G., Newman, R. S., & McVey, K. A. (1982). Learning the functional significance of mnemonic actions: A microgenetic study of strategy acquisition. *Journal of Experimental Child Psychology, 34,* 490–509.

Pascual-Leone, J. (1969). *Cognitive development and cognitive style: A general psychological integration.* Unpublished doctoral dissertation, University of Geneva, Geneva.

Pascual-Leone, J. (1970). A mathematical model for the transition rule in Piaget's developmental stages. *Acta Psychologica, 63,* 301–345.

Pascual-Leone, J., & Goodman, D. (1979). Intelligence and experience: A neopiagetian approach. *Instructional Science, 8,* 301–367.

Pascual-Leone, J., Goodman, D., Ammon, P., & Subelman, I. (1979). Piagetian theory and neopiagetian analysis as psychological guides in education. In J. M. Gallagher & J. Easley (Eds.), *Knowledge and development: Vol. 2. Piaget and education* (pp. 243–289). New York: Plenum Press.

Pascual-Leone, J., & Smith, J. (1969). The encoding and decoding of symbols by children: A new experimental paradigm and neopiagetian model. *Journal of Experimental Child Psychology, 8,* 328–355.

Pearson, P. D., & Gallagher, M. C. (1983). The instruction of reading comprehension. *Contemporary Educational Psychology, 8,* 317–344.

Perfetti, C. A., & Lesgold, A. M. (1977). Discourse comprehension and sources of individual differences. In M. Just & P. Carpenter (Eds.), *Cognitive processes in comprehension* (pp. 141–183). Hillsdale, NJ: Lawrence Erlbaum Associates.

Perfetti, C. A., & Roth, S. (1981). Some of the interactive processes in reading and their role in reading skill. In A. M. Lesgold, & C. Perfetti (Eds.), *Interactive processes in reading* (pp. 269–297). Hillsdale, NJ: Lawrence Erlbaum Associates.

Piaget, J. (1926). *The language and thought of the child.* London: Kegan Paul.

Piaget, J. (1929). *The child's conception of the world.* New York: Harcourt, Brace.

Piaget, J. (1980). The psychogenesis of knowledge and its epistemological significance. In M. Piattelli-Palmarini (Ed.), *Language and learning: The debate between Jean Piaget and Noam Chomsky* (pp. 23–34). Cambridge, MA: Harvard University Press.

Polya, G. (1945). *How to solve it.* Princeton, N.J.: Princeton University Press.

Pylyshyn, Z. W. (1984). *Computation and cognition: Toward a foundation for cognitive science.* Cambridge, MA: MIT Press.

Quinsaat, M. G., Levin, J. A., Boruta, M., & Newman, D. (1983). *The use of a word processor in classrooms.* Paper presented at the meeting of the American Educational Research Association, Montreal.

Reddy, R., & Newell, A. (1974). Knowledge and its representation in a speech understanding system. In L. W. Gregg (Ed.), *Knowledge and cognition* (pp. 253–285). Potomac, MD: Lawrence Erlbaum Associates.

Reichman, R. (1978). Conversational coherency. *Cognitive Science, 2,* 283–327.

Rentel, V., & King, M. (1983). Present at the beginning. In P. Mosenthal, L. Tamor, & S. Walmsley (Eds.), *Research on writing: Principles and methods* (pp. 139–176). New York: Longman Inc.

Rieger, C. (1977). Spontaneous computation in cognitive models. *Cognitive Science, 1,* 315–354.

Robinson, F. G., Tickle, J., & Brison, D. W. (1972). *Inquiry training: Fusing theory and practice.* Toronto: OISE Press.

Rohwer, W. D., Jr. (1973). Elaboration and learning in childhood and adolescence. In H. W. Reese (Ed.), *Advances in child development and behavior* (Vol. 8.) (pp. 1–57). New York: Academic Press.

Rose, M. (1981). Sophisticated, ineffective books—The dismantling of process in composition texts. *College Composition and Communication, 32,* 65–74.

Rumelhart, D. E. (1975). Notes on a schema for stories. In D. G. Bobrow, & A. M. Collins (Eds.), *Representation and understanding: Studies in cognitive science* (pp. 211–236). New York: Academic Press.

Rumelhart, D. E. (1980). Schemata: The building blocks of cognition. In R. J. Spiro, B. C. Bruce, & W. F. Brewer (Eds.), *Theoretical issues in reading comprehension* (pp. 33–58). Hillsdale, NJ: Lawrence Erlbaum Associates.

Sacks, H. (1976). On getting the floor. *Pragmatics Microfiche, 1,* 7–8. (April, D11–E5).

Samuels, S. J., & Eisenberg, P. (1981). A framework for understanding the reading process. In F. J. Pirozzolo, & M. C. Wittrock (Eds.), *Neuropsychological and cognitive processes in reading* (pp. 31–67). New York: Academic Press.

Scardamalia, M. (1973). *Mental processing aspects of two formal operational tasks: A developmental investigation of a quantitative neo-piagetian model.* Unpublished doctoral dissertation, The Ontario Institute for Studies in Education, Toronto.

Scardamalia, M. (1975). Two formal operational tasks: A quantitative neo-piagetian and task analysis model for investigating sources of task difficulty. In G. I. Lubin, J. F. Magary, & M. K. Poulsen (Eds.), *Piagetian theory and the helping professions* (pp. 19–27). Los Angeles: University of Southern California Publications Dept.

Scardamalia, M. (1977). Information processing capacity and the problem of horizontal decalage: A demonstration using combinatorial reasoning tasks. *Child Development, 48,* 28–37.

Scardamalia, M. (1984). *Knowledge telling and knowledge transforming in written composition.* Paper presented at the meeting of the American Educational Research Association, New Orleans.

Scardamalia, M., & Baird, W. (1980). *Children's strategies for composing sentences.* Paper presented at the meeting of the American Educational Research Association, Boston.

Scardamalia, M., & Bereiter, C. (1979). *The effects of writing rate on children's composition.* Paper presented at the meeting of the American Educational Research Association, San Francisco.

Scardamalia, M., & Bereiter, C. (1981). *The transition from conversational to literary schemata in children's writing.* Paper presented at the meeting of the American Educational Research Association, Los Angeles.

Scardamalia, M., & Bereiter, C. (1982). Assimilative processes in composition planning. *Educational Psychologist, 17,* 165–171.

Scardamalia, M., & Bereiter, C. (1985a). Development of dialectical processes in composition. In D. R. Olson, N. Torrance, & A. Hildyard (Eds.), *Literacy, language and learning: The nature and consequences of reading and writing* (pp. 307–329). Cambridge: Cambridge University Press.

Scardamalia, M., & Bereiter, C. (1985b). Research on written composition. In M. Wittrock (Ed.), *Handbook of Research on teaching.* (3rd ed.). New York: Macmillan Education Ltd.

Scardamalia, M., Bereiter, C., & Fillion, B. (1981). *Writing for results: A sourcebook of consequential composing activities.* Toronto: OISE Press. (Also, LaSalle, IL: Open Court Publishing Company, 1981.).

Scardamalia, M., Bereiter, C., & Woodruff, E. (1980). *The effects of content knowledge on writing.* Paper presented at the meeting of the American Educational Research Association, Boston.

Scardamalia, M., Bereiter, C., Woodruff, E., Burtis, P. J., & Turkish, L. (1981). *The effects of modeling and cueing on high-level planning.* Paper presented at the meeting of the American Educational Research Association, Los Angeles.

Scardamalia, M., & Bracewell, R. J. (1979). *Local planning in children's writing.* Paper presented at the meeting of the American Educational Research Association, San Francisco.

Scardamalia, M., Cattani, C., Turkish, L., & Bereiter, C. (1981). *Part-whole relationships in text planning.* Paper presented at the meeting of the American Educational Research Association, Los Angeles.

Scardamalia, M., & Paris, P. (1985). The function of explicit discourse knowledge in the development of text representations and composing strategies. *Cognition and Instruction, 2,* 1–39.

Schank, R. C. (1977). Rules and topics in conversation. *Cognitive Science, 1,* 421–441.

Schmidt, R. A. (1975). A schema theory of motor skill learning. *Psychological Review, 82,* 225-260.

Shatz, M. (1977). The relationship between cognitive processes and the development of communication skills. In B. Keasey (Ed.), *Nebraska Symposium on Motivation* (pp. 1-42). Lincoln, NE: University of Nebraska Press.

Shaughnessy, M. P. (1977). *Errors and expectations: A guide for the teacher of basic writing.* New York: Oxford University Press.

Shaw, R., & McIntyre, M. (1974). Algoristic foundations to cognitive psychology. In W. Weimer & D. Palermo (Eds.), *Cognition and the symbolic processes* (pp. 305-362). Hillsdale, NJ: Lawrence Erlbaum Associates.

Shaw, R., & Turvey, M. T. (1981). Coalitions as models of ecosystems: A realist perspective on perceptual organization. In M. Kubovy & T. Pomerantz (Eds.), *Perceptual organization* (pp. 343-415). Hillsdale, NJ: Lawrence Erlbaum Associates.

Siegler, R. S. (1976). Three aspects of cognitive development. *Cognitive Psychology, 8,* 481-520.

Siegler, R. S. (Ed.). (1978). *Children's thinking: What develops?.* Hillsdale, NJ: Lawrence Erlbaum Associates.

Siegler, R. S. (1981). Developmental sequences within and between concepts. *Monographs of the Society for Research in Child Development, 46* (2, Serial No. 189).

Simon, H. A. (1972). On the development of the processor. In S. Farnham-Diggory (Ed.), *Information processing in children* (pp. 3-22). New York: Academic Press.

Simon, H. A. (1974). How big is a chunk? *Science, 183,* 482-488.

Simon, J. (1973). *La langue ecrite de l'enfant.* Paris: Presses Universitaires de France.

Smith, F. (1982). *Writing and the writer.* New York: Holt, Rinehart & Winston.

Smith, N. V. (1979). Syntax for psychologists. In J. M. Morton & J. C. Marshall (Eds.), *Psycholinguistics: Vol. 2. Structures and processes* (pp. 3-65). London: Paul Elek.

Spelke, E. S. (1982). Perceptual knowledge of objects in infancy. In J. Mehler, E. C. T. Walker, & M. Garrett (Eds.), *Perspectives in mental representation: Experimental and theoretical studies of cognitive processes and capacities* (pp. 409-430). Hillsdale, NJ: Lawrence Erlbaum Associates.

Spelke, E. S., Hirst, W., & Neisser, U. (1976). Skills of divided attention. *Cognition, 4,* 215-230.

Spiro, R. J. (1977). Remembering information from text: The "state of schema" approach. In R. C. Anderson, R. J. Spiro, & W. E. Montague (Eds.), *Schooling and the acquisition of knowledge* (pp. 137-165). Hillsdale, NJ: Lawrence Erlbaum Associates.

Spiro, R. J., Bruce, B. C., & Brewer, W. F. (Eds.). (1980). *Theoretical issues in reading comprehension.* Hillsdale, NJ: Lawrence Erlbaum Associates.

Stallard, C. K. (1974). An analysis of the writing behavior of good student writers. *Research in the Teaching of English, 8,* 206-218.

Staton, J. (1980). Writing and counseling: Using a dialogue journal. *Language Arts, 57,* 514-518.

Stein, N. L. (1979). The concept of a story: A developmental psycholinguistic analysis. In R. J. Bracewell (Chair). *Recent approaches to writing research: An evaluation and forecast.* Symposium conducted at the meeting of the American Educational Research Association, San Francisco.

Stein, N. L., & Glenn, C. G. (1979). An analysis of story comprehension in elementary school children. In R. O. Freedle (Ed.), *New directions in discourse processing* (Vol. 2.) (pp. 53-120). Norwood, NJ: Ablex Publishing Corporation.

Stein, N. L., & Trabasso, T. (1982). What's in a story: An approach to comprehension and instruction. In R. Glaser (Ed.), *Advances in instructional psychology* (pp. 213–267). Hillsdale, NJ: Lawrence Erlbaum Associates.

Sternberg, R. J. (1980). Sketch of a componential subtheory of human intelligence. *Behavioral and Brain Sciences, 3,* 573–614.

Strunk, W., Jr., & White, E. B. (1959). *The elements of style.* New York: Macmillan.

Swaney, J. H., Janik, C. J., Bond, S. J., & Hayes, J. R. (1981). *Editing for comprehension: Improving the process through reading protocols.* (Tech. Rep. No. 14). Pittsburgh, PA: Carnegie-Mellon University, Document Design Project.

Tetroe, J. (1981). *The effects of children's planning behavior on writing problems.* Paper presented at the meeting of the American Educational Research Association, Los Angeles.

Tetroe, J. (1984). *Information processing demand of plot construction in story writing.* Paper presented at the meeting of the American Educational Research Association, New Orleans.

Tetroe, J., Bereiter, C., & Scardamalia, M. (1981). *How to make a dent in the writing process.* Paper presented at the meeting of the American Educational Research Association, Los Angeles.

Thomassen, A. J. W. M., & Teulings, J. L. H. M. (1983). The development of handwriting. In M. Martlew (Ed.), *The psychology of written language* (pp. 179–213). Chichester: John Wiley & Sons.

Trabasso, T., Stein, N. L., & Johnson, L. R. (1981). Children's knowledge of events: A causal analysis of story structure. In G. Bower (Ed.), *The psychology of learning and motivation: Advances in research and theory* (Vol. 15.) (pp. 237–282). New York: Academic Press.

Van Bruggen, J. A. (1946). Factors affecting regularity of the flow of words during written composition. *Journal of Experimental Education, 15,* 133–155.

van Dijk, T. A. (1980). *Macrostructures: An interdisciplinary study of global structures in discourse, interaction, and cognition.* Hillsdale, NJ: Lawrence Erlbaum Associates.

van Dijk, T. A., & Kintsch, W. (1983). *Strategies of discourse comprehension.* New York: Academic Press.

Voss, J. F. (1984). On learning and learning from text. In H. Mandl, N. L. Stein, & T. Trabasso (Eds.), *Learning and comprehension of text* (pp. 193–212). Hillsdale, NJ: Lawrence Erlbaum Associates.

Vygotsky, L. S. (1962). *Thought and language.* (E. Haufmann & G. Vakar, Eds. and Trans.). Cambridge, MA: MIT Press.

Vygotsky, L. S. (1978). *Mind in society: The development of higher psychological processes.* (M. Cole, V. John-Steiner, S. Scribner, & E. Souberman, Eds. and Trans.). Cambridge, MA: Harvard University Press.

Wason, P. C. (1980). Specific thoughts on the writing process. In L. W. Gregg & E. R. Steinberg (Eds.), *Cognitive processes in writing* (pp. 129–137). Hillsdale, NJ: Lawrence Erlbaum Associates.

Whitehead, A. N. (1929). *The aims of education.* New York: Macmillan.

Wickelgren, W. A. (1979). Chunking and consolidation: A theoretical synthesis of semantic networks, configuring in conditioning, S–R versus cognitive learning, normal forgetting, the amnesic syndrome, and the hippocampal arousal system. *Psychological Review, 86,* 44–60.

Widdowson, H. G. (1978). *Teaching language as communication.* Oxford: Oxford University Press.

Widdowson, H. G. (1983). New starts and different kinds of failure. In A. Freedman, I. Pringle, & J. Yalden (Eds.), *Learning to write: First language, second language* (pp. 34–47). New York: Longman Inc.

Wilensky, R. (1983). Story grammars versus story points. *Behavioral and Brain Sciences,* 6, 579-623.

Wilkins, A. J., & Baddeley, A. D. (1978). Remembering to recall in everyday life: An approach to absent-mindedness. In M. M. Gruneberg, P. Morris, & R. N. Sykes (Eds.), *Practical aspects of memory* (pp. 27-34). London: Academic Press.

Woodruff, E., Bereiter, C., & Scardamalia, M. (1981). On the road to computer assisted compositions. *Journal of Educational Technology Systems, 10,* 133-148.

Woodruff, E., Scardamalia, M., & Bereiter, C. (1982). Computers and the composing process: An examination of computer-writer interaction. In J. Lawlor (Ed.), *Computers in composition instruction* (pp. 31-45). Los Alamitos, CA: SWRL Educational Research and Development.

Woods, W. A. (1980). Multiple theory formation in speech and reading. In R. J. Spiro, B. C. Bruce, & W. F. Brewer (Eds.), *Theoretical issues in reading comprehension* (pp. 59-82). Hillsdale, NJ: Lawrence Erlbaum Associates.

Wooton, A. (1975). *Dilemmas of discourse.* London: Allen & Unwin.

Writers at Work: The Paris Review Interviews, (2nd Series). (1963). New York: The Viking Press.

Yau, M., & Bereiter, C. *The effect of writing in a second language on complexity of content.* (In preparation).

Young, R. E., Becker, A. L., & Pike, K. E. (1970). *Rhetoric: Discovery and change.* New York: Harcourt, Brace & World.

Zbrodoff, N. J. (1984). *Writing stories under time and length constraints.* Unpublished doctoral dissertation, University of Toronto, Toronto.

Author Index

Subject Index